Commentary on ROMANS

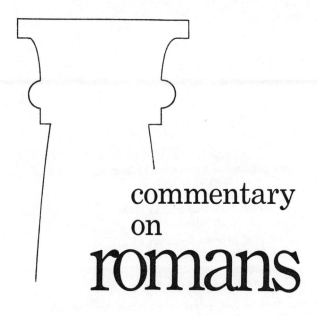

commentary
on
romans

Anders Nygren

FORTRESS PRESS/Philadelphia

First published as *Romarbrevet* by Verbum,
Stockholm, 1944.

First American edition 1949
Ninth printing 1967
First paperback edition 1972
Sixth printing 1983

COPYRIGHT © 1949 BY FORTRESS PRESS

Library of Congress Catalog Card Number 49-48317
ISBN 0-8006-1684-7

452C83   Printed in the United States of America   1-1684

Contents

PART THREE

9:1—11:36

1

Introduction

1. THE EPISTLE TO THE ROMANS, "THE CLEAREST GOSPEL OF ALL"

In his preface to Romans, Luther characterizes this letter as "rightly the chief part of the New Testament and the clearest gospel of all"; and he adds that it would be well worth memorizing, so that a Christian could recite it by rote, word for word. Thus it is the judgment of Luther that this epistle sets forth the gospel more clearly than any other writing in the New Testament.

But since his time we have not lacked voices that have declared that Luther is guilty of overstatement in his appraisal. He personally owed very much to the Epistle to the Romans; and he found in it the highest support for the position upon which his work as reformer rested. It was thus natural that he should see in it the chief part of the New Testament and the clearest gospel of all. But in this judgment, it is said, we cannot follow him. If one is to call anything the chief part of the New Testament, that must without doubt be the Gospels.

This objection is tempting; to many its truth seems self-evident. But upon closer examination it is seen that to some degree at least it rests on a false presupposition. Behind it

1

often lies the belief that in the Gospels—particularly in the Synoptics—we have the original reports of the life and teachings of Jesus, and that this primary material was subsequently used by Paul in a way that was not true to its proper meaning. In this way, on the simple narratives about Jesus there arose the belief in Him as the Christ and the Son of God. If that were really the fact, it would of course have to be admitted that the clearest gospel is found in the Synoptics, and that Paul beclouded it. However, this whole idea is nothing but an unhistorical postulate. The actual fact is, on the contrary, that belief in Christ is assumed by the Gospels as well as by Paul. Had that faith not been present, we should have had no Gospels. The Gospels are not descriptive records in the interest of history; they are a witness to Christ, born of faith in Him and aiming to evoke in others the same faith. "These are written that you may believe that Jesus is the Christ (ὁ Χριστός), the Son of God, and that believing you may have life in his name." So it is affirmed in the Gospel according to John (20:31), and the same is true for all the Gospels. The difference between Paul and the Synoptics consists only of this, that Paul fixed the content of that faith more clearly and unequivocally. It is the same gospel; but the Synoptics are the easier to distort. He who is willing to lay hold of them with profane hands can do so. Here man found it possible to undertake the construction of a purely historical "life of Jesus" out of the Gospels, for which faith was not necessary—that is, to pare off the gospel from the Gospels. For all such attempts the gospel according to Paul is a stumbling block. The gospel which is comprehended in the Gospels and gave them their name is brought forth by Paul and set in the foreground in a manner that does not leave room for misunderstanding.

2

The history of the Christian church is consequently witness to the fact that the Epistle to the Romans has in a peculiar way been able to supply the impulse for the renewal of Christianity. When man has slipped away from the gospel, a deep study of Romans has often been the means by which the lost has been recovered. It is enough to recall what the epistle meant, in such connection, to Augustine or to the men of the Reformation. Upon further consideration, therefore, one finds it necessary on purely objective grounds to concede that Luther was right in his judgment. What the gospel is, what the content of the Christian faith is, one learns to know in the Epistle to the Romans as in no other place in the New Testament. Romans gives us the gospel in its wide context. It gives us the right perspective and the standard by which we should comprehend all the constituent parts of the Gospels, to arrive at the true, intended picture.

In a treatment of Romans, dating from the time when man thought that in the Synoptics was to be found "the historical Jesus" and in Paul a view that departed from the teaching of Jesus, it was said, "How fortunate that we have the gospel not only as Paul proclaimed it!" Now we happily find ourselves in the better position that we do not have to choose between Paul and the Gospels. It is closer to the truth to say, "How fortunate that we also have the gospel as Paul proclaimed it!"

2. THE GENERAL CHARACTER OF THE EPISTLE

Among Paul's epistles, Romans has a peculiar position, inasmuch as it is the only one he wrote to a congregation that was strange to him. When and how the Christian congregation in Rome was established we do not know; only this can be said, that it did not happen through Paul or any of his closest fellow-workers. It is natural to assume that the Roman congregation's origin was related to Rome's peculiar position at the crossroads of the world's traffic. In the account which Acts gives of the outpouring of the Holy Spirit, mention is made of "visitors from Rome" among those who witnessed the Pentecostal sermon of Peter (2:10). Beyond that we know very little about the Roman church; its constitution and its special situation. What we know is almost wholly limited to what we can learn from the letter itself. As aid to our understanding we can count on no additional light from without.

Under such circumstances one is tempted to think, "Too bad that we know so little about the congregation to which Paul directed this epistle! How much better we should understand Romans if we had a clearer insight into the situation within the congregation at Rome, if we knew the different groups and trends which Paul had in mind as he wrote." But however spontaneous that thought may be, it is nevertheless misleading. For if one seeks the key to the epistle in certain special conditions within the congregation at Rome, one thereby shows that the attention is directed away from that which is central. The characteristic and peculiar thing about Romans, differentiating it from the rest of Paul's epistles, is just the fact that it was not, or was only in slight degree, aimed at circumstances within a certain congregation. Its purpose is not to correct maladjustments. Nor does Paul here, as in the Epistle to the Galatians, give battle to opponents who would alienate the congregation from him and from the gospel he preached. In Romans, Paul undertook to write to a congregation that was strange to him. This is a fact which ought never to be overlooked;

it has set its mark on the whole epistle and given it a uniquely objective character.

But what was the occasion for Paul to write this long, richly freighted letter to a congregation as yet strange to him? He has himself given us certain intimations as to the answer. In the introduction to the epistle he tells that he had long yearned to come to Rome and to establish closer acquaintance with the Christian congregation there. To be sure, he elsewhere acted on the principle "not to preach the gospel where the name of Christ was already known" (15:20). But with Rome there was a different situation. Although there, in the capital city of the world, a Christian congregation had arisen without his co-operation, perhaps even before he began his missionary work, that fact did not constitute a hindrance for him. He had been called of God to be the apostle to the Gentiles, to the heathen; so he must go to the central point of the heathen world, where men of all peoples and tongues thronged together. To this must be added another circumstance. When Paul, from Corinth, writes his letter to the Christians at Rome, he stands at the high point of his activity. His third missionary journey lies behind him, and he considers his work in the East concluded. Now it is his plan to shift his work to Spain. En route he will realize his intention to visit the Roman congregation, and he anticipates that by it he will "be equipped for the journey" to Spain (15:24). Furthermore, Rome would be the base, it would seem, for his new missionary work, as Antioch had been for his work hitherto. Before he could undertake the journey, only one thing remained, namely to go to Jerusalem "with help for the saints," which was being gathered in Macedonia and Achaia (15:25f.). To prepare the congregation at Rome for his coming he now sends this letter. As yet he has no premonition of what is to happen to him in Jerusalem and that he will come to Rome in a manner quite other than he expected—as a prisoner.

The immediate occasion for the writing of the letter is thus relatively clear. But even here one must be careful not to draw erroneous conclusions as to the epistle's general character and contents. For it would otherwise be easy to reason about as follows. Everything depends, for Paul, on getting the support of the congregation at Rome for his new missionary plans; so with all his might he must seek to win their confidence. This he does by his letter, giving them thereby a demonstration how he had preached the gospel. In this fact one would see the reason for the didactic character of the epistle. Or one may say that Paul here gives account, to the Christians at Rome, how he had preached the gospel; above all he is eager thereby to make clear his attitude to the law. This was the more necessary for him because he always had to reckon with the fact that his old opponents among the Jewish Christians could undermine him in Rome too, and thereby rob him of the congregation's support.

To reason so is to stretch the significance of the outward occasion for the letter, at the cost of the actual contents of the epistle. There is nothing to indicate that the contents of the letter are due to Paul's desire to justify himself before the Roman congregation. Paul is here dealing with a great, actual problem, with questions of such compass and significance as no one after him has had to grapple with in the history of Christianity. In view of that fact, to offer as the real explanation of the letter the accidental circumstances, of a more personal character, which supplied the occasion for its writing, does not contribute to the deeper understanding of its contents; but quite the contrary. In like manner, it is a misunderstanding of Romans to see in it a typical example of Paul's missionary preaching. This epistle was written to a congregation which already knew the gospel and did not need an underlying missionary proclamation. And if anyone replies that Paul wrote such, not because the congregation at Rome needed it, but to give an example of how he presented his missionary preaching, that he might thereby recommend himself to them, then the epistle is itself the most effective refutation of such a view. The Epistle to the Romans is anything but an exhibition. Paul is dealing with problems on which life hangs both for him and for the congregation to which he writes. Since it is essential to understand these problems, it is only a disservice if, instead of looking deeply into them, one concerns himself with the external and incidental circumstances which gave Paul the occasion for dealing with the problems. That some, in interpreting Romans, have let its outer occasion play so large a role is probably due to the fact that so little is known about such outer circumstances. In Paul's own explanation interpreters have had one sure point about the occasion for the letter. It was tempting to use it to the uttermost. But the result was that that sure point was made to support much more than it really could.

It has often been regarded as a limitation in the epistle that it has so little of the quality of a real letter. It rather impresses one as a doctrinal writing, a theological treatise, which is only externally clad with the form of a letter. Doubtless what one has in mind, in such a comment, is the epistle's objective character, referred to above. It is true that Romans does not deal, or deals only in slightest degree, with the

7

conditions within the Roman congregation. But it is nevertheless a real letter with which we are confronted. That which it offers is not doctrines and explanations, presented with theoretical intent; it contains precisely that which Paul, in the moment of writing, found most necessary to say to his readers.

He is about to write to a congregation largely unknown to him. With what area shall he deal? He cannot make it his aim to shape the congregation's life by specific directions, counsel, and admonitions; for he knows them but slightly, and they stand under no obligation to him. But there are quite other thoughts to which he does give expression. The great problem of his life rises up; and it is at the same time the great problem of all Christendom. What is the new that entered with Christ? What is it that the congregation has by faith in Him? And what is the relation between the new way of salvation, the way of faith, and the way in which the people of God had hitherto walked, the way of works? These were questions which Paul, in his work, always had to face anew; and the congregation greatly needed the answer to them.

We have no reason to lament that Romans contains so few concrete references to the situation in the congregation at Rome. We owe it to that fact that we have what is much more vital. Instead of the special problems of the congregation at Rome, we confront Paul's own life problem. Instead of an accounting with his opponents, we see Paul's accounting with himself, with his past; for he too had formerly walked the way of salvation by works. To the very fact that he had been hindered from realizing his purpose to visit the Roman congregation, and therefore had to write to it as a congregation that was strange to him, are we indebted for our possession, in this epistle, of Christianity's incomparably remarkable document, where the gospel speaks, more clearly than anywhere else, against the law as a background.

3. The Fundamental Concept of the Epistle: Righteousness from God

Until quite recently it was customary for theology to draw a sharp line between Jesus and Paul. Jesus preached the coming of the kingdom of God; but Paul, it was said, changed this to the doctrine of justification by faith. Now there is room for no doubt that that view is false, and that the continuity between Jesus and Paul is essentially unbroken. When, therefore, we seek to fix the basic thought in Paul's view of the gospel, it is quite proper to point out how it has both its origin and its anchor in Jesus' proclamation about the kingdom of God.

If there is anything which the newer exegetical study has clearly established, it is the extraordinary significance which the eschatological had for early Christian faith. At the center of Jesus' message stood the proclamation of the kingdom of God and the beginning of the new age. In hope the pious who "looked for the consolation of Israel" had reached forward toward that day when God himself would institute His kingdom and take command. In that tense expectation the proclamation of Jesus is heard, "The time is fulfilled, the kingdom of God is at hand" (Mark 1:15). When Jesus talks about the kingdom of God, it is no longer a matter of something distant, which shall some time come. "This age" has already reached its end, and "the new age" stands at the door. With Jesus himself the messianic age has arrived. With reference to the messianic prophecy about "a year of grace from the Lord," He could say, 'Today this scripture has been fulfilled in your hearing" (Luke 4:21). That He was "He that should come" is seen in that the messianic signs were already at hand, "the blind receive their sight and the lame walk, lepers are cleansed and the deaf hear, and the dead are raised up, and the poor have good news preached to them" (Matt. 11:5). Even if one can at the same time speak of the kingdom of heaven as something that shall come and is approaching, it is nevertheless also a present reality; the forces of the kingdom of heaven are already in operation. It is not through human achievements that the kingdom of God comes, but by God's wonderful intervention. It comes as a gift from God. Therefore Jesus can call His disciples blessed, "for theirs is the kingdom of heaven" (Matt. 5:3, 10). They have the right of domicile in the new age. They need not fear, for it is the Father's good pleasure to give them the kingdom (Luke 12:32).

The kingdom of God comes. But therewith is also given a *new righteousness:* the righteousness of God. Jesus' disciples "hunger and thirst after righteousness" (Matt. 5:6); they do not think, like the Pharisees, that they have the righteousness by virtue of which they can stand before God. But Jesus calls them blessed, "for they shall be filled." The kingdom of God is approaching, and in it they will receive God's righteousness as a gift from Him. For just as the kingdom of God can come only through God's mighty intervention, so God's righteousness can become man's possession only in that he receives it as a gift from God. Jesus does not at all deny that the Pharisees also have a kind of righteousness; it was zealous for God's law and sought for the realization thereof in all of life's relationships. But that is not the righteousness which belongs with the kingdom of

God. Therefore it is written, in Matthew 5:20, "Unless your righteousness exceeds that of the scribes and Pharisees, you will never enter into the kingdom of heaven." So inseparably do the new kingdom and the new righteousness belong together. In Matthew 6:33 we also hear how Jesus directly couples these two in the exhortation, "Seek ye first the kingdom of God and his righteousness."

But what is the inner content of that "righteousness of God" which is so inseparably joined with the kingdom of God? *That is Paul's problem.* Above all it is his problem in the Epistle to the Romans.

No one else was so well qualified as he to solve this problem. The rest of Jesus' disciples had all alike come out of circles which at least to some degree stood in criticism against the piety of the Pharisees. They had, to begin with no righteousness of their own to appeal to. To receive the righteousness of God, which was proffered to them through Jesus, was for them like a development of their earlier piety, which had humility before God as its most distinctive quality. Attachment to Jesus therefore required of them no total break with all their earlier religious life. Therefore the new did not seem to them something absolutely new. There was an element of continuity. For Paul the situation was different. He came directly from the ranks of the opposition, from the status of the Pharisees. During his pre-Christian period righteousness had been the great passion of his life. It was in the service thereof, and to establish the righteousness of the law, that he persecuted the Christian congregation. So when, at Damascus, he received the Lord's revelation, it meant a total collapse of all that he had labored for up till then. If Jesus was the Messiah, the kingdom of God was already at hand. The new age had come. But then the righteousness which had made Paul a persecutor of the Christian community was a false righteousness. God himself had condemned it as sin; in its place He now proffered in the kingdom which had come a totally new righteousness—the righteousness of God. From this position it is easy to comprehend what an exceptional task was Paul's in the history of Christianity. Only one like Paul, himself on the contrary way of salvation, the way of righteousness by the law, was capable of making clear for Christianity the new way of salvation which God had opened through Christ, and of setting forth the righteousness of God in its absolute newness.

Paul knew both ways of salvation. From his former life he knew the law and the righteousness which it could effect; from his present experience he knew the gospel as the power of God unto salvation to everyone who believes. Out of his own experience, therefore, he was able to set one against the other. But Paul was not a convert of the usual sort that after conversion can only paint the former life in dark colors. As a Christian, Paul is still just to his pre-Christian life. He never forgets that then, too, he had a kind of righteousness, namely, such righteousness as comes by the law. In this connection it is especially useful to cite Philippians 3:4-9, where we read, "If any other man thinks he has reason for confidence in the flesh, I have more: . . . as to the law a Pharisee, as to zeal a persecutor of the church, as to righteousness under the law blameless. But whatever gain I had, I counted as loss for the sake of Christ. Indeed I count everything as loss because of the surpassing worth of knowing Christ Jesus my Lord. For his sake I have suffered the loss of all things, and count them as refuse, in order that I may gain Christ and be found in him, not having a right-

12

eousness of my own, based on law, but that which is through
faith in Christ, the righteousness from God that depends
on faith."

The first thing one notices in this statement is that there
is no trace of resentment. Yet many have thought of Paul's
development somewhat as follows: Originally he set forth on
the way of the law. After many fruitless efforts to achieve
righteousness by keeping the law, he finally had to give up
and launch out on another way. The law, which had formerly been his pride, now appeared to him the very enemy.
His own failure was thus regarded as the reason he rejected
the law as a way of salvation. In that situation it dawned
upon him as a liberating insight that it is not by the fulfillment of the law, but through faith, that man is justified
before God. Whereupon a great burden fell from his
shoulders. But in the passage cited from the Epistle to the
Philippians we hear from Paul himself the direct opposite.
There actually is a righteousness which is to be achieved
by virtue of the law; and in relation to that he had *not*
failed, but was a "man without reproach." So the law had
not been for him a stumbling block, on which he had fallen;
it belonged rather to that which Paul considered genuine
achievement. His attitude to the law, when he had to give
up the way of righteousness by the law, was not negative
but positive. It was a sacrifice which was required of him,
not a heavy burden which he cast off with satisfaction and
release. Thus the antithesis is so much the greater when,
through Christ's revelation, he is constrained to give up that
which is beloved and precious to him, that he may instead
win Christ and be found in Him. When Paul says, "For his
sake have I suffered the loss of all things," one senses immediately how difficult it had been for him to forsake this

hard-won righteousness.

No one else has seen as clearly as Paul the new in Christianity and its contrast to that which went before. It is to misunderstand him when, as has often happened, many have interpreted his contrast between the righteousness of faith and the righteousness of works (the law) as if he meant to say that a human being cannot achieve righteousness before God by reason of his works, but that on the contrary he becomes righteous by his inner quality, by his faith. The latter would still be a matter of man's own righteousness. No, the contrast Paul sees is much more radical. In the last analysis it is the antithesis between *his own righteousness and the righteousness of God*. He had sought to establish his own righteousness by the way of the law; but God had rejected that and established a new righteousness, when He sent Christ. The new righteousness is not a righteousness that comes from us, but one that can only be characterized with the word *"righteousness from God."*

Man ought to note carefully what a mighty religious reversal is encompassed in the word "righteousness from God." In practically all that is spoken of as religion we are met by man's effort to establish his own righteousness that he may thereby establish himself before God and win His favor. Christianity brings everything like that to an end when it speaks of "the righteousness of God" or "righteousness from God." Here a totally new kind of fellowship with God has appeared, a fellowship with God in which it is not man and his works but God and His work that stands at the center. We are not here dealing with a thought speculatively arrived at, but with a work of God, when He, quite contrary to man's effort to open a way to God, himself from His side, in Christ, laid down a way for mankind and opened a new way to fellowship with Him. It is this total reorientation in the religious relationship which Paul, in the Philippian passage cited above, formulated with such definitive clarity, "*not by my own righteousness* which comes by the law, but by the righteousness which comes through faith in Christ, *the righteousness from God.*"

In that expression, "the righteousness from God," the very foundation thought of the Epistle to the Romans is encompassed. That is affirmed by Paul himself when in 1:17 he states the theme for his letter. He does so with the following word, "The righteousness of God is revealed through faith for faith; as it is written, 'He who through faith is righteous shall live.'" And the whole epistle, as it proceeds, is nothing but a clarification of the contents of this "righteousness from God," and the consequences for the Christian life of the new righteousness of God which was revealed through Christ, and which is shared by him who believes in Christ.

More clearly than anyone else, Luther saw that that which is more vital than all else in the Epistle to the Romans is the antithesis between the egocentric and the theocentric fellowship with God, between the righteousness which we ourselves offer and the righteousness which comes from God. The first point in Luther's exposition of Romans consists of an explanation of that which is the essential summary of the epistle (*summarium huius epistole*). He writes, "The sum total of this epistle is to destroy, root out, and bring to naught all carnal wisdom and righteousness." If both among Jews and Gentiles man is concerned to establish a righteousness of his own, we have to learn the direct opposite from the Epistle to the Romans: "Here it is vital that our own righteousness and wisdom be brought to naught and rooted out of our hearts." With reference to Jeremiah 1:10, "You shall root out and pull down, destroy and throw down, build up and plant," Luther explains, "All that is in us is to be rooted out, pulled down, destroyed, and thrown down, i.e., all that delights us because it comes from us and is found in us; but all that is from outside of us and in Christ is to be built up and planted." And Luther proceeds, "God will not save us through our own righteousness and wisdom, but through that which comes to us from outside of ourselves; through a righteousness which has neither come from us nor been produced by us, but which comes to us from elsewhere; which did not grow on this earth, but comes from heaven. Hence man must learn a righteousness which is completely from without and foreign to us. And therefore one's own personal righteousness must first be rooted out."

4. THE TWO AEONS

What is the principal content of the letter to the Romans? From the beginning evangelical Christianity has spoken clearly on that point: justification by faith. That answer is correct; and that which has been said above has given support to it. But by itself that answer is far from enough to assure a right interpretation of the epistle.

An interesting observation has been made by Adolf Schlatter, one of today's foremost exegetes. He declares that evangelical theology's interest in Romans lapses as soon as it has reached the beginning of the fifth chapter; that it concerns itself only with the apostle's teaching about justification and its fruitage—that we have peace with God through our Lord Jesus Christ. But, Schlatter says, there is much more in this epistle. In the remaining chapters Paul discusses many other requirements central to the Christian life;

and these demand to be heard within the Christian church. "We have not come through to a full understanding of Paul if we hear only that he says, 'We have peace with God.'"

About this declaration it must be said that there is in it something that is right and something that is not right. It is manifestly right to say that we must listen to the epistle in its entirety, and not stop arbitrarily with its early chapters. It was of course not by accident that Paul did not stop with the eleventh verse of chapter five.

Nevertheless it would not be right to say that Paul goes on to talk of many other and important things; for from beginning to end in this epistle he discusses only one and the same thing. There is a great, unbroken unity in this letter, an inner consistency the equal of which is to be found neither in other Christian literature nor in the whole compass of literature. It would be impossible to mention another document so utterly unitary and so filled to its limits with crucial thoughts. But the consistency noted is more than consistency of thought. It is rather the harmony of an utterly consistent life. It is of the same kind as Luther's amazing consistency. But Luther had Paul and the Epistle to the Romans by which to stand. Paul had no such support on which to fall back. He stood on the immediate fact of God's work for us in Christ, and he put that fact into words on which subsequent ages have been able to live. It is because he has this one tremendous fact to proclaim that his presentation shows its unbreakable unity.

Nevertheless Schlatter's observation may well serve as a wholesome reminder, even though Romans is marked by such rigorous unity, centering throughout in our new righteousness through God, and revealing the single, central theme of justification by faith. For if we recognize the inclusive unity of the epistle, the fact that interest is not sustained to the end of it is unequivocal evidence that it is falsely understood; justification is not interpreted as Paul meant it. Two things in particular should be noted. For one thing, there is the frequent mistake of thinking that Paul here presented a particular—even though central—point in the Christian faith. Justification is not, in Paul's mind, merely an article in Christian doctrine. It is the basic reality on which the whole of Christian life rests. That I am justified means that through Christ I have become possessed of the new righteousness which comes from God, and am incorporated as a member of the kingdom of God. The attrition of the years has changed this reality, which includes and transforms the whole of life, to a theoretical doctrine about man's justification.

The second point to be noted is perhaps even more fateful. Perhaps with the purpose of giving justification reality in man's life, it is often viewed as a subjective, psychological experience. It is thought of as a change within the soul of man. Such an interpretation is utterly alien to Paul's meaning. For him justification is not something which occurs within the soul. He sees it in a great, universal perspective.

Here we are face to face with a view which holds the greatest dangers for a correct understanding. Such concepts belong to the thought-forms of neither Paul nor the rest of early Christianity. They are strange to Paul, even as his manner of thought is strange to us. But it is hardly possible to avoid misconstruction of Paul's meaning, if we come to it with today's thought-forms and axiomatic propositions. To words which he used with definite intent we give meanings that are not true to his mind. We give dogmatic and psychological meanings to his words, without being aware of the violence we do him. If without other preparation than our traditional conceptions, we turn to the reading of Romans, the strange likelihood is that, in the first four chapters, we shall find the understanding of justification with which we approach it. We look upon his words as if they were directed to certain mundane and psychological issues. All his crucial words—for example, such words as faith, righteousness, life, peace with God—are given a significance that was not Paul's. Faith is generally thought of as an inner quality, present in man or required of man; perhaps even a religious organ whereby one receives the grace of God. In any case, it is considered a subjective condition necessary for justification. Righteousness is viewed as a state of ethical well-being. Life is thought to be a new spiritual activity. Peace with God is held to be a psychological state of tranquility, etc. But that which is overlooked by such a view is precisely the characteristic Pauline meaning pervading all these terms. To avoid such error, as far as possible, we here give an introductory discussion of a passage taken from the heart of the epistle, choosing this because it most clearly gives expression to the basic position taken for granted by Paul and manifest throughout the letter. We thus, in a sense, let Paul interpret himself, when we use as background for our interpretation a passage where he clearly discloses the presuppositions on which he builds.

For this purpose we use Romans 5:12-21—exactly the passage where Schlatter says the interest of evangelical theology fails. In these verses Paul sets Adam and Christ in juxtaposition. Here interpreters of the New Testament have found their greatest difficulties. Because this thought is apparently introduced abruptly, without connection with what has preceded, exegetes have hardly known what to do with it. And other difficulties are seen. It is said that, in such comparison of Adam and Christ, Paul fell back into the rabbinical manner of thought. Others have affirmed, in the light of comparative religions, that Paul here used a modification of the familiar Hellenistic concept of original man.

The net result has been to leave scholars in perplexity. Some have thought the passage an epilogue to what has preceded. Others have called it a prologue to what follows. But the truth is that this passage is actually the high point of the epistle, in the light of which the whole is best to be understood. That we here confront something central and basic for Paul is evident in the very abrupt introduction and eruptive breaking forth of the idea expressed, as if no ready expression was adequate. It is complained that Paul does not at all demonstrate the parallelism between Christ and Adam, to which he appeals. But the very failure to do so, the accepting of the parellelism as self-evident, is itself evidence that Paul is here presenting something which he considers decisive and axiomatic. It is too basic to be capable of formal demonstration. One does not prove an axiom. Paul does not move from Adam to Christ, but from Christ. In the comparison of the two he is not trying to assure a unique position for Christ. Had that been his aim, there would be reason for the demand that he defend his logic in making the parallel. But the authority of Christ is to him utterly clear, quite independently of a line of reasoning. Rather is his purpose in such a comparison emphatically to affirm that Christ does occupy a status given Him by God.

Paul thinks in terms of aeons. Two realms stand over against each other. One is the dominion of *death* over all that is human, the age of Adam. The other is the dominion of *life*, the age of Christ. The question to which Paul is here addressing himself is to inquire what it is that has come about because Christ has been given to us. His answer is clear: the new aeon, the aeon of life, has come upon us. Thereby have they who stand with Christ, in faith on Him, been taken out of the dominion of death which overshadows Adam's race. This is the fact which was written to the Colossians (1:13), "He [God] has delivered us from the dominion of darkness and transferred us to the kingdom of his beloved Son." This is the *universal* significance of Christ. If the word did not already have other meaning for us, we could call it Christ's "cosmic" significance. Paul himself uses the word in this connection, "cosmos," the world. It is precisely this universal and cosmic aspect of Christ and His work which Paul is seeking to declare by the comparison with Adam. When Adam departed from God, it was not something which concerned only him as an individual; but in his act sin and death were made regnant in the cosmos, in the world, in the human order as a whole. Now through Christ, says Paul, in the same all-inclusive way, yea even much more, has *life* become regnant in the human order.

Some have discussed Paul's concept of history in this connection. But Paul is here treating of much more than a philosophy of history. His perspective looks far beyond the purview of such. The customary meaning of our terms, when we speak of a view of history or a concept of historical movement, has reference to what, for Paul, belongs wholly to the old aeon, the aeon of death. Even the most inclusive of philosophies of history do not look beyond that area. The two aeons or ages of which the apostle speaks can of course not be equated with our traditional division of time, time before the birth of Christ and time after that event. This traditional division is indeed the result of man's feeling that Christ's coming had decisive significance for humanity; that by His coming the status of humanity was changed. But this division nevertheless falls short of the Christian view of mankind. It sees history, both before and after the birth of Christ, as the history of the children of Adam. It sees only that which, in Paul's view, belongs to the world of sin and death.

If we are rightly to understand the contrast between death and life, between the aeon of death and the aeon of life, between the two ages, we must realize that Paul here sees in death a meaning much deeper and much more pervasive than we ordinarily understand by the term. He does not mean merely the termination of this life. He pronounces the judgment that rests on this life too. He is not saying merely that we have life for a time, after which life ends in death; nor is he aiming to explain the fact of such death. What Paul had to say to the effect that sin came into the world through Adam, and death through sin, has often been interpreted as if he, with theoretical interest, looked into the past for an explanation of the phenomenon that man must die, after he has lived for a longer or shorter time. But this is certainly to misunderstand his words. What he is saying is rather that all that we call life, with all that it encompasses, lies under the dominion of death. He finds that all humanity's life, from Adam till now, is lived under the mark and condition of death. Death rules supreme in this world—and it is to miss the point to ask whether this means physical, spiritual, or eternal death. Death is the status of all who belong to this world, the children of Adam.

Against this background the meaning of the gospel is

seen most clearly. To us who are in bondage to the dominion of the age of death comes the gospel with its message
that the new age, the age of life, has burst upon us. As
death became the lot of all through one man, Adam, so God
now bestows life on us through one man, Christ. Just as
Adam stands at the head of the old aeon (ὁ αἰὼν οὗτος), so
Christ stands by reason of His resurrection, as the author
and perfecter of the new (ὁ αἰὼν ὁ μέλλων). As long as men
had to look forward toward Him "who was to come," the
new aeon could only be called "the coming age." But now,
after He has come, it is no longer merely something that is
to be. Since the resurrection of Christ the new aeon has
become actual fact in our world. Christ stands at the frontier
between the two ages, outdating the old and blazing the
way for the new. In Christ we belong to the new aeon. In
II Corinthians 5:17, Paul expresses this fact thus, "If any
one is in Christ, he is a new creation; the old has passed
away, behold, the new has come."

In summary, we can say that Adam and Christ signify
for Paul these two aeons, the old age and the new. In the
old aeon, which began with Adam, death rules with unlimited power over all the children of Adam. In the new aeon,
which burst upon man with the resurrection of Christ, life
has come to dominion still more mightily.

In this connection a word should be said as to terms.
When we use the expression "the two aeons," despite the
strangeness thereof, we do so not merely because Paul uses
that noun, but even more because it is a better word than
"age" or "era" to express what is under discussion. In the
use of the word "age," there is danger that attention is
directed to different events in time. But Paul's word helps
to make clear that he speaks of two different orders of exist-

ence, one under the dominion of death and the other under the dominion of life.

The truth is that it is not only the verbiage that seems strange to our minds. The underlying meaning is extremely difficult for us to grasp. The whole manner of thought about the two aeons is quite alien to us. The reason lies in the secularizing of the thought of western civilization during the last several centuries. The roots of that process of secularization lie much further back in history; but the results have become clear only in recent centuries. It is very germane to consider secularization in this connection; for *saeculum* is of course the Latin equivalent for the Greek aeon (*aἰών*). Step by step man's life has come to be looked upon in mundane perspective. *This* world, *this* age, this *saeculum* came to be the only one man thought of. The result was an unprecedented foreshortening of man's perspective. Many have spoken of the characteristic "short perspective" of early Christianity; and it is true that, with its eschatological expectation of the early end of the present age, early Christianity had no thought of an ongoing mundane development, in the evolutionary sense. And yet the truth is that is was early Christianity that thought in terms of the long perspective; for it recognized not only the earthly, but also the supraworldly, the eternal. It is the secular view that thinks in the short perspective of man, imprisoned and enmeshed wholly in the mundane.

It hardly needs to be confessed that the secularizing of man's outlook has left its mark on theology and the interpretation of Christianity. The result has been that the gospel has for many come to have importance only for the earthly scene. It has been regarded as one view of the world, side by side with others; or as a static doctrine about God and

His nature. An earthly view of religion is prone to regard it as a subjective experience in the soul of man which must be nurtured and protected if it is to be well with man's whole life. But such is not Christianity's own view of itself. If one comes to the New Testament with such a false assumption, he can arrive only at a distorted idea of its meaning. Over against such a secularized view of Christianity it must be insisted that the gospel is not merely a doctrine about the nature of God, a high ethical standard, or the way to an enriched and refined spiritual life, or the like. The gospel is the proclamation of the work wrought by God when He sent Jesus Christ into the world. It is the message about the dynamic activity which God thereby introduced into our existence. The gospel is the declaration that God brought something wholly new into this age, that through Christ he brought the new age among us—an age begun in our midst, but to be fulfilled in glory.

For the men of the Reformation this understanding of the gospel and the consciousness of the two aeons were both living facts. They operated with the same basic assumption as Paul and were therefore in harmony with his view. But because of the current secularism our age has largely lost that meeting of minds with Paul and can recover it only by painstaking effort. Yet it may be that it is easier just now than it has been before in modern times to come eye to eye with Paul's meaning. We can now ask whether we must, like Paul, see the sharp dualism between the old aeon and the new. Are they really the ages of death and of life, respectively? Is actual experience really like that? Does the natural life of man really belong to the realm of death? Have we not failed to see how much of abiding value human culture has achieved? With such thoughts as these, men, in optimistic and culture-conscious times, have rejected the word about the two aeons. They have believed that, with human resources, we can build the kingdom of heaven on earth, giving dominion to life.

But now the state of the world has taught us to judge more realistically. And we can see more readily that this world, left to itself, stands under the sovereign dominion of death. People pour down death on people in order that, on the ruins that result, something else may be raised up. In this it is evident to Christian insight that both that which is ruined and that which is built on the ruins bear the mark of death and carry in themselves their own judgment and dissolution. Paul says that death is the sovereign ruler of this world. The facts demonstrate that his judgment presents the most realistic picture of human existence and circumstance.

If one would understand what Paul has to say in this epistle, he must from the start take seriously this affirmation about the two aeons. Basic to this view of Paul's are two facts: one, that in this world we belong to death's domain; the other, that through Christ, God has burst in upon this world with the dominion of life, calling us by the gospel to enter into it with Him. When Paul's background and basic outlook are thus seen, we can express in brief compass the line of thought he follows in this epistle.

5. The Line of Thought in the Epistle to the Romans

Before taking up our consideration of the several divisions of Romans, it may be well to present a brief orientation as to the rigorously consistent line of thought we shall encounter. Otherwise, as happens to many, we may be aware of the affirmations here found, but treat them like pearls strung, one by one, on a thread. We fail to see the rigorous harmony in which they stand. Part of the responsibility for such atomistic treatment may lie with the external fact that the text has been cut up into verses. Such division is of course at the same time a gain and a loss. It aids greatly in the quotation and location of texts and it helps in the memorizing of Scripture. But, on the other hand, it may also lead us to think that we are dealing with separate, independent statements, a collection of scriptural declarations. Such atomistic treatment becomes particularly bad when we deal with a document like Romans. Paul is not here giving us a collection of aphorisms pertinent to life's varied situations. Paul never wrote such a collection of declarations—least of all in Romans. Step by step, persistently and consistently, he hews his way through the flood of thoughts which present themselves to him as he undertakes to explain the meaning of God's work in Christ. It will pay us best to give open-minded attention to what Paul actually says, rather than to thoughts of our own that may be awakened by what he says. The distraction of associations that may cling to words removed from their context must be avoided. Step by step we must resolutely follow Paul's thought and observe as he builds up his message. The individual declarations cannot otherwise be understood, for they depend for their meaning on the context which they serve.

The best place to begin, for an inclusive view of the meaning of Romans, is, as said above, the fifth chapter's comparison of Adam and Christ. This gives the key to the whole epistle. We have already labeled this passage the high point of Romans. When we attain to its height, all that precedes and all that follows spread out before us in one inclusive view. We see how part fits directly into part, how Paul's thought moves from step to step under its inherent compulsion. With this passage as our point of orientation we can with surer understanding peruse the epistle from beginning to end.

It is immediately clear to us what the apostle means when, in 1:17, he gives his motto and text for the whole epistle: ὁ δὲ δίκαιος ἐκ πίστεως ζήσεται, "He who through faith is righteous shall live." The context makes clear that the righteousness mentioned is that already referred to, "the righteousness of God." That is the utterance of the immediately preceding words, δικαιοσύνη θεοῦ. As to him who has that righteousness through faith, it is said that he shall live. The meaning is clear from what we have already pointed out: he is removed from the dominion of death and received into the relationship of the new life, which is revealed and realized through Christ. It is noteworthy that the declaration which Paul makes the motto of his letter is taken from the Old Testament, from Habakkuk. Already in the Scripture of the old covenant Paul finds reference to that which he will here set forth and explain: "He who through faith is righteous shall live." It is only to such that entrance into the aeon of life is promised. That the righteous shall live and that the sinner stands under the power of death, man already knew. Man knew that righteousness and life, like sin and death, belong together. But God opened a new way to life for us when He raised up Christ and let Him, as the first fruit, triumph over death, destroying its power and bringing life and immortality to light. It is not he who is righteous through his own works who shall live, but he who through faith is righteous, who through faith belongs to Christ. Here our own righteousness and God's righteousness, "the righteousness of God," stand in opposition. The good and right which we do are our own righteousness; but that does not help us to enter into life. That is a righteousness which has its value for this age. But one does not enter into the kingdom of God by reason of any righteousness of his own. That is possible only through a wholly different righteousness. *Christ is the righteousness of God.* He who believes on Him has with Him been set free from the power of death. He who believes on Him has through Him been received into the realm of life. He already in this life shares in the new aeon, and he shall live in it when it is made perfect in glory. Such is the meaning of the theme of Romans. The whole letter is devoted to the development of that theme: "He who through faith is righteous shall live." That development falls into four great divisions.

(1) Paul's first endeavor is to characterize him who through faith is righteous. This he does in chapters 1:18– 4:24. He confronts us immediately with the antithesis of the two aeons. As background for his teaching about righteousness through faith, he describes the condition of the old aeon, before the "righteousness of God" was revealed— man under the wrath of God, under the dominion of death. It is true of the heathen (1:18-32). They forsook God and did not seek to honor or worship Him. Therefore God gave them up. But the same is also true of the Jews (2:1–3:20). They boasted that they had God's law and believed that by it they could attain unto life. But, like the heathen, they too stand under the dominion of death and the wrath of God. Therefore the apostle must "charge both Jews and Greeks, that they are all under sin" (3:9). Nor can the law effect any rescue from this state. Rather was it given "that every mouth may be stopped, and the whole world may be held accountable to God. For no human being will be justi-

fied in his sight by the works of the law" (3:19f.). Both the unrighteousness of the heathen and the Jews' righteousness of the law stand under the wrath of God. This is man's state in the old aeon.

But then came the great change, when "the righteousness of God" was revealed through Christ. In 3:21 we read, "But now the righteousness of God has been manifested apart from the law . . . through faith in Jesus Christ." That change, that complete transformation has not occurred by any achievement of ours. "For there is no distinction; since all have sinned and fall short of the glory of God" (3:22f.). The change, the transformation, has been effected by an approach from God's side. At the point of time fixed in His own counsel He sent into the world of death Him who is the Prince of life. And now He lets the proclamation sound to all the world. "Believe the gospel, believe the glad message that the time of bondage is past." He who believes on Him and becomes His has passed from the realm of death unto life.

We have earlier said that the difference between the old age and the new is not the same as the division of time by the birth of Christ. There was faith even in the time of the old covenant. Paul himself draws his word as to the righteousness of faith from Old Testament prophecy. And in the passage just cited about the great transformation effected by the intervention of God there is a word that points back to the Old Testament. We now return to examine it. When Paul speaks of the revelation of the righteousness of God through Christ, he adds, a righteousness of which "the law and the prophets bear witness." In Paul's thought, the law and the prophets do not stand against faith in Christ, but bear witness of Him. How this happened Paul indicates in the fourth chapter, where Abraham, though he lived before Christ, is presented as a type and example of those who through faith are righteous. He did not look to himself and his own possibilities, but to what God would do; and he believed on Him "who gives life to the dead and calls into existence the things that do not exist" (4:17). By such faith he honored God (4:20). Therefore Abraham could be set forth as the father of each and every one "who does not work, but trusts him who justifies the ungodly" (4:5). Though he was an Old Testament patriarch, he belonged to the new aeon, or, in the words of the Gospel according to John, "Abraham rejoiced to see the new day, the day of Christ; he saw it and was glad."

(2) The theme of the epistle reads thus: He who through faith is righteous shall live. The first half thereof received its exposition in the first four chapters. That part came to its conclusion in Paul's presentation of Abraham as the father of all the believing. Thereby the picture of him who through faith is righteous is made concrete.

In the second chief division, which includes the next four chapters, 5-8, the other half of the theme is developed. It is the affirmation as to him who through faith is righteous that *he shall live*, ζήσεται.

What this means is indicated at once in the mighty affirmation with which chapter 5 begins: "Therefore, since we are justified by faith, we have peace with God through our Lord Jesus Christ. Through him we have obtained access to this grace in which we stand, and we rejoice in our hope of sharing the glory of God." The new life is the diametrical opposite to the old. In the old, the wrath of God (ὀργὴ θεοῦ) was revealed from heaven against ungodliness and wickedness of men, as the first chapter says. In the new, there are access to the grace of God and peace with God. In the old, men fall short of the glory of God (δόξα θεοῦ). In the new, says the apostle, we rejoice in the glory of God, though it be as yet only in hope. The kingdom of God has come upon us, though it is not yet established in its fullness.

He who through faith is righteous *shall live*. What do these four chapters say about that? And what is meant by living in Christ? Most simply, and closest to Paul's own way of answering, the meaning can be stated as follows: to live in Christ means

1) to be free from the wrath of God (chap. 5)
2) to be free from sin (chap. 6)
3) to be free from the law (chap. 7)
4) to be free from death (chap. 8)

Here we offer just a brief comment on each of these chapters.

In chapter 5 we meet the crowning point. The new life is stated in its essential terms: grace, peace, and the hope of the glory of God; and its basis is God's love. The wonder of God's love Paul sees revealed supremely in the cross. The uniqueness of that love is that it is bestowed, not in consideration of any merit of man, but, on the contrary, upon such as deserve God's wrath. It is given to the sinful and the weak, the ungodly, the enemies of God. But, Paul continues, if while we were His enemies, God demonstrated such love to us through Christ, much more "since we are now justified by his blood . . . shall we be saved by him from the wrath of God." The wrath of God is removed from those who are in Christ. Then follows that which has all the time stood in the background, the presupposition on which all that has preceded rests—the passage about the two aeons, about Adam and Christ, about the sovereign power of death in this world and the sovereign power of life which has come to us in Christ.

There is a question which confronts Paul when, in the final verses of chapter 5, he points out that the law belongs to the old aeon, which is superseded in Christ: are we then to continue in sin? That is the issue for the sixth chapter. The law is the power that stands against sin. When the modest role of the law in God's plan of salvation is seen, is not the result to set sin free from its restraint? "By no means!" says Paul, pointing out that in baptism we are incorporated into Christ, becoming one with him. "The death he died he died to sin, once for all, but the life he lives he lives to God. So you also must consider yourselves dead to sin and alive to God in Christ Jesus" (6:10f.). Here we have the familiar juxtaposition of death and life, applied directly to sin. Sin belongs to the old aeon, from which we have escaped through Christ. The law sought to prevent sin, but it could not—for it too belongs to the old aeon. Christ has set us free from the bondage of sin and made us ministers of righteousness. Thus Paul, in the final verse of this chapter, affirms the absolute opposition between sin and life in Christ, "The wages of sin is death, but the free gift of God is eternal life in Christ Jesus our Lord" (6:23).

Having made clear the opposition between the Christian life and sin, Paul can—in the seventh chapter—freely and without fear of misunderstanding discuss the Christian's freedom from the law. This chapter has always been a crux in interpretations. Men have asked as to whom Paul said, "I am carnal, sold under sin. . . . For I know that nothing good dwells in me, that is, in my flesh. I can will what is right, but I cannot do it." Luther held that Paul here speaks of his life as a Christian. In later times men have tended to hold that Paul here speaks of the conflict that ruled his life while he was under the law. Could Paul speak so disparagingly about the Christian life? Could he have so low a concept of Christ's power to overcome sin in the new life? The cause of this difficulty is that men have overlooked the background of what Paul here says, that is, the fact of the two aeons. Men seem to have assumed that the apostle here gives a psychological description of a discordant state of the soul. But the real meaning is simple and clear, if we but give heed to the context and background. The tension here described is only an expression of the tension between the two aeons; and a recognition that the Christian's life is conditioned by both. The new aeon has indeed come upon us through Christ; but this does not mean that one who has been justified is now free from the old. Paul can at the same time say, "Wretched man that I am! Who will deliver me from this body of death?" and "Thanks be to God through Jesus Christ our Lord" (7:24f.).

Then, despite his realistic view of the circumstance of the Christian life, Paul begins the eighth chapter with the triumphant word, "There is therefore now no condemnation for those who are in Christ Jesus." It is the law that condemns. But it is not by the law that the Christian is justified, but through that which God has done in Christ. "For God has done what the law, weakened by the flesh, could not do: sending his own Son in the likeness of sinful flesh and for sin, he condemned sin in the flesh" (8:3). Thereby the dominion of the law was abolished. For even though, in the present age, we are still subject to the power of death, the sufferings of this present time are not worth comparing with the glory, God's δόξα, which is to be revealed in the new creation. We still long for our sonship, deliverance from this body of death. But in all this we gain a glorious victory through Christ Jesus our Lord.

In this Paul reaches the end of the second section of his epistle. He has completed the circle and is back at the point in the fifth chapter, the juxtaposition of the dominions of death and of life. He has made clear what it means to live in Christ. He who lives in Christ has passed from the dominion of death into life. It might seem that that is the final word in the theme, "He who through faith is righteous shall live." But Paul has not yet reached the end. He has two more inclusive things to add.

(3) It has long been held that chapters 9-11 are a long parenthesis. Scholars have made all kinds of efforts to explain how Paul got switched from his main argument to such a sidetrack. But the truth is that these chapters are not a parenthesis at all, or a digression. They are a consistent development of the very thought with which Paul is dealing.

Paul proclaims that God's promise his been fulfilled in Christ. The new aeon is the time of fulfillment. The promise was given to Israel. "To them belong the sonship, the glory, the covenants, the giving of the law, the worship, and the promises" (9:4). But now Paul is faced by the mystery that, in the very moment the promises should be fulfilled, they appear to be unrealized. For the result of the coming of Christ was not Israel's restitution but her rejection. Is the righteousness which is by faith then contrary to God's promises? Does God, through His new revelation, cancel His earlier promises? Paul rejects such thoughts: "It is not as though the word of God had failed" (9:6). No, the righteousness which is by faith is in utter agreement with the promises, if only we understand rightly. In this context Paul presents three great arguments, which are entirely in harmony and confirm each other. 1. It is false to appeal to the promises against God who gave them; for God's sovereignty is seen in the very promises. In His sovereignty God decreed, when He gave the promises, that they should be fulfilled to those who believe in Christ. They alone are "the children of promise." 2. But if, when God has decreed that righteousness is to come by the way of faith, Israel seeks after righteousness by the way of the law, the fault is Israel's if she be rejected and fail of the fulfillment. 3. Her rejection is not final but points forward to eventual acceptance. Yet Israel must first be rejected. For as long as there was anything to which she could appeal—be that the fulfillment of the law, lineage, covenant, or the promises given to the fathers—so long was the way to God barred. But Israel's rejection opened the way for Israel's eventual acceptance by God's free mercy. "For God does not repent of His call."

Only now has the adopted theme been presented fully, when it has been made quite clear that the righteousness of works will not suffice; that only he who through faith is righteous shall live. Paul has arrived at the point from which he can address his admonitions to the church at Rome. This he does in his fourth section.

(4) After our observation of the great message of Romans, it does not surprise us to hear Paul introduce his admonitions with the inclusive exhortation, "Do not be conformed to this world, but be transformed by the renewal of your mind" (12:2). This is the basis of Paul's ethics. All that follows thereafter is only the fuller development of this basic mandate that the Christian be not conformed to this aeon, but be transformed into harmony with the new. How does life come into harmony with the new aeon? That is attained when we live "in Christ," as members of "the body of

Christ." A Christian is nothing by himself. What he is he is "in Christ." "So we, though many, are one body in Christ, and individually members one of another" (12:5). But to live "in Christ" is to live in love. "Love one another with brotherly affection" (12:10). It is the Christian's responsibility, in the midst of the present age and its orders, to live the life of the new aeon. He must live in love to his neighbor, for "love is the fulfilling of the law" (13:10).

After Paul has thus shown, by his admonitions, what the Christian's renewal means in actual life, he returns to the point where he started: "It is full time now for you to wake from sleep. . . . . The night is far gone, the day is at hand. Let us then cast off the works of darkness and put on the armor of light" (13:11f.). The night is far gone; that is, this age approaches its end. The day is at hand; that is, the new age stands at the door, indeed it has already begun to enter. That fact is to be manifest in our behavior: "Let us conduct ourselves becomingly as in the day" (13:13). If we believe in Christ and that, through Him, God's new kingdom has come upon us, our life must be transformed into harmony therewith. Therefore Paul commands, "Put on the Lord Jesus Christ" (13:14).

That even Paul's admonitions fall perfectly within the frame of the course of thought presented is perhaps the clearest evidence of all as to the utter consistency that characterizes this epistle from beginning to end.

Further to fix the course of Paul's thought, and to keep it the better before us, we give an outline of the contents of the epistle. And with it we give a parallel outline using the terms that are characteristic for Paul.

Outline of the Epistle

Parallel Outline

Introduction: Paul's obligation to preach the gospel

Theme: ὁ δίκαιος ἐκ πίστεως ζήσεται

I. ὁ δίκαιος ἐκ πίστεως

    1. The old aeon—ὀργὴ θεοῦ
        (1) ἀδικία τῶν ἀνθρώπων

        (2) δικαιοσύνη ἐκ νόμου

    2. The new aeon—δικαιοσύνη θεοῦ

        (1) Revealed through Christ

        (2) Witnessed to by the law and the prophets: Abraham as type for ὁ δίκαιος ἐκ πίστεως

II. ὁ δίκαιος ἐκ πίστεως ζήσεται

    1. ἐλεύθερος ἀπὸ τῆς ὀργῆς Ἀδάμ, ὁ τύπος τοῦ μέλλοντος

    2. ἐλεύθερος ἀπὸ τῆς ἁμαρτίας

    3. ἐλεύθερος ἀπὸ τοῦ νόμου

    4. ἐλεύθερος ἀπὸ τοῦ θανάτου

III. The righteousness of faith does not
                violate God's promise   9:1 –11:36

   1. In His very promise God shows His
      sovereignty: the promise is only to
      those who believe   9:6 – 9:29

   2. Israel is herself responsible for her re-
      jection, because she seeks her right-
      eousness through the law   9:30–10:21

   3. When her time is come Israel will be
      accepted by God's free compassion 11:1 –11:36

IV. The behavior of those who through faith are righteous
                                    12:1 –15:13

   1. In conformity to the new age   12:1 –13:14

     (1) In Christ (as members in the body of Christ)
                                12:3 –12:8

     (2) In love   12:9 –12:21

     (3) Even in the present aeon with its institutions
                                13:1 –13:7

     (4) Love, the fulfillment of the law 13:8 –13:10

     (5) "Put on the Lord Jesus Christ" 13:11–13:14

   2. Specific applications: the weak and the strong
                                14:1 –15:13

Conclusion   15:14–16:27

III. δικαιοσύνη ἐκ πίστεως does not violate God's promise

   1. In His very promise God shows His sovereignty: only οἱ ἐκ πίστεως are τέκνα τῆς ἐπαγγελίας

   2. Israel is herself responsible for her rejection because she seeks her δικαιοσύνη ἐκ νόμου

   3. When her time is come Israel will be accepted by God's free compassion

IV. ὁ δίκαιος ἐκ πίστεως περιπατεῖ

   1. κατὰ τὸν αἰῶνα τὸν μέλλοντα

      (1) ἐν Χριστῷ (as members of σῶμα Χριστοῦ)

      (2) ἐν ἀγάπῃ

      (3) Even in ὁ αἰὼν οὗτος with its institutions

      (4) πλήρωμα νόμου ἡ ἀγάπη

      (5) ἐνδύσασθε τὸν κύριον Ἰησοῦν Χριστόν

   2. Specific applications: the weak and the strong

Conclusion

II

Introduction to the Epistle

Paul's Obligation to Preach the Gospel in Rome

1:1-15

Inasmuch as, in this letter, Paul addresses himself to a church with which he had hitherto had no direct personal relation, it is necessary for him to begin by giving his reasons. It is therefore entirely natural that his habitual salutation is, in this case, considerably extended. There are, in particular, two things which induce him to such expression. First he must here introduce himself in a way not necessary elsewhere. And he must make clear what right he has to claim this church's attention. These two reasons center in the same fact. He refers both to the grace given to him and to his apostleship. These, more than giving him the right, lay upon him a special responsibility to bring the gospel to the church in Rome. That fact gives unusual weight even to his introductory words. They are much more than a formal introduction. Again and again the tremendous theme of the letter appears in them. The great issue is at hand from the beginning.

Like the rest of his letters, this one begins with Paul's name. But it is not in his own name that he comes. He comes on behalf of his Lord and by His commission, the "servant of Jesus Christ." In the very coupling of these two names, Jesus and Christ, we encounter something unprecedented. It is easy for us to slip over that fact, because that coupling of names is taken for granted, tradition having made it a commonplace. For us the name "Christ" usually means only a proper name for the familiar figure of Jesus Christ. The two names are fused into one, and considered only a name. But for Paul and his age the Christ-concept, the Messiah-concept, had a vital meaning, a reality independent of Jesus and prior to Him. When Paul couples the name Christ with Jesus he means something unprecedented —that the Messiah whom Israel had awaited for centuries had now come, and the messianic age with Him. Thus in Paul's own day God's greatest miracle had occurred; and Paul had been appointed by God to proclaim this fact. Christ is Lord ($\kappa\acute{\nu}\rho\iota\sigma$), and Paul is His bond servant ($\delta\sigma\hat{\nu}\lambda\sigma$). For many the passing of subsequent centuries has worn thin the meaning of calling Christ Lord and man His bond servant. It was different with Paul. To him those terms expressed life's greatest and most revolutionary reality. What it means for Paul to be bond servant is implicit in the fact that Christ is Lord. The two terms, Lord and bond servant, are correlative. In this case "bond servant" has more than its usual meaning, because Christ is more than other lords. He is *the Lord* in the absolute sense; He is Kyrios. What the term signifies for Paul can be seen in Philippians 2:9ff.: "God has highly exalted him and bestowed on him the name which is above every name." God has given Him the name which is reserved for God himself, the name Lord, Kyrios. Ever after Paul met the Lord on the Damascus road, he was not his own; he was the Lord's bond servant. The all-commanding task thereafter was to tell all the world the message about the Lord Jesus Christ.

Paul had not simply taken this task upon himself; God had called him especially for it. Therefore he says "called to be an apostle." For him the call to the apostolic office had followed immediately upon his call to discipleship. While Jesus walked upon earth, He gathered a circle of disciples who were to be His witnesses and messengers. Foremost among them were the twelve, and to them He gave the apostolic mission. Paul was aware that he too had received an equally direct call. But whereas they had been sent to Israel, he was sent to the world of the Gentiles. A compelling consciousness of his election is evident in what Paul says about his call to be an apostle. His commission was utterly unique, without counterpart elsewhere. The task given to him was peculiar, and appropriately God called him in utterly unique manner. In a passage in Galatians, Paul lets us see his sense of election. When he had spoken of his pre-Christian period and of the persecutions he practiced against Christians, he added, "But when he who had set me apart before I was born, and had called me through his grace, was pleased to reveal his Son to me, in order that I might preach him among the Gentiles . . . I went" (Gal. 1:15f.).

The same word which Paul used there to affirm that God chose him for a special work, the word "to set apart," he also uses in Romans in direct connection with what he says about his apostolic office: "set apart for the gospel of God." His use of that precise word was not unintended. "Set apart" (ἀφωρισμένος) has the same root meaning as Pharisee (φαρισαῖος). Even before his becoming a Christian he had been "set part." As a Pharisee he had set himself apart for the law. But now God had set him apart for something

entirely different, "for the gospel of God." In the Swedish
translation Paul's words read, "set apart to preach the gospel
of God." But the Greek says simply "for the gospel," not "to
preach the gospel." This loose translation might lead us to
place emphasis at the wrong point; that is, on the preaching.
Paul does not say that he was set apart as preacher. He says
he was "set apart"; the difference indicated will be clear.
Paul, who had set himself apart for the law, is set apart by
God for the gospel. Thus in the very first verse of this epistle
we encounter the letter's basic juxtaposition of law and gospel which, from one point of view, is the theme of Romans.

The gospel is the great new reality which God has now
brought to us. And yet this new reality is not unrelated with
what has gone before! It does not come without preparation. Already through the prophets God had promised such
a gospel. The gospel comes as the fulfillment of promises
given earlier. What had once been a promise has now become reality.

Many have had difficulty as to what really was Paul's
attitude to the Old Testament. On the one hand, Christ
has outdated it. The way of the gospel shows the way of
law to be a false road to salvation. And yet Paul does not
abandon the Old Testament. He holds fast to it as God's
own revelation. To a purely static and impersonal view
this might look like a contradiction. But to Paul, with his
living concept of God, there is here no contradiction. God
does not always have to deal with men in the same way, or
give all at one time. He is the living and active God, and
by His activity He brings forth that which is new. When it
pleased Him to give to us what He had not given to the
people of the old covenant, we need not minimize it as if
it were not really new—for the sake of continuity with the

old—nor need we scorn the old, that what is now given may be seen to be something utterly new. It is the same God who speaks in both situations. That is to be seen in the fact that the new which He gives is the fulfillment of the old promise. The promise and the gospel point to each other. The promises portend the gospel; the gospel is the accomplishment of the promises.

For Paul, as for early Christians in general, there was something vital in the fact that the Old Testament scriptures thus recorded the promises of that which God now effected in their midst. Thus Paul writes, in I Corinthians 15:3f., that "Christ died for our sins in accordance with the scriptures, that he was buried, and that he was raised on the third day in accordance with the scriptures." The repeated insistence that these things occurred "in accordance with the scriptures" shows how vital this was to Paul. There is another enlightening passage in Acts 13:32ff., where we read, "We bring you the good news that what God promised to the fathers, this he had fulfilled to us their children by raising Jesus, as also it is written . . ." Here we see why the earliest Christian theology to so large a degree took the form of scriptural proof. Men searched the Scriptures to find evidence as to Christ.

The gospel has a single center around which all revolves. From beginning to end it treats of *the Son of God.* It was through His coming that the new age entered. The law speaks about man and what he must do. The gospel speaks about God and what He has done by sending His Son into the world. So Paul can simply characterize the content of the gospel of God: it is the gospel about the Son of God. As man, sharing our common humanity (κατὰ σάρκα), He is descended from David—in harmony with the Old Testament

47

promise which calls the Messiah the son of David. But
Christ does not belong only to our common humanity.
Through Him God has permitted something utterly new
to enter our world. It would therefore be false to see in
Him only that which belongs to the old age. It does not
suffice to say what Christ is "according to the flesh" (κατὰ
σάρκα). Something greater must be said about Him "according to the Spirit," "according to the Spirit of holiness" (κατὰ
πνεῦμα, κατὰ πνεῦμα ἁγιωσύνης). He who according to the
flesh, in His human existence, belonged to the seed of David,
was ordained by God for something different and higher.
God designated Him "Son of God in power." That was
certified to Him by His resurrection. To be sure, from the
beginning He was Son of God, but in weakness and lowliness. The divine glory, which formerly was hidden, was
manifest after the resurrection. From that hour He is the
Son of God in a new sense: He is the Son of God "in power,"
Son of God in glory and fullness of power.

To Paul the resurrection of Christ is God's mightiest act.
It is by it that the new age decisively arrived. In Ephesians
1:19-21 we encounter a range of thought which gives clear
view of Paul's attitude on this. He speaks of "the working
of his great might which he accomplished in Christ when
he raised him from the dead and made him sit at his right
hand in the heavenly places," making Him Lord over "every
name that is named, not only in this age but also in that
which is to come."

When Paul speaks of the resurrection, here in the beginning of Romans, he uses what may appear a very surprising
expression. We should have expected him to say "his
(Christ's) resurrection from the dead." But instead of that
he quite generally says, "the resurrection of those who are

dead." We should have expected ἐξ ἀναστάσεως αὐτοῦ ἐκ νεκρῶν; but he says ἐξ αναστάσεως νεκρῶν. Now the resurrection of Christ and the resurrection of those who are dead are two very different things. The expression "the resurrection of Christ" points to an event at a single point in history. His resurrection from the dead means, as the word states, that He was removed from the community of the dead. The dead remained where they were, but He was removed "from the dead." The expression "the resurrection of the dead" (those who are dead), on the other hand, refers to an all-inclusive event which is thought of as placed at the end of time, "the last day," wherein all the dead are recalled to life. So we are confronted with the peculiar fact that when Paul refers to the resurrection of Christ, he says, "the resurrection of the dead." He says about Christ that He was designated Son of God in power by the resurrection of the dead. But he clearly means "by his resurrection from the dead."

Various expedients have tried to meet this difficulty. According to one explanation, he chose the expression purely for euphemy and brevity. Another suggests that Paul actually did not mean to refer to a single event in history, the resurrection of Christ. By reference to the resurrection of the dead he rather meant only to indicate the quality of the event through which Christ reached His dignity as Son of God in power. Paul's expression would then mean that, through a resurrection of the kind and character which is in prospect for all the dead, Christ should attain to the power and glory commensurate with His status as Son of God. Still other explanations hold that Paul was simply guilty of inaccuracy in expression, since he manifestly meant the resurrection of Christ but said the resurrection of the dead.

But it is really quite unnecessary to fall back on such half-apologetic explanations. The words, just as they stand, give expression to a characteristically Pauline view. It is obvious that Paul refers to the resurrection of Christ as an accomplished fact. The resurrection is the frontier over which Christ passed to the status of Son of God in power. But, just as he says, Paul also means "the resurrection of the dead" in the usual sense of those words. But how can he mean both of these things? The explanation lies in the fact that for him the resurrection of Christ and the resurrection of the dead are not two totally different things. In the final analysis they are one and same truth. *For Paul the resurrection of Christ is the beginning of the resurrection of the dead.* Through Christ the resurrection age has burst upon us. He who believes in the Son of God "has passed from death to life" (John 5:24). Paul too could say that. The recently cited passage in Ephesians gives guidance here. Right after the declaration that God raised Christ from the dead and set Him above every name that is named, not only in this age but also in that which is to come, follows the statement about Christ as the head of the church and the church as His body (Eph. 1:22f.). That which has happened to the head also happens to the body. In Christ we are the children of the resurrection. Here we reach the full significance of the comparison of Adam and Christ. As Adam's death meant death for all his race, so Christ's resurrection means resurrection for those who through Him have become members of the new age. The resurrection has thus already begun. As yet it is limited to the Head; but it is true and meaningful for all who are members of His body. On

this fact Paul built his argument in I Corinthians 15. There
were some who admitted the resurrection of Christ but
denied the resurrection of the dead. But if there be no resurrection of the dead, then Christ is not risen; for His is the
first act in the resurrection of the dead. But if Christ is not
risen, our faith is vain. We are still in our sins. If Christ
did not rise nothing real and momentous has happened to
transform our world. "But," Paul declares, "in fact Christ
has been raised from the dead, the first fruits of those who
have fallen asleep. For as by a man came death, by a man
has come also the resurrection of the dead" (I Cor. 15:20f.).

All that is needed to resolve the difficulty here under
discussion lies in the statement that Christ is "the first fruit."
Christ arose as the first fruit. Through His resurrection
comes the resurrection of the dead. Thus we see how well
chosen and how fitting the words of Paul are when he speaks
of "the resurrection of the dead." If by His resurrection
Christ was designated Son of God in power, it was not by
reason of His own resurrection alone, as if the exaltation
involved only Him individually. Christ became Son of God
in power in the fact that it was by His resurrection that the
aeon of the resurrection and life burst upon this world of
death. So *the resurrection is the turning point in the existence of the Son of God.* Before that He was the Son of God
in weakness and lowliness. Through the resurrection He
became the Son of God in power. *But the resurrection is
also the turning point in humanity's existence.* Before this
the whole race was under the sovereign sway of death; but
in the resurrection of Christ life burst forth victoriously, and
a new aeon began, the aeon of the resurrection and life.

It may justly be said that in Romans 1:4 we have the
whole message of the epistle in a nutshell. Paul's intent is

to make clear the content of the gospel and to show what it is we possess in the fact that Christ was given. In one short affirmation, in the fourth verse, Paul gives his understanding, pointing to the resurrection of Christ as the starting point for a new age and a new humanity.

The meaning of this verse is not so clear from the translation used in the Church of Sweden. Paul's thought is particularly obscured by the translation of his "according to the Spirit" and "according to the Spirit of holiness" (κατὰ πνεῦμα ἁγιωσύνης) by the words "as a holy spiritual being." And, besides, the word "power" is not coupled with "Son of God" —as it is by Paul—but the verb: "with power designated Son of God." Even though that reading is not grammatically impossible, the word order makes it less likely; and the meaning would thereby be made less clear and good. And finally the Swedish version mentioned renders "the resurrection from the dead." The last two points referred to have already been treated sufficiently; but something should be said about the first.

Paul contrasts "flesh" and "spirit" (σάρξ, πνεῦμα). With our inherited mode of thought we are particularly prone to understand these terms as referring to two different parts of man's being. "The flesh" is regarded as being the bodily side of our life, the lower, sensory nature. "The Spirit" would likewise be the higher, spiritual capacities, our rational nature, our inner essence. When Paul says that "according to the flesh" Christ was born of the seed of David, he is understood to mean that His body belonged to the seed of David. And when he says that "according to the spirit" Christ was designated Son of God in power, that is thought to affirm that Christ as a spiritual being was the Son of God. Then it is thought that the resurrection freed Christ from all that was lower and physical and exalted Him as a spiritual being. As man He had both body and spirit, but after the resurrection, which set Him free from the body, He was pure spirit.

About such a view it must be said that it totally misses what Paul means to say. The whole inclusive viewpoint which is the background of such a thought, is totally alien both to Paul and to the Scriptures in general. Of course Paul and the other New Testament authors recognized the difference between the external and inner in man. But it is not to that difference that reference is made when "flesh" and "spirit" are contrasted. To grasp correctly what is meant thereby one must remember the Old Testament background. There is never any thought of a contrast between different parts of man's nature. The contrast is between God and man. God is "Spirit." And man is "flesh"—and that is true of everything human, without differentiation between higher and lower. "The flesh" means man in his totality—the external and the inner, the physical and the psychical, the sensory and the rational. "The flesh" means the impotence and futility of man when left to his own resources. And another meaning is very close to this; for "the flesh" also characterizes man in his sinful state, his alienation from God, and his will to live only for himself and by his own devices. To live thus without God is to live according to the flesh. But to live according to the Spirit is to live in fellowship with God and His will and to receive all from His hand.

We are immediately struck by the similarity of the flesh-spirit contrast with that of the old and new aeons. The old aeon is the realm of the flesh; but the Spirit is regnant in the new. Even where the terms "according to the flesh" and "according to the Spirit" are used without such reference, the thought of the two ages is never wholly absent. It is so

in the passage we are now considering. When Paul here
says that Christ is born of the seed of David "according to
the flesh," the apostle is declaring that as a man Christ belongs to the line of David; He belongs to our common
humanity and to the present age. And when it is said that
He was designated Son of God in power "according to the
Spirit" by the resurrection of the dead, it means that through
His resurrection He entered into sovereign power in the
new aeon, the resurrection aeon which itself began with His
resurrection.

Since the whole gospel has the Son of God as its center,
Paul can gather it all up in the name "Jesus Christ our Lord."
The whole gospel is encompassed in the fact that Jesus is
the Christ, the promised Messiah, and that God designated
Him Son of God in power by the resurrection and gave Him
the name which is above every name, the name Lord. We
have already discussed the significance of that name, to give
the right understanding of Paul's meaning in calling himself
the bond servant of Jesus Christ. But Paul himself first uses
the title for Christ in the verse we have been discussing.
That which he there ascribes to Jesus Christ is nothing less
than the Old Testament name of God, "the Lord" (Adonai=
JHVH), which the Septuagint translates Kyrios.

It is thus as "a servant of Jesus Christ, called to be an
apostle, set apart unto the gospel," that Paul addressed himself to the church in Rome. He characterizes the gospel by
pointing to the Son of God who by His resurrection was
exalted as Kyrios, Lord, to whom all power is given in
heaven and in earth. When Paul then returns, in the fifth
verse, to the subject of his apostleship, the fullness and
breadth of that office can be seen in the light of the message
he has to proclaim. It was from *the Lord* that Paul received

grace and apostleship. Both of these terms are essential for him, for not everyone who receives grace is made an apostle. But for Paul the two did come together. He was not first called to be a Christian, and called later to be an apostle. When the Lord revealed himself on the Damascus road, Paul received his double call at one and the same time, by that one act and in that one revelation. The Lord had chosen him for a special mission. For that reason he received that extraordinary revelation, given only to him. His mission was to the Gentiles. It was from the Lord who is over all things, in this age and in that which is to come, that Paul received his apostleship. But his commission was inclusive in its outreach. Among all the Gentiles, to the end of the earth, he is to preach the gospel concerning the Lord and His sway. He is to bring the Gentiles to faith in the Lord and obedience to Him. When God exalted Christ and gave Him the name which is above all names, it was in order that every knee should bow and every tongue confess that He is Lord. This is likewise the objective in Paul's preaching, "to bring about obedience to faith" in Christ.

There has been dispute about the meaning of the expression "obedience of faith." But the context should make that quite clear. Obedience is always required of man in his relation with God. It was so in the Old Testament. There it was particularly obedience to God's law, obedience to the covenant. But obedience is also necessary in the new aeon ushered in by Christ. But now obedience has a new significance. Now it comes to mean primarily that one receives in faith that which God proffers us through Christ. This is the "obedience of faith." Paul is aware that he is sent to bring the Gentiles thereto.

Now Paul has come to the point where he can address

himself directly to the church in Rome. As the apostle to
the Gentiles he has a special responsibility as to the church
in Rome. The Romans were Gentiles, and the Gentiles had
their center in Rome. They belonged to his field of labor.
This was reason enough for his writing to them. But he
addresses them, not as Gentiles, but as Christians. By divine
call they had become Christ's. Paul recognizes that with
three terms: they are "called," "God's beloved," and "saints."
We must examine each of these characterizations.

They are "called." How does one become a Christian?
We are prone to answer by making reference first to man's
voluntary attitude. It is different with Paul. For him, as for
early Christians in general, it is clear that it is not primarily
by the will and effort of man, but by the mercy of God, that
one becomes a member of the kingdom of Christ. Whatever
efforts one may make, however he may seek and strive after
righteousness before God, by his own zeal he is borne further and further away from God. The Jew, with his zeal
for the law, is an example of this. There is help for man
only in the fact that God intervenes and lets His call go forth
to man. Thus for Paul "the called" has become a technical
designation for Christians. It is by God's call that they have
come to belong to Christ. What the term signifies is seen
most clearly in II Timothy 1:9f.: "God . . . called us with a
holy calling, not in virtue of our works but in virtue of his
own purpose and the grace which he gave us in Christ Jesus
ages ago, and now has manifested through the appearing
of our Saviour Christ Jesus."

They are also "God's beloved." It is not hard to find the
reason why Paul applies that name. It is in harmony with
the dominant position his thought accords to the concept of
God's love, God's *agape*. This central concept sets its clear

mark on this epistle. The entire message of Romans is that through Jesus Christ God has set us free from the powers that held us prisoners in the old aeon and given us the righteousness of God and a new life in the new aeon—and that the love of God is both the sole cause and ultimate ground thereof. It was love which impelled God to give His Son for our sake (8:32). "God shows his love for us in that while we were yet sinners Christ died for us" (5:8). That which happened thus was the turning point in the history of humanity. By the intervention of God's love we have been removed from wrath, sin, the law, and death. We have been removed from all those powers which ruled in the old aeon and translated to the new, where pure love rules. In Colossians 1:13 this is expressed thus: "He has delivered us from the dominion of darkness and transferred us to the kingdom of his beloved Son." It is important to give heed to the expression which is here used about Christ. He is God's beloved Son, or, to translate literally, "the Son of His love" (ὁ υἱὸς τῆς ἀγάπης αὐτοῦ). In Christ God has intervened into our existence and made its conditions entirely new. To belong to Christ is therefore to be "God's beloved." In the high point of Romans Paul writes to the Christians, "God's love has been poured into our hearts through the Holy Spirit which has been given to us" (5:5). That love now encompasses their entire life. Henceforth no power whatever can separate them from the love of God in Christ Jesus (8:35-39). When Paul addresses the Christians as "God's beloved," he uses that word in its deepest and most inclusive sense. That name characterizes their entire existence as Christians.

Finally, they are "saints." A subtle danger of misunderstanding lurks near that word. When we hear the term "saints," our thoughts are prone to move in a moralistic direction. We think of an ethical quality in man, perhaps even approaching sinlessness. But it must be affirmed that all such thoughts are false to Paul's meaning. He knows no "saints" in the Roman Catholic sense of the term. He does not mean to apply the term only to such Christians as have advanced far in personal sanctification. *All* Christians, without exception, are saints. But it is not by virtue of their own efforts or their ethical quality that they are such. They are saints only by virtue of God's call. Thereby they have been taken out of this world and set apart as God's own. Through God's call and election they have become members of God's holy people. Therein, and alone therein, their holiness lies.

Instead of bringing his thought to a conclusion with a traditional greeting, Paul breaks forth into the apostolic blessing, "Grace to you and peace from God our Father and the Lord Jesus Christ." This is related to the Jewish salutation of peace, but Paul broadens it and fills it with Christian content. It is clear that it is mistaken to think of this "peace" as simply an inner state of the undisturbed soul. Nor is this benediction only a powerless wish. It speaks of an actual sharing of a spiritual reality. In this benediction at the beginning of his letter we see, in concise form, the content of the gospel which is to be developed as the letter continues.

The full significance of these words may best be grasped by viewing them in the light of Jesus' own form of the salutation of peace. To Him peace is a *gift* which He imparts to His disciples: "Peace I leave with you; my peace I give to you" (John 14:27). That gift His disciples were to pass on. When He sent them forth, He instructed them to begin their preaching with the greeting, "Peace be to this house" (Luke 10:5). That this is more than a wish; that it is the sharing of a spiritual reality is clear from the further statement that if the gift be not accepted it is to return to the disciples. Paul proceeds in like manner. His first word addressed directly to the church at Rome is the salutation of peace. With that "peace" he probably mentions "grace" because of the central place which it holds in his theology. But it should be remembered that grace and peace are already coupled in the Aaronic benediction (Num. 6:25f., "be gracious unto you and give you peace"). Paul may have been drawing upon that source. Grace and peace here constitute a unity, giving inclusive expression to salvation in its fullness. It comes from God and it has come to us through Jesus Christ.

From early days this benediction has been considered one of the surest evidences that Paul affirmed the deity of Christ. Only for that reason was it possible for him, without qualification, to place Christ beside the Father. That observation is correct beyond doubt; and it finds support in the fact that, according to Paul, Christ has the right to the divine name "Lord." In that name lies the most unequivocal confession of Christ's divine majesty.

We have now come to the end of the first and more important half of the introduction. As to the latter half (vss. 8-15) we can speak more briefly. It presents neither major theological problem nor difficulties of interpretation.

Paul begins with thanksgiving to God, and that definitely for the church at Rome. "In all the world," wherever he went on his far-reaching mission he heard about their faith. Particularly for him who ventured his life to preach the gospel of Christ to the ends of the earth was it a fountain of joy that that gospel had been received with faith in the very capital of the world. When Paul says that the faith of the church in Rome is spoken of in all the world, his statement is often taken as a testimony that that faith was especially strong, and that he therefore holds up that church as an example for others. But there is no evidence for that in the text. The fact that the gospel had found its way to Rome and there been received with faith is cause enough for Paul to thank God. Even though he is not susceptible to this world's power and glory, and though Rome has therefore no lure for him in that way, he is realistic enough to sense what it would mean for the Christian mission that there is in the capital of the world a church that believed in Christ. He had naturally yearned for opportunity to come into contact with the Christians in Rome. Therefore he has prayed to God that he might succeed in coming to them.

When Paul here, as was customary in ancient correspondence, follows his salutation with his thanksgiving to God on account of those to whom he writes, he would not have them think that what he says in holy zeal is only conventional form. He calls God to witness. God knows that for a long time, indeed for years, the church at Rome has ever been in the apostle's thoughts and prayers.

There is another reason for wishing to make contact with this church. His plans include Spain; but of that he says nothing as yet. He does not come to that till near the end of the letter (15:24). In the introduction he speaks only of his longing to reach Rome. There was motive enough for that, apart from further missionary ambitions toward the west. Paul explains his desire to go to Rome, saying that he would share with them something of the spiritual gifts he has received, to strengthen them. He does not mean that he alone has something to bestow, while the church at Rome only receives. He hastens to add, "that is, that we may be mutually encouraged by each other's faith, both yours and mine."

It has been customary to see an example of tact and sensitiveness in what Paul says about mutuality in their relationship. When he ventures to say that he would impart to them some spiritual gift, he is aware that it may seem much too pretentious and awaken their displeasure. So he immediately guards against such misunderstanding by assuring them their fellowship would be good for him too. To be sure, his words do give a good example of his sensibility and tact. But we should be wrong if we see insinuation or calculation here. His sensibility and tact lie rather in the fact that he states the real truth of the situation. That as the Lord's apostle he has something to impart is the simple and inescapable fact. No false modesty keeps him from saying so. But that is no denial of mutuality. He too derives strength and comfort from their relationship. As he proceeds, he tells them about the profit he anticipates from presence with the Christians at Rome. He says he expects to "reap some harvest" among them as well as among the rest of the Gentiles. It would not be possible to say more clearly that he receives as well as gives. But there is no retraction of his first statement, that he will impart to them some spiritual gift. That calls for no modification. He must only guard against misunderstanding. Retracting neither affirmation, he sets them side by side. Only so can the full truth be made clear.

As he says in 1:13, he had often intended to go to Rome; but something had always prevented. He stresses the fact that he had long been willing; but it had not been God's will. Thus far God had given him other tasks. It is interesting to observe that it is not only in Romans that we have evidence of his intention. In Acts 19:21 his words are quoted, "After I have been there [Jerusalem], I must also see Rome." The feeling that he "must" is also evident in Romans. But why is it so necessary for him to affirm his readiness to visit Rome? Why does he declare so emphatically that it is not by his own will that has not yet come? It has been suggested that enemies (Judaizers?) seized the opportunity to put him in a bad light with the Roman church, declaring that he either would not or dare not come to Rome with his gospel. The reason for Paul's fervor would then lie in his desire to defend himself against the attack. Evidence of this might be seen in 1:16, "I am not ashamed of the gospel." As to this matter we have no certain knowledge. What we do know is that, by this letter, Paul is preparing them for his coming; and it is necessary to make clear to them that failure to come earlier was not evidence of indifference on his part.

Paul would also make it clear that the reason for his coming is greater than his own wish. The fundamental reason is his consciousness of an inescapable duty. Only when that has been pointed out does he come to the end of his introduction. That is the objective of all he has said up to this point. The background of what he says about this duty is his recognition of Jesus Christ as Lord and of himself as His bond servant. Jesus Christ, the gospel, and his own apostolic office all lay his duty upon him. Accordingly his introduction reaches its culmination in the declaration, "I am under obligation both to Greek and barbarians, both to the wise and to the foolish; so I am eager to preach the gospel to you also who are in Rome." The question has been raised, to which group the apostle thinks the Romans belong —to Greek or to barbarians? to the wise or the foolish? Such an inquiry is completely uncalled for. The apostle's idea is not at all to differentiate certain categories of men, that the Romans may accordingly be assigned to their place. Paul simply means to acknowledge the inclusive character of his responsibility. None are excepted therefrom. Paul knows he has a responsibility for all, be they Greeks or barbarians, educated or unschooled. The Romans were also included when Christ called him and gave him the Gentile world as his field of labor. By virtue of such call and responsibility he now writes to prepare them for his coming.

In his exposition of this passage Lietzmann says, "We see this entire introduction in its true light only if we set it in relation to 15:14-24." Though he was the apostle to the Gentiles, Paul avoided any church which he had not himself established (15:20) lest he "build on another man's foundation." But now, for the first time, naturally enough he forsakes that principle—in the case of the capital city of the world. Therefore he must explain the step. Therefore he is almost excessive in his modesty (1:12). But therefore also the change from his prior habit (1:13) and the consequent inability of exegetes to be quite certain what Paul wants in Rome and what he does not want. He does not say clearly, nor can he. The difficulty lies in his own situation, not in the peculiar status of the Roman congregation. We must insist that quite the opposite is true. Paul says very clearly what it is that drives him to Rome. All that he has said up to this point aims at that. Paul addresses himself to this church by virtue of the authority which his apostolic office confers. His task is "to bring about obedience to the faith among all the Gentiles." This is exactly what now takes him to Rome. As already stated, he does not yet make any mention of the help he expects his visit to Rome to give to his mission to Spain. For the time being he addresses himself to the Romans for their own sake, and only for that reason.

With this, Paul's introduction is completed, and we arrive at the point where the apostle gives concise statement to the theme of the epistle.

III

The Theme of the Epistle

"He Who through Faith is Righteous Shall Live"
1:16-17

When Paul, after his detailed introduction, turns the attention to the main theme of the epistle, his transition is made with the words, "I am not ashamed of the gospel." With them he again touches upon an idea which he had already treated in detail in I Corinthians 1:17–2:16. To those who do not believe, the gospel is foolishness. But that cannot dissuade Paul from proclaiming the gospel, for he knows that "it is the power of God for salvation to every one who has faith." His transition is well chosen. In his introduction he had already approached his central theme that the gospel is the power of God for salvation, doing so to contradict false assumptions as to the reason why his visit to Rome has been so long delayed. "Almost silently he slips over from the personal reference to that which he teaches" (Jülicher).

And yet one must be careful not to exaggerate the importance of these words. Their function is after all only to serve as a good transition. Looked at formally, they can indeed be regarded of prime significance, and the epistle as Paul's explanation why he is not ashamed of the gospel. One cannot of course think that this alone is the purpose of this letter. But influenced by the feeling that this affirmation is of cardinal importance, some have given it altogether too much emphasis and made it the occasion for all sorts of baseless psychologizing embellishments. It has been supposed that Paul was held back by reluctance to come with so simple a gospel to so resplendent a cultural center as Rome; and to combat that feeling of uncertainty he had to remind both himself and the Roman church that the gospel comes with the power of God. Despite its lowly form, it is nothing of which to be ashamed. But such an idea finds no support in the text. There is nothing to suggest that Paul has such worldly motives for preaching the gospel. A. Schlatter has rightly said, "Reasons for deliberating whether he ought to be ashamed of the gospel were as real in the lowliest house of worship of the Jews as they were in the Roman Forum. Their root lay in the message he came with, in what he called its foolishness."

The gospel—that is what Paul will speak of in this letter. We remember how, in the introduction, he characterized the content and purpose of the gospel. It treats of the Son of God, who by the resurrection became "the Son of God in power," υἱὸς θεοῦ ἐν δυνάμει; and it treats of the new age which He ushered in. For that reason Paul can call the gospel "the power of God for salvation," δύναμις θεοῦ εἰς σωτηρίαν. These correspond with each other—"the Son of God in power" and the gospel as "the power of God for salvation." The gospel receives its power from Christ and from the act of power which God effected through Him. To grasp the full meaning of the word, one ought to note how for Paul the gospel always stands in inescapable relation to the law. Wherever the gospel is, the law always stands in the background. This we saw in the introduction.

Paul set himself apart for the law; God set him apart for the gospel. When Paul now speaks of the power of the gospel, the awareness of the law's weakness and inadequacy lies in the background. "What the law could not do" (τὸ ἀδύνατον τοῦ νόμου), that God did when He sent His Son (8:3). There God intervened with power for our salvation. It is this message which the gospel brings us. And yet it is not enough to say that it treats of God's power; it is itself the power of God, God's δύναμις. Whenever the gospel is preached, the power of God is effective unto salvation. The gospel is not the presentation of an idea, but the operation of a power. When the gospel is preached, it is not merely an utterance; it is something that occurs. The power of God is at work for the salvation of men, snatching them from the powers of destruction (δυνάμεις ἐξουσίαι), and transferring them into the new age of life.

To whom does the gospel become God's saving power? Paul answers, "to every one who has faith." To believe is simply to accept the gospel and thereby to become participant in the new life in Christ. In the introduction Paul said his task was "to bring about obedience to the faith." Now, in his main theme, he takes up the concept of faith, which concept is to occupy so decisive a place in what follows. He gives particular stress to this word by repeating it not less than four times in these two verses. It is of utmost importance to attend to what Paul says, and what he does not say, about faith; for if we misinterpret here our understanding of the whole epistle will be distorted. What, then, is meant by the words "every one who has faith"?

Interpreters have been in rather complete argreement that Paul here meant to affirm what is required of man if he is to be saved. Faith is then looked upon as a necessary

condition required for salvation. Paul has been thought to
say that the power of God for salvation does indeed come
to us in the gospel; but if it is to be effective man must meet
the condition implicit in the requirement that he have faith.
Even though salvation is wholly God's work and is offered
to man without price, man must at least do what is required
of him—he must believe what the gospel proclaims. How
common this view is can best be shown by presenting representative examples.

"Faith is the indispensable and only condition for salvation" (Althaus). "Faith is declared to be the only and
unfailingly effective condition for the attainment of salvation" (Jülicher). "Faith is the condition on the part of man
without which the gospel cannot have power for him" (B.
Weiss). "Nothing but faith is demanded in order that man
may experience the righteousness of God" (von Hofmann).
"The gospel is operative for salvation to every one that has
faith; effective without exception for all men under the
condition of faith." "Here it needs only to be said that beside
the conditions daily fulfilled independently of man, when the
gospel is preached, the faith of him who hears is also an
inescapable condition" (Zahn). E. Kühl speaks with like
intent about "The Achievement of Faith" as the condition
on the part of man for justification. And O. Moe affirms
what Paul is saying that "there is no other demand but
faith." In other words, the issue is "the sufficiency of faith
for salvation."

There is such an agreement in the chorus of interpreters
as to what Paul meant when he used the word "faith" in
this connection. It is agreed that he was declaring what is
required on the part of man as the prerequisite and condition of his salvation. But against this it must be declared

with utmost emphasis that nothing was further from Paul's mind than this. For him faith is not something that man offers as the condition of his justification. Even on their surface can be seen the difference between Paul's words and the interpretation thus given to them. What Paul says is wholly positive when he speaks of the gospel as the power of God for salvation to every one who has faith. But there is something negative about interpretations and formulations quoted: without faith the gospel cannot be effective as a saving power; only on the condition of faith is a man saved, and so on. And the situation is not much improved by speaking more positively about "the sufficiency of faith for salvation"; for the negative is heard through it: "there is no other demand but faith."

It might perhaps seem that there has been only a rather inconsequential shift of accent. Paul clearly says that the gospel is a saving power for every one who has faith. Is it really a vital change if one says "only for him who has faith is the gospel a saving power"? And is one then not justified in saying that faith is the condition which is required of man for his salvation? The difference might seem to be fine-spun. But the truth is that there lurks in it a fateful distortion of the whole Pauline view. In this way Paul's words are made to mean the exact opposite of what he intended.

When one speaks of "the sufficiency of faith for salvation," he clearly intends to say what Luther meant by *sola fide*, "by faith alone." It is by faith that man is justified, and not by the works of the law. Thus far one is also in agreement with Paul. And yet in that expression lies something which is utterly foreign to both Paul and Luther. The intention of the expression *sola fide* is to withstand everything legalistic. And yet even *sola fide* can be understood legalistically. That is the case as soon as faith is thought of as something which is demanded of man. When one says "it is enough to believe," its meaning is legalistic, if faith is held to be a different—and perhaps lighter—requirement than that which the law makes. A legalistic outlook betrays itself in the fact that it is customary to declare that faith leads to the doing of all that the law requires, wherefore there is no peril in calling "faith alone" the way of redemption. It is said that faith at its fullest is more than *assensus*, the intellectual affirmation of a truth. There must also be *fiducia*, the heart's trust in the grace of God in Christ. Such *fiducia* carries with it man's moral renewal; and it is only by virtue of this ethical fruitage that faith is "sufficient" as the one condition of salvation. But that view brings us right back into the legalism which Paul was opposing with his affirmation as to faith, and against which Luther stood with his word about "faith alone."

The reason one thus loses his way in interpreting what faith meant to Paul clearly is due to the fact that he approaches the word with a fixed, dogmatic concept of faith and forthwith decides that it is this that Paul is saying. From such a source has come the psychological view of faith which makes it a subjective quality in man, necessary as the condition of his salvation. Starting from that view, some have assigned co-operative roles to God and man, attempting to determine what each must contribute in the work of salvation. In the gospel God meets man with His message of salvation: but as long as man has not taken his stand as to that message it remains a powerless word. So the crucial question is how man on his part reacts to the gospel. Only when he reacts with faith does the gospel become a power for salvation.

Paul's thought is utterly different from this. When he

says that the gospel is "the power of God for salvation to every one who has faith," he has no thought of apportioning to God and man respective contributions to salvation. For him faith is not a subjective quality which must be present in man if the gospel is to be able to show its power. It is truer to say that one's faith is evidence that the gospel *has* exercised its power on him. It is not man's faith that gives the gospel its power; quite the contrary, it is the power of the gospel that makes it possible for one to believe. Faith is only another word for the fact that one belongs to Christ and through Him participates in the new age. Paul looks at faith in a much longer perspective than we usually do, a perspective resting on his view of the two ages.

In the old age man stands under the powers of destruction, the δυνάμεις, ἐξουσίαι and ἀρχαί which rule in this world of sin and death. There is is no possibility that he can do anything to set himself free. His whole course of life is under the control of these powers under which he lives; he is wholly surrendered to their might. Paul's view of man is the same as that expressed by Jesus, in Luke 11:21f., "When a strong man, fully armed, guards his own palace, his goods are in peace." There cannot be deliverance and freedom unless "one stronger than he assails him and overcomes him." That is what has taken place through Christ. He is the strong one who has overcome the powers which held us prisoners. Such is the dynamic view which lies behind Paul's statement that the gospel is the power of God for salvation to every one who has faith. It gives both salvation and faith their precise meaning. Salvation does not lie in the fact that certain thoughts and ideas are proclaimed to us and we then give them our loyalty and help them to victory. Were that true, one might properly say that faith is the condition

necessary for salvation. But salvation means that Christ, by
the power of God, delivers us from the bondage of the old
aeon and brings us into the new aeon. This is what occurs
through the gospel. And thus to be removed from the realm
of darkness and received into the kingdom of Christ is precisely what faith is.

"To every one who has faith" says the apostle, adding
immediately, "to the Jew first and also to the Greek." Greek
is here set in contrast with Jew. It has an inclusive meaning,
signifying the Gentiles as a whole. It is the more natural for
Paul to use the word in that meaning, because the Hellenistic
world represented the Gentiles to him. In his missionary
labors to the Gentiles he had for the most part met Hellen-
ists. It is chiefly such that he has in mind as the chapter
proceeds to describe the situation among the Gentiles. To
contrast Jews and Greeks also serves the purpose Paul has
in mind, to show that both Gentiles and Jews are under the
wrath of God and that salvation is offered to both through
faith in Christ.

When Paul thus mentions the two groups into which
mankind can be divided, from the religious point of view,
Jews and Gentiles, he does so also to show that there is no
difference between them. How completely unlike they were!
The Jews had God's revelation and had received His promise. God had entered into covenant with them; and they
had shared a holy history with Him. The Gentiles had none
of these. The Jews had the law of God and were zealous
for righteousness. The Gentiles were given over to unrighteousness. There is no denying that such differences were
real and deep. But they all vanish and are nothing before
the gospel. When, as Paul says in 1:17, the gospel comes
with a new righteousness, "the righteousness of God," the

difference pales between the legal righteousness of the Jews and the unrighteousness of the Gentiles. Both lack the righteousness of God on which all depends; and when that is proffered to them, it is for both an equally great and unmerited gift of God. Here there is no difference. The identity of both finds verbal expression in Paul's words τε—και. That which is true of one group is just as true of the other.

But if Paul really means to assert that the difference between Jew and Gentile vanishes when confronted by the gospel, why does he add the specific and apparently differentiating word πρῶτον, "to the Jews *first*"? Does this after all mean that the Jew has special preference in salvation? That cannot be what Paul means. The word may refer to Israel's special history. In that case their priority is now abolished with the coming of Christ. "There is neither Jew nor Greek." All are one in Christ Jesus (Gal. 3:28). He has created one new man in place of the two (Eph. 2:14f.). Faith makes the status of the Jew new, as well as that of the Gentile. Thus the priority of the Jew is abolished.

One may be surprised that Paul, who was the apostle to the Gentiles and counted the Romans among them (1:5f.), should be so eager to discuss the position of the Jew, and that he seems to recognize a certain priority by saying "to the Jew first." But the explanation of his eagerness is his purpose to make clear that salvation is the same for them too. He would make it impossible for any to think that the gospel is only for the Gentiles, while the Jews should find their salvation through the law. Paul denies that the law is a "power for salvation." Even Abraham was not justified by the law (chap. 4). Now that the promise is fulfilled in Christ, it does apply "to the Jew first." But this is not to say that it is in any way to mean less to the Gentiles. It is because

Paul's thought thus encompasses Jew and Gentile that he at the same time says πρῶτον and τε—καί—which seem to contradict each other. Paul means to declare the same about both Jew and Gentile. The Jew, indeed "the Jew first," is called through the promise to receive the new righteousness which God proffers through Christ. But the Gentile is just as truly called. Neither is preferred to the other.

Now Paul has come to the point where he can declare his central idea, "the righteousness of God." Righteousness is always the central matter in the relation between God and men. It was so in the time of the old covenant. It was the focal issue of the law. Righteousness is precisely what the law demands. One's relation with God is right only if he fulfills God's requirements. And now that Christ has come and brought the new aeon, righteousness is still the crucial issue. It is a misunderstanding of the gospel to think that it is less concerned about righteousness than the law is. The direct opposite is the truth. The gospel is concerned about nothing else. That is suggested by what Jesus said to the disciples, "Unless your righteousness exceeds that of the scribes and the Pharisees, you will never enter the kingdom of heaven." But the righteousness here spoken of is of another kind than the "righteousness of the law." It is not man's own righteousness, but "the righteousness of God." It is the righteousness of the kingdom of heaven, the new age. It does not originate in us and come into being through our works and our fulfillment of the law. It is a righteousness which God has effected for us through His work in Christ. To put it concisely, it is not our own righteousness but a "righteousness from God."

The best help for the interpretation of this concept which is so central for Paul, "the righteousness of God," Paul has himself supplied in these words "not having a righteousness of my own, based on law, but that which is through faith in Christ, the righteousness from God that depends on faith" (Phil. 3:9). This quotation shows us both how this concept was rooted in Paul's own life—cf. pp. 12ff. above—and its juxtaposition of opposites: "the righteousness from God" is contrasted with man's own righteousness and the righteousness of the law. "The righteousness of God" is the same as "the righteousness from God," δικαιοσύνη θεοῦ and δικαιοσύνη ἐκ θεοῦ; both are contrasted with δικαιοσύνη ἐκ νόμου.

We are hereby delivered from the very great danger of another suggested interpretation. It is no longer necessary to ask, "Does Paul mean God's own righteousness in the sense of a property belonging to Him, or does he mean that man thus has a righteousness by reason of which he can stand in God's presence?" It is certainly God's own righteousness of which he speaks, but not in the sense of a property that lies in Him. Such a view is very natural for us, with our persistent Greek way of thinking; but it is utterly foreign to Paul's view. The righteousness of God is a righteousness which He reveals to us and permits us to share. Hence it is indeed man's righteousness too. The clearest evidence that this is the case is Paul's simultaneous reference to the "righteous" who shall live. It is man's righteousness, not in the sense that it is of himself, achieved by him, but in the sense that it is proffered to him and accepted by faith. It must, however, be added that the meaning is not that, having had a divine gift infused into him, he now has it as property or inner quality. His righteousness is an objective relationship, proffered to us through Christ and into which we are received through faith in Him. Just as the kingdom of God came through Him, so too has the righteousness of God. This righteousness is not merely something individual; it is the universal mark of the new age, of God's kingdom which has come through Christ.

Already in his rabbinical period Paul was familiar with the idea that righteousness is the characteristic of the messianic age. In the Old Testament he had met the name "The Lord our righteousness," the name of the expected Messiah: "Behold, the days come, saith the Lord, that I will raise unto David a righteous Branch, and he shall reign and deal wisely and shall execute judgment and justice in the land. . . . And this is his name whereby he shall be called, The Lord is our righteousness" (Jer. 23:5f.; cf. 33:15f.). Now that promise has been fulfilled through Christ. In Him God has revealed His righteousness. In His own person He is "The Lord our righteousness," or, as Paul expresses it in I Corinthians 1:30, He is "made our righteousness." The end of His redemptive work, as Paul says, is "that in him we might become the righteousness of God" (II Cor. 5:21).

It is of righteousness in this sense that Paul speaks here. In summary fashion we could say, "the righteousness of God" is a righteousness originating in God, prepared by God, revealed in the gospel and therein offered to us. It is the righteousness of the new age. In Christ it has come to us, and he who through faith belongs to Him has it as his righteousness. It is his, not as a righteousness he has himself effected, but precisely a "righteousness from God." But hereby there is given to the concept "the righteous" a totally new meaning. One is not "righteous" because he has made himself right before God by the fulfillment of the law, but because he belongs to Christ through faith. For it is only "in Christ" that the new age with its righteousness is at hand. The righteous is thus "he who through faith is righteous." "The righteousness from God" is synonymous with "the righteousness of faith," δικαιοσύνη θεοῦ with δικαιοσύνη ἐκ πίστεως.

In the beginning of verse 17 Paul brings together four extraordinarily important concepts: the gospel, the righteousness of God, revelation, and faith. "In it the righteousness of God is revealed through faith for faith." It is vital to see how an intellectualistic and static understanding could confuse and misconstrue these words and give to each one of them, and to all of them together, a meaning entirely different from Paul's. Thus the gospel has been thought of as a "doctrine" or as the proclamation of timeless religious truths; the righteousness of God as a property residing in the divine nature; revelation as the communication of facts and ideas formerly hidden; and faith as the acceptance of such doctrine as true, as assent to universally valid religious ideas. But if Paul is to be understood, such a static and intellectualistic interpretation must be rooted out so thoroughly as to leave no trace of it. The gospel is—as we have already had occasion to point out—not merely a proclamation of ideas but God's mighty work, the power of God, whereby He snatches the victim of sin and death from his master and sets him in the new relation of righteousness and life. The righteousness of God is not a property resident in God, but God's mighty intervention into our existence, which results in a total change in its condition. "The righteousness from God" is a reality which God has raised up in our midst. As the wrath of God is effective in the old aeon, so the righteousness of God is effective in the new. When Paul speaks of that righteousness as "revealed," he does not think of revelation as meaning intellectual illumination. His concept of revelation is not intellectualistic and static, but dynamic.

Revelation is an *action* on the part of God. It is not Paul's thought that God is unknown to us, as if hidden behind a veil, and that the drawing aside of the veil then reveals Him, whereby we perceive what God is like, that He is righteous. God's revelation is rather a mighty manifestation of His will; once—in the old aeon—showing His wrath against the godlessness of men; and now—in the new aeon—showing His righteousness in and through Christ. And as far as faith is concerned, the meaning is not that affirmations about the gospel are held to be true, but rather that men are gripped and constrained by God's power, and thereby borne into the new age, into life with Christ.

The gospel and faith belong together inseparably. Therefore we may not speak of faith as something which could exist apart from the gospel. Faith is not a state of the soul which man must have, that by its aid he may receive the gospel. It is the gospel which is primary, which creates faith and awakens it in us. When one hears the gospel and is conquered by it, that is faith. Faith is not prior to the gospel and independent of it. It arises only through one's meeting with the gospel.

In speaking of faith, Paul here uses the double expression "through faith for faith"—ἐκ πίστεως εἰς πίστιν. What is the reason for this, and what does he aim to express? This is a point on which there have been many interpretations wide of the mark. Is it right to view these two phrases separately, as if Paul meant to say one thing with the first and something else by the latter? They are clearly inseparable in the sentence. And their manifest effect is to give particular emphasis to the word "faith." Faith is both the beginning and the culmination. The manner of expression suggests something like *sola fide*. When the righteousness of God is revealed in the gospel, it is to faith and faith alone.

"Through faith," ἐκ πίστεως, is Paul's usual phrase when he speaks about justification. He means to preclude all thought of a righteousness of our own, attained through law and works, δικαιοσύνη ἐκ νόμου or ἐξ ἔργων. But the church's history shows many examples of the fact that it is possible to believe in justification by faith in a way that still leaves room for works-righteousness. For instance, there is the view that God's purpose in sending Christ was to make it possible for us to fulfill the law. The reasoning runs like this. Man does not have in himself the ability and power to fulfill God's law; so there is no possibility of justification by his own works. The only hope is in "faith alone," in the fullest sense of those words. Through faith man receives the power that he lacked; and then he is justified through the fulfill-ment of the law, by the power which has become his through faith. We see that the affirmation of "justification by faith" has not kept this reasoning from ending with trust in a righteousness of the law. The fulfillment of the law is the object; faith is degraded to the status of a means to that end. Such a view is precluded by Paul's assertion that the righteousness of God is revealed not only "through faith" but also "for faith"; to ἐκ πίστεως is added εἰς πίστιν. By this coupling of phrases the last trace of works-righteousness is uprooted. For that coupling proclaims that faith is the end, not merely the means. The great and wonderful gift which God gives us through Christ is not that by Him we are enabled to fulfill the law. The wonderful fact is just this—that God gave Christ to us, and that through faith we be-come His and share the righteousness revealed through Him.

What word in the sentence does the expression "through faith for faith" modify? The answer is not self-evident. The sentence structure would permit the conclusion that the expression modifies the verb which precedes it. The purpose would then be to make more clear the way in which the revelation of the righteousness of God takes place; that that which was hidden is revealed "through faith for faith." But there is good reason to ask whether these phrases modify any single word. As said before, the repetition of the word "faith," with the different prepositions, gives that word special emphasis. It may also be added that the whole expression "through faith for faith" has special emphasis and stands there in relative independence. In some translations this is suggested by separating the expression from the foregoing by a comma. The result is to suggest a relative independence, and that these words do not modify any single part of the preceding clause, but the whole of it. It might be written thus, "In it the righteousness of God is revealed—and that through faith for faith." Inasmuch as the accent is definitely on "the righteousness of God," the consequence is that the mind most naturally joins there to that which is said about faith in the end of the clause. If it is more important to observe the thought which is being presented than the sentence structure, it would help to express it thus, "In it the righteousness of God is revealed—a righteousness through faith and for faith." There is support for this in Romans 3:21. There Paul returns to the thought of 1:17; and there it is not only in his thought but in specific words that faith is connected with "the righteousness of God." He says, "But now the righteousness of God has been manifested apart from the law . . . the righteousness of God through faith in Jesus Christ." By his repetition of the phrase "the righteousness of God" he removes all doubt as to the connection pointed out. This connection is also clear from the prophetic quotation in 1:17. Professor O. Moe has rightly said, "If what Paul says in the first part of verse 17 is to harmonize with what he quotes in the latter part of that verse, it is necessary that ἐκ πίστεως modifies the expression δικαιοσύνη θεοῦ." Be it remembered, too, that for Paul δικαιοσύνη ἐκ πίστεως came close to being a technical term (cf. 9:30; 10:6). The righteousness of God he here speaks of may also be spoken of as a righteousness of faith. The central thought is about faith, and only about faith, "through faith for faith."

The whole message of this epistle is contained in 1:17, particularly in the prophetic quotation: ὁ δίκαιος ἐκ πίστεως ζήσεται, "He who through faith is righteous shall live." That statement is properly called the theme of the epistle. On that scriptural text the apostle constructs his letter.

It would hardly be possible to find another declaration that has had so distinctive and varied a history. Time after time it has played a decisive role in the great turning points of 2,500 years of religious development. Here we can refer to only a few of the most important in the eventful history of this affirmation.

1. We meet it first in Habakkuk 2:4. Confronted by the great Chaldean invasion, the prophet stands watch to see what the Lord has to say to him. The Lord declares that the arrogant and proud conqueror shall fall; but "the righteous shall live by his faith." Because of the peculiar way in which this declaration is introduced, some have believed that behind this prophetic affirmation they detect a concept already current. They have thought that the prophet here uses an old proverb which ran about like this: Pride goes before a fall, but righteousness saves from death; the promise of life is given to humble and faithful devotion to righteousness. Here that proverb is applied to the concrete

situation produced by the strong and arrogant usurper. Be that surmise as it may, as the declaration is used by Habakkuk it is applied to the Jewish, theocratic nation. Since pride leads a people on to destruction, faithful devotion to God and His commands leads to life and safety.

2. In the synagogue the declaration that "the righteous shall live by his faith" came to play a very significant role. It was interpreted as the summary and highest expression of the righteousness of the law. This is illustrated very well in the following Talmudic tradition: On Sinai Moses received 613 commandments. King David came and summed them up in eleven (Ps. 15). Then came Isaiah and summed them up in six (Isa. 33:15f.). Micah came and summed them up in three, "He hath shewed thee, O man, what is good; and what doth the Lord require of thee, but to do justly, and to love mercy, and to walk humbly with thy God?" (Mic. 6:8). Again came Isaiah and summed them up in two, "Keep ye judgment, and do justice" (Isa. 56:1). Finally came Habakkuk and summed them all up in one, "The just shall live by his faith."

It should be noted that the Old Testament commandments themselves are looked upon as coming to their highest expression in this prophetic word. *In Habakkuk 2:4 the synagogue finds the adequate expression of righteousness by the law and its works.* It sees here a witness to the saving power of the law. He who keeps the commandment shall live. The righteous have the right to life because of their fidelity to the law and the covenant. It is by such a faith, by faithfulness, that the just shall live.

3. Now, what does *Paul* do with this prophetic word? *He takes it out of the hands of the representatives of the righteousness of the law and makes it the motto and crown-*

ing expression of a view which is the direct opposite, of the righteousness of faith.

How could he do that? Before we can answer, we must observe his manner of interpreting the expressions of Scripture. Paul was brought up on rabbinic thought. From that source he got the concept that Scripture has several meanings. First, it has its evident, historical significance. But he who would really understand Scripture must not stop there. There is often a deeper meaning hidden in figures of speech and prophetic expressions; and it is the interpreter's task to discover this deeper sense. But the quest must not stop even with that. The word is God's; therefore the vital thing is to discover what God meant to say by any particular expression. The human agent through whom God spoke the word may not have been aware of this divine meaning. It is in this fact that Paul finds the interpreter's deepest task. Scripture aims at more than a report on what God did with the fathers, and what He said to them. Beyond that it has a word to say to us "upon whom the end of the ages has come" (I Cor. 10:11). In the light which Christ sheds we can now see that Scripture spoke of old about the righteousness of faith. "Scripture, foreseeing that God would justify the Gentiles by faith, preached the gospel beforehand to Abraham, saying 'In thee shall all the nations be blessed' " (Gal. 3:8). When that promise was first made, its deepest meaning was not evident. But the veil which had formerly hidden Scripture's profoundest meaning has been removed by Christ (II Cor. 3:14). Now we can also see the deeper significance in a declaration like Habakkuk 2:4. Even if the prophet himself did not apprehend the full truth about the faith which he spoke, it was God's purpose to speak of faith and the righteousness which is by faith. To us that deeper meaning is revealed, because we live in faith with Christ, and he has removed the concealing veil.

As the caption and theme of his epistle Paul sets the declaration, "He who through faith is righteous shall live," ὁ δίκαιος ἐκ πίστεως ζήσεται. In so doing he combines these two phrases ὁ δίκαιος and ἐκ πίστεως into one indissoluble concept: ὁ δίκαιος ἐκ πίστεως, "he who through faith is right-eous"; and as to such an one the affirmation is ζήσεται, he shall live. What this means we have already discussed in our introductory statement about the line of thought of the epistle—pages 28ff. above. Here it is only necessary to call attention to the difference between Paul's interpretation and that of Judaism.

The veil has not been removed, in the thought of Juda-ism; so Habakkuk's declaration is understood to speak of righteousness by the law. Accordingly, the prophet's refer-ence to faith is interpreted to mean the just man's faithful-ness and steadfastness in his righteous course. But Paul dissents from this. Making use of the accepted rabbinic manner of interpretation, we might say he cries, "Do not, with the synagogue, understand the prophet to mean that 'the righteous shall live by his faith (i.e., his faithfulness),' but see, with the church, that the affirmation means that 'he who through faith is righteous shall live.'" The Greek should not be written thus, ὁ δίκαιος | ἐκ πίστεως ζήσεται, but rather ὁ δίκαιος ἐκ πίστεως | ζήσεται.

It is not to be denied that there are certain difficulties in the way of our view. They are indeed so real that most interpreters have rejected the idea that Paul thus couples ἐκ πίστεως with ὁ δίκαιος. The chief objection is that Paul's word order is all against it. It is said that, if he had meant to say what we have affirmed, he would not have said it so poorly, ὁ δίκαιος ἐκ πίστεως; he would have written ὁ ἐκ πίστεως δίκαιος, or ὁ δίκαιος ὁ ἐκ πίστεως. Under the circumstances we have to ask whether there is any sufficient reason for not doing the natural thing of joining ἐκ πίστεως with the verb. What reason have we for coupling ἐκ πίστεως with ὁ δίκαιος? We reply that the reason is not merely good enough to be persuasive; it is decisive.

First and foremost, the context demands that the words be thus coupled. As already pointed out, the word πίστις is repeated not less than four times in these two verses which state the theme of the epistle. A particular emphasis is thus given to this word. He is speaking about the righteousness which is by faith, δικαιοσύνη ἐκ πίστεως. When he quotes Habakkuk 2:4 in this connection, he shows that he understands the prophet to have said what he himself is saying. The effect of the quotation is to declare, *"It is written."* If he had thought of ἐκ πίστεως as joined with the verb, in the ordinary manner, the quotation would have given no confirmation to his own view. What he is trying to emphasize, and to support by Scripture, is not that "the just" shall live. As to that his Jewish opponents were as certain as he—though, to be sure, their view of "the just" was quite different from his, for they thought of him who is righteous through the keeping of the law. What Paul really wants to reinforce is the fact that "he who through faith is righteous" shall live; and this he understands Habakkuk to say. It is clear enough that this is the only possible interpretation. It is surely not the case that Paul invokes a passage of Scripture that does not at all say that which he is setting forth as a decisive point.

In the second place, we encounter the still weightier fact that in the very development of the letter Paul supplies the most unequivocal commentary on the meaning of the passage. When he develops the theme so concisely stated in this verse, he does so in a manner that removes all doubt as to the word-coupling suggested above. *The very structure of Romans and the letter as a whole are proof that in its theme ἐκ πίστεως is connected with ὁ δίκαιος and not with ζήσεται.* In the first part of the epistle, to the end of chapter 4, Paul gives himself with great precision to the first half of his theme; he discusses the man who through faith is justified. In the second part (chap. 5-8) he affirms the second half of the theme, what is to happen to the one thus justified: he "shall live."

It might of course easily be suspected that a zeal for systematic construction had read this clear division into the apostle's discussion. Are we guilty of subjectivity and an unrestrained impulse to systematize? Or is the construction actually supported and set forth by Paul? A purely objective statistical observation can answer that question. If it is true that chapters 1-4 discuss not merely righteousness and "the just," but specifically him "who through faith is righteous"; and if it is true that chapters 5-8 declare how he "shall live," one would expect that the word "faith," πίστις, would occupy a definite prominence in the first four chapters while the word "life," ζωή, would appear with no such frequency. And as to the next four chapters one would similarly expect the word ζωή to occupy the dominating position, while the word πίστις falls into the background, or at least that it is not here the central word. Do the facts support such an anticipation? The result of a word count is truly surprising! In chapters 1-4 πίστις (or its correlative πιστεύειν) appears at least 25 times. In chapters 5-8 it is found only twice. One of these two places is in 5:1, where its use gives emphasis to the contrast.

This verse is the transition from the first part of the epistle to the second. True to his habit, Paul here recapitulates in a few words the burden of that which has preceded. It is for that reason that he uses the word πίστις in this verse. He is only about to enter into the matter to which he devotes the next part of the epistle. 5:1 is thus a summation of the central thesis of the first part.

As to the word ζωή (with its related ζῆν, ζωοποιεῖν), we find exactly the opposite. Not counting the thematic verse, the word is used only twice in chapters 1-4; but in chapters 5-8 we find it 25 times. It is thus established with a clarity that cannot be overemphasized, that the theme for chapters 1-4 is ὁ δίκαιος ἐκ πίστεως and for chapters 5-8 ζήσεται. It follows that in 1:17 Paul's thought joins ἐκ πίστεως to ὁ δίκαιος, and not to ζήσεται.

In addition to such compelling considerations there are others of a more formal character which confirm the correctness of this conclusion. Of these, mention may be made of the following. Standing at the transition from the first part of the letter to the next, and casting his eye over the former, Paul sums it up thus: δικαιωθέντες οὖν ἐκ πίστεως "since we are justified by faith" (5:1). Here there is precisely that coupling of ὁ δίκαιος (=δικαιωθείς) with ἐκ πίστεως. Paul himself joins them.

When set over against the reasons which force us to the interpretation "he who through faith is righteous," the objections which can be raised seem slight indeed. For instance, it is objected that if Paul actually intended to say "he who through faith is righteous," he would have changed his words to say ὁ ἐκ πίστεως δίκαιος or ὁ δίκαιος ὁ ἐκ πίστεως; but for answer it suffices to remember that Paul is here using a quotation. The objection would have point if Paul had been

freely formulating his own statement. Had he been doing
so he would doubtless have used one of the suggested
phrases. But he is presenting a quotation. So he is not free
to do violence to it; he must be true to his source. Or another
(Schlatter) has said, "There is no evidence at all that Paul
did not understand this Semitic affirmation," and then attempted to show what Paul means by giving the prophet's
meaning. To this we reply that it is not suggested that Paul
did not grasp the literal sense of the statement, but rather
that he also saw in it a deeper significance. Nor, in the next
place, can it be maintained that we are offering an interpretation which would have seemed forced to Paul's day. It is
in entire accord with exegetical principles then recognized,
to which rabbinical literature supplies manifold examples.
(This fact is specifically pointed out by our foremost authority on rabbinical literature, Professor Hugo Odeberg.)

Thus the reading "he who through faith is righteous shall
live" assumes that ἐκ πίστεως is not joined with ζήσεται but
is coupled with ὁ δίκαιος. Both parts of this contention have
been met with objections.

It is said, for one thing, that to couple ἐκ πίστεως with
δίκαιος is to affirm a contrast which the apostle has neither
prepared for nor implied. The expression "he who through
faith is justified," if it is to have real meaning, must stand
over against another "he who through the law is justified."
But Paul has as yet said nothing about that in this connection. It is indeed true, in a sense, that he has not here expressly spoken of him "who through the law is righteous" in
contrast with him "who through faith is righteous." Yet that
does not disprove that something of that contrast is already
to be sensed in what Paul says. How could it be otherwise?
This is not the first time that Paul uses Habakkuk 2:4 as

support for the righteousness of faith. In Galatians, when he
is deep in the conflict against a righteousness of the law and
of works, he has used the same expression and used it specifically in contrast to the righteousness which is through the
law: "Now it is evident that no man is justified before God
by the law, for 'He who through faith is righteous shall live'"
ὁ δίκαιος ἐκ πίστεως ζήσεται. Paul had been in the thick of that
fight, and is in some degree still engaged in it. He has steadily set "the righteousness of the law" over against "the righteousness of faith," δικαιοσύνη ἐκ νόμου against δικαιοσύνη ἐκ
πίστεως. He divides men into two classes—those who belong
to the realm of the law, οἱ ἐκ νόμου, and those who belong to
the realm of faith, οἱ ἐκ πίστεως. How would it have been
possible for him to set these two words, δίκαιος and ἐκ πίστεως,
side by side without thinking of the righteousness of faith
and of its opposite, the righteousness of the law. His primary
thought here is not to speak of this opposition; so it is not
strange if all that the prophetic quotation signified for Paul
does not immediately appear on the surface. But as he advances he has abundant occasion to introduce the readers
to it. More and more pointedly he sets forth the contrast
between the righteousness of faith and the righteousness of
the law.

Likewise it has been said that to separate ἐκ πίστεως from
ζήσεται is to rob the latter of all emphasis and to "make it
entirely meaningless to the context." But the diametrical
opposite is the case. To say "the just shall live by faith"
leaves the word "live" with relatively little emphasis. But if
we say, "he who through faith is righteous shall live," that
final word receives a decided emphasis which cannot be
overstated. It is made clear that one is not speaking of life
in general; it is of life in its eschatological sense that the

affirmation is made. Any modification of that one word "live" is a weakening of it. When Paul says of him who through faith is righteous that he "shall live," the meaning is that he is removed from death's realm and received into life's aeon, which God has brought near in Christ. Thereby that which verse 16 said about salvation, σωτηρία, is thus carried forward to its full meaning. Not till then is it clear how the gospel can be the power of God unto salvation to every one who believes; for through the righteousness of faith thus revealed admission is granted into the age of life.

4. Still another time was Habakkuk 2:4 to play a decisive role in a turning point in the history of Christianity, namely in the Reformation. The crucial significance of Romans 1:17 for Luther's religious development is well known. It was this word that supplied him with the key to the gospel. Here he found the basic witness as to justification by faith, as to the God who in Christ makes the sinner righteous. Before this time this scriptural declaration had had a wholly different meaning to him. When he read about "the righteousness of God" revealed in the gospel, he understood it to mean that God righteously rewards the righteous and punishes the sinner. The very meaning of the gospel was hidden from him. He himself says, "I labored diligently and anxiously as to how to understand Paul's word in Romans 1:17, where he says that the righteousness of God is revealed in the gospel. I sought long and knocked anxiously; for the expression *justitia Dei* 'the righteousness of God,' blocked the way." He says further, "As often as I read that declaration I wished always that God had not made the gospel known." But as the beginning of 1:17 was the stumbling block for him, it is interesting to note that he was helped to right understanding by the 2,000-year-old prophetic word in Habakkuk 2:4.

In one of his table talks Luther gives a vivid description of how he came to clear understanding. Long he hung in uncertainty, until he was confronted by this prophetic word: *justus ex fide vivet.* "That helped me," Luther adds. For now he saw what the righteousness is about which Paul here speaks. The text first confronted him with the abstract word "righteousness"; and it was in this word that all his difficulty centered. But then the text spoke concretely about "him who is righteous" and about the significance of faith for him. "Then taking the abstract and the concrete together, I became certain, seeing the difference between the righteousness of the law and the righteousness of the gospel." He discovered the meaning of the gospel by letting the word of the prophet about "the just" shed its light on the concept of "the righteousness of God": it is through faith that one is justified before God. Thus it was Habakkuk 2:4 which showed Luther the difference (*discrimen*) between law and gospel, between the righteousness of the law and the righteousness of faith. "When I saw the difference, that law is one thing and gospel another, I broke through." The stumbling block was thus removed from his way, and—as Luther elsewhere expressed it—it was as if he found a door opened wide and leading into paradise. "And as I had formerly hated the expression 'the righteousness of God,' I now began to regard it as my dearest and most comforting word, so that this expression of Paul's became to me in very truth a gate to paradise."

Through the years the gospel has advanced in peculiar ways. Paul gave the prophetic word of the Old Testament its particular meaning and made it customary thereby to express the gospel's truth. And when, after a millennium and a half, the gospel was beclouded and Paul's declaration endangered, this Old Testament word was the means by which the gospel was again discovered so that Paul's proclamation of the righteousness of faith is heard again.

PART ONE

"He Who through Faith Is Righteous"
1:18—4:25

The first part of the epistle treats of him who through faith is righteous. But who is he who through faith is righteous? It is he who shares in "the righteousness of God" revealed through Christ, the righteousness which is from God. In its very nature it is "the righteousness of faith."

On the surface it might appear as if Paul here speaks of something quite different. That which first meets us in 1:18 is the affirmation about the wrath of God and the ungodliness and wickedness of men. Here is support for our earlier statement that we note a juxtaposition in what Paul says about "him who through faith is justified." At the time we were discussing the contrast between "the righteousness of faith" and "the righteousness of the law (works)." But as the righteousness of *God* it stands over against all that man can effect, against both his attempt to offer a righteousness of his own making and all his wickedness. In opposition to *"the righteousness of God"* which Paul proclaims stands (1) unrighteousness and (2) the righteousness of the law. Here is the outline for Paul's treatment. First he discusses human life both in its lack of all righteousness, its unrighteousness, and in its trust in a righteousness of its own making, a righteousness of the law. Then, against this background, Paul presents the new "righteousness of God."

We must take note of the point of view characteristic of

Paul. From what we have said it would be natural to expect that, when he wanted to set forth the righteousness of *God*, he would set over against it the character of *man*, as it is seen both in its unrighteousness and its trust in the righteousness of the law; that his outline would be like this:

1. *Man:* (a) his unrighteousness
          (b) the righteousness of the law
2. *God's righteousness*

But Paul's outline is somewhat different. It is always of God that he speaks, even when he sets forth man's unrighteousness and man's works-righteousness. It is not one thing human or another which is in juxtaposition to the righteousness of *God*; but in contrast to the righteousness of *God* stands the wrath of *God*. This is the controlling viewpoint for Paul. His outline is therefore as follows:

1. *The wrath of God:*
          (a) against unrighteousness
          (b) against the righteousness of the law
2. *The righteousness of God*

To live in unrighteousness and to live in the righteousness of the law both stand under the wrath of God. By these the old aeon is characterized. But the characteristic of the new aeon is "the righteousness from God."

IV

Under the Wrath of God

1:18–3:20

What the new aeon is Paul can tell only by first making clear what the old aeon is. What "righteousness from God" means he can make clear only by first pointing out the wrath of God which rests on all where "righteousness from God" is not found. For this reason the concept of "the wrath of God" occupies an unusually prominent place in the beginning of Romans. It is the subject not only of the section characterizing the unrighteousness of men, but also in like manner of the following section which discusses the righteousness of the law. It stands as the peculiar caption of that part of the epistle which ends with 3:20. What does this concept of "the wrath of God" mean to Paul?

To begin with, it may be said that, in general, "the wrath of God" is the same as His holy displeasure at sin. But if it be thus described, we must realize that it means more than a passive discountenancing of sin. To Paul the wrath of God is a terrifying reality. "God is not mocked, for whatever a man sows, that he will also reap" (Gal. 6:7). This idea about the wrath of God is not an unimportant appendage to Paul's view, which could be dropped without serious loss; it stands in indissoluble relation to his whole faith in God.

As long as God is God, He cannot behold with indifference that His creation is destroyed and His holy will trodden underfoot. Therefore He meets sin with His mighty and annihilating reaction. But one thing more must be said. Just as "the righteousness of God" or "righteousness from God" means the whole situation which exists where man is in right relation with God, so "the wrath of God" signifies the total situation that obtains, the lost condition, where man has departed from God. His whole existence gets its character from the fact that he stands under the wrath of God. And this perspective is widened to include all humanity. For of the old man, steeped in sin, it is true that he stands under the wrath of God. Thus Paul can forthwith use "the wrath of God" to characterize a whole order of existence, the old aeon. To live in this age and according to its nature is to stand under the wrath of God. This is true of all without exception. In that which comes later Paul distinguishes clearly between the unrighteousness of the Gentiles and the Jews' righteousness of the law. But in the final analysis, in that which is decisive there is no difference between them. Both alike and in like measure stand under the divine wrath, and to both alike salvation from wrath is proffered through the righteousness of God revealed in Christ.

1. THE WRATH OF GOD AGAINST UNRIGHTEOUSNESS
1:18-32

(1) The unrighteousness of the heathen

The first thing Paul has to affirm is that the wrath of God is revealed against unrighteousness. In this, too, it is a matter of divine revelation, as, just before this, mention was made of the revelation of 'the righteousness from God." ἀποκαλύπτεται in verse 17 has its counterpart in ἀποκαλύπτεται

in verse 18; and thus the wrath of God stands in juxtaposition to the righteousness of God. Even though the content
of the revelation is diametrically opposite in the two cases,
the revelation is nevertheless of the same active, dynamic
kind in both. Where God through Christ reveals His righteousness, then, as was said above, it means not merely a
theoretical sharing of knowledge, but God's active intervention for the salvation of man. In corresponding manner,
when God reveals His wrath against human unrighteousness,
this is not merely an intellectual disclosure that God is an-
gered by sin; but this too is God's active intervention. The
wrath of God, also, is a divine dynamic, a power of God, but
unto destruction, not unto salvation.

When and how is the revelation of the wrath of God
made? Does Paul think of it as taking place in time? Or
does wrath in this context, as in 2:5, have an eschatological
meaning? Is it a wrath which overtakes the unrighteous
now, in this life? Or is it a wrath which shall overtake him
"in the day of wrath"? As to this, interpreters have differed.
On the one hand, it has been insisted that the revelation of
wrath here spoken of is in the present. The parallelism with
verse 17, which speaks of a revelation now taking place in
the gospel, forbids us to construe verse 18 as referring to
other than a present disclosure of the wrath of God. On the
other hand, it has been affirmed just as positively that for
Paul the wrath of God is without doubt an eschatological
concept, and that the parallelism with that which follows—
of which 2:5 is a clear example—makes any other view
impossible.

There can be no doubt that the problem thus posed is
artificial and without basis in the text. Paul gives no occasion to set up such an alternative between God's wrath as

either present reality or eschatological event. It is not a case of either—or. It is both—and. The clearest evidence for this is precisely the parallel in verse 17. Just as "the righteousness from God" is both a present reality in this world and yet a reality that awaits complete fulfillment in eternity, so too is the case with the wrath of God. The wrath of God is already revealed in the present against human unrighteousness, as Paul says with increasing definiteness as he advances. Yet the final revelation of God's wrath is not made until "the day of wrath." There is no reason to limit the meaning of the expression to the one sense or the other. Precisely because Paul uses it as the characterization of the condition of the old aeon, its meaning transcends the antithesis between present and future.

The cosmic significance of the divine wrath appears still more clearly when Paul says it is revealed "from heaven." Manifest before all who have eyes to see, and inescapable to any, God intervenes with His judgment of wrath, when men neglect Him in His holy will. It is the Almighty himself who acts in doom. From one point of view one may say, to use Luther's expression, that wrath is "God's strange work," because only love is "God's own work"—in which God's own and peculiar will shows itself in its inmost purpose, unaltered by anything alien. But from another point of view one both can and must say that wrath is also God's own work, which He himself discloses from heaven. It is God, and not some alien powers, who has laid the old aeon under condemnation.

This has come about because of the ungodliness and unrighteousness of men. Because Paul here uses both "ungodliness" (ἀσέβεια) and unrighteousness" (ἀδικία), many have naturally thought that he means to refer to two different occasions of God's wrath. Such interpreters have felt that they could best make his meaning clear by letting un-godliness signify irreligion and unrighteousness signify immorality. But it can be said with certainty that that is not what Paul means. Even if these two words, if taken out of the context, may bear something of the suggested meanings, nevertheless it is quite foreign to the thought of Paul to make the sharp distinction between irreligion and immorality which seems so natural to contemporary interpreters. And farthest from the truth would be to find in the proposed distinction a reason for saying that Paul held irreligion's deepest cause to lie in immorality. Quite to the contrary, Paul is at pains to say that a wrong relation to God is the ultimate cause of man's corruption. We come closest to Paul's thought if we regard the two words as simply an emphatic expression of one and the same thing. No view could be wider of the mark than to consider "unrighteousness" as immorality, without reference to the religious fact of man's relation to God. It is just the fact of wrong relationship with God that Paul means to include by the use of the word ἀδικία. This unrighteousness of men is set in contrast to "righteousness from God," of which the apostle has just spoken. By this opposition to δικαιοσύνη θεοῦ the concept ἀδικία ἀνθρώπων gets its significance and color.

Though Paul does not say expressly that he here speaks of the Gentiles, the context makes that fact clear. God reveals His wrath from heaven against the unrighteousness of the Gentiles. But how can God let His wrath fall on those who do not know Him? Over those who do not know His will, and thus live in all manner of unrighteousness? Is not such wrath unjustified? No, God does not reap where He has not sown. He has not concealed the truth. Men by their unrighteousness have suppressed the truth, not wanting to

know it. In the interest of autonomy, man sought to cast off
dependence of God. It was not because of lack of divine
revelation that men have forsaken God. "What can be known
about God is plain to them, because God has shown it to
them." Though God is invisible, man can know Him, for
He has not left himself without witness. Ever since the creation of the world He has revealed His eternal power and
deity. He has made himself known in His works.

Romans 1:20 is one of the places in the New Testament
which has been subject to the worst misunderstanding. From
what Paul says about God's self-revelation to the Gentiles
men have sought to educe an entire "natural theology" or
"natural religion." But Paul has also been misunderstood
by those who deny that there is any natural theology in his
thought. We must give further attention to this matter. Is
it proper in any sense to speak of a "natural theology" or a
"natural knowledge of God" in Paul? Before we can answer
that question we must examine the problem which confronts
us in the concept of a natural knowledge of God.

Belief that man is able to attain to knowledge of God
grew up outside of Christianity and in a wholly different cli-
mate of thought. When this view is confronted with God's
revelation in Christ, the question arises as to the relation
between the natural knowledge of God and the divine revelation mediated through Christ. We meet that question
again and again in the history of Christianity. For instance,
we see it in orthodoxy's distinction between *articuli mixti*
and *articuli puri,* holding that some things in our knowledge
of God can be attained by human reason while others rest
on special divine revelation. We see it again in the Enlightenment's "natural religion" or "religion of reason," in which
the natural knowledge of God tends to usurp the whole field,

making any special Christian revelation more or less unnecessary. But we come upon it too in the more recent effort to
reject all thought of a natural knowledge of God, denying
that God reveals himself other than in Christ. For the issue
is the same, even though the answer is different. It is not
hard to show that this is the case. If in orthodxy there was
a kind of balance between natural knowledge of God and
revelation in Christ, in the Enlightenment the emphasis
moved toward the natural knowledge of God, with the place
of revelation moving towards the zero end of the scale. In
the recent theological view mentioned above, the emphasis
moves in the opposite direction, tending to reduce the possibility of a natural knowledge of God to zero. It is thus only
the conclusion that is different; but the way of looking at
the problem is the same.

Men have come to the interpretation of Paul with such
a preconceived formulation of the problem. Thus they ask
whether or not he speaks of such a natural knowledge of
God. But the result is a misunderstanding of Paul, whether
the answer be yes or no. It is clear that he cannot be made
an advocate for any sort of natural theology or natural religion in the accepted meaning of these terms. But, on the
other hand, he of course does say here that ever since the
creation of the world God's eternal power and deity have
been manifest and can be known by His works. And in the
second chapter he says that the "Gentiles who have not the
law do by nature what the law requires . . . They show that
what the law requires is written on their hearts." Does not
Paul, then, after all recognize a natural knowledge of God
and a natural morality?

In a case where it seems necessary to answer both yes
and no, it is probably true that the problem has been stated

incorrectly. We are dealing with such a case. Paul does not deal at all with the issue as it has been stated. They who have thought that he did understood his words thus because they came to him with their own concept of natural theology. But the fact is that Romans does not set itself to discuss a range of dogmatic issues of that kind, in the pursuit of which the apostle formulated a doctrine as to the natural knowledge of God. We are bound to misunderstand him if we treat his words as "scriptural proof" of a completed dogmatic view. They must not thus be torn out of context and used to answer an issue of our own making. They must be seen in the context that evoked them, with attention to the purpose for which the author used them.

We are not left in the dark about the apostle's purpose. He tells how God through Christ has, in the new aeon, revealed a new righteousness and thereby bestowed life on us. But formerly, in the old aeon, the wrath of God was revealed from heaven against all unrighteousness. It is in connection with this declaration about the wrath of God that verse 20 speaks. Why is the wrath of God manifested? Because men in their iniquity suppress the truth. Throughout the whole history of mankind God has ever made himself known in His works. He does so at all times, also when He manifests His wrath against unrighteousness. But is the result that men have really learned to know God? No, rather have men "exchanged the truth about God for a lie" (vs. 25). But, for the very reason that God set forth His truth that men might see it, men are without excuse when they do not follow it. The problem which Paul does face here, as to which he declares his position, is this: How can the wrath of God come upon the Gentiles, victims of ignorance and blindness not of their own making? But, says Paul, it is of their own

making! They are without excuse, for through His mighty
works God has revealed himself and appeared before them.

In this connection it is interesting to observe a detail
in Paul's expression. Our translation of εἰς τὸ εἶναι αὐτοὺς
ἀναπολογήτους (vs. 20) reads, "So they are without excuse."
Though that rendering is possible, it would fit the apostle's
thought better to understand him as saying that God has
made himself known to them "that they may be without
excuse." Though that is the most natural translation, it was
probably avoided because it seemed unreasonable that such
should be the meaning and intent of God's self-revelation.
But according to Paul it is actually the will of God that he
who turns away from God be without excuse; and by His
self-disclosure He has removed all possibility of such from
man. In exactly the same way, in 3:19, Paul speaks of the
purpose of the law: "that every mouth may be stopped, and
the whole world may be held accountable to God." The
finality of Paul's expression fits well with the purpose he has
in mind as he speaks of God's revelation in this connection.

In so far as he touches the question of a natural knowledge of God, he does not do so with the positive intent of
declaring that natural man is possessed of the ability to
come to a knowledge of God. As to that his thought is found
clearly stated in I Corinthians 2:14; the natural or "psychic"
man cannot understand the truth about God. Paul has rather
the negative purpose of declaring that man is without any
excuse. He affirms that man rightly stands under the wrath
of God. "Without excuse," ἀναπολόγητος is the decisive
word here.

Paul *touches* the problem of the "natural knowledge of
God." But does he actually get into it? It is certainly not
his idea that "the natural man" has the ability to find his own

way to God. What is the result when the man who has
turned away from God would be pious and Godfearing?
Paul answers that such a man searches creation and turns
to the worship of idols. Paul never says that the natural man
finds the marks of God in nature. That idea, imposed on his
words by "natural theology," is quite opposed to his meaning.

Does Paul then mean that God revealed himself only
in Christ, and nowhere else? No, for he says expressly,
ἀποκαλύπτεται γὰρ ὀργὴ θεοῦ, the wrath of God is revealed
from heaven. This is truly a revelation of God, but of another kind than that given in Christ. Paul also speaks of a
divine revelation which leaves man without excuse. This
too is of another kind than that given in Christ.

It is clear that Paul breaks down the familiar alternatives in this problem. Ever since man posed the issue of a
"natural theology" and a "natural knowledge of God," he has
thought of such alternatives. Either there is a natural knowledge of God in the sense that the natural man has knowledge
of God, so that one can affirm a revelation of God apart from
Christ; or, if one denies the natural man's knowledge of God,
he must deny that there is any revelation of God except in
Christ. Paul recognizes no such alternative. He knows that
God reveals himself in all His works, in creation, in temporal
blessings, in wrath and judgment, and in salvation. But just
because Paul believes in God's revelation, he cannot follow
the way of "natural theology" and seek God *behind* His
creation, leaving us to find our way to the Creator by following His tracks in that which He made. Man's failure is not
that he has neglected to speculate about God, that he is
remiss in finding his way, after the manner of natural theology, back to the Author of the world, *via causalitatis, via
negationis,* and *via eminentiae.* Man's fault, which justly

places him under the wrath of God, is rather this, that, however God has revealed himself in His mighty works, man does not honor Him and thank Him as God. "Natural theology" belongs to that of which Paul says, "Claiming to be wise, they became fools." The god whom man finds in such manner is only an empty and vain idea, nothing more than an idol created in man's own image.

It is thus easy to see why Paul can have no dealings with "natural theology." The reason is not that it deals with an inclusive, divine revelation, while Paul limits the area of revelation, finding none except in Christ. On the contrary, as we have seen, Paul's view of God's revelation is much more inclusive than that of any natural theology. He believes in God as living and ever active. He has no thought that God has limited His self-disclosure to a single point. The reason why there is no bond between Paul and natural theology is that they hold to entirely different concepts of God.

Natural theology assumes a deistic view. It postulates a God who, after creation, withdrew from the world and concealed himself behind that which He had made. And it looks upon men as left to themselves and desiring nothing more than to find God by means of the evidence of Him which creation bears; for they would worship and serve Him.

But Paul believes that God is living and ceaselessly active. Ever since creation He has been active in the life of man. In His work He reveals His eternal power and glory. As to mankind, Paul holds that, though God ever comes to meet with him, man does not honor Him as God or give thanks to Him. In his pretended wisdom, which is really folly, he has "exchanged the glory of the immortal God for images resembling mortal man or birds or animals or reptiles."

It is really necessary to consider in such detail Paul's position as to natural theology. It is now so much a part of our own mental habit that we assume quite unreflectively that Paul was also occupied with this issue. But if we let this issue set the trend of our discussion, we distort his thought, whether we take affirmative or negative position as to the possibility of natural theology. Nor is this the only point on which current views do violence to the apostle's thought. Another illustration is his view of heathenism.

The concept of heathendom has lost its pregnant significance under the influence of the modern study of comparative religions. This discipline thinks of heathendom as "the non-Christian religions," or "the religions outside Christianity." These religions are looked upon as preparatory to Christianity. If Christianity presents God's revelation in Christ, they present His natural revelation. In them we find God's general revelation, as we find His special revelation in Christianity.

Paul knew himself called as apostle to the heathen world. What was his view thereof? In it he saw no divine revelation at all. It is not God who is revealed in the "non-Christian religions" but the corruption of man; not God's truth but man's falsehood. "They exchanged the truth about God for a lie and worshiped and served the creature rather than the Creator, who is blessed forever! Amen" (vs. 25). To bracket Christianity with the human religions, perhaps as the highest step in a developing series, is utterly different from Paul's concept of "the religions outside Christianity." For to look upon them as in a lower stage of development than Christianity is to see in them a measure of truth. But

Paul characterizes them as "a lie." They are not a lower stage of truth or a preparation for the full truth; they are a distortion of the truth, the direct opposite of truth. To be sure there is a relation between them and the truth; for they could not be if God had not revealed His truth. But that is not to accord them any positive value. It only leaves their adherents without excuse before God, the just object of His wrath. Far from seeing any positive value in the worship of the heathen, Paul considers it evidence of man's deepest corruption. Man can descend to nothing lower than to despise and dishonor God in His majesty by worshiping and serving the creature rather than the Creator. What matchless contempt of God Paul sees in this is seen most clearly in the fact that he breaks out into a doxology, in reaction. It is such contempt of God that above all else evokes God's wrath.

(2) *The reaction of God's wrath*

How does the wrath of God show itself? In its ultimate form it will be disclosed in "the day of wrath." But even now in history God makes His wrath operative. Paul indicates this by repeating three times the fateful words, παρέδωκεν αὐτοὺς ὁ θεός, "God gave them up." When man does not turn to God, God punishes him by giving him up to sin. At first glance that may be a surprising and difficult thought. Let us again call to mind the radical difference between Paul and the thought of the present. When we hear the word "unrighteousness," we are most apt to think of moral evil, of injustice, which men commit against one another and thereby undermine the foundations of society. And when it is said that divine punishment is visited on the unrighteous, this statement is understood in corresponding manner. God

does not allow the unrighteous to prosper. Punishment follows upon evil-doing, either in the form of present misfortune, or as eternal banishment from God's fellowship. That
fellowship is regarded as man's "greatest good," the felicity
that answers man's inmost desire.

But Paul's thought is the direct opposite on practically
every point. One is tempted to say, with some oversimplifi-
cation, that it is as if the two concepts "unrighteousness"
and "divine punishment" had been interchanged. In the first
place, "unrighteousness" is not, for Paul, a moralistic concept. Its opposite is not human righteousness, man's moral
well-doing, but the righteousness of God. The deepest meaning of unrighteousness here is that man has turned away
from God, that he did not seek God, and "did not see fit to
acknowledge God" (vs. 28). And how does God punish
this unrighteousness? Paul replies, "by giving man up to
sin." Then he describes this punishment by painting in glar-
ing colors just such conduct as we usually call wicked. When
he tells how God discloses His wrath against unrighteousness, he does not say that God withdraws His blessing and
permits misfortune to overtake the wicked. He simply says
that God gives him up to sin; and that sin itself disgraces
man (vss. 24-27) and disturbs human society (vss. 28-31).

Man thinks himself free when he in selfishness and vain-
glory rejects God's authority and withholds faith and obedience from Him. But Paul considers that only a vain delusion.
We are apt to think that God deals only with the faithful,
but not with those who have turned away from Him in unbelief and disobedience—as if man could depose God; as if
anything whatever could slip out of His hands! No, even
they who turn away from God are ever in His almighty
hand; but they stand under the wrath of God because of

their unrighteousness. When they turn to sin they follow their own choice; but they are by no means free, but doubly bound. He turns exactly to that to which the wrath of God gives him up and his punishment falls fully on him. It is God, the omnipotent Judge, who gives him up to sin and commits him to the power of sin.

When man attempts to escape from God into freedom, the result really is that he falls a prey to the forces of corruption. Among these forces Paul first names *the wrath of God*; and that which follows after is intended to show what it means to stand under it. Next to the wrath of God Paul places *sin*. Sin is not an individual misstep or a human act that falls short of a standard. Paul considers it a universal power of corruption into whose might God in His wrath gives over the unrighteous man. Thus the wrath of God and sin are most closely related. In the last verse of this chapter there is reference to two other powers which hold man in bondage. There it is said of the unrighteous that "they know God's decree that those who do such things deserve to die." *The law* stands over against the unrighteous. To such the holy law of God becomes a condemning law, a power of destruction which hands the wicked over to *death*.

Wrath, Sin, Law, Death—these are the four terrifying powers of destruction which rule over man in the old aeon. As the epistle advances Paul has much to say about these powers. When man finds that the way he is traveling leads to destruction, he may conclude that by a fresh act of will he must launch out on another. Of course he considers himself free. So he feels that the new course is quite possible for him. But this is a delusion which Paul is at pains to correct. Man is not free. He is given over to the powers of destruction. Sin is not something which man has under control, so

111

that he can choose for or against it. It is a power which holds him in thralldom. All that he does and wills stands under the wrath of God, under the condemning power of sin, law, and death. A new status is possible only if God effects it, if God reveals His righteousness. It is that which God has done through Christ. In Him the new aeon has come, in which it is not God's wrath that rules but God's righteousness. Precisely by the fact that Paul makes it clear that, in the old aeon, man is utterly in the power of hostile forces, it becomes even clearer that righteousness cannot be effected by man. "The righteousness from God" is revealed in the gospel. It alone can give deliverance and life, σωτηρία and ζωή. Thus the best introduction to that which Paul has to say about the righteousness from God in the new aeon is what he has said about the wrath of God in the old.

It is a dark page which Paul writes about the unrighteousness of the Gentiles. He had gathered the material from conditions that were manifest to anyone who observed them, their idolatry and their moral waywardness. He could have found the same in the Old Testament and the wisdom literature of the Jews (cf. especially the Book of Wisdom, chaps. 13-14). They direct attack against paganism with its idolatry. They marshal tables of indictments. But is not this dark picture of heathenism one-sided? Did not the Gentile world also have the brighter aspects—e.g., Greek culture—as to which Paul says nothing? He who asks that question ought to note that Paul does not mean to describe the morals or the culture of the Gentiles. Had that been his purpose, he could fairly be charged as intimated. He does not attempt a careful objective characterization of a people with its lights and shadows. Nor was it his purpose to blacken the natural man, to show how poor and lost he is. His purpose was rather to say what it means to stand under the wrath of God. It is for that reason that he sets forth that by which the wrath of God against ungodliness and unrighteousness is revealed. And as to that, what he says is utterly fitting. This anyone can see for himself in the life of those who have turned away from God. "A religion which lives on false-hood, a body which is defiled, a society in which hate and war are at home, these are the revelation of the wrath of God" (A. Schlatter).

2. THE WRATH OF GOD AGAINST THE RIGHTEOUSNESS OF THE LAW
2:1–3:20

(1) The Jews are also without excuse

The Jews could agree immediately and entirely with all that Paul has thus far said against the Gentiles, with their idolatry and unrighteousness. The Gentiles are without excuse in their ungodliness and moral transgression. The wrath of God overtakes them justly. But now Paul directs the same charge against the Jews themselves. The very fact that the Jew agrees so entirely with Paul's charge against the Gentile shows that he himself is without excuse and subject to the wrath of God.

We assume that at the beginning of the second chapter the apostle turns his attention to the Jews; but that is not exactly self-evident. Not until verse 17 does he speak explic-itly to the Jews. In the earlier part of the chapter he uses the general address, "O man." Formally it is possible to refer 2:1-16 either to that which precedes, as to the Gentiles, or to that which follows, about the Jews. Both positions have been taken among interpreters. But it is pretty certain that Paul here turns his attention to the Jews. In support of this we point out that this view gives a clearer and less forced meaning to the words, and also the relation of these verses to the Book of Wisdom, chapters 11-15. The latter consideration is quite decisive. These chapters in the Book of Wisdom clearly supply the key to the second chapter of Romans.

Earlier we called attention to the relation between what Paul says about the idolatry and immorality of the Gentiles and the comparable statements in the Book of Wisdom, chapters 13-14. The parallels are striking. Both speak of the folly of idolatry and how creation bears witness to the Creator. "For verily all men by nature were but vain who had no perception of God, and from the good things that are seen they gained no power to know him that is, neither by giving heed to the works did they recognize the artificer. . . . If it was through astonishment at their power and influence, let them understand from them how much more powerful is he that formed them" (Wisd. 13:1, 4). Both insist that the Gentiles are without excuse (Rom. 1:20, Wisd. 13:8), and both present catalogues of indictments against their moral corruption. But one would not venture to assert, on the basis of these facts alone, that Paul makes direct reference to this chapter in the Book of Wisdom. Like declarations appear in many places in Jewish propaganda literature. But that Paul's view does stand in very special relation to this book becomes quite clear when we turn to the second chapter of Romans, where he addresses himself to the Jews. What use does the Book of Wisdom make of its declarations about the Gentiles, when it directs its attention to the Jews? Four things must be noted. (1) The wrath of God rests on the Gentiles, but not on the Jews. (2) It is the Jews' knowledge of God and His will which saves them from His wrath. (3) Even in His condemnation God is forbearing, to give His foes opportunity to do better. (4) When the Jew judges others, he ought to remember the goodness and mercy of God.

We illustrate each of these points by quotations. (1) The wrath of God rests on the Gentiles, but not on the Jews. "For when they (the Israelites) were tried, albeit but in mercy chastened, they learned how the ungodly were tormented, being judged with wrath: for these as a father, admonishing them, thou didst prove; but those, as a stern king, condemning them, thou didst search out" (Wisd. 11:9f.). "While therefore thou dost chasten us, thou scourgest our enemies a thousand times more" (12:22). (2) It is the Jews' knowledge of God and His will which saves them from His wrath. "For even if we sin, we are thine, knowing thy dominion . . . for to be acquainted with thee is perfect righteousness" (15:2f.). (3) Even in His condemnation God is forbearing, to give His foes opportunity to do better. "Thou hast mercy on all men, because thou hast power to do all things; and thou overlookest the sins of men to the end that they may repent" (11:23). "Judging them by little and little thou gavest them a place of repentance, not being ignorant that their nature by birth was evil, and their wickedness inborn, and that their manner of thought would in no wise ever be changed, for they were a seed accursed from the beginning" (12:10f.). (4) When the Jew judges others, he ought to remember the goodness and mercy of God. ". . . to the intent that we may ponder thy goodness when we judge" (12:22).

Against that background the words of Paul in the second chapter have a particularly clear and definite meaning. It is not against an imaginary opponent that Paul contends. He is not putting his own words into the mouth of the Jews. He merely presents what they had themselves said. When

he says, "O man, you who judge," he addresses himself to
the Jew's manner of life, as we see it in the Book of Wisdom.
The Jew feels that he enjoys an abiding advantage over the
Gentile. He sees himself on God's side, assenting to God's
judgment on the Gentile's sin. In the exercise of that judgment he feels very safe before God. God pours out His
wrath on the heathen. "Pour out thy wrath upon the heathen
that have not known thee, and upon the kingdoms that have
not called upon thy name" (Ps. 79:6). But He saves His own
people. To the Jew, who thinks like that, Paul says, "The
fact that you pass judgment does not make you safe before
God. On the contrary, in the very fact that you agree in the
judgment of the unrighteousness of the Gentiles, you have
pronounced judgment on yourself too."

This interpretation overcomes a difficulty which has
greatly troubled the exposition of this passage. Paul enters
upon his course of thought here with a "therefore," a διό. It
would seem from this that the thought which he now presents springs from that which has gone before. Interpreters
have felt that they faced the following alternative: *either*
we must stand by the logical significance of this word, and
understand 2:1ff. as referring to the Gentiles, *or*, if this passage has reference to the Jews, we must overlook the logical
conjunctive character of the word and regard διό as a careless transitional particle, by which the writer turns from one
idea and takes up another. But even though the latter view
be possible, we have shown how an emphatic "therefore"
fits the context. *Precisely "therefore,"* because that which
has been said about the Gentiles is also true as to the Jews,
"therefore" the Jew is himself without excuse, when he
judges. In passing judgment on others he condemns himself. For, as we read in the Book of Wisdom, the Jew con-

fesses that he too sins. But he expects God to judge him
and the Gentile in different ways. "For even if we sin we
are thine, knowing thy dominion" (Wisd. 15:2). With bit-
ing irony Paul says, "Do you suppose, O man, that when you
judge those who do such things and yet do them yourself,
you will escape the judgment of God?" (vs. 3). No, God's is
a true judgment, corresponding with reality (κατὰ ἀλήθειαν,
vs. 2). For "God shows no partiality" (vs. 11).

The Jew says, "Thou, our God, art good (χρηστός) and
true, patient (μακρόθυμος) and directing all with mercy."
To this he adds the citation from the Book of Wisdom,
"For even if we sin, we are thine, knowing thy dominion"
(15:1-2). Paul answers, "Do you presume upon the riches
of his kindness and forbearance and patience?" (vs. 4).

The Jew says, "God is merciful and forbearing in judgment, giving his foes opportunity for repentance," εἰς
μετάνοιαν (Wisd. 11:23). Paul replies, "Do you not know
that God's kindness is meant to lead *you* to repentance?"
(μετάνοιαν, vs. 4).

The Jew says, "God judges the heathen in his wrath; but
it is different with us. We are saved from his wrath. When
he chastises us, he does so in gentleness" (Wisd. 11:9f.; cf.
12:22). Paul replies, "By your hard and impenitent heart
you are storing up wrath for yourself on the day of wrath
when God's righteous judgment will be revealed" (vs. 5).

That which has been presented is enough to show that
the apostle here addresses himself to the Jews. The situation
is like this: When, in 1:18-32, Paul spoke of the wrath of
God against unrighteousness, he referred primarily to the
heathen and his unrighteousness. Even though he did not
make specific mention of the Gentiles, what he said made it
clear that is was of them he was speaking. In exactly the

same manner, he now goes on, in 2:1ff., to speak about God's wrath against the righteousness of the law. Though he does not specifically mention the Jews—saying here only, "O man" —what he says makes it clear that he has the Jew and his legal righteousness in mind.

Both—the Jew and the Gentile—stand under the same judgment. Even as Paul said that the Gentiles are without excuse (ἀναπολογήτους, 1:20), he now says the same about the Jews: "Therefore you have no excuse," (ἀναπολόγητος, 2:1). And as he said that the wrath of God is revealed against the unrighteousness of the Gentiles, so he now says the same about the Jews, "You are storing up wrath for yourself in the day of wrath." Both stand under the same condemnation before God, under the same divine wrath which rules in the present aeon. Neither has any excuse which can stand between him and God's wrath.

What Paul is here especially concerned about is to break down the supposed protection on which the Jew depended. There is no escape for the Jew in the fact that he aligns himself with God in judging the unrighteousness of the heathen. On the contrary, in judging another, he condemns himself. He has no right to appeal to the goodness and forbearance of God, for God's judgment is true and without partiality. But, furthermore, Paul puts his finger on the sorest point of all when he asserts that there is no protection against the wrath of God in the fact that the Jew has the law of God. Verse 17 says, "You call yourself a Jew and rely upon the law." That is the issue to which the apostle devotes the entire second chapter: the Jew's trust in the law, his righteousness by the law. We must now give closer attention to that, observing Paul's attack upon it.

(2) The law does not protect against the wrath of God

The Jew was deeply convinced that the wrath of God rests on the Gentiles who do not have the law and do not know the true God. But as for himself, on the other hand, he counts it his greatest credit that he knows God and has the law. It is for this reason, above all else, that he is assured of his superiority to other people. The Gentiles "shall hear all these statutes, and say, 'Surely this great nation is a wise and understanding people.' For what nation is there so great, who hath God so nigh unto them, as the Lord our God is in all things that we call upon him for? And what nation is there so great, that hath statutes and judgments so righteous as all this law?" (Deut. 4:6-8). To be sure, the Jew is not so foolish and blind as to assume that he keeps all the law of God perfectly. When he puts his trust in righteousness by the law, it is not that he feels that his own deeds would enable him to stand before the Judge, if strict justice were to pronounce the verdict. Righteousness by the law is not to be understood in that extreme sense. We must be careful not to make that mistake. The Jew is well aware that he fails in many ways, and he will be lost unless God in His mercy judges leniently. But it is precisely the fact that he has the law and knows God that fills him with confidence and gives him a feeling of safety. He is aware that he knows the right way; and unlike the heathen, he has not strayed away from God. In this way, he is sure, he is fundamentally right with God; in that sense he is righteous. Beyond that he trusts that God's leniency will overlook his failures.

We find a good expression of such thought in the Book of Wisdom (15:1-4): "Thou, our God, art gracious and true, longsuffering, and in mercy ordering all things. For even if we sin, we are thine, knowing thy dominion. But we shall

not sin, knowing that we have been accounted thine; for to
be acquainted with thee is perfect righteousness, and to
know thy dominion is the root of immortality. For neither
were we led astray by any evil device of men's art, nor by
painters' fruitless labor (idols)." Here we see reference both
to the perfect righteousness which consists of knowledge of
God and His will—which the Jew has, but not the heathen—
and to the sin and errancy which must appeal to God's
mercy.

But now Paul directs his attack against the Jew's confidence because he *knows the law*, against his trust in righteousness by the law. It is not only when we come to verse
17, or to verse 13, that we see this. It is apparent from the
beginning of the chapter. *To know God and His will is not
perfect righteousness.* For the law everything depends on
performance. Therefore, from the first verse and repeatedly
throughout the chapter, Paul comes back to the matter of
behavior and accomplishment. "You, the judge, are doing
the very same thing" (vs. 1). "The judgment of God rightly
falls upon those who do such things" (vs. 2). "You judge
those who do such things and yet do them yourself" (vs. 3).
Likewise throughout the whole chapter.

On the day of judgment it will be demonstrated that God
is a just judge. It will then do no good to point out that
one has had the law and known God's will. It is written,
"Thou renderest to every man *according to his work*" (Ps.
62:12). Paul points out what this will mean. "To those who
by patience in well-doing seek for glory and honor and immortality, he will give eternal life; but for those who are
factious and do not obey the truth, but obey unrighteousness, there shall be wrath and fury." They who seek for
the things that belong to God—glory (δόξα), honor, and im-

mortality—are contrasted with those who are self-seeking (οἱ ἐξ ἐριθείας). This thought has a close parallel in 1:18ff. Self-seeking leads to the suppression of the truth in unrighteousness; and against such the wrath and fury of God are revealed. Paul repeats this contrast, in reverse order, in verses 9f., "There will be tribulation and distress for every human being who does evil, . . . but glory and honor and peace for every one who does good." As to the repetition, as to both, of the words, "the Jew first and also the Greek," cf. 1:16.

So God makes no distinction between Jew and Gentile when they come to judgment. Both will be judged on the same basis: Have they done the good or the evil? "For God shows no partiality." With God there is no such favoritism or bias as the Jew assumed. But must there not be a difference, after all, between him who knows the law and him who does not? Indeed there is—but not to the Jew's advantage! For, "all who have sinned without the law will also perish without the law, and all who have sinned under the law will be judged by the law" (vs. 12). God is not unright-eous; He does not judge those who have not the law as if they had known it. But the Jew knows the law—and sins against knowledge. Therefore he will be judged by the law. Far from being safe because he knows the law, the Jew will stand under the judgment of the law. It is the law, in which he reposed his confidence, which is the power which condemns him and turns him over to the wrath of God. His knowledge of the law takes away from him all excuse for his sin. The law cannot save him from doom. "For it is not the hearers of the law who are righteous before God, but the doers of the law who will be justified" (vs. 13).

In the last analysis, then, there is no basic difference in

the judgment of Jew and Gentile. They are basically in the
same situation. Is the Gentile to be held responsible for the
fact that he does not have the law? One might rather ask,
will not the fact that he does not have the law protect him?
No, says Paul, he too is without excuse. To be sure, he will
not be judged by the law; yet he will receive the proper
reward for his deeds. He who sins without the law is lost
without the law. But should the Jew, who sins despite the
fact that he has the law, escape punishment? Will the law
be his refuge? No, he will be judged by the law. Thus the
law becomes his accuser, his destruction.

The Jew's advantage is that he has the law, while the
heathen does not have it. Paul does not deny that difference.
He speaks of him who sins with the law and of him who sins
without it. But he reduces this one difference to its proper
significance. Though the heathen does not have the law, he
is not without knowledge of God's will. Of that he knows
enough that he is without excuse for his evil-doing. As early
as 1:20ff. Paul pointed out that that is the case. Now he
takes up the matter of the recognized difference between
the Jew and the Gentile. It is not only the Jew who can
differentiate between right and wrong. The Gentile also
knows that difference and acknowledges it in his daily life.
As to this Paul says, "When Gentiles who have not the law
do by nature what the law requires, they are a law to themselves, even though they do not have the law. They show
that what the law requires is written on their hearts, while
their conscience also bears witness and their conflicting
thoughts accuse or perhaps excuse them" (vss. 14f.).

But it is of greatest importance to note carefully what
Paul does say on this point, and what he does not say. Here
is a point where thoughts and presuppositions foreign to him

have often been ascribed to him. It has been said, for instance, that Paul here speaks of a *lex naturae,* after stoic
fashion. It is pointed out that he says that heathen may by
nature (φύσει) fulfill the law, and that because the natural
law, *lex naturae,* is written on their hearts. This is only another illustration how, when one comes with an accepted
theory, he finds it where it is really not intended, or even
where the opposite is meant. That such is the case is clear
enough if one gives heed to the context. As we say, Paul is
here criticizing the Jews because they trust in the law and
boast themselves of God. To them he says that God shows
no partiality. They who have sinned without the law shall
perish without the law; and they who have sinned under the
law shall be judged by the law, for it is not the hearers of
the law but the doers of the law who are righteous before
God. The emphasis is not on having the law but on keeping
it, on fulfilling the law. Then Paul continues—and what he
presents is not an imaginary case, but actual fact which none
can deny, because it is seen very, very often—when a heathen,
though he does not have the law, does just what the law says
one ought to do—when, for example, he honors his parents,
as many among all peoples do, whether they have the law
or not—would God say, "He does not have the law, so what
he does is evil?" No, the vital thing is that he keeps the law;
so it must be said, as to that heathen, that his harmony with
the law is quite different from that of a Jew who has the law
but does not keep it. In the fact of his action that heathen
does, in natural and straightforward way, something which
is good and in keeping with the law. At another time he
violates the law; but that is not Paul's point. When he acts
in harmony with the law, his solidarity with the law is fully
certified. It could not be said better or more forcefully than

Paul does: he *is* a law unto himself. That is not in the least
to say that he *has* the law. Paul specifically says he does not
have it, and that so insistently that he does so twice in verse
14 alone. Nor is Paul speaking of a law written in the heart;
for then the heathen would indeed have the law, and that
in a more intimate way than the Jew has it. The latter had
it on tables of stone or in a holy book. Manifestly what Jeremiah 31:33 says about the law written in the heart influenced
Paul; and yet he does not specifically say that "the law" is
written on the heathen heart. He does not say ὁ νόμος, but
τὸ ἔργον τοῦ νόμου. Not the law itself, but the work of the
law which the heathen does, is written on his heart.

It is clear that Paul's thought here has nothing to do with
the question of a *lex naturae*. He was not advancing a general theory as to the heathen, to the effect that they by nature do what the law commands. He is only talking about
the particular situation when a heathen, in the situation
where nature places him, does something which the law does
command. The heathen's actual *doing* of what the law requires, even when he does not have the law, is what Paul is
contrasting with the Jew's confidence in the mere fact that
he *knows* the law. For the same reason that Paul does not
speak of "natural theology," he does not speak of a *lex naturae*. Both of these concepts are foreign to Paul's concept
of God. The concept of *lex naturae* also implies a deistic
conception of God. It thinks of God as having written certain ethical principles on the human heart, at the creation.
Even when he is out of fellowship with God he has these
principles in him and can direct his life accordingly. But
Paul believes in God as living and ever active with man,
even with the heathen, in life's concrete situations, showing
him what is good and what is required of him. God has not

written "the law" in the hearts of the Gentiles, in the sense
that they have by nature a universal principle to which to
subject life and from which to draw conclusions as to how
they ought to live. He has written "the works of the law"
in their hearts so that, if they do otherwise in the concrete
situation, they are aware that they have done evil. "Their
conscience also bears witness." Paul does not think that the
heathen live in utter darkness, unable to tell right from
wrong, white from black. Just because what the law requires
is written on their hearts, they have a sense of how they
ought to act in the specific situation. When they act contrary to the right, and seek to justify themselves before
others and even before themselves, they know within themselves what the fact really is. The heathen's conscience
stands as an objective witness beside him, showing that he
actually knew that he did wrong. So Paul also speaks of the
conflicting thoughts that rise, accusing or excusing the heathen. If, when he has done something good and right, he
be accused as if it were evil, his thoughts rise up to defend
him against the charge; and if the evil he has done be approved, he may maintain a good exterior, but his inmost
thoughts accuse him nonetheless.

There are three that bear witness: (1) the act which
shows that "what the law requires" is written in the heart;
(2) conscience; and (3) accusing or excusing thoughts.
These three agree and show that the Gentile is without excuse when he does evil. Therein it is demonstrated that the
judgment of God is just when the Gentile, as well as the Jew,
falls under the wrath of God.

To what he has just asserted Paul then adds immediately,
"on that day when, according to my gospel, God judges the
secrets of men by Christ Jesus." The connection here pre-

sents a problem. It is clear that, beginning with verse 5, Paul speaks of "the day of wrath," referring to the final judgment. But verses 14-15 seem to apply to the present, as they speak of that which is written on the heart and of accusing or excusing thoughts. Why then does Paul immediately add verse 16, which seems to defer that which has been said to the day of judgment?

The difficulty has led to the suggestion that verses 14-15 are an aside or a parenthesis, verse 16 belonging immediately with verse 13. According to that suggestion the sense would be "It is not the hearers of the law who are righteous before God, but the doers of the law who will be justified . . . on that day when, according to my gospel, God judges the secrets of men by Christ Jesus." Another suggestion is to the effect that what is here said about the heathen is not yet evident to all, but that will be manifested on the day of judgment. That is in harmony with the Swedish translation of Romans, which inserts, "Thus it will be found to be" on that day, etc. Such is of course not part of the Greek text. Still another—most doubtful—suggestion makes verse 16 itself refer to the present, not to the final judgment: whenever the gospel is preached Christ judges the secrets of men. That this is not the meaning is clear from Paul's reference to "the day of wrath" in verse 5. He cannot have expected the reader to understand anything but a reference to the day of judgment in what he says about "that day when, according to my gospel, God judges the secrets of men by Christ Jesus." Had his meaning been otherwise, his expression would have been different. But none of the other suggestions is entirely adequate. No one can be absolutely certain what the connection of verse 16 was for Paul himself. We cannot go beyond the suggestion that Paul was so filled with the thought of the day of judgment that he continues with it, after his declaration as to the heathen.

We here have Paul's own words as evidence that he regards the declaration about judgment as part of the gospel. Many have felt that Paul's proclamation of justification by faith is irreconcilable with and must exclude all thought of judgment, especially any judgment as to the works of men. So it has been proposed that what he says here is not what he really believes, but an accommodation to the current Jewish view. But this suggestion rests on a misunderstanding of the apostle's thought. For him, as for the rest of the New Testament, the last judgment is an inescapable fact, which nothing can put in question. It is only in the judgment that the creative and redemptive work of God comes to completion. And even that final judgment belongs to the work of Christ. Paul's position is the same as that stated in John 5:27, "The Father has given him authority to execute judgment, because he is the Son of man." God will judge the world through Christ. Judgment has universal relevance. It is not only for Jews and Gentiles. Even as to Christians it is said, "We must all appear before the judgment seat of Christ, so that each one may receive good or evil, according to what he has done in the body" (II Cor. 5:10).

For Paul there is no contradiction between justification by faith and judgment. The former does not make the latter unnecessary for the Christian's account. By justification by faith God has not abolished the judgment of the works of men. "For we shall all stand before the judgment seat of God. . . . So each of us shall give account of himself to God" (14:11f.). Justification does not mean carte blanche for the Christian, so that God no longer asks as to his works. Rather is the thought of judgment to keep the Christian alert. He must never forget that he must some day give account of his deeds before God.

But does not Paul mean that man is to be judged according to his faith or unbelief? Such a question also rests on a misunderstanding of Paul. For him faith is not something which man offers in lieu of works. To think that is to remain in the legalistic position, merely substituting one requirement for another. Without hesitation Paul can speak of the judgment of man's works simply because that word—as Luther expresses it—does not stand *in loco justificationis*. His thought cannot be paraphrased in the formula of P. Althaus, "All comes from faith; yet all depends on works." That is Augustine's position, not Paul's. Paul would never say, like Augustine, that the law was given that men might seek grace, but grace was then given that the law might be fulfilled. Paul does not combine the law and the gospel in that way, that the law embodies the true will of God which man cannot fulfill; wherefore God gives man the gospel that by its help he may keep the law and be justified at last by the works that were thus made possible. Paul never considers faith in Christ simply as a means to something else on which all finally depends. For him faith is both the beginning and the end. All comes from faith and all depends on faith. Paul himself has given the best expression of that, ἐκ πίστεως εἰς πίστιν, "from faith—to faith." To believe in Christ, to live "in Christ" and through Him to share in the new aeon is in and of itself full and complete justification. In and of itself that is already "righteousness from God"; it does not merely become such by virtue of works that are thereby affected. For Paul all actually depends on this—that one "is in Christ." But of that he is not yet speaking in this connection—and for good reason. It would have been preferable in every way if interpreters, following Paul's example, had refrained from introducing here the thought of justification by faith. But it is by this time traditional practice to confront what Paul says about judgment with his proclamation of justification through faith. This has usually resulted in a blunting either of what he says about judgment or of what he says about justification, or of both. To forestall this, if possible, it has been necessary to deal with this problem.

If we now look back to verses 12-16, we may note that two different tendencies stand over against each other. This is the reason why that which Paul says about the Gentiles yields, from one point of view, a very positive impression, but, from another viewpoint, a negative impression. It has aroused surprise that Paul can speak so favorably of the heathen, in view of the fact that in the first chapter he so unsparingly set the unrighteousness of the Gentiles under the wrath of God. The reason is clearly that he now gives attention to the Jew's righteousness through the law. It is not because Paul wants to speak of the Gentiles' fulfillment of the law that he refers to them. His purpose is rather to show by reference to them that the Jews' trust in the law is not well founded. It is true that the Jew has the law, while the Gentile does not have it. But what is the difference, since ultimately all depends on the doing of that which the law requires? As a deathblow to the Jew's confidence because he *has* the law, Paul points out that the heathen, though he does not have the law, sometimes *does* by nature what the law requires. The specific meaning of what the apostle is saying rests on the context of the second chapter which contrasts the *knowing* of the law with the *keeping* of it.

Nevertheless Paul does not forget that these words also

are part of a more inclusive context, and that a negative one. Both the Jew and the Gentile are sinners; both belong to the old aeon and stand under the wrath of God. This negative quality leaves its mark on these verses. We see it first in verse 12, "All who have sinned without the law will also perish without the law, and all who have sinned under the law will be judged by the law." "Under the law" and "without the law," that is the difference. All have sinned, therein is the similarity. It is not by accident that Paul speaks negatively. It would not have been equally true to say, "All who have done right without the law will also be justified without the law, and all who have done right under the law will be justified under the law." Why not? Because Paul knows that both the Jews and the Gentiles are all under sin (3:9). He knows that all have turned away and become worthless, and that "no one does good" (3:12). He knows that "no human being will be justified in his sight by works of the law" (3:20). In the last analysis whatever can be said positively about Jew and Gentile turns into something negative. About the Jew the positive is that he knows the law; but that very fact becomes the basis of his condemnation. About the Gentile the positive is that he is a law to himself; but for that very reason he is without excuse before God, since he is also a sinner.

From the Gentile, who has not the law, Paul turns in verse 17 to the Jew who has the law, saying, "You call yourself a Jew and rely upon the law and boast of your relation to God and know his will and approve what is excellent, because you are instructed in the law, and if you are sure that you are a guide to the blind, a light to those who are in darkness, a corrector of the foolish, a teacher of children, having in the law the embodiment of knowledge and truth" (vss. 17-20).

With that Paul has come to the point at which he has aimed from the beginning of the chapter. We could use as motto and superscription of chapter 2 the opening words of this section, "You call yourself a Jew and rely upon the law." In the long list of the Jews' advantages, which now follows, many have felt that they detected a bit of irony. But that is not Paul's intention. The special status of the Jews, through the works and revelation of God, he does not consider as something unimportant or paltry about which one might speak ironically. It was that which he himself, in his pharisaical period, considered his "gain"; and he turned away from it not as one gives up something valueless, but as one offers that which is precious to gain the one thing which is essential (Phil. 3:4-9; cf. above pp. 12ff.). To know God and His will, to be instructed in the law so that one may judge what is best, these are beyond question something great and significant. With full justice Israel may look upon herself as a teacher of peoples, because in the law she has by divine revelation the right expression of knowledge and truth. Paul of course knows that there is much carnal pride in the Jews' pride that they belong to God's chosen people; and it is especially against the Jews' confidence because they know the law that Paul speaks. He knows that when the Jew "boasts himself of God" he is guilty of censurable self-esteem. But it is not for the sake of irony that he refers to the Jews' advantage. He uses it rather as background and emphasis for the contrast which he draws between knowing the law and keeping the law. The Jew's mistake was not that he prized the law and esteemed the knowledge of it a great advantage. It was right to thank God for that. His mistake was to let it stop with merely knowing the law. His mistake was that he *put his trust in the law.* It is not the law in which one should trust, for sin reigns despite the law. "You then who teach others, will you not teach yourself? While you preach against stealing, do you steal? You who say that one must not commit adultery, do you commit adultery? You who abhor idols, do you rob temples?" (vss. 21f.). The great wrong in the life of the Jew was that while, on the one hand, he "boasts of his relation to God," and "boasts in the law," on the other hand he "dishonors God by breaking the law." So Paul adds the word of Scripture, "The name of God is blasphemed among the Gentiles because of you." The more the Jew boasts of his relation to God, while he at the same time disobeys His will, the more will they who do not know God despise Him. Must not God's wrath rest on such?

(3) Circumcision does not shield from the wrath of God

Everything to which the Jew can appeal to shield him from the wrath of God accordingly seems useless and ineffective. It does not help him that he assents to God's judgment on others. Nor does it shield him to appeal to the longsuffering of God, for to do so that one may continue in sin is a blasphemy against God which cannot but evoke His wrath. And now we have seen and know God's law gives no security, but rather leaves the sinner utterly without excuse.

But is not *circumcision* an effective shield against God's wrath? Did not God himself establish the covenant with Israel and designate circumcision as the seal of this covenant? Is it possible for God to be angry at His peculiar people, who bear the mark of circumcision as evidence that they belong to Him? Is circumcision to be denied all meaning? Indeed circumcision is an advantage, Paul says. But the

covenant, of which circumcision is the sign, is a covenant of
law. Therefore, as he says, they of the circumcision must
fulfill the law. "Circumcision indeed is of value if you obey
the law" (vs. 25). But the trouble lies just there. And what
is the consequence? Should God, as the Jew seems to feel,
out of partiality for him because he is circumcised in the
flesh, close His eyes to the Jew's disobedience? Must not the
just God rather, when a Gentile keeps the law, regard him
as circumcised, while the Jew transgresses the law as if he
were not circumcised?

Thus the positions are reversed. As we saw at the beginning of the chapter, the Jew felt called upon to judge the
Gentile. Now Paul says, "Then those who are physically
uncircumcised but keep the law will condemn you who
have the written code and circumcision but break the law"
(vs. 27). In Matthew 12:41 we read, "The men of Nineveh
will arise at the judgment with this generation and condemn
it; for they repented at the preaching of Jonah." It is as if
Paul has this word of Jesus in mind. At any rate he uses the
same thought here against those who put their trust in the
law and circumcision: the uncircumcised, who have not the
written code and circumcision, shall stand with you in the
judgment and condemn you.

Men have asked who these uncircumcised are who nevertheless fulfill the law. It has often been said that the reference is to Gentiles who come to believe in the gospel; for
only of such can it be said that they really fulfill the whole
law: νόμον τελεῖν. "Paul clearly speaks of the actual fact that
some, born in heathendom and uncircumcised, in their col-
lective relationships obey God's command. But where are
they to be found, heathen who thus fulfill the law and thereby put the Jews to shame? In the emphasis given to ἐκ

φύσεως it is implied that something new has been added to their natural state, a spiritual circumcision. They are still heathen only in the way Peter and Paul, according to Galatians 2:15, are still Jews (by φύσει). That which has delivered them from their natural heathen state can only be their Christian faith" (O. Moe, in agreement with Zahn). It is quite clear that such an interpretation misses just that which Paul means to say here. For one thing, it does violence to the context. Such a reference to Gentiles who believe in Christ and their fulfillment of the law is out of place in the closely knit thinking which Paul develops from 1:18 to 3:20. He limits himself to speaking of the wrath of God in the old aeon. The idea does not fit here. But it is quite as wide of the mark to say, on the other hand, that this view is utterly beyond Paul's thought. The real point is that the Jew, who passes judgment on the Gentile and unlike him thinks himself safe from the wrath of God because of his possession of the law and circumcision, must be told that the Gentile who fulfills the law will condemn him. But if one says "the Gentile who is converted to Christ" will condemn the Jew, the point of the contrast is lost. And, to mention a third consideration, it would be impossible (despite Phil. 3:3) for Paul to say of the Christian that he is regarded by God as circumcision. The statement that the uncircumcised is reckoned by God as circumcised can have meaning only for him who still belongs to the old aeon. For in Christ, in the new aeon, the very issue between circumcision and uncircumcision has lost all meaning (Gal. 5:6).

"Man looks upon the outward appearance, but God looks upon the heart." Paul applies this word to circumcision. "For he is not a real Jew who is one outwardly, nor is true circumcision something external and physical. He is a Jew who is one inwardly, and real circumcision is a matter of the heart, spiritual, and not literal" (vs. 28f.). What Paul says there is not essentially new. Like affirmations occur in various places in the Old Testament, e.g., Deuteronomy 10:16; 30:6; Jeremiah 4:4; 9:25f. But he is reminding the Jew in his trust in circumcision that the Scriptures themselves declare that the vital thing is not external membership in God's peculiar people. When Paul thus distinguishes between the Jew who is rightly so called and a Jew who is one of God's chosen people only in outward things, he shows most clearly how far he is from irony. For Paul too to be called a Jew is a matter of honor, which God accords only to one whose heart is circumcised and purified. Of such he says, "His praise is not from men but from God."

There is no shift of thought in the transition from the second chapter to the third. The division of chapters at this place is more confusing than helpful. It is natural for the reader to look for a new issue when he takes up a new chapter. But that is not true here; 3:1-20 belongs rather with what has been under discussion in chapter 2, only serving to carry the thought further. It is with 3:21 that we go on to something new.

The Jew puts his trust in the law. To this Paul says that merely to have the law is no shield against the wrath of God. That is the first stage in Paul's discussion. With 2:25 he enters on his second step. The Jew trusts in circumcision. To this Paul says that circumcision is likewise no shield from God's wrath. It is of value only if you obey the law. That is the same as he has said as to the law. The matter of circumcision is referred to question as to the law.

But does Paul really mean to say that circumcision is without significance? In 2:25 there is at least the implica-

tion that circumcision may be of value. If one who has the
law from God disobeys it, the law is manifestly no help to
him, for it condemns him. But the situation looks different
as to circumcision. It is God's sign, for He instituted circumcision. Thereby He set apart Israel as His peculiar people. What advantage would it be if everything depends on
fulfilling the law? Does not that make circumcision insignificant in comparison with the law? The law does of course
play a vital role in circumcision. By faithful fulfillment of
the law one shows that he is true to the covenant. But that
is not the whole matter. Circumcision involves two things.
One is God's promise; the other is the requirement of the
law. If man fails in the latter, he has, for his part, broken
the covenant. Paul has pointed that out in what has preceded. But is that enough to abolish God's action and promise in circumcision, leaving the Jew then as if God had never
established the covenant or given His promise? It is to this
question that Paul turns, at the beginning of the third
chapter.

"What advantage has the Jew? Or what is the value of
circumcision?" he asks. What he has already said might lead
one to think the answer would be, "None at all!" He has
been at pains to remove from the Jew all reason to boast and
to put him on the same plane with the Gentile. But now
Paul replies, "Much in every way!" The Jew's advantage
does not rest on what he does, but on what God has done
with him. The fact that God chose Israel as His peculiar
people and gave her His promises can never be undone.
Even if the Jew has no right to appeal to what God in times
past did with the fathers, as if that could now give him a
favored status before God's judgment, the fact that God
established that relationship still stands; He gave Israel a

unique place in the history of redemption. That is not a
matter of light esteem. Insistent as Paul has been to show
that Jew and Gentile stand alike under God's judgment. he
by no means intends to deny the real differences between
them. The Jew has an advantage which can never be taken
away, that is that it was to him that God first gave His word
of promise. Thereby circumcision is seen in a new light. By
the circumcision Israel became the people of promise. As a
precious trust they received the promise which applied not
merely to them but to all people; and that promise has now
been fulfilled through Jesus Christ. This fact too has now
been entrusted to them; and even if they do not accept the
trust, God's faithfulness is not thereby done away. Paul here
touches on an issue which he will discuss thoroughly in chapters 9-11. Here he merely answers the question, "Does their
faithlessness nullify the faithfulness of God? By no means!"
He gives his thought immediately to the affirmation that
man's faithlessness makes the faithfulness and truthfulness
of God the more manifest.

This truth is obscured somewhat by the translation of
verse 4, "Let God be true though every man be false." Paul
is more emphatic. "Let God become true and every man a
liar." The fact that translators have softened Paul's expression is probably because it may seem offensive in two ways.
First of all, it may seem improper to say that God may "become true," as if He were not so already. And, secondly, it
does not seem possible that Paul wished every man to become a liar. But neither of these objections is weighty. Paul
does not speak here of truthfulness as a property of God;
He speaks of God's promise, which would cease to be true
if man's faithlessness could destroy its validity; but it remains
true because God fulfills it despite man's faithlessness. Paul

gives striking expression to this thought by saying "Let God become true." Then he adds, "Let every man become a liar." The thought that all men are liars Paul finds in Psalm 116:11; but he gives it a deeper meaning. He actually would that everyone stand as a liar before God. That is the background against which the truthfulness of God stands in all its glory. It is also the presupposition for man's salvation. To him who stands against God, salvation does not come from his vindication before God or from his effort to put himself right with God. It roots in the fact that he is condemned as wrong. God lets him become a liar, a sinner. That is so central for Paul's thought that one need not doubt that he means what he says, "Let every man become a liar."

It is by man's falseness, not in spite of it, that the truthfulness of God is glorified. That may seem strange; but Paul knows that it is so, and that Scripture bears witness to it. He thinks particularly of the great penitential psalm, 51, David's confession of sin, after the prophet Nathan had made him aware of his depravity. After confessing, "Against thee, thee only have I sinned and done this evil in thy sight," he continues immediately, "that thou mightest be justified when thou speakest" (Ps. 51:4). God's intent, when He let David fall into sin, was that the divine righteousness be revealed. Paul does not cite the complete passage, assured that passing reference to the familiar psalm will be enough for every reader. He gives only the latter part of the passage, as it appears in the Septuagint, "That thou mayest be justified in thy words and prevail when thou art judged." Though man's sin is rebellion against God's will, it must yet serve to magnify the divine truthfulness and righteousness.

But here we confront two additional questions. First, if it actually is true that man's sin thus magnifies God's glory, is it not unjust for God to visit His wrath on man? And secondly, ought not man to sin the more, that God's glory may be the greater? Paul raises both questions, and rejects both with dispatch. He does not consider them worth discussing.

The first he expresses in two ways. With reference to our unrighteousness and God's righteousness he says, "But if our wickedness serves to show the justice of God, what shall we say? That God is unjust to inflict wrath on us?" It is clear how meaningless and shallow that seems to Paul. That is the significance of his parenthetic "I speak as a man," κατὰ ἄνθρωπον λέγω. Perhaps he also means to protect himself against seeming blasphemous enough to speak of unright-eousness in God. At any rate, he lets the reader know that there is something manlike, too manlike about the question itself. Otherwise every one would be able to see that it is one thing for man to do evil, and something else when God over-rules and makes the evil to serve His purpose. Man may reason like this: wrongdoing is really excusable, since, by God's overruling, it leads to good consequences. It is there-fore unjust for God to punish the offender anyway. This all too human way of looking at evil Paul disavows. "By no means! For then how could God judge the world?" God is to judge the world. He passes judgment on unrighteousness. How can one imagine that He will punish some iniquities and overlook others? And how can one accuse Him of injus-tice when He manifests His wrath against unrighteousness, though the evil be overruled; for the evildoer was not aiming to serve the will of God. Verse 7 deals with the same prob-lem in another form, contrasting the truthfulness of God with man's falseness. "If through my falsehood God's truthfulness abounds to his glory, why am I still being condemned as a sinner?"

By this he is brought to face the other question. If our sin can contribute to the glory of God, ought we not to sin the more that God's honor may thereby be magnified? With apparent justice men felt they could draw that conclusion from Paul's proclamation of grace. In 5:20, for instance, he says, "Where sin increased, grace abounded all the more." But in chapter 6 Paul demonstrates thoroughly that no such deduction may properly be drawn from his thought. But in our immediate context he simply says, "Their condemnation is just."

(4) The result: The whole world lies in guilt before God

Romans is, as we have already said, marked by an extraordinary unity and consistency of thought. This is especially evident in two ways. (1) When Paul introduces a thought he does so with a concise statement to serve as a caption for what is to be presented; (2) at the close of the discussion, he gathers up its result in brief summary statement.

Interpretation is greatly helped by recognition of this procedure. By these introductory propositions and conclusions, Paul sets up his own signboards for our guidance. We need not puzzle about his meaning, unless we ignore these helps which he supplies.

We have now reached the conclusion of that which begins in 1:18. It is illuminating to see how Paul has marked the course of his thought.

His caption is "the wrath of God." It confronts us in the very first verse. "The wrath of God is revealed from heaven" (1:18). What he does from 1:18 to 3:20 is to show how everything in the old aeon, without exception, stands under the wrath of God. Everything and every one stand under God's wrath. It is true of Gentile and Jew in like measure. It is not hard to show that the heathen stands under the divine wrath. It is enough to call attention to that which all can see; so no lengthy argument is needed. The second half of the first chapter suffices. The Gentile stands under God's wrath, with no excuse to which he can appeal. The real difficulty, however, appears when Paul turns to consider the Jew, to show that he stands under the same condemnation. The Jew does have something to which to appeal, and he considers it a defense against the wrath of God. Paul's task is to show the Jew that he is not justified in his expectation from the undeniable advantage which God has given him. This is where Paul bears down. He considers thorough discussion necessary; so he devotes to that point all of chapter 2 and most of chapter 3. The Jew appeals to the law; but the law does not shield him. And he appeals to circumcision, that sign of the covenant which God himself ordained; but there is no refuge for him here either.

And now Paul has come to the end of this point. He can sum up and draw his conclusion. He asks, "What then? Are we Jews any better off?" And he answers, "No, not at all; for I have already charged that all men, both Jews and Greeks, are under the power of sin." In this they are alike, and therefore the wrath of God rests on both. And when the Jew tries to avoid this bracketing with the Gentile, Paul calls his attention to Israel's own Scriptures, as they speak of the universal sinfulness. He offers six quotations.

1) "None is righteous, no, not one;

no one understands, no one seeks for God.

All have turned aside, together they have gone wrong;

no one does good, not even one." Psalm 14:1-3

2) "Their throat is an open grave,
   they use their tongues to deceive."   Psalm 5:9

3) "The venom of asps is under their lips."   Psalm 140:3

4) "Their mouth is full of curses and bitterness."   Psalm 10:7

5) "Their feet are swift to shed blood,
   in their paths are ruin and misery,
   and the way of peace they do not know."   Isaiah 59:7-8

6) "There is no fear of God before their eyes."   Psalm 36:1

The Jew might of course seek to escape by insisting that these Scriptures refer to the Gentiles, not to the Jews. But Paul forestalls that. "Now we know that whatever the law says it speaks to those who are under the law" (vs. 19). That is, the passages cited refer specifically to the Jew. The Scriptures convict them of sin. Despite any differences between Jews and Gentiles, both alike are sinners and both under the wrath of God. The Jew is wholly in error when he trusts the law to shield him against divine wrath. God certainly did not give the law that man might boast himself of its possession or use it for an excuse. It is truer to say that the opposite was God's purpose, namely, "that every mouth may be stopped, and the whole world may be held accountable to God." The intent is that man be silent before God, recognizing the justice of His judgment. Let man be silent as to his own righteousness and his claim of advantage; let him rather confess that he is a sinner.

As long as it is the law that determines man's status before God, only one judgment is possible. "Enter not into judgment with thy servant; for in thy sight shall no man living be justified" (Ps. 143:2). In a free reference to that verse, Paul says, "For no human being will be justified in his

sight by works of the law." Anyone who thinks, like the
Jews, that he can attain to righteousness through the law,
has not understood the significance of the law. As Paul says,
it is given "that every mouth may be stopped." But, the Jew
asks, what good is the law, if it does not help man to attain
to righteousness? Paul answers, that sin may be unmasked
and man brought to a consciousness of it. And this means
more than the unmasking of individual sins which man
commits. In other words, the issue is not sins in a moralistic
sense, but sin as a power, a dynamic force. In the old aeon
sin rules with limitless sway. But it is only by the law that
man can see that fact, that sin is the ruling power of his life.
That is Paul's meaning when he says, "through the law comes
knowledge of sin." The law makes it clear to man that he
is a sinner.

It is manifest enough that the Gentiles, who have not the
law, are sinners and under the wrath of God. When, therefore, the law stops the mouth of those who have the law,
compelling them to confess that they are the veriest sinners,
the result is clear. "The whole world is held accountable to
God," and all without exception stand under His wrath.

V

The Righteousness of God

3:21–4:25

Paul has now come to the decisive matter of the transition from the one age to the other. Up to this point he has dealt only with the old aeon. His entire presentation has been concerned with the wrath of God manifest in like measure against the Gentiles' unrighteousness and the Jews' righteousness by the law. All this led to the conclusion that the whole world stands guilty before God. The wrath of God is the inclusive judgment on the old age.

"But now," Paul says, something utterly new has entered human history. "The righteousness of God has been manifested," δικαιοσύνη θεοῦ. With that the new age has appeared. "The old has passed away, behold, the new has come." These words from II Corinthians 5:17 apply most pointedly here, as do also those which follow immediately thereon, "All this is from God." The new situation is in no way man's achievement. As Paul has said, all that man was able to effect stands under God's wrath. The change is brought about by God's intervention, by the work which He effected through Christ.

The strongly emphasized "now" with which Paul opens the present passage has temporal as well as logical significance. "Now," in Paul's own day, the miracle had happened.

144

God had intervened in an entirely new way. Formerly he had revealed His wrath from heaven; now He has revealed His righteousness in Christ. That He has done so does not simply mean that we now know a characteristic of God which was formerly veiled from us. It is rather an action of God which constitutes this new revelation. This is clear, for instance, from the juxtaposition with the wrath of God. Like God's wrath in the old aeon, so the righteousness of God in the new is in highest degree an active and effective entry of God, by which the whole existence and circumstance of man are affected.

True to his habit, Paul places his caption over the new line of thought. The capital words ὀργὴ θεοῦ, the wrath of God, which govern the entire passage 1:18–3:20, meet us in the first verse thereof. In like manner now the first verse of the passage 3:21–4:25 gives us the thematic rubric, "the righteousness of God." And then, not satisfied to give only that, Paul makes further statement to indicate the line of his thought. Verse 3:21 has two things to say about the righteousness of God: (1) it is revealed through Christ, and (2) the law and the prophets bear witness to it. Both of these are developed in what follows—the former in the rest of chapter 3, and the latter in chapter 4.

1. THE RIGHTEOUSNESS OF GOD, REVEALED THROUGH CHRIST
3:21-31

(1) The righteousness of God is not by the law

Messiah has come. The kingdom of God is at hand. The righteousness of God is revealed. All these, which have a common meaning, indicate the character of the great change which Paul says has come. But what is their meaning? They mean that God has established an entirely new relationship

with man; and this relationship is characterized not by
God's wrath, but by His righteousness. The old age under
the wrath of God is succeeded by a new age ruled by the
righteousness of God.

The term used here, δικαιοσύνη θεοῦ, "the righteousness
of God," indicates with exceptional clarity that the vital
thing is not merely a new relationship among men. It would
be easy to fall into such a misunderstanding. When we think
of righteousness we habitually think of something which
stands in opposition to sin. Then, since sin is certainly real
in man's life and expresses his inner condition, we readily
think of righteousness also as a quality of man. If sin may
be described as a perverted state of mind, an inner condition
which makes man displeasing to God, it is easy also to view
righteousness simply as a state of mind, an inner quality
which makes one acceptable to God. But that view certainly
misses Paul's idea entirely. Likewise his view of sin is quite
different. Sin is more than an inner state; it is an objective
power of corruption which has man in its clutch. And, in
even higher degree, there is a corresponding truth as to
righteousness. It is not an inner quality of man's, but an
objective power by which God has given man a new status
through Christ. Righteousness is primarily God's rather
than man's. Paul here speaks of "the righteousness of God,"
not of man's righteousness. Indeed, Paul contrasts "the
righteousness of God" not merely with man's sin, but with
man's own righteousness. Thus it is of God that Paul speaks
all the time—first of the wrath of God, and now of the righteousness of God. That does not mean that he is silent about
man. Rather does he also speak of man at all times—formerly
of man under the wrath of God, and now of man translated
to the realm of the righteousness of God.

We may say, therefore, that by the expression "the righteousness of God" Paul does not refer to something which is solely a property of God, or solely a property or inner quality of man. The latter is precluded by the very words. It is "the righteousness of God," not of man. But to also preclude the former—that righteousness is solely a property of God—it is truest to translate δικαιοσύνη θεοῦ as "righteousness *from* God." The righteousness of God is a reality in our midst, which God has manifested on earth. It has come from God and is revealed through Jesus Christ. Just as "the wrath of God" is the inclusive state of the old age, so "righteousness from God" is the characteristic of the new.

Already in 1:17, where Paul states his theme, he introduces the concept of "righteousness from God," indicating that it is the basic concept of the entire epistle. Because of its central position we have already had to deal with that concept repeatedly. Here we must be content to refer to the earlier discussions, especially on pages 9ff. and 74ff.

How has this righteousness of God been manifested? How has this reality come among us? In answer, Paul insists first that it is the direct opposite of a righteousness achieved through the law, and it has come without any intermixture of the law.

From the very introduction of the concept of "the righteousness of God" in the theme of the epistle, one senses its contrast with righteousness through the law—the more so since the former is also spoken of as "righteousness of faith." But now Paul says so clearly and without circumlocution. When God reveals His righteousness He does so "apart from the law." That is of central importance to Paul. Its intent is not to agree that there are other ways beside the law by which one may attain to the righteousness of God. He does not mean to say that the righteousness of God may be reached *with* the law or *apart from* it. The truth is rather that the righteousness of God can *not* be reached by the law. Wherever the righteousness of God is found, it has come apart from any co-operation of the law. It has come, and been revealed, through Christ; and in that the law claims no share. It has come, in the deepest sense of the word, "apart from the law." The righteousness of God and righteousness by the law are opposite to each other and absolutely exclude each other. Where the one is, the other cannot be. For Paul it is of utmost importance for every one to understand that the new situation of which he now speaks has come about "apart from the law." The law always speaks about that which is required of man. But now, in the new aeon, it is no longer a matter of law, but of Christ and of faith in Him; not of what man does or does not do, but of what God has done through Christ. Where the law rules, there is the wrath of God, not the righteousness of God. Where Christ rules— or where faith is, which means the same—there, and only there, is the righteousness of God.

God has revealed His will in the law. That, Paul does not at all deny. In that sense the law is not abolished by the gospel. But the question now is how the "righteousness from God" has been revealed and become ours. The answer is that this has not happened through the law, but only through the gospel, only through God's act in Christ. To affirm that the righteousness of God comes and is manifest "apart from the law" is neither to depreciate nor to assail the law. For who has said that man is to be justified through the law? That is only the opinion of sinful man. God did not say so. In His Word He says the contrary. Paul refers to the holy Scriptures of the old covenant, to "the law and the prophets," as he says in the traditional terms of the two main divisions of the Old Testament. Righteousness by law is not found in them. Even "the law and the prophets" bear witness to the righteousness of God, which is now revealed through Christ, in the fullness of time. The basic witness for his gospel Paul draws from these two divisions of the Old Testament. From "the prophets" he has taken the theme of his epistle, in its most concise form: "He who through faith is righteous shall live" (1:17). And from "the law," from the Mosaic books, he draws his illustrations for the picture of "him who through faith is righteous." Abraham, as he is characterized in Genesis, is for Paul the very representative and archetype of "him who through faith is righteousness" (cf. chap. 4). Thus both the law and the prophets bear witness against righteousness by the law.

(2) The righteousness of God is the righteousness of faith

Paul has presented the negative side: the righteousness of God is not righteousness by the law. When God revealed His righteousness He did so "apart from the law." Now Paul goes on to present the positive side: the righteousness of God is the righteousness of faith. What "the law and the prophets" had foreshadowed of old has now become present reality through Christ. Through Him "the righteousness from God" has been manifested. When Paul speaks of that revelation, he does not mean merely the impartation of theoretical knowledge, as we have already pointed out. The righteousness from God is not revealed just to give us knowledge of it, but that it may be shared with us and become ours. For that very reason it becomes ours in a way wholly different from that in which we receive the law. It becomes ours through *faith*.

149

As works belong with law, faith belongs with Christ. In I Corinthians 1:30 Christ is presented as the righteousness from God. But it is not merely on His own account, but for us, that He is such, "so that in him we might become the righteousness of God" (II Cor. 5:21; cf. p. 76 above). It is this which takes place when we believe in Him: His righteousness becomes ours.

It is manifestly Paul's profound concern to make clear that everything depends on faith. He therefore is not content merely to say that the new righteousness is a "righteousness of God through faith in Jesus Christ." That says all that must be said. But Paul is insistent that we note that what he speaks of is a matter of faith, and of nothing else. So he continues in a way that at first seems redundant. He adds "for all who believe." Perhaps what Paul thus added was originally even more detailed and therefore still more pointed. On this verse manuscripts show differences. There is much to indicate a fuller form, εἰς πάντας καὶ ἐπὶ πάντας τοὺς πιστεύοντας, "unto all and upon all who believe." Since any additional statement may appear redundant and superfluous, it is easier to think that one of the phrases which is so like the other—εἰς πάντας and ἐπὶ πάντας—was dropped, than that what already seemed unnecessary was enlarged to include two phrases so similar. It is quite characteristic of Paul to repeat a noun with different prepositions for the sake of special emphasis. 1:17 gives us an example by its parallel use of ἐκ πίστεως and εἰς πίστιν, "through faith for faith."

If our conclusion is correct, that the fuller form was the original, we face the question of what Paul meant to say by the use of the two prepositions εἰς and ἐπί. What does he mean when he says, "for all who believe"? And what more does he mean in saying "upon all who believe"?

It is of course not self-evident that he meant each of these to mean something different. He may have intended nothing more than extra emphasis. The word which he repeats is "all." The most evident effect of the repetition is to stress the universality of the righteousness of faith. That is what Paul has already said in his theme in 1:16. There he declares that "the gospel is the power of God for salvation *to every one who has faith,*" παντὶ τῷ πιστεύοντι. When the gospel is preached, when the righteousness of God is revealed, when Christ comes, salvation is already under way for him who believes—for every one who believes, for every one without exception or difference. That places an extraordinary emphasis on faith. It is on faith, and on faith alone, that all depends. Paul's thought may be stated most simply by *sola fide,* "by faith alone." That sets forth the contrast with which he is dealing: apart from the law—through faith.

That the righteousness of God comes "to all who believe" on Christ, and becomes theirs, is a simple and clear idea which presents no difficulty in interpretation. But the meaning is less clear as to the expression "upon all." Many have expressed their surprise at Paul's use of the preposition "upon" in this context. It does not seem to apply well to what is said about righteousness. What can it mean to say that the righteousness of God is revealed "upon all who believe"? The answer may be found in 1:18, which presents an exact parallel to the verse now under consideration. There it is said that "the wrath of God is revealed from heaven against all ungodliness and wickedness of men." These two passages make precisely parallel affirmations as to the old age and the new, respectively. They are equally universal. *All* are under the wrath of God; and *all* who be-

lieve in Christ share in the righteousness of God. In both
cases the same preposition is used, ἐπί, "upon." The juxtaposition is manifestly intended by Paul; he makes the statements parallel point for point. *Upon* the old aeon in its entirety the wrath of God rests; and *upon* the new aeon in its
entirety the righteousness of God. As in the old aeon *everything* lies under the power of sin and death, so in the new
aeon *everything* is included in the saving power of the righteousness of God. From above, from heaven, comes the wrath
of God upon all unrighteousness. And from above comes
the righteousness of God upon all who believe. That righteousness has its source in God and comes to us through
Christ. In both cases ἐπί refers to something which comes
upon man from above, possesses him and directs him. Thus
the expression "upon all who believe" becomes another witness as to the nature of the righteousness which is revealed
through Christ. By faith in Him we are recipients of the
righteousness which comes down to us from God. It is not
an inner quality of our own, but an active intervention of
God by which He transforms our existence and renews its
circumstances. Formerly the wrath of God from heaven
pursued man who was doomed to death. Now through
Christ the heaven of righteousness and life stretches out
over all who believe. By the grace of God man is included
in God's own righteousness. Just as wrath is an objective
power which exercises its might to the destruction of man,
so the righteousness of God is also an objective power which
exerts its might for redemption and life.

While men stand under the law there are always differences among them. There is the difference between the
righteous and the sinners, between those who strive to fulfill
the law and those who break the law. As to the fulfillment

or the violation of the law there is an endless gradation of more or less. But all such differences pale before the new righteousness of God. "There is no distinction." Without exception all are sinners before God. "All have sinned." That is the point of departure for the whole redemptive work of God. No one has anything to offer which could elicit the love of God. In that respect all are alike. Man's own righteousness, though it be of great importance within human relations, does not serve at all to motivate God's work of salvation. That depends wholly on God himself. The only motive is in God himself, in His gracious will.

This fact is made the clearer by the declaration that "all have sinned and fall short of the glory of God." Wherever God is, there is His glory, δόξα θεοῦ. The kingdom and the power and the glory are God's. But we are called to be partakers of that glory. God has not created us to live under the thralldom of alien powers, in darkness and death, but to live in His kingdom and share in His glory. "Glory and honor and peace for every one who does good"—thus, in 2:10, Paul states God's intention as to man. But sin has kept that intention from realization. Because all have sinned, they have come short of that which God purposed for them. They are submerged in the power of sin and death.

Such was the situation when God revealed His righteousness. This Paul regards as of the greatest importance. All that can be said about man, in this respect, is that "all have sinned and fall short of the glory of God." If God nevertheless clothes them with a new righteousness, or—to say the same thing—justifies them, there can be no thought that man has for his part contributed anything to that end. In the deepest sense of the word it is *sinners* who are justified. How does that happen? "They are justified by his

grace as a gift, through the redemption which is in Christ
Jesus." It strikes us clearly that there is a negation behind
this affirmation. In what he has already said Paul has been
at pains to exclude any idea that man has in some way
merited justification. His purpose is still the same, now that
he asserts that the positive basis of justification is God's action in Christ. He expressly piles up qualifications to bar all
thought of human merit or worth. He does so with the positive intent of making clear that that of which he speaks is a
gift. It is something which is bestowed on us freely, without
our merit, by the grace of God. Entirely without our doing,
God has placed us in a new situation. When Paul adds that
this has come about "through the redemption which is in
Christ Jesus," we hear in the word "redemption" a reminder
of the thralldom in which man lies, by reason of which he
cannot make his own way to the righteousness of God.

Thus the positive and the negative lead to the same point.
When Paul wants to make clear that justification is the act
of God, he can say so effectively only by repeating steadily
that it is not by man's doing. Every negative assertion as
to the law and good works, every word about man's sin and
his falling short of the glory of God serves the positive purpose of glorifying God's work in Christ. There Paul's thought
is summed up in one great affirmation. Righteousness comes
down from above, from God. If it were a righteousness
achieved by man, it would be the basis of distinctions among
men and lay claim to commendation. One might offer more
righteousness, another less. But now every such righteousness from below, every righteousness achieved by man, is
precluded. "All have sinned," and the wrath of God rests
on all. In this negative status all are comprehended without
exception. But not only in this negative status. When God

reveals His righteousness in Christ there is again "no distinction." All are justified by grace, through faith in Christ. All
who are "in Christ" are alike partakers of His righteousness,
one neither more nor less than the other; for it does not
depend on what man does, but on what he receives of God's
free grace. What man *does* leaves him a sinner before God;
but by what he *receives* from God he is righteous.

We return to Paul's words about "the redemption which
is in Christ Jesus." This redemption and the righteousness
of God belong indissolubly together. As in I Corinthians
1:30 which says that Christ was made our righteousness and
redemption, Paul also joins those concepts here. It is a redemption, a liberation, which has taken place "in Christ."
This word—ἀπολύτρωσις, redemption—is not used carelessly.
Its use recognizes man's condition in the old aeon, his slavery
to the powers of destruction; and its purpose is to show how
that condition has been completely changed "in Christ."
"The redemption which is in Christ" is something which has
entered into human history at a precise point; but it also
stretches on throughout that history. Here that which happened once in the death and resurrection of Christ is also
looked upon as that which always happens when by faith
men are incorporated into Him and become members of His
body. "In Christ" the sway of the powers that oppose God
was broken once for all. Therefore it is also true that they
who are "in Christ" are thereby free from all those forces
which held man captive in the old aeon.

In chapters 5-8 Paul has abundant occasion to take up
this theme again. There he has much to say about the powers
of destruction from which we are freed "in Christ": Wrath,
Sin, the Law, Death. Here in chapter 3 he limits himself to

showing how our liberation was effected and how it happened that the righteousness of faith was revealed.

(3) How the righteousness of faith was revealed

What did God do when He manifested His righteousness? Paul says that *before all the world He set forth Christ as a "mercy seat."*

In this connection Paul uses a word whose general meaning is clear enough, but whose particular use here has been variously understood—the word ἱλαστήριον. The difficulty of knowing certainly what Paul meant by the word is the greater because it is so rarely used in the New Testament. Besides in this verse—Paul's only use of it—it appears only once in the New Testament, in Hebrews 9:5. Some translations of the Bible suggest that Paul uses ἱλαστήριον in a general sense: God has given Christ to us as a means of atonement. Another interpretation, appearing in other translations, finds support among the Greek fathers (e.g., Origen), and was accepted by Luther. It holds that Paul uses the word in its specific sense of "mercy seat." Convincing reasons support the latter. It should be noted that the Septuagint uses ἱλαστήριον as the technical term for the "mercy seat," the cover of the ark of the covenant, behind the veil, in the Holy of Holies. In Hebrews 9:5 the word is used with the same meaning. It is natural to conclude that Paul gives it that significance. It fits the context particularly well, and it fits Paul's thought and mode of expression better than the other, which has little Pauline flavor about it.

The greatest reason for not giving the word its natural, concrete meaning is that interpreters have hesitated to think that Christ is here likened to an object of temple furniture such as the mercy seat. And it is further argued that the verb "put forward" is also against such a view. The mercy seat was very definitely not "put forward" into general view. On the contrary, it was concealed in the Holy of Holies, where the public could not see it. But such objections have little weight indeed, if only we give heed to the point Paul is making. It is said that, since the significance of the expression is here uncertain, it is best to use the general word "expiation" and let the context supply its real purport (Lietzmann). But the answer is that it is exactly the context that shows that Paul means "mercy seat." He here speaks steadily in concepts that cluster about that thought. Comparison with the Old Testament allusion makes that clear at once.

The mercy seat was the place where God manifested His presence in Israel. In Exodus 25:22 God said to Moses, "There will I meet with thee, and I will commune with thee from above the mercy seat, from between the two cherubims which are upon the ark of the testimony, of all things which I will give thee in commandment unto the children of Israel." God manifests His glory at the mercy seat. When on the Day of Atonement the high priest enters the Holy of Holies, he must bear incense with him, "that the cloud of the incense may cover the mercy seat that is upon the testimony, that he die not" (Lev. 16:13); and he must sprinkle the blood of the victim seven times before the mercy seat, to make atonement for the people and turn away God's wrath at their sins.

These are the thoughts that Paul has in mind. He presents the same concepts—the manifestation of God, God's wrath, His glory, the blood, the mercy seat. Just before this he has spoken of mankind under the wrath of God, which "falls short of the glory of God" (vs. 23). But now God has manifested His righteousness to man, in that He presents

Christ as a mercy seat. In Christ God reveals himself in His glory. Now He does not, as before, hide it behind a cloud of incense in the Holy of Holies. On the contrary, He has now put Christ forward before all the world as our ἱλαστήριον, our mercy seat. Whoever believes in Him is no longer under the wrath of God, but, as Paul says in 5:2, he can rejoice in hope of sharing the glory of God.

When Paul says that God put Christ forward as our mercy seat, he has in mind a precise point in history. It is not primarily Christ's incarnation but His death. The crucified and risen Christ is our *redeemer* and *reconciler*. It is essential to say both; and Paul does that in this connection. But it is no less important to note that he does not conceive of redemption and reconciliation as two different things. In one breath he speaks of both. He speaks of "the redemption which is in Christ Jesus whom God put forward as a mercy seat (= reconciler)." The work of Christ is called redemption because by it we are delivered from bondage to the hostile powers. But since the same act of Christ delivers us from the wrath of God and gives us peace with Him, it can also be spoken of as reconciliation (cf. 5:1, 9ff.). Here as elsewhere it is affirmed that reconciliation is God's own work. It was God who put Christ forward as our mercy seat. "God was in Christ reconciling the world to himself" (II Cor. 5:19).

What did God intend when He thus put Christ forward as a mercy seat? Paul answers that He thereby meant to manifest His righteousness before all the world. We must notice how central is the idea of manifestation, the public presentation and demonstration, in this passage 3:21-31. The caption of these verses says that "the righteousness of God has been manifested" through Christ; and that thought is thereafter repeated in a variety of ways. It is stated that God openly and manifestly set Christ forth as a mercy seat. And now Paul says that God thereby shows His righteousness. Thus, ever since the death and resurrection of Christ, the righteousness of God is a reality present and manifest in our world. The new age of fulfillment, grace, and righteousness has come.

According to Paul there is a relationship between what God did before and now. The old aeon was the time of God's wrath. But that does not mean that man then experienced nothing but His wrath. God in His longsuffering passed over the sins of men, whom He spared from immediate destruction. This God did in anticipation of that righteousness which He would reveal through Christ, in the fullness of time. The whole history of God's dealings with mankind looks forward toward this new manifestation. So in the age that has now come, in the new aeon which has burst upon us through Christ, God reveals His righteousness, both that He may be righteous and that He may justify him who believes in Jesus as the Christ.

This line of thought, which in mode of expression is one of the more difficult passages of the epistle, gives us good insight as to what Paul means by δικαιοσύνη θεοῦ, "righteousness from God." It was difficult to apprehend this, as long as we set up the alternative: *either* righteousness is a property of God, *or* it is a condition in man which makes him acceptable before God. Then the meaning would be about as follows. God's righteousness would properly require that He annihilate sinful mankind. But then His purpose for man would come to nought. Therefore in mercy He has come to terms with sin and overlooks man's unrighteousness. But to do so is beset with peril. For it might seem that

God had really not been in earnest about His judgment on
sin—and that God is not truly righteous. So it was necessary
that He "show his righteousness." This He did by putting
Christ forward as a means of atonement. By Christ's atoning
death it was made utterly clear that God actually judges sin
and yet can forgive without sacrificing His righteousness.
"Both purposes are fulfilled. God shows himself as the righteous One; and He imputes righteousness to the sinner who
believes in Christ" (Althaus). Through Christ, God has
justified His action; He has shown His righteousness beyond
doubt. Even though it might appear otherwise, from the
fact that He is longsuffering and has come to terms with the
fact of sin, He has now demonstrated by the death of Christ
"that he himself is righteous."

There is in this line of thought a clear and harmonious
meaning. One could certainly apply the Anselmic judgment
nihil rationabilius. It is a consistent demonstration of the
necessity of the death of Christ, if we start from God's puni-
tive righteousness. But it suffers a double weakness. It lacks
support in the text and its meaning is not true to Paul's
thought. Paul is not trying to give a rational demonstration
of the necessity of Christ's death. He speaks of what God
has done, not of what He *had* to do. He does not talk about
something that God did to justify himself, but about what
God has done to justify us. Men have looked here for a
theodicy, a defense of God's dealings with humanity before
Christ. But Paul knows nothing of a theodicy; not even in
chapters 9-11, and still less here. The text does not say that
God wished to show that He really is righteous, as some
translators would understand it. Paul says rather that God
put forward Christ as a mercy seat thereby to let His righteousness openly appear (εἰς ἔνδειξιν τῆς δικαιοσύνης αὐτοῦ).

The righteousness of which verse 25 speaks is no other than that spoken of in verse 21. It is the same righteousness which is affirmed throughout the epistle. It is always "the righteousness of God," with all that that implies. And when verse 26 sums up the purpose of God when He gave us Christ as a mercy seat, Paul does not say "that God might be found to be righteous," but simply that in so doing "he himself is righteous and that he justifies him who has faith in Jesus." The righteousness which God manifested through Christ is God's own righteousness. God is himself righteous; and through Christ He now lets us share it "within the realm of faith," as one might perhaps most helpfully translate the expression used here, τὸν ἐκ πίστεως.

Thus the whole of Paul's thought is gathered up in a great unity. All has its source in God's righteousness. Through Christ "the righteousness from God," which He is in His own person, has come to us and is manifested in our world. And οἱ ἐκ πίστεως, they who through faith have become members of Christ and live their life "in Christ," are justified through Him; like Him they become "righteousness from God." But their righteousness is not their own, as if they had themselves effected it. It is God's and has come from God. It is not righteousness by the law, but the righteousness of faith, δικαιοσύνη ἐκ πίστεως.

Here, perhaps more clearly than in any other place, we see how Paul's concept of "the righteousness of God" abolishes the traditional alternative, "God's righteousness *or* man's righteousness." The righteousness of the new age is at once God's own righteousness and the righteousness which was bestowed on us through Jesus Christ. It is God's own righteousness; yet it is a reality in our midst, even as the

wrath of God is a reality in our world as long as the old
age lasts.

(4) The righteousness of faith excludes all boasting

"Then what becomes of our boasting?" That is Paul's
next question. From his pharisaic period he knew how easy
it is for righteousness to slip into boasting. The Jew prides
himself on the very fact that he has the law (2:23). For
even if he does not keep the law, the possession of it puts
him into a certain relation with righteousness. But even
more he who fulfills the law and is righteous has something
to boast of, according to the Jew's idea.

This makes Paul's question inevitable. Through Christ
righteousness has come into our world. It meets us, not
merely as a demand or as an ideal, but as a fact, as a present
reality. He who believes in Christ *is* righteous. What then
becomes of our boasting? Is there any place for that? No,
"it is excluded," Paul replies. That that must be the answer
is clear from what he had already said. "There is no distinction; since all have sinned and fall short of the glory of
God." And when they are justified it is "a gift"; so there is
no occasion for them to boast. But now that he has stated
clearly what God did when He showed His righteousness,
Paul can show even better than before why there is no room
for boasting.

All boasting is excluded. The very possibility of it has
vanished. How did that happen? Or—to quote Paul literally—"On what principle? On the principle of works? No,
but on the principle of faith." "The principle of works" is
only another name for "the law." So it is not the law which
excludes all boasting. To be sure, the effect of the law has
indeed tended to strike down and eliminate all boasting. In

that direction its result has been considerable. We recall that Paul has already said that "through the law comes knowledge of sin." The function and purpose of the law, he says, is "that every mouth may be stopped, and the whole world may be held accountable to God." The commission to eliminate all boasting the law carried out with extraordinary effectiveness. When one would boast of anything before God, the law confronts him with its demand for holiness, and he is silenced.

Yet Paul says that it is not by the law that boasting is excluded. Why? Because the law cannot remove the roots of boasting. It can *actually* bring our boasting low, but it cannot remove it *in principle*. In situation after situation the law can make man see that he has not measured up to God's demand; that there is here nothing for him to boast of, for he has not attained to complete righteousness. But as long as it is on the basis of the law that one lives, there is always the theoretical possibility that he may henceforth keep the law better. Every word of judgment, which for the present stops his mouth and takes away any right to boast, becomes at the same time a demand for increased efforts to attain to righteousness. And if man could in that way achieve righteousness—for it is that which the law insists on—he would have something about which to boast. At least hypothetically then man could look forward to a time when boasting would be justified. It is in the very nature of the law that it cannot remove that possibility. For "the works of the law" are man's own works; righteousness by the law is man's own righteousness and a basis for boasting.

But faith excludes all that once for all. Here is a righteousness which is not merely hypothetically possible. It is a righteousness which is already actual. It is already present on earth, not merely prospective. But in that fact there is no occasion for boasting, for it is not a righteousness effected by man. It has come to him from above, from God. Even though, since it has been given to him, it is in a sense his own and in Christ he is "the righteousness of God," it is his purely as something which he has received and for which he must thank Another. There is no cause for him to boast. It is only when this fact is seen that boasting becomes impossible.

The deepest reason why all boasting is excluded Paul states in verse 28: "Man is justified by faith apart from the works of the law." The exclusion of the works of the law and the exclusion of boasting are correlative. If there were any place for the works of the law in justification, there would also be place for boasting. But now, with the words χωρὶς ἔργων νόμου, Paul has banished from this area both the law and the works of the law. To use Luther's apt expression, *in loco justificationis*, the works of the law can effect nothing. In justification it is a matter of faith and of *faith alone*.

Roman Catholics have, as is well known, attacked Luther sharply because he translated verse 28 with the expression *allein durch den Glauben* (*sola fide*). Indeed, they have specifically accused him of falsifying the text. But quite the contrary is true; for the words *sola fide*, "by faith alone" express exactly what Paul says here. He means precisely that in the matter of justification everything is excluded except faith; and that is just what the expression "by faith alone" says. That that is what the text means is seen from the fact that, long before Luther, various interpreters, of varied points of view, made unconditional use of *sola fide* to express Paul's meaning. It will suffice, on this point, to mention Origen, Pelagius, and Marcilio Ficino. That these

men, holding views so diametrically different from those of
the Reformation, naturally and without ulterior purpose
used the words *sola fide*, shows more clearly than anything
else that when Luther said "by faith alone," he was not
guilty of smuggling in an alien idea to help the Reformation.
The expression is simply the natural way to say what Paul
means.

It is the opposition to *sola fide* which is guilty of manifest
distortion of the apostle's thought. What is the reason for
objecting to "faith alone"? To make way for "faith formed
by love," for *fides caritate formata*! And why is there such
eagerness to bring in the idea of "love" into a context where
Paul speaks only of "faith"? Because "love is the fulfillment
of the law." Men have not been satisfied to leave the law
out, despite Paul's repeated declaration that, when God revealed His righteousness, He did so without the works of
the law (χωρὶς νόμου, vs. 21; χωρὶς ἔργων νόμου, vs. 28).
They have not been able to feel that faith in Christ is full
and complete righteousness. They have insisted that if
through faith we become participants in the righteousness
of God, it must be because faith carries with it "the fulfillment of the law." But that is to say just the opposite of what
Paul says here.

In faith in Christ, Paul has found that which binds Jews
and Gentiles together, overcoming the great hostility between them. Christ abolished "in his flesh the law of commandments and ordinances, that he might create in himself
one new man in place of two, so making peace, and might
reconcile us both to God in one body through the cross"
(Eph. 2:15f.). From this point of view, too, it is important
that the law is excluded. If the law counts, the Jew would
have a real advantage; for, unlike the Gentile, he had re-

ceived the law. Hence it was essential for Paul to affirm that this fact did not open to the Jew a way of righteousness and salvation other than that open to the Gentile. The righteousness of God is given only in Christ, only through faith in Him. "Or is God the God of Jews only? Is he not the God of Gentiles also? Yes, of Gentiles also." As there is only one God, so there is only one way of salvation for all mankind. There is no distinction here between Jew and Gentile.

Paul has gainsaid righteousness by the law and affirmed the righteousness of faith. Has he then overthrown the law? No, quite the contrary! We have earlier pointed out that "the law and the prophets" cannot be used as authorities for righteousness by the law. The law itself bears witness *against* righteousness by the law, and *for* the righteousness of faith. Now, by what Paul has presented, he has opportunity to state his meaning more exactly. God's purpose in giving the law to a humanity that stood under the bondage of sin was to bring men to a knowledge of their sin "that every mouth may be stopped, and the whole world may be held accountable to God." Righteousness by the law flies in the very face of the meaning of the law. It leads to man's boasting himself before God. So we here face the peculiar fact that righteousness by the law, which thinks it esteems the law so highly and is zealous for its fulfillment, really overthrows the law. But the righteousness of faith, despite superficial appearances, really works in the same direction as the law, when the law is rightly understood. The righteousness of faith accomplishes what the law would effect: it excludes all boasting. It shows that the law is right when it stops every mouth. Thus it upholds the law and makes it effective. Paul will later have further occasion to show how in another sense there is a positive relation between the law and the righteousness of faith. In the present context, where he aims to show that the righteousness of faith excludes all boasting, it is enough for him to make it clear that, in this, faith and the law support each other and lead to the same result. Faith in Christ does not overthrow the law. It rather confirms it and helps it to achieve its intended result.

2. THE RIGHTEOUSNESS OF GOD, WITNESSED TO BY THE LAW AND THE PROPHETS
4:1-25

(1) Abraham's righteousness was the righteousness of faith

The entire history of God's saving work is, for Paul, a great unity. There is an inner unity between the old covenant and the new. The law and the righteousness of faith support each other. The righteousness of faith strengthens the law and makes it effective. That was the point with which Paul concluded chapter 3. Now, in chapter 4, he takes up the question from the other side, showing, as he said in 3:21, that the law and the prophets support the righteousness of faith. How does he proceed to do so?

At an earlier point we saw him in a similar situation. That was when, in 1:17, he took the theme of his epistle from an Old Testament declaration. That prophetic word—"the just shall live by faith"—the Jews' righteousness by the law had seized and used as a summary of its own point of view. But by his interpretation—"he who through faith is righteous"—Paul takes this affirmation away from the representatives of righteousness by the law and makes it the caption and motto for the righteousness of faith (cf. above, p. 83). His procedure is just like that here too.

In Abraham the Jews saw their relation to God embodied in an ideal figure. With pride they could call themselves

"Abraham's children." He was not merely their progenitor from whom the Jews had their origin in the natural sense (κατὰ σάρκα). From him they also derived their spiritual advantage. It was with him that God had made the covenant on which rested Israel's unique position as God's chosen people. That act of divine election was also the source of "the law and the prophets." When they wanted to show what was meant by righteousness before God, they could point to Abraham. That Abraham was "righteous" in eminent degree was shown from both Scripture and Jewish theological explanations. And since God's covenant with Israel was a covenant of the law, Abraham became the type for those who are righteous through the law.

Paul acknowledges that Abraham was righteous and recognizes his typical significance as the progenitor of the chosen people; but he denies that the Jews had any right to appeal to Abraham's righteousness as an example of their own righteousness by the law. What Paul does in the fourth chapter can be stated most simply as follows. He takes Abraham away from the representatives of righteousness by the law and sets him forth as the type of *those who through faith are righteous.* Thereby he refers to what he recently said about boasting.

"What then shall we say about Abraham, our forefather according to the flesh? For if Abraham was justified by works, he has something to boast about." Here again is the matter of boasting, as to which Paul had just declared that both the law and faith work together to make it impossible and to exclude it. But it is of course inescapable that, if it was by works that Abraham won his status as righteous, he really has something about which to boast. In that case he has something of his own on which to build.

But this is exactly what Paul denies most pointedly. Abraham may have something of which to boast before men; "but not before God." Before God there cannot be any boasting at all. Paul can deny the conclusion, because he denies the premises on which it rests. For by its very nature Abraham's righteousness was not by the law or by works, but by faith. Not only does Paul say so, but Scripture testifies to that. Paul has "the law and the prophets" on his side in what they have to say about Abraham and his righteousness. "For what does the scripture say? 'Abraham believed God, and it was reckoned to him as righteousness.'" In the passage cited (Gen. 15:6), nothing is said about Abraham's works; only his faith is noted. He believed God when He made His promise to him: "So"—as innumerable as the stars in the skies—"shall thy descendants be"; and his faith was reckoned to him as righteousness. It was in this way, according to Scripture, that Abraham became "righteous." In the very expression that it was "*reckoned*" to him, Paul sees the implication that we here witness an action of divine grace. "Reckon" means the same as to "reckon because of grace." Therefore Paul continues, "Now to one who works, his wages are not reckoned as a gift but as his due. And to one who does not work but trusts him who justifies the ungodly, his faith is reckoned as righteousness."

With that Paul has reached a point which is of utmost importance in his interpretation. Here he can tolerate no mistiness. He must insist on clear and precise characterization. He tolerates no indecision between faith and works. He sets forth a clear either—or. *Either* it depends on works— and then boasting may continue, since it is not by grace but by his own merit that man is judged righteous. *Or* it depends on faith—and then all else is excluded, works, merit,

wages, boasting; and then it is indeed the justification of the
sinner. In other words, it is no longer a matter of *our* works,
but of *God's*. Faith always has the action of God as its correlative. Faith is what it is because of its dependence on
God. When Paul speaks of faith, he never means, so to say,
a mere psychological operation; for faith is always determined by its object. Thus he speaks, in this connection, of
faith as "faith in him who justifies the ungodly." Only in
this way, that God acts and we allow Him to act, can the
righteousness of God come to us. Thus, by the nature of
the case, the righteousness of *God* cannot be other than the
righteousness of *faith*. Scripture testifies for Paul, in the
passage cited, "Abraham believed God, and it was reckoned
to him as righteousness."

There has sometimes been surprise that, when talking
about the righteous Abraham, Paul speaks so pointedly about
God's justification of "the ungodly." Where does Scripture
say that Abraham was "ungodly"? But that question is quite
unnecessary. For Paul clearly does not mean to say that
Abraham was sinful in special degree. Let it be noted that
"the ungodly" does not refer directly to Abraham, in the
text. What Paul would support by his appeal to Scripture
is the fact that Abraham's righteousness was a righteousness
of faith. Having made that clear, Paul goes on to speak in
general of the nature of the righteousness of faith. That it
is the sinner, "the ungodly," who is justified by God, is quite
in harmony with what Paul has said. That of course seemed
a blasphemy to his pharisaical opponents; but for Paul it was
the inescapable truth with which his entire gospel stands
or falls. For if righteousness is by God's action, and not by
ours, then it follows that God gives His righteousness to him
who has it not, to him who stands under the power of sin.

Man is not righteous, nor can he make himself so. "All have sinned and fall short of the glory of God; they are justified by his grace as a gift."

For Paul the essence of justification is the *forgiveness of sins*. When God lays sin to one's account, that means that he stands under the wrath of God and the dominion of death. But when sin is forgiven and not laid to one's account, that means that he is delivered from the wrath of God and placed under His righteousness. That righteousness is reckoned to one, or that sin is not reckoned to one, is one and the same thing, stated positively in the former and negatively in the latter. When God forgives sin, He in so doing establishes righteousness. On the other hand, sin can be forgiven only because God reveals his righteousness. As Paul has earlier said that righteousness is reckoned unto man through an action of divine grace and supported his statement with a reference to Abraham, likewise he now uses another scriptural reference that speaks of the forgiveness of sins. "Blessed are those whose iniquities are forgiven, and whose sins are covered; blessed is the man against whom the Lord will not reckon his sin" (Ps. 32:1f.). That which joins this declaration with what Paul has already said is that in both cases he is speaking of "reckoning" or "not reckoning."

Thus both Abraham, the eminently "righteous," and David, "the man after God's own heart" (I Sam. 13:14), could be used as witnesses for the righteousness of faith. Abraham was righteous because faith was reckoned to him as righteousness; and David was righteous because God did not reckon his sin against him. Both cases show that the righteousness, as to which "the law and the prophets" witness, is the righteousness of faith. Before God there is no righteousness except that of faith.

But the Jews, just as the children of Abraham, trusted in two things: *circumcision* and *the law*. In chapter 2 Paul discussed both and refuted the claims based on them. Neither circumcision nor the law can shield from the wrath of God. Now he returns to the point and shows that the Jews have here no right to appeal to Abraham. It was neither through circumcision (vss. 9-12) nor through the law (vss. 13-17) that Abraham was righteous.

(2) Not through circumcision was Abraham righteous

For the Jews Abraham was the great dividing point in history. Before him humanity was, so to say, an undifferentiated mass. From that mass Abraham was called out by election. The foundation was thereby laid for something new; and this was handed on to his successors by circumcision. This was the sign and promise that Abraham's successors should be his progeny, not merely in the natural sense, but also in the spiritual. They should be one with him and share in the blessing bestowed on him. Through circumcision Israel was marked with God's own seal. Circumcision is the external mark of belonging to God's peculiar people. Thus Abraham marked the parting of the ways in God's history with mankind. From there on humanity was divided into two groups: (1) the *circumcised,* who belonged to God's chosen people; and (2) the *uncircumcised,* whom God allowed to go their own way. Such was the Jewish view as to the position of Abraham and the significance of circumcision.

But now the question arises, does that which was said above as to the forgiveness of sins and the reckoning of righteousness apply only to the circumcised, only to those who by natural descent belong to Abraham and have cir-

cumcision's mark and seal as evidence that they belong to
the people of God? Or does it apply also to the uncircumcised, to the Gentiles? For Paul the answer to that question
depends entirely on how Abraham himself became righteous. How did it happen that "faith was reckoned to him as
righteousness"? What was his situation when this came to
him from God? "Was it before or after he had been circumcised?" On that point Scripture gives clear answer. Paul
refers to the order of the declarations in Genesis. In chapter 15 we read that Abraham believed God and it was
reckoned to him as righteousness. Not before chapter 17 do
we find the account of the institution of circumcision. Between these two there lay a considerable interval of time.
So it is clear that it was not through circumcision that Abraham was made righteous. That occurred while he was still
uncircumcised, before he could appeal to circumcision or
was bound to the law by it. Faith and the righteousness of
faith came first. Circumcision came later "as a sign or seal
of the righteousness which he had by faith while he was still
uncircumcised."

It is interesting to note what Paul's attitude to circumcision is. Though one might expect him simply to oppose it,
that is not the case. There is a certain parallelism between
his concept of circumcision and his concept of the law. Just
as the law, rightly understood, is not contrary to the righteousness of faith, but bears witness to it, so circumcision,
rightly understood, is not contrary to the righteousness of
faith; it is rather, as Paul says here, "a seal of the righteousness of faith." But it is vital that it be rightly understood.
For circumcision can be understood and evaluated in a way
that does set it in irreconcilable opposition to the righteousness of faith.

Paul does not wish to take circumcision away from the Jews. But their use of it must be changed. Otherwise it comes into conflict with faith. When the Jews try to force circumcision on the Gentiles, they show that they use it in the wrong way. They trust in circumcision, rather than in God and Christ. That puts them on one side, while Abraham and the Gentiles both trust to faith. If the Jews say that since there is only one way to blessedness and righteousness, and that way is by circumcision, the Gentiles must therefore be circumcised before they can belong to the people of God, Paul replies that there is indeed only one way, for Jew and Gentile alike—and that way is through faith.

The Jews boast that they are the children of Abraham and hold that he is the father only of the circumcised. But the Scriptures say that Abraham himself was not circumcised at the time when his faith was reckoned unto him as righteousness. That is, they place him in the same status as Gentiles who believe. But by that fact the perspective is broadened. The promise to Abraham about his "seed" includes more than was seen at first glance. It means more than that he would be the progenitor of a whole nation. By faith he would be the father of all who believe, of οἱ ἐκ πίστεως without exception, whether Jew or Gentile, circumcised or uncircumcised.

It was indeed the intention that circumcision was to be a strong bond between Abraham and his posterity. But be it noted that that is said of Abraham as a man of faith. Circumcision was given as a sign of faith and of the righteousness of faith. Therefore it would not suffice for those who came after him merely to be circumcised. Abraham was not merely circumcised. He *believed;* and his faith was the basis of his circumcision. When his successors are only circumcised, they have only the sign but not the reality. They have that which is external; but the inner bond between Abraham and them is broken. He believed; but they are beyond the pale of faith. His righteousness was the righteousness of faith; but they strive to effect righteousness by the law.

Whose father is Abraham then? In the outer sense, κατὰ σάρκα, he is of course the father of his posterity. But this was not the particular meaning of God's promise to him. The promise meant rather that he should be the father of all who believe, of all who follow in the footsteps of his faith. The situation is not that by the promise Abraham became the father of all the circumcised, on the one hand, and, on the other hand, of such of the uncircumcised as follow him in faith. The promise applies only to those who believe. Even for the circumcised it is faith that unites them with Abraham. Only they who believe are actually, and in the sense of the promise, the children of Abraham.

The Jews looked upon Abraham as the great dividing point in the history of mankind. But according to Paul, Abraham through his faith became the great rallying point for all who believe, whether circumcised or uncircumcised. There is no distinction; all who are justified are justified by faith, by faith alone.

(3) *Not through the law was Abraham made righteous*

What has been said establishes the point that it was not through circumcision that Abraham became righteous. But, Paul continues, it was not through the law either. When Paul looks back to the promise given to Abraham (Gen. 12:2f.; 13:14ff.; 15:5, 7, 18ff.), he does not find reference anywhere to the law. What is affirmed is that Abraham believed God. Here Paul sees a decisive witness for his thesis: *not through the law, but through the righteousness of faith,* οὐ διὰ νόμου, ἀλλὰ διὰ δικαιοσύνης πίστεως.

What was really the promise that was given to Abraham? The answer Paul gives says, "He should inherit the world," or "He should be heir of the world." The promise is actually not found in the Old Testament in just that form; but Paul here refers to the traditional exposition by Jewish theology. That he could do the more readily because there was no danger of confusing his understanding with that exposition. For Paul all nationalistic aspirations had disappeared from such a statement. To him the promise that Abraham should inherit the world refers to the dominion of Christ over the world. That is inseparably tied up with His position as Messiah. In this connection we should recall words from the Sermon on the Mount, "Blessed are the meek, for they shall inherit the earth" (Matt. 5:5). In this sense it is true as to Christ and all who believe on Him, or follow in the path of Abraham's faith, that they shall inherit the world.

That which concerns Paul right here is not so much the content of the promise, but the question who are included in it and on what condition it is fulfilled. Who are the heirs of the promise? The choice is between the people of the law and the people of faith, between οἱ ἐκ νόμου and οἱ ἐκ πίστεως. But what would be the result, if it were the people of the law who should inherit the world? Faith would be void and vain. And besides that, the promise itself would lose its force and validity. In the very fact of the promise Paul sees reference to faith. It is implicit in the nature of the promise that the law does not belong with it. To speak of the law, in connection with the promise, is to introduce an alien element which robs the promise of its meaning. To make this clear, Paul sets up two series, each with three links. They are so presented that the links in either series belong inseparably together, but are clearly out of place in the other. On the one side Paul sets faith—the promise—grace; on the other, the law—transgression—wrath. The promise is given by grace and can therefore be accepted only by faith. But the operation of the law is the precise opposite: "The law brings wrath." As to that it is not necessary for Paul to speak at length here. He has done that earlier in discussing the old aeon. He has pointed out that the wrath of God is revealed not only against unrighteousness, but also against righteousness through the law. The wrath of God is of course revealed against sin even where the law is not known. But the idea that through the law one can escape the wrath of God is the more unreasonable, according to Paul, because the law does not remove sin, but makes it greater. Sin does exist even where the law is not known; but there cannot be transgression, because that implies a law which is transgressed. What happens, when the law is made known, is that sin is intensified to transgression. Therefore the law also intensifies the wrath of God.

Thus Paul shows the connection within the one series; the law, sin, and wrath are inseparable. Now he turns to the other series, showing concisely that an unfailing unity exists here too, and that this unity demonstrates the necessity of faith. "That is why it depends on faith, in order that the promise may rest on grace and be guaranteed to all his descendants." The three links in this series—faith, grace, and the promise—are closely joined in the Greek. Literally translated it would read, "Therefore by faith, in order that by grace, to the end that the promise may stand fast."

The promise that was given to Abraham said that he should be "the father of many nations." The immediate

meaning of that promise was that in the physical sense he
should be the father of many. But now the promise has
found much greater and more glorious fulfillment. Abraham has really become the father of "many nations," the
father of all who believe. He is not only the father of all
those who have received circumcision and the law, who in
an outward way are his physical progeny, his seed κατὰ
σάρκα. He is also the father of all who follow in the footsteps of his faith.

It happened first in Paul's own day that the promise to
Abraham was fulfilled in its deepest meaning; for then the
Gentiles came to believe in Christ and thus became the children of the faithful Abraham. In Galatians 3:8 Paul writes,
"The scripture, foreseeing that God would justify the Gentiles by faith, preached the gospel beforehand to Abraham,
saying, 'In thee shall all nations be blessed.'" Thus Paul
understands the meaning of the Scriptures. They speak not
only of the past; they apply even more to the present. They
speak of that which is now taking place. Because Scripture
foresaw that the Gentiles are to be justified through faith,
not through works, it speaks beforehand about Abraham's
faith and promises that he is to be the father of all who
believe. So it has come about that the promise abides for
all his seed, παντὶ τῷ σπέρματι. If it had depended on the
law, the promise would have applied only to οἱ ἐκ νόμου,
"only to the adherents of the law." But now, since it depends
on faith, the promise continues for οἱ ἐκ πίστεως, "also to
those who share the faith of Abraham."

(4) Abraham the type of him "who through faith is righteous"

The first part of Romans treats of ὁ δίκαιος ἐκ πίστεως, of
him "who through faith is righteous." Now Paul has come

to the end he has had in view in the whole discussion; he can point to Abraham as the type and pattern for him "who through faith is righteous." The characteristic which gave Abraham his peculiar position in the history of the people of God was the fact that "he believed." By this faith he became the father of all who believe.

Accordingly Paul's purpose in the following verses (17-25) is to show what faith is, and what it means, with Abraham as his example. Wnat was Abraham's situation, in which his faith could prove itself? God had given him a promise. He had promised Abraham that he should be the father of many nations: "So shall thy descendants be." But when Abraham contemplated himself and his human capacities, what God promised looked simply impossible. How could he become the father of many nations, now that the capacity for parenthood was as good as dead both in him and in Sarah? Yet he did not doubt but believed.

What is it, then, that characterizes Abraham's faith? That he believed the impossible, it has sometimes been said. It was not that which, from human point of view, was reasonable that he believed, but rather that which seemed improbable, even absurd. The basic quality of faith, it has been said, is that it flies in the face of human calculations and probabilities. Faith and paradox are interchangeable concepts. One could then express Paul's idea of faith with the sentence, *"Credo quia absurdum."*

But in this customary form the statement is not true. It is not the sheer fact that one believes the improbable, the impossible, the absurd, that constitutes the faith of which Paul speaks. Nor was that the nature of Abraham's faith. He had *God's promise*, and it was that which he believed. Only in the light of that fact can one properly speak about

what is humanly impossible. Since he had the divine promise, he could not be made to doubt God by the fact that he
saw clearly that human resources were not equal to its fulfillment. *This is faith*, to hold to God's promise, even if man
has no human ability to build on, even if all human calculations contradict. When Abraham believed, it was not
because he had reason to hope, from the human point of
view. On the contrary, he believed, even though by human
judgment there was no hope. Though the circumstances
were such that hope seemed utterly impossible, he nevertheless held to his hope; and he could do this because it was
only on God's promise that he based it. This double fact—
that, on the one hand, there was no hope, but, on the other,
he still hoped—is, according to Paul, something essential for
faith. "In hope he believed against hope" (vs. 18). The
Greek is very expressive, παρ' ἐλπίδα ἐπ' ἐλπίδι ἐπίστευσεν.

Without hope, and yet with hope: that is the real mark
of faith. Only where these stand over against each other is
faith found. Where man can manage with his own resources,
it is not a matter of faith; faith is not self-reliance. Faith is
rather the direct opposite of self-reliance, the opposite of
confidence in one's own adequacy and resources.

Many have thought that it is characteristic of faith that
it turns away from the actual, that it closes its eyes to sensi-
ble, tangible reality and soars to another world. In keeping
with this thought many have inserted a negation into the
text, a "not" which is absent from the best manuscripts. The
meaning would then be that because Abraham did *not* look
on his own incapacity, he became strong and was able to
hold fast to God's promise. But Paul says quite the opposite.
For him faith does not mean to close one's eyes to the facts.
Faith has no kinship with optimistic self-deception or with

the easy idea that things always come through in one way or another. Abraham saw the situation as it really was, including that which seemed to make God's promise absurd. But, Paul says, "He did not weaken in faith" (vs. 19); "He grew strong in his faith," the next verse adds.

How does it happen that faith grows weak? And how does it grow strong? We should take note that Paul here gives quite a different explanation from what we would expect. One might naturally think that faith would weaken when confronted by mounting difficulties; that faith would yield before doubts when the difficulties become so great that the promise seems impossible of fulfillment. Conversely, one might expect that if the prospect brightens and fulfillment seems at least possible, faith again grows stronger. But Paul affirms the opposite! When our own possibilities fail, faith increases; for it does not rest on ourselves and our own adequacy, but on God and His promise. It was just because Abraham did not trust in his own powers that he could face the impossibilities in his situation without losing hope. He had God's promise to hold to. That is the way faith acts, according to Paul.

God and faith! According to Paul these belong together. There can be no talk of faith without awareness of God. Faith is what it is, because it depends on God. From this it follows that, for Paul, faith can never be just a function of the soul or an inner condition in man. In Paul's meaning it is impossible to separate the action of faith (*fides qua creditur*) and the object of faith (*fides quae creditur*), as if they were two independent things. There is no action of faith if we lose sight of the object of faith—of God and His promise. But when it is said that faith is always faith in God, it must also be said that it is not a matter of a general and indefinite belief in God, but precisely belief in the God "who gives life to the dead and calls into existence the things that do not exist" (vs. 17). It was in Him that Abraham believed. He believed that God was able, by His promise, to give life to his body and to Sarah's maternal capacity, thereby enabling them to become the ancestors of many nations.

By believing in God, Abraham gave Him the honor that was due to Him. Honor ($\delta\acute{o}\xi a$) and glory are qualities of God. "To him be glory and dominion for ever and ever." It was of that honor that the sin of man had robbed God. Paul had already affirmed (1:21, 23) that "although they knew God, they did not honor him as God," but exchanged the glory of God ($\delta\acute{o}\xi a$ $\theta\epsilon o\hat{v}$) for images to which they offered their worship. But what sin thus withheld from God, faith accords Him. Faith recognizes His divine glory. It is for God to give the promise, and for us to receive it. This is the only honor man can give to God. Only in faith is man "right" in his relation with God. For that reason Paul can at the same time speak of Abraham's faith and of righteousness: "He gave glory to God, fully convinced that God was able to do what he had promised. That is why his faith was 'reckoned to him as righteousness'" (vss. 20-22).

Thus Paul speaks of Abraham and his faith. But it is not meant that the statement applies only to *him*. Abraham's example is referred to only because he is the type for everyone "who through faith is righteous." Therefore Paul continues, "But the words, 'it was reckoned to him,' were written not for his sake alone, but for ours also. It will be reckoned to us who believe in him that raised from the dead Jesus our Lord, who was put to death for our trespasses and raised for our justification" (vss. 23-25).

According to Paul there is precise correspondence between faith as we see it in Abraham and faith in those who believe in Christ. Abraham believed in the God "who gives life to the dead." Here, Paul holds, is the point where Abraham's faith has significance as example and type. Something similar is to be true of us who, through Christ, belong to the new age. When we believe in Jesus as "put to death for our trespasses and raised for our justification," we believe in the God "who gives life to the dead." God first raised Jesus from the dead. But this divine act had meaning not alone for Jesus personally and individually. By His resurrection from the dead, Jesus became "our Lord," the head of the new humanity. That which happened to Him also has its meaning for us. By faith in Him we are included among the children of the resurrection. We have passed from death to life.

Thus faith in Christ does not mean only that we believe in Him as risen from the dead. We also believe that through Him we are removed from the dominion of sin and death and received into the age of righteousness and life. God has dealt with us through Christ; He has made us, who were dead, alive with Christ. Concisely put, that is the meaning of justification. Justification is the revelation of the new righteousness of God. The sinner, who stood under the wrath of God, is through Christ incorporated into the new reality which gets its character from "the righteousness of God." Now we see clearly why, according to Paul, justification must indeed be justification of the *sinner*. It is he who is dead, whom God raises to life. "Even when we were dead through our trespasses, he made us alive together with Christ" (Eph. 2:5).

It should be observed that Paul here sets our justification (δικαίωσις) in closest connection with Christ's resurrection, just as, on the other hand, he connects our sins with

Christ's death. He "was put to death for our trespasses and raised for our justification." Otherwise we generally find justification coupled with the death of Christ, in Paul's thought (cf. 3:24f. and 5:9). Hence it has been asked how Paul can here connect justification with the resurrection. But that question reveals a manner of thought which is foreign to Paul. Paul recognizes no such alternative. To him the death and the resurrection of Christ belong together inseparably. Taken together they constitute the basis of justification. How was it that God revealed His righteousness and ushered in the new age? 3:24f. answers that God presented Christ as our mercy seat. That is a reference to Christ's death. But Paul also says that it took place when God raised Christ from the dead: for that is the beginning of the new age of the resurrection and life (cf. 1:4). Without the resurrection, the death of Christ would be nothing to Paul. "If Christ has not been raised, your faith is futile" (I Cor. 15:17; cf. Rom 8:34).

PART TWO

PART TWO

"He Who through Faith Is Righteous Shall Live"
5:1–8:39

The theme of the epistle (1:17) says, "He who through faith is righteous shall live." In that part of the letter which has engaged us up to this point, Paul has presented the first half of this theme. He has painted the picture of him "who through faith is righteous." That was the purpose served by what chapter 4 said about Abraham; for he was presented as the type of him "who through faith is righteous." Paul's task, in the first four chapters, was to state how we, who stood under the *wrath of God* because of our sin, have now, through Christ, been included in the *righteousness of God*. What has happened through Christ is that we are now under the dominion of the righteousness of God. It is that which Paul means, and nothing else, when he says that we are justified through Christ. If as Christians we are called righteous, that has no other meaning than to say that we have been justified. In the very concept of justification it is implied that righteousness is not originally a property in us; it comes to us through an action of God. Not by what we have done, but by what God has done in Christ are we righteous. That righteousness did not come through what we have done can also be expressed by saying that it was revealed without the works of the law, χωρὶς νόμου; it is not a righteousness through the law, not δικαιοσύνη ἐκ νόμου. That it has come through that which God has done is the same as to say that it has come through the gospel; it is the righteousness of faith, δικαιοσύνη ἐκ πίστεως. "Righteous" is he who believes in Christ. He can be called righteous, not by reason of his own ethical excellence and sinlessness, but because he is justified through God's act in Christ. The "righteous" is he who is "justified"; ὁ δίκαιος is ὁ δικαιωθείς.

All this Paul has made clear in the first part of his presentation. Now in chapter 5 he enters upon a new part. The task of the next four chapters is to show what it means to say that he who through faith is righteous "*shall live*" (ζήσεται). Where the wrath of God rules there is *death;* where the righteousness of God rules, there is *life.* Paul has already declared the former in many ways. Now he turns to the discussion of the latter. He who believes in Christ has passed from death to life. Christ lives in him (Gal. 2:20), and he lives in Christ (ἐν Χριστῷ). Through Christ he has been delivered from the age of death and received into the age of *life.* What does it mean to "*live,*" in this pregnant sense? That is the question Paul is about to discuss. Each of the next four chapters has its contribution to make to the answer. Chapter 5 says it means to be free from *wrath.* Chapter 6 says it is to be free from *sin.* Chapter 7 says free from *the law.* And chapter 8 says we are free from *death.*

It is particularly interesting to note how Paul joins the two, when he now turns from the first part to the second. "Raised for our justification," he says in closing the first part. In so saying Paul has coupled justification, righteousness, with the resurrection of Christ. But since the resurrection of Christ is the beginning of the new age of *life*, we see that Paul has carried his presentation precisely to the point where, in the next section, he must show what the new life means. In the concluding statement of the first part, one can already glimpse the issue to which the second part supplies the answer. What does it mean to say that he who through faith is righteous *"shall live"*?

But as the final word of the first part carries us up to the issue to be discussed in the second part, so the opening statement of the new section points back to the former and summarizes its message. We have already noted Paul's habit of gathering up the contents of a discussion in a concise summary. He does the same here: "Therefore, since we are justified by faith," δικαιωθέντες οὖν ἐκ πίστεως. All that he has said from 1:18 to 4:25 can be summed up in the expression "he who through faith is righteous." Should there be any lingering doubt on that point, it must yield when we now, at the transition to the next section, hear Paul's own summary. He uses almost the same identical word in discussion and summary: ὁ δίκαιος equals ὁ δικαιωθείς.

He who through faith is righteous *"shall live."* What does that really mean? We must now attend to the four answers which Paul gives. The first of these says that he shall *live free from the Wrath of God.*

VI

Free from the Wrath of God

5:1-21

That it means *freedom from the wrath of God* is the first thing Paul affirms when he takes up the description of the life into which we enter through Christ. To some degree this has already been made clear in the discussion that has preceded. He set in juxtaposition the old age, marked by the wrath of God, and the new age, marked by the fact that the righteousness of God is revealed through Christ. It is clear that to be under God's wrath and to be in the righteousness of God are diametrically opposite and mutually exclusive. Where the righteousness of God rules there is no longer room for the wrath of God. But Paul is insistent that this fact be made utterly clear. He is not satisfied to let the fact appear clearly in what he has said. He devotes special attention to it in the present connection. He develops his thought in three steps. First he states positively what freedom from the wrath of God means: "Since we are justified by faith, *we have peace with God*" (vss. 1-4). Next he shows how our new situation has its basis in *God's love* (vss. 5-8). And finally he points out the consequence for the eternal status of the Christian; even *on the day of judgment he is saved from the Wrath of God* (vss. 9-11).

1. Saved from the Wrath of God by God's Love
5:1-11

(1) Peace with God

"Since we are justified by faith, we have peace with God." With these words Paul begins his new discussion. Where the wrath of God has been taken away, peace with God reigns. "Peace with God" is thus the mark of the new life.

When we hear the word "peace," it is very easy for us to think of it as expressing a certain subjective state of the soul. Peace is the opposite of disturbance and unrest. It is a calm, exalted, and peaceful mood of the soul. It is not to be denied that this is included in Paul's words. But we have not laid hold of his deepest meaning if that is all we see. For Paul, peace is not merely an inner condition. Peace is a concept which implies relationship. It speaks of the mutual relationship between man and God. If one stands in right relation with God, it follows also that his inner condition is one of calm and rest; but this is a consequence and not the basic fact. That which is fundamental is the relation of peace with God; and it is primarily of this that Paul speaks.

Before Christ came and brought us peace with God, strife reigned. The relation between God and men was marked by disunity and enmity. The relationship was disturbed on both sides. Paul does not speak of enmity on the part of God—God has never been our enemy—but he does speak of the wrath of God against a humanity that is hostile to God. But on the part of man, it is a matter of actual enmity to God. It was "while we were enemies" that we were reconciled to God through the death of His Son (vs. 10). But now, through the reconciling work of Christ, the relationship between God and men has been set right on both sides. He who through faith is righteous no longer stands under the wrath of God; nor is he any longer, on his part, hostile to God. Both of these aspects are included in the fact that he has peace with God. But for Paul the accent manifestly falls on the objective side, on the fact that Christ has taken away the wrath of God. To live in Christ is to be free from the wrath of God. In this connection, be it remembered that to Paul the wrath of God means more than the expression of God's feeling of displeasure at sin; it is an effective action which places sinful humanity under God's condemnation. The wrath of God is an objective power of destruction. From that power Christ has freed us; He has taken us out of that condemnation. One is not giving Paul's meaning, if he, with a subjective theory of the atonement, says that Christ's redemptive action only sought to remove man's hostility to God, while no change needed to be made on God's part. Paul knows that the wrath of God is a terrible reality, and, if it be not removed, no change on the part of man can effect a real fellowship between him and God.

We encounter in the text a word which might seem to imply the subjective. For this reason it needs special attention. This expression, which our translation renders "we have peace," appears in the most numerous and best manuscripts in the form εἰρήνην ἔχωμεν; but the context would lead us to expect εἰρήνην ἔχομεν. That is, the manuscripts present the verb in the subjunctive mood. For this reason some have translated it, "Let us have peace with God," or "Let us remain at peace with God." But even if we overlook the difficulty of fitting such a translation into the context ("quite meaningless, in this context," says Lietzmann), grammar itself excludes it. For εἰρήνην ἔχειν is quite another thing from εἰρήνην φυλάσσειν. But even if it could be shown that

the letter originally said ἔχωμεν, that would not prove that
Paul meant it this way. Paul did not of course write the
letter with his own hand; he dictated it. Lietzmann rightly
says, "Since, as early as the first century, men no longer
made any difference between long and short 'o,' it cannot be
proved that there was a long 'o' in the original; and even less
can it be shown that Paul so dictated it. He may have said
'echomen,' meaning ἔχομεν, but Tertius wrote ἔχωμεν. This
could be the case, even if the ω could be traced back to the
original. The meaning here must carry more weight than
the letter. Only ἔχομεν gives Paul's real meaning."

"Through our Lord Jesus Christ," says Paul, "we have
peace with God." Again and again, in these four chapters,
he repeats the words, "through Jesus Christ our Lord." It is
particularly to be noted that each of these chapters ends
with these words. When Paul here speaks of the new life
of the Christian, he is at pains to say that all which he is
affirming is true only "in Christ" and through Him. Without
Christ we would always remain in bondage to the powers
of this world. But when Christ has become our Lord, He
brings to an end, once for all, the dominion of the powers of
destruction. We are no longer in their grip. When Christ
is our Kyrios, there can no longer be any other κυριότης. All
the old tyrants—Wrath, Sin, the Law and Death—are cast
down, and we become Christ's and live under Him in His
kingdom, serving Him in eternal righteousness. We are set
free from the powers of destruction; we are free from wrath,
the power of destruction which Paul has particularly in
mind in this chapter.

That we have peace with God also means that we have
access to God's grace. For Paul, grace and peace are inseparable. Even before this, we have met that unity in Paul's

salutation to the church in Rome (1:7); there too he couples
grace and peace. To "stand in grace" with God is the opposite of standing under His wrath. Paul carries that contrast
to its utmost consequences when he speaks of "the glory of
God," ἡ δόξα τοῦ θεοῦ. That is the ultimate and the highest
that can be affirmed about the Christian life, that it shares
in "the glory of God." Glory, δόξα, is of the very nature of
the divine life; and through Christ we are made to share in
it. As, in the old aeon, it could be said that "all have sinned
and fall short of the glory of God" (3:23), so now, since
Christ has come bringing the new aeon with Him, it can be
said that *we boast of the glory of God.* This is the great,
positive fact which Christ has brought to us, that He makes
us sharers in God's own eternal life. But as yet, Paul adds,
this is ours only "in hope." It is of the nature of the new life
to be, at the same time, both present and coming, something
that is both at hand and waiting for its fulfillment. With
Christ the new age has come into this world as a reality.
With the resurrection of Christ, the aeon of the resurrection
has begun. But, since "glory" is an essential quality of it,
it has not yet reached its consummation. Toward that end
Christian hope reaches forward, not as to something uncertain, but to something absolutely certain, of which it may
already rejoice.

"More than that, we rejoice in our sufferings," Paul continues. Life in Christ reaches forward toward consummation
and "glory." But that does not mean flight from the world.
Even this present life is made new through the Christian
hope. To him who lives his life only in the *present* age and
in *this* world, the sufferings which come to him can only be
something negative. But for the Christian, suffering is precisely the point where the power of hope most clearly proves

itself. He knows "that the sufferings of this present time are not worth comparing with the glory that is to be revealed to us" (8:18). Suffering receives a new meaning. It becomes a means in God's hand to carry us on toward the consummation. When God lets the weight of suffering rest on us, He does so to exercise us in patience and endurance. Suffering has the very effect of making the Christian hope the more eagerly for the "glory" which God has promised him. Suffering is thus not something of which we must be ashamed. Hope makes it something positive, in which we can actually rejoice. If there were no suffering, hope would never have opportunity to attain to its full strength. It is by suffering that hope is tested and strengthened. The role of suffering in the Christian life is to develop endurance, "and endurance produces character, and character produces hope."

(2) God's love

In what has gone before, Paul has shown how, through Christ, God has established a new relation, marked by righteousness and peace. But how is it possible for God to receive into His covenant of peace those who have always been His enemies, and have stood under His wrath? In that there is something hard to comprehend. But that is just what God has done through Christ. It would never have occurred to us to conceive it, if God had not actually done so.

What is the basis of that divine action? Here Paul refers to *God's love*. But, it could further be asked, what is the basis for God's love? To the latter question we have no answer. God's love has its basis only in God himself. It cannot be referred to something still more ultimate, or ascribed to anything beyond what God is. There is no help in rationalizing and seeking to make God's love more understandable by referring to human parallels. There really is no human parallel. If we persist in the attempt, the result is certain to be a distortion of God's love. All human analogies and parallels fail. To be sure, Paul also compares the divine love with the human; but he does so to show that they are different.

But if divine love, of which Paul speaks, is utterly distinctive in kind and can be included in no human categories, how is it possible to talk about it at all? We can speak of it, because God has himself revealed it. It must be remembered that what is meant is not an intellectualistic kind of knowledge. God has shown His love in concrete action. "God shows his love for us in that while we were yet sinners Christ died for us" (vs. 8).

Unless we come to this passage (vss. 5-8) with our own presuppositions, it must be clear that it speaks of God's own love, the love which He has shown to us through Christ. About that, verse 5 says, "God's love has been poured into our hearts through the Holy Spirit which has been given to us." The expression "God's love," ἡ ἀγάπη τοῦ θεοῦ, is to be viewed as a subjective genitive, not an objective genitive. It speaks of God's love to us, not of our love to God.

But a contrary interpretation has often been given on this point. Augustine has had an unfortunate influence. His view may be stated briefly as follows.

All in all, love is the most elementary expression of human life. To love is to seek one's welfare and contentment in something. To Augustine that is equivalent to saying that "there is not anyone who does not love." But it all depends on what one loves, toward what object one directs his love. Love may be either good or bad. Good love is love to God. As a creature of God, man is intended to seek and find his

well-being in God, for God is by nature the highest good;
in Him is comprehended all that man could wish or strive
for. The true love is therefore that which is directed upward.
This Augustine called *caritas*. But in sinful man love moves
in the opposite direction. By nature he is not prone to love
God above all else. He rather seeks his satisfaction in lower,
earthly things. This love which is directed downward is
the false love. This Augustine calls *cupiditas*. This is the
only love of which man, by his own powers, is capable, since
the fall. It is natural to him, because earthly things are so
close to him; they exercise so irresistible an attraction for
him that he cannot but love them and seek them rather than
God. The inevitable consequence is that man, because of
the downward direction of his love as it seeks its good in
earthly things, suffers failure and loses the good which he
seeks. For earthly and perishable things can never actually
satisfy the heart that was made for eternal values. The heart
must always remain restless until it finds rest in God. Since
man is bound to the sensory, the true love that reaches up
toward God can arise only if God creates and stirs it up
within man. God does that when he gives the Holy Spirit
to man; for that means that God, who is love, infuses love,
caritas, into man. By virtue of that, man is enabled to direct
love's desire upward towards God and heavenly things. All
this Augustine thinks he finds in Romans 5:5, which, he believes, speaks of love to God and how it arises in man by
God's infusion of it into the heart. This is therefore the text
to which Augustine returns again and again. On it, above
all others, he rests his teaching about grace which infuses
love into man (*infusio gratiae, infusio caritatis*).

But this entire interpretation is utterly untrue to Paul.
In this view Augustine has less of Paul than of the old *eros*

concept of love. Augustine's starting point is human love, interpreted as desire, always seeking to find satisfaction. But Paul's view of love is the direct opposite; love does not seek its own (I Cor. 13:5). Paul's view starts with God's love, manifested most clearly in His giving of Christ. Because they thus start from different points, Augustine and the theological tradition that builds on him cannot correctly understand what Paul means when he speaks of love.

As for 5:5, it is evident that Paul there talks about love in God himself. When we realize that he never uses *agape* to express man's love to God, we shall not think that it is of man's love that Paul speaks in this verse. *Agape*, the love which God showed us in Christ, is for Paul so tremendous a fact that he regularly refrains from using the same word to express our love to God. In the fact that where the text says "poured *out*" (ἐκχέειν), Augustine and the tradition that follows him use the verb "poured *in*," we can at once see sign of the distortion. Paul has a double reason for saying here that love is "*poured out.*" In the first place, the expression is often met in the discussion of God's wrath. As in the old aeon God poured out His wrath upon His enemies, so He has now, in Christ, poured out His love. In the second place, it is the technical term for "the outpouring of the Holy Spirit." That Paul was mindful of that is evident from the fact that to the statement about the outpouring of God's love he immediately adds the explanation that this was done "through the Holy Spirit which has been given to us."

In Christ, God's love has filled the cup to overflowing and been poured out on us. It has poured forth from the heart of God and sought its way to our hearts, true to the very nature of love. God's love now has a representative in our hearts, "the Holy Spirit which has been given to us."

The function of the Holy Spirit, according to Paul, is to be a "guarantee" in our hearts that we belong to Christ and are "in Him" (II Cor. 1:21f.). When God's love is present with us as an unfailing reality, that is the work of the Holy Spirit.

But Paul does not stop with the active presence of God's love with us. He turns our attention back to the mighty action of God, whereby His love made its way to us. If we ask what God's love, God's *agape*, is, Paul answers by pointing us to Christ and His death for us. Nowhere else is there a revelation of God's love like Christ's death on the cross. There, and there alone, we learn to know the deepest meaning of God's love. What Paul says here is like the declaration in I John 3:16, "By this we know love, that he laid down his life for us." If we had not met the love which reveals itself in the cross of Christ, we should not have known what *agape* is. We might have known a general love, but not divine love.

The nature of this divine love appears very clearly, if we observe the condition of those to whom God showed His love by Christ's death. Paul says, "While we were yet helpless, at the right time Christ died for the ungodly" (vs. 6). We were helpless and ungodly when Christ offered Himself for us. Here it is most clear that divine love is quite different in kind from man's. "One will hardly die for a righteous man—though perhaps for a good man one will dare even to die" (vs. 7). Paul does not deny that human love may lead one to die for another. But it would require a strong motivation. One does not lay down his life for anybody at all; hardly even for a righteous man, even though his worth might seem to justify it. One would be most likely to make the sacrifice for a relative or a benefactor. But for whom did Christ sacrifice His life? Not for benefactors, but for enemies; not for the righteous, but for sinners and the ungodly. This is truly the "unmotivated" love. To be sure, in the deepest sense, this love is not without its own motive. There is something which sets it in action. But it is proper to call it "unmotivated," because there is in the object to which it is directed nothing at all to which appeal can be made to explain this love. Man's enmity to God, his sin, and his ungodliness certainly do not merit God's love.

Paul is eager to show this "unmotivated" character of the divine love. With this in mind he piles up negative expressions to indicate how unworthy they were for whom Christ died. He calls them helpless and ungodly (vs. 6), sinners (vs. 8), and enemies of God (vs. 10). Luther used an exceptionally striking expression to indicate the difference between divine love and human love. The latter he speaks of as gained, the former as spontaneous or springing forth. God's love springs forth spontaneously from its own fountain. It is not called into action by any good characteristic or state in man, to whom God gives it.

In the preceding we have spoken interchangeably about the love of Christ and the love of God. We could do this because to Paul both are expressions of the same thing. The love revealed in the death of Christ is not independent of God. God is himself the subject of that love. It was not the case that Christ showed only *His own* love by giving His life for us. Paul says, *"God* shows his love for us in that Christ died" (vs. 8). Christ's action is God's action. Christ's love is God's love. When God in His love would save mankind from the dominion of the powers of destruction, He did so by giving His Son for us, and made Him our mercy seat. That is the greatest and most incomprehensible act of God's love. After the sacrifice of Christ we could not speak conclusively about God's love without referring to the cross of

Christ; and as little could we speak about the love revealed
in Christ's death without seeing in it God's own love. The
two are one and the same. Paul has stressed this more than
anyone else; and the passage here under discussion may be
called the classic text on the oneness of God's love and
Christ's cross. The simplest expression for this is "the love
of the cross."

(3) Saved through Christ from the wrath to come

Now follows the application of what has been said. Paul
states the meaning thereof for the Christian's status before
the judgment that is to come.

When, in vss. 5-8, he spoke of God's love which was revealed to us in Christ's death, he did so because God's love
is the ultimate basis for the removal of God's wrath and our
reception into the new relation of peace with God. It is
because of it that we have access to His grace and can
already "rejoice in our hope of sharing the glory of God"
(vss. 1-4). But the wrath of God is a reality which applies
not to this life only. Certainly the wrath of God is even now
revealed from heaven against all human godlessness and
unrighteousness. But the time of God's wrath lasts as long
as this temporal life itself—as do also God's patience and
forbearance. That means that the last word as to God's
wrath has not yet been uttered. A day will come when the
heat of God's wrath will consume all that is evil. Paul calls
that "the day of wrath" (2:5), adding that it will then be
manifest that God is a righteous judge who will render to
every man according to his works. How will it then be with
him who has become a member of Christ and "lives in Him"?
Through Christ he has been freed from the wrath of God in

the present age. Will he also be able to stand before God "in the day of wrath"?

The answer to that question seems to Paul a plain consequence of what he has already said about the love God has shown through Christ. If it is really so that, while we were still His enemies and served unrighteousness, God manifested such love to us that He sent His Son to die for us, how could it possibly be that He would surrender us to wrath's eternal power of destruction, now that we are no longer enemies but participants in His righteousness? Therefore Paul's conclusion says, "Since we are now justified by his blood, much more shall we be saved by him from the wrath of God" (vs. 9).

The connection with what has preceded is evident. With the words δικαιωθέντες οὖν, "since we are justified," the chapter began. In verse 9 Paul refers to that. He repeats the same words and links them immediately with our freedom from God's wrath: δικαιωθέντες νῦν, "since we are now justified, much more shall we be saved by him from the wrath of God." This is accordingly the status which is bestowed on us through Christ: (1) We no longer stand under wrath's destructive power; we are delivered from the old aeon where the wrath of God (ὀργὴ θεοῦ) rules, and received into the new aeon, where the righteousness of God (δικαιοσύνη θεοῦ) and peace reign. That is to say, we are justified (δικαιωθέντες). (2) But this also has its effect on the day of judgment. Then too we shall, through Christ, be freed from wrath in its last and conclusive manifestation (σωσθησόμεθα ἀπὸ τῆς ὀργῆς). "When the wrath of God cleanses humanity of all evildoers, Jesus will be the Saviour of the justified, not because of what they have done in His service, but because He died for them" (Schlatter). The wrath of which Paul here speaks, from which we shall be saved through Christ, is the same as what he elsewhere calls *"the wrath to come"* (ἡ ὀργὴ ἡ ἐρχομένη, I Thess. 1:10). Thus he speaks of salvation as something in the future. He who believes in Christ is certainly saved now; but salvation is full and final only when one is delivered from the wrath to come. It is only then that Christ's work for us attains its fullness.

Once more Paul repeats this fact in other words and at the same time carries the matter one step further. "If while we were enemies we were reconciled to God by the death of his Son, much more, now that we are reconciled, shall we be saved by his life" (vs. 10). Jesus died to take away enmity and bring about reconciliation. Reconciliation took place, Paul says, "while we were God's enemies." That is a troublesome statement for every subjective theory of the atonement which sees in the atonement only a change in man's attitude to God. When Paul speaks of the atonement, he does so in a way that breaks down the traditional alternative "subjective or objective atonement." The atonement does not consist either in a change of God's mind because man makes satisfaction, or in a change of man's mind because he sees God's love in Christist. The atonement is not brought about by the change of our mind from enmity against God to love for Him. It has already taken place, and when it took place we were yet enemies of God. But, on the other hand, there can be no talk of a change in the mind of God through the atonement, for the atonement is, to Paul, exclusively the work of God. "All this is from God, who through Christ reconciled us to himself. . . . God was in Christ reconciling the world to himself" (II Cor. 5:18f.). The objectivity which Paul recognizes is quite different in kind from that in the alternative mentioned above. He knows that the wrath of

God is an objective reality, which rested heavily on a humanity sunk in sin. But he also knows that God had thoughts of peace with those who were His enemies, and that, through Christ, He made a new covenant of peace with them. That, too, is an objective reality. Peace with God is not merely a state of feeling in us. When we believe in Christ, we thereby have, in a purely objective sense, a new status before God. We are justified, that is to say, set under the sway of God's righteousness; and we are reconciled with God, that is to say, delivered from His wrath and placed in a relation of peace with Him. Properly these two expressions, justification and atonement, are one and the same fact, looked at from different points of view. They who, through faith in Christ, are justified are no longer at enmity with God, but reconciled with Him. They are at the same time δικαιωθέντες and καταλλαγέντες.

Thus, though there is precise correspondence between verses 9 and 10, so that both say exactly the same thing, nevertheless the matter is carried an essential step futher in the latter. That happens by the introduction of the thought about Christ's life, which is set beside the thought of the death of Christ and in juxtaposition therewith. We were justified by His blood, that is through His *death* (vs. 9). We were reconciled with God "by the *death* of his Son" (vs. 10). But if all this was effected by Christ's *death*, "much more shall we be saved by his *life*," Paul continues. About him who through faith is righteous, it is said that he *"shall live."* That is because of his oneness with the living Christ. Christ lives in us, and we in Him (ἐν αὐτῷ, ἐν Χριστῷ). Through His life (ἐν τῇ ζωῇ αὐτοῦ) we possess final salvation. To live in Christ is to be free from the wrath of God. That is to be delivered both from the present wrath which God reveals

from heaven against all human ungodliness and unrighteousness, and from "the wrath to come," which will be revealed
on "the day of wrath."

It is this of which a Christian may rightly boast. All
boasting of oneself is excluded (3:27). But through Christ
he can "rejoice in God." God is no longer against him, but
for him. He cannot boast before God, but he can rejoice in
in God. He has nothing of his own to stand on, neither his
works, his ethical character, nor his religious faith. He rests
on God and on what God has done through Christ, and will
do. Therefore, when Paul says how we "have received our
reconciliation" and been freed from the wrath of God, he
is eager to affirm decisively, once more, that this has been
accomplished only and alone "through our Lord Jesus
Christ." Those same words spoke to us in the first verse
also. To make sure, Paul repeats them here, and as he proceeds he has occasion to repeat them again and again that
it may never be forgotten that we owe our liberation from
the powers of destruction to Christ alone and to His redemptive work. Only because Christ has become "our Lord," our
Kyrios, have other powers lost their dominion over us.

The words "through our Lord Jesus Christ" indicate that
the matter which Paul took up at the beginning of this chapter has now come to its conclusion. These words are the
final chord of his hymn of praise. In each chapter, from 5
to 8 inclusive, these words occupy a similar position and
serve the same function.

2. The Two Aeons: Adam and Christ
5:12-21

(1) Adam the prototype of "him who should come"

We have seen that in 5:11 Paul brought to a conclusion

the point which he took up at the beginning of the chapter. His purpose was to show that he who through faith is righteous lives his life "in Christ," free from the wrath of God. But now a surprise is in store for us. Paul does not turn from this point to the statement of the next, that the Christian is free from sin. He takes up again the first point and discusses it in a way that, for the moment, seems to overleap the bounds of the issue. Verses 12-21, viewed formally, are perhaps the most peculiar in all the epistle. Paul's thoughts leap forth here like a torrential mountain stream. They rush on with such force that they do not always come to carefully formed expression. In these ten verses comes together all that Paul had discussed in the preceding chapters, both about the wrath of God and God's righteousness, and all that which he is about to present in the chapters that follow. Here the whole problem of Romans is brought together in this brief passage that is filled to overflowing with vital thought.

It is therefore not strange that interpreters have had difficulty with these verses. Many have had a feeling that they lie somewhat outside of the main thought of the epistle. Unfortunately the passage has therefore been viewed as a parenthesis, as an epilogue to what has gone before, or as introductory to that which follows. In either case the result has been to look upon the passage as one which could be passed by without special loss. Luther did not otherwise minimize the significance of these verses; but even he, in his famous preface to Paul's Letter to the Romans, called them "an entertaining outbreak and excursion."

But it is not only as to its form that this passage has confronted interpreters with difficulties. The real meaning of it has been quite as troublesome. The parallelism which

Paul draws between Adam and Christ has seemed so strange and unmanageable that it has made scholars the more willing to treat this section as a parenthesis. More or less consciously interpreters have acted on the assumption that something, which is so foreign to today's thought as to seem unreal, cannot have been of decisive importance to Paul either. To explain how he happened in on the digression, reference has, for instance, been made to the important place which "the Adam-speculation" came to play in rabbinical thought. Then it is assumed that Paul here simply fell back into a rabbinical way of thinking. Still another opinion has said that Paul is here making use of the familiar Hellenistic view of "primeval man." But whether one has accepted one explanation or the other, what Paul here says about Adam and Christ is looked upon as a departure from characteristic Pauline and biblical thought. So scholars have thrust the whole passage aside.

Whether Paul did derive a certain impulse from Jewish or Hellenistic ways of thought is a question whose answer is extremely difficult. We should not forget that Paul read about Adam on one of the first pages of his Bible; so it is not necessary to look for remoter sources from which the idea might have come. But be that as it may, it is entirely clear that the meaning of his thought about Adam and Christ is entirely different from either Jewish or Hellenistic concepts. It is rather the direct opposite. For instance the Hellenistic concept of primeval man expected that he would reappear in the final times. But Paul does not look on Christ as an Adam redivivus. He sets up Adam and Christ in this parallel, not to affirm their identity, but contrariwise to point out the contrast between them. When once one comes to realize what that means to Paul, he forthwith discovers that this passage is by no means a parenthesis or a digression in the apostle's thought. Rather do we here come to the high point of the epistle. This is the point where all the lines of his thinking converge, both those of the preceding chapters and those of the chapters that follow.

It was because of the importance of this passage for the understanding of the whole epistle, that we used it in the introduction as the key to our exposition. In that way it shed its light on the preceding chapters. For the main idea of the passage we can here refer to our earlier treatment (pp. 16-26). But certain points must be discussed in the interest of full understanding.

A problem confronts us in the very first word. The passage begins with a "therefore," διὰ τοῦτο. The question is to what, in that which has preceded, Paul here refers. What has already been said that could call forth the juxtaposition of Christ and Adam to which Paul now proceeds? Some interpreters look back to what immediately precedes this verse; others to all of the passage 5:1-11; and still others to all that followed 3:21. The idea would then be that since the redemptive work described issued from Christ, *therefore* Paul feels justified in according Him a position that may be compared with Adam's. "In view of the great affirmations that can be made about the new order of salvation and its works, there is between Christ and Adam, in respect to developments issuing from them, such a parallel that Christ may be called the second Adam, the beginner of a new humanity" (E. Kühl). But that is to ascribe to Paul a line of thought which, by all the evidence, is alien to him. There is no intimation that Paul regarded Adam's position so highly that he sought, by peculiar reasoning, to claim a comparable position for Christ. The very fact that there is no clear agreement as to what, in that which has preceded, the word under discussion refers, argues strongly against the suggested interpretation. For that reason some interpreters have simply held that διὰ τοῦτο is an unimportant expression of transition, intended to refer to nothing in particular in the foregoing. But that looks too much like an escape from a real problem. It simply refrains from attempting an explanation. It is safe to conclude that Paul has had in mind something which made it natural for him to use this particular expression which would otherwise have been a transition phrase of no importance. The explanation is not hard to find.

All the time Paul has been speaking out of a very definite presupposition. All that he has said in the preceding chapters rests on the difference between the two aeons. Paul has said what we human beings are, as members of Adam's lost race; everything human is sunk in sin and stands under the wrath of God. But, on the other hand, he has declared what we have become through Christ; by faith in Him we have been delivered from the dominion of wrath and received into the kingdom of righteousness and life. "He who through faith is righteous shall live." The idea of the two aeons has formed the background for all this; but it has not yet been explicitly stated. It has actually been implied throughout; but thus far it has only been glimpsed. But now it breaks out of the background into full view. Adam and Christ stand there as the respective heads of the two aeons. Adam is the head of the old aeon, the age of *death;* Christ is the head of the new aeon, the age of *life.* As sin came into the world through one man, Adam, and death through sin, so also through one man, Christ, the righteousness of God came into the world, and through righteousness life. This is the great fact of which the latter part of this chapter speaks

Now a thought, long held back, breaks forth with vigor—half unintended. For this idea of Christ and Adam is not an organic part of the exposition of the freedom from the wrath of God which righteousness gives. But, on the other hand, it is not out of place here. It only broadens the perspective of what has preceded. It may well be asked where this line of thought could better have been introduced.

It might be thought that Paul might better have introduced it at the beginning of the first chapter, introducing the discussion of the status of man in the old aeon. Then what he says about Christ could have introduced the chapters in which the apostle discusses the new aeon. But such procedure would not have been possible for Paul. For Adam did not signify to Paul something independent of Christ. It is Paul's intention to discuss Adam only as the antitype to Christ; hence he cannot discuss Adam till he has spoken of Christ.

One might likewise think that the right place for this discussion of Adam would have been at the beginning of the fifth chapter. Then the statements of the Christian's deliverance from all that belongs to the old aeon—from Wrath, Sin, the Law, and Death—would have followed as specific examples of what this section affirms. Even though such an arrangement might seem better, from an outward view of an outline, it must be conceded that Paul's order is actually preferable. The culminating declaration of the exposition about man's status in the old aeon was "the wrath of God." The question immediately arises as to the new aeon; so it is most natural that the answer be given at once: the Christian is free from the wrath of God. One might see it as finesse in the presentation that the answer is given first, and then the background against which it must be viewed. Probably

Paul engaged in no such reflections as to form of composition. At this point in his discussion the thought that formed its background simply pushed its way to the front, demanding expression. But this certainly does not deny that it came to expression at the place which best served the purpose in view.

But we return to the word with which the passage begins, διὰ τοῦτο. With the background stated, we see that this word has a particularly simple and good significance. On the one hand there is the fact of relationship with what has preceded. But, on the other hand, the reference is not to any particular verse or statement, but precisely to the unstated presupposition which underlies all that has been said. Perhaps our best way to indicate its meaning would be by a strongly emphasized "thus": "Thus—as death came through Adam, so life has now come through Christ."

Also in the very next word we face another problem: ὥσπερ, "as." The word implies that a comparison is being presented. But we are immediately confronted with the fact that the second member of the comparison is missing. The chief clause is not there, and the statement ends in an anacoluthon. There is of course no doubt as to the meaning. The context makes that quite clear. And furthermore, the comparison is again taken up in verse 18. The missing clause can easily be supplied. But the structural irregularity is there. The conjunction ὥσπερ is not accompanied by the expected οὕτως.

Some have dealt with the problem by simply dropping the word ὥσπερ, thus changing the comparison into a plain declaration. But by so doing they lose something essential, for it is indeed a comparison which is here being made. The word "as," ὥσπερ, serves the vital function of showing that here, as in all that has already been said, Christ is the central person. Adam is mentioned only as antitype for Christ.

If we would understand the benefaction which God, through Christ, has spread abroad to all mankind, we do well, according to Paul, to take note of the condemnation which has passed from Adam to all men. That comparison helps us to see the universal scope of the work of Christ. But we cannot grasp Paul's thought unless we observe that his view of man is quite different from the present individualistic and atomistic concept. Paul does not think of humanity as a chance gathering of individuals, comprehended under an inclusive concept. He sees mankind as an organic unity, a single body under a single head. It is in such a view that Adam has meaning for him. Adam is not merely a single individual who lived long ago. Adam is significant as the head of the "old" humanity, as the head of the present aeon (ὁ αἰὼν οὗτος). That which happened to the head involves the body also. Humanity's fate was determined in Adam. Through one man sin entered the world, and through sin everything human became subject to death. Ever since Adam the fate of the race has been to lie in thralldom to the powers of destruction. When man lives in sin, he deludes himself with the belief that he is himself in control; that he is free and can choose sin in one moment and good in another. But in reality the sin which he commits is evidence that sin is the master and man the slave. So also as to death. Man would save his own life; he is always looking out for himself But all that he does still serves death. Death is the sovereign who rules over man's whole existence. Such is the common lot of man since Adam.

When Paul says how sin and death came into the "cosmos," achieving unlimited sway in the whole human realm, he uses two verbs which must be noted, especially since we shall have occasion to return to them toward the end of the chapter. About sin he says it "came in," εἰσῆλθεν. And then he adds that death "spread to all men," διῆλθεν, and took complete mastery over them.

The end of verse 12 presents still another problem. What is the meaning of the words, ἐφ' ᾧ πάντες ἥμαρτον? No one can answer absolutely. Two interpretations are possible here. Ever since Origen it has been customary to interpret ἐφ' ᾧ as ἐπὶ τούτῳ ὅτι. This is the case in our Bible translation, "because all men sinned." According to the other, which is perhaps better, the expression is understood to mean, "it was under these circumstances, under these auspices, that all sinned." But whichever view we choose, Paul's main idea is entirely clear and beyond doubt: it was through one man, Adam, that all men are sinners and are subject to death. If we choose the first interpretation, the meaning is not that the result of Adam's sin was merely that he himself became subject to death, and thereafter, "because all men sinned," they too suffered the same fate. For in that case the statement would retract what Paul has just been affirming. And the view becomes still more impossible, if one remembers the parallelism between Adam and Christ. Paul declares that as through the fall of one man (Adam) death became the lot of all, so now through one man's (Christ) righteousness, life holds sway. But if Paul had meant that all became subject to death because of the sins which they themselves committed, the conclusion would logically be that all would enter into life by reason of the righteousness which they themselves achieved. That is an idea which is certainly the utter opposite of all that Paul says. If we are to keep the translation "because all men have sinned," we shall have to understand it as Augustine did, "all men have sinned in Adam." In any case, this much is settled for Paul: humanity's fate rests on what happened in him who was its head and representative. Any interpretation that dilutes that thought, or departs from it, is definitely *false*.

That this is true is further evident from that which Paul goes on to say: "Sin indeed was in the world before the law was given, but sin is not counted where there is no law. Yet death reigned from Adam to Moses, even over those whose sins were not like the transgression of Adam" (vs. 13f.). Adam had received definite commandment from God, instructing him as to his behavior. Therefore when he sinned, his action had the character of direct "transgression" (παράβασις, παράπτωμα). Before there can be talk of "transgression," there must be a command or a law. Such there was in Adam's case, but not in the case of those who came later, until the law was given through Moses. In the meantime, says Paul, there was sin in the world; but sin was not counted where there was no law. But during that time sin nevertheless held unlimited sway over mankind. It reigned "even over those whose sins were not like the trangression of Adam." Sin and death are in the world as tyrants, who do not ask man whether he will serve them, but rule autocratically.

What Paul is here interested in, above all else, is the contrast between the one man, through whose action such a condition was brought about, and all of mankind which was affected by what that man did. The transgression and the fall happened through one man; but the consequences are of *cosmic* dimensions. Adam's action affected the "cosmos," as Paul says it, that is, all the world of humanity. That which happened in him became decisive of the fate of all who belonged to his race. When Paul here speaks jointly of sin and death, it should be observed that, in this connection, he is thinking chiefly of death and its power. Death is "the last enemy," ἔσχατος ἐχθρός (I Cor. 15:26). The great contrast, as to which Paul speaks throughout the epistle, is the contrast between *death,* under whose power we stand by nature, and *life,* which is given to us through faith in Christ. "He who through faith is righteous shall *live.*" That which occupies Paul is thus the question how it happened that death came to hold sway in the world of mankind. That came about through the agency of sin. Sin is the servant who goes ahead to prepare the way for death. When through one man sin came into the world, the result was that Death came into control. Sin is "the sting of death" (τὸ κέντρον τοῦ θανάτου, I Cor. 15:56). It is the tool and weapon by which death has brought humanity into its power. Through sin death got the human race into its grip, and is now its real master. Death has ascended the throne in this world; and now, with sovereign authority, it uses its power with terrifying effects. In this chapter Paul repeats again and again, with increasing pointedness, that death has attained to royal control in our world (ἐβασίλευσεν ὁ θάνατος, cf. vss. 14, 17, 21).

From the foregoing it follows that, for Paul, death is not only an event which comes upon us and puts an end to life. Death is a power, a ruler. That is what is suggested by spelling the word with a capital—Death. About the same is true as to the other powers of destruction referred to more or less extensively in this chapter—Wrath, the Law, and Sin. Wrath is not only a feeling or an expression of displeasure on the part of God; it is a destructive power. One is in a state of total perdition when God allows His holy displeasure to overtake the sinner. Sin is not only—as moralism thinks—the evil deeds one does; it is an objective power under which the man who is hostile to God stands, and as a result of which all that such a man does is sinful. And the 'aw is not only the total of God's will; it is an objective power which places man under the judgment of condemnation.

As Adam is the head of the old aeon (ὁ αἰὼν οὗτος), so Christ is the head of the new (ὁ αἰὼν ὁ μέλλων). It is with a view to making that juxtaposition that Paul here discusses Adam and his position in the human race. Adam concerns Paul here only as "a type of the one who was to come," as τύπος τοῦ μέλλοντος (vs. 14). The expression "one who was to come" (ὁ μέλλων or ὁ ἐρχόμενος) is one of the usual designations of the expected Messiah. "Are you he who is to come?" John the Baptist, speaking through his disciples, inquires of Jesus. That Jesus saw the messianic nature of the question is clear from His answer. He refers to the signs of the Messiah that were already at hand (Matt. 11:3-6). When Paul speaks about the new aeon, it is not usual for him to refer to it as "the coming aeon" (ὁ αἰὼν ὁ μέλλων). But here we glimpse the idea in his characterization of Christ as he "who was to come"; for as ὁ μέλλων He is the head of ὁ αἰὼν ὁ μέλλων.

In Adam and in Christ the two aeons stand in sharp contrast to each other. As the old aeon is the kingdom of death (ἡ βασιλεία τοῦ θανάτου, cf. ἐβασίλευσεν ὁ θάνατος, vss. 14, 17, 21), so the new aeon is the kingdom of life (ἡ βασιλεία τῆς ζωῆς, cf. ἐν ζωῇ βασιλεύσουσιν vs. 17). Now, in what follows, we shall see how Paul confronts these two kingdoms with each other.

217

(2) The kingdoms of death and of life

Adam is Christ's prototype. Or, to speak more exactly, he is Christ's antitype. Adam is "a type" for Christ, and Christ is Adam's antitype. In the idea of type-antitype a certain double meaning is expressed. On the one hand, a correspondence is suggested; and on the other, a contrast. In a way Adam and Christ belong together; and yet they are diametrically opposite to each other. What is true of Adam is true of Christ, but in a directly opposite sense. Adam is the head of mankind. But precisely the same is true of Christ. Adam is the head of mankind in the sense that in him mankind was lost. Christ is the head of mankind in the opposite sense, that in Him mankind was saved. Adam is the head of mankind, from which the contagion of sin and death spreads to all its members. Christ is the head of mankind, from which righteousness and life come to all the members. Paul's line of thought here is closely related to that in I Corinthians 15:21f.: "For as by a man came death, by a man has come also the resurrection of the dead. For as in Adam all die, so also in Christ shall all be made alive." The fall of Adam was the beginning of the age of death; the resurrection of Christ was the beginning of the resurrection of the dead (cf. 1:5), the beginning of the new resurrection-aeon, the age of life. "In Adam," we all stand under the sovereign dominion of death; and "in Christ" under the sovereign dominion of life.

If this concept of "type-antitype" presents a complicated coupling of correspondence and contrast, the complication grows deeper when it is seen that the parallel between Adam and Christ falls short in the very point where it was intended to apply. The reason for this is not that Paul chose a poor illustration, but the very nature of the case. It is inevitable that every human comparison with Christ fails. In the final analysis there is nothing that can be put in the same category with Him. There is only one who can be compared with Him in universal significance, namely Adam; and it is just he whom Paul has used for his parallel. But even he is not equal to that role, for *Christ is infinitely greater.* There is only one thing which can be compared with the blessing which Christ brings, namely, the condemnation that came by Adam. But that comparison also fails, for the *blessing which comes from Christ is incomparably greater.* Again we confront a double fact. On the one hand, a parallel is attempted; but on the other hand, it is impossible, because that which is used for the purpose is not at all equal to that of which it was to serve as a type. Adam is called τύπος, a pattern or model for Christ; but Christ burst all patterns. There is nothing which is like unto Him.

In view of such facts it is not strange that Paul has particular difficulty with his presentation here. He barely gets to ὥσπερ, "as," in verse 12, before he breaks off with the comparison. And when, in the end of verse 14, he returns to the comparison with the statement that "Adam was a type for the one who was to come," he drops it again and seems to give it up entirely. To be sure, verse 15 also makes a comparison; but its meaning is precisely the opposite of what the foregoing would have led us to expect. We might have expected something like the following: as it was then with the fall, so it is now with the gift of grace. But that is not what Paul says; he affirms the exact oposite. "But the free gift is not like the trespass. For if many died through one man's trespass, much more have the grace of God and the free gift in the grace of that one man Jesus Christ abounded for many" (vs. 15). On the one hand, it is a mat-

ter of a *human* action, effected by one man, but entailing
incomprehensible consequences for the whole human race.
On the other hand, it is a matter of *God's* action, effected by
Him through one man, Jesus Christ. Great as were the
consequences of Adam's action, they did not match that
which God has effected through Christ. For "the grace of God
and the free gift" there is no human measure, however great
such measure be. In comparison with the greatest and most
fateful that enters man's life, even in comparison with the
condemnation which came by Adam's fall, God's blessing
through Christ stands forth as "abounding."

Paul has one thing more to add about the difference
between Adam's action and Christ's. How much greater the
latter is one can see, if he gives attention to the difference in
starting point for the two. Behind Adam's action lay no preceding history; man's life was still as an unmarred page.
Behind the action of Christ lie "many trespasses," that is,
all the sin and transgression of human history. Adam went
on to his sin without any prior handicap; but his action involved such consequences that the judgment it brought on
him led to the condemnation of his whole race. But how
much greater is the action of Christ! He comes to His work
when all mankind is sunk in doom. The situation into which
He enters is anything but free from handicap. He is faced
not with the fall of one, but of the many. All that was thus
destroyed He must restore. But His grace was adequate,
not only to restore all to what it once was for Adam, so to
say, to undo all that had happened thereafter. It was also
sufficient beyond that to establish the righteousness of God
among us. From this point of view too, the blessing which
comes from Christ must be called "abounding."

But since "the grace and the free gift" do so abound,

Paul can use the terrifying consequences of the fall as an encouragement for the church. For the church can thereby see how great is the gift that has been bestowed on it. It can thus get some sense of the dimensions of the work of Christ. If the fall had such results, the abounding grace and gift must be much greater still. Therefore Paul continues, "If, because of one man's trespass, death reigned (ὁ θάνατος ἐβασίλευσεν) through that one man, much more will those who receive the abundance of grace and the free gift of righteousness reign in life (ἐν ζωῇ βασιλεύσουσιν) through the one man Jesus Christ" (vs. 17).

Paul's thought here could be expressed most simply in this way: If *the dominion of death* was great in Adam's race, *the dominion of life* shall be *much greater still* for those who are Christ's. But Paul expresses himself in another way. The reason is not hard to find. There is another difference between the dominions of death and of life which he would not pass without notice. Death is a power of destruction, a tyrant, under which man lives and in whose bondage he finds himself. And life is also a power, under which man is set by Christ; but it is not a tyrant. For him who is subject to the dominion of life, the time of bondage is past; he is free. That difference between the realms of death and of life determines Paul's formulation; it is the reason why he adopts a construction different from what we would expect. When he speaks of death, he talks only of *its* dominion; for they who are subject to that have no share in the dominion; they are simply slaves. But as to life he expresses himself differently. As to those who from Christ receive grace and the free gift of righteousness, he says that they "will reign in life." Here, too, the realm of life shows its infinite superiority.

From the foregoing it is as plain as one could wish that Paul has no idea at all that, by a comparison with Adam, he is assuring a more honorable place for Christ. He is not attempting to prove the greatness of Christ, as many a commentary has held. It is far from his thought that such a comparison could lend strength to a claim of Christ's greatness. On the contrary, he shows again and again that the comparison breaks down because Adam can in no way measure up to Christ. It is rather the case that that which can be said for Adam is much truer of Christ, and in a much higher way. It is Christ who stands first for Paul; and Adam enters only as "a type of the one who was to come."

It is good here to look back to verse 12. If we be likely to interpret its statement "because all men sinned" to mean that, according to Paul, death has its dominion over all men because they have all sinned, then we meet the direct refutation of any such interpretation in verse 17. For here it is said clearly that it was not through the fall of the many, but through the fall of one, that death reigned. This is the common fate of all the children of Adam; and the Christian shares in it, as long as he lives in this age. But it is not only in this that he shares. Through Christ he shares in the new aeon, in which life has broken through to power. But in this too it is true that it has come, not through many, but through one alone, Jesus Christ. "He who through faith is righteous shall live." But his righteousness is not his own, achieved by him. It is here spoken of as "the free gift of righteousness." But this gift, "righteousness from God," Christ has brought to us; and with this righteousness comes life. Therefore they who through faith have become members of Christ shall reign with Him in life's new aeon.

In verse 12 Paul took up his comparison between Adam

and Christ, but he got no further than the beginning. The comparison which he began with an ὥσπερ ("as"), he breaks off in an anacoluthon. And in his presentation he has called our attention much more to the contrast between Adam and Christ, rather than to resemblances between them. But now that the points where the parallel breaks down have been pointed out so carefully, Paul can return to his comparison, without fear of being misunderstood. This he does in verses 18 and 19. Here we again meet the ὥσπερ (ὡς) with which he had begun. But this time it does not stand alone; it is followed by an οὕτως. The second member of the comparison, which was missing in verse 12, we find here. Paul gathers up his comparison concisely in these words, "Then as one man's trespass led to condemnation for all men, so one man's act of righteousness leads to acquittal and life for all men. For as by one man's disobedience many were made sinners, so by one man's obedience many will be made righteous."

Despite all the limitations which Paul has indicated, the parallel between Adam and Christ has given him the chance to show clearly what significance Christ has for our justification and our participation in the dominion of life. Just as Adam's whole existence was determined by his falling away from God, i.e., by a "fall," so Christ's whole existence is determined by the fact that He stands in right relationship with God, i.e., that He in His own person is the realization of "the righteousness of God." Against Adam's παράπτωμα stands Christ's δικαίωμα. And just as the condemnation, which rests on all men in the old aeon, and the dominion of death, which reigns there, are based on the fall of one, Adam, so likewise is the righteousness of one, Christ, the basis for the justification which is now given to us in the new aeon, and for the dominion of life which reigns there. To express the blessing which is given to us through Christ, Paul uses the words δικαίωσις ζωῆς, "the justification of life."

In that concise expression Paul gathers up the whole of his message. We who "in Adam," and because of his disobedience, came to stand as sinners, have now "in Christ," and because of His obedience, come to stand before God as righteous (δίκαιοι, vs. 19). And this justification is a "justification of life," in harmony with the declaration, ὁ δίκαιος ἐκ πίστεως ζήσεται, "He who through faith is righteous *shall live*."

(3) The intervention of the law

Adam and Christ express the two great opposites in the history of mankind. Each of them stands in the forefront of his own age. What is the role of the law, in this contrast? That issue already appeared in verses 13f. Reference is made to the time "from Adam to Moses." Is it not thus that the law constituted an epoch in God's history with mankind? The condition after the law was given was essentially different from that which obtained before. And so too the condition under the law is different from that which came with Christ. It is written, "The law was given through Moses; grace and truth came through Jesus Christ" (John 1:17). Would it not follow from this that it is not enough to speak of two ages? Ought we not to distinguish three ages, ruled by the names of Adam, Moses, and Christ? This is the idea that lies behind the traditional threefold division, "without the law," "under the law," and "under grace."

But that would be, according to Paul, a complete misunderstanding of the role of the law. Adam and Christ are the opposites who rule over all. The dominion of death and the dominion of life are such total opposites that they leave place for no third. In that sense the law did *not* constitute an epoch. Paul says it has come in *beside* these two great opposites. In verse 12 he said that sin and, through sin, death "came into" the world ($\epsilon i\sigma\hat{\eta}\lambda\theta\epsilon\nu$) and "spread" to all men ($\delta\iota\hat{\eta}\lambda\theta\epsilon\nu$). Now he says about the law that it "came in," but only *beside* the other ($\pi\alpha\rho\epsilon\iota\sigma\hat{\eta}\lambda\theta\epsilon\nu$). In actual fact the law is of great moment, for it is an expression of God's holy will. But when it is seen in the perspective of the two aeons, its place in God's plan of redemption is relatively modest. It can by no means constitute an age of its own.

The law has come in between Adam and Christ, between the dominion of death and the dominion of life, between the age of sin and the age of righteousness. In what relation does it stand to these mutually antagonistic powers? The law pronounces judgment on sin and demands righteousness. It aims to set up a barrier against sin and to assist righteousness to triumph. To that extent it manifestly stands on the side of righteousness. But on the other hand, the law itself belongs to the old aeon; wherefore it is not able to call forth any genuine righteousness (cf. $\tau\dot{o}\ \dot{\alpha}\delta\acute{\nu}\nu\alpha\tau o\nu\ \tau o\hat{\nu}\ \nu\acute{o}\mu o\nu$ in 8:3). To this fact, that the law belongs to the old aeon, its impotence is due. The law can demand the good, but it cannot bring it about. But it was never God's intention that the law should be a way to righteousness and life. "For no human being will be justified in his sight by the works of the law," Paul says in 3:20; and that is intended to be not merely a recognition of man's weakness and inability to fulfill the law, but the declaration of a principle as to the function and meaning of the law. Paul always insists that there is no law which can give life (Gal. 3:21).

According to Paul, the law is God's curb against sin. But

now the peculiar thing happens that the law, whose function it was to work against sin, comes to work hand in hand
with sin. For what is the result of the coming of the law?
Has sin perhaps been diminished? Manifestly the opposite
is the case. The law has increased sin, in unprecedented degree and in several ways. Paul has already said that there
was sin in the world before the law came; "but," he adds,
"sin is not counted where there is no law" (vs. 13). The law
has the effect of increasing sin to actual "transgression"
(παράβασις). And, further, experience shows that the commandment of the law actually provokes to sin. The real result of the coming of the law then was that the fall became
greater and sin could really abound.

How shall we understand this? Has the law then had an
effect quite contrary to what God anticipated? No, says
Paul, what has been affirmed was not only the real effect of
the law, but exactly the effect that God *intended*. "The law
came in *to* (ἵνα) increase the trespass." That statement is
completely incomprehensible and seems more like a blasphemy against God and an attack on the law, as long as one
stands in the position of legalism. But to Paul, whose eyes
have been opened by faith in Christ to see that there is
something greater than the law, it is clear that the situation
is truly as stated. God has actually given the law the mission
to evoke sin and lead it to develop all its powers. There was
indeed sin before the law came in; but it lay as if dead and
inoperative. But it is God's will that, where there is sin, it
be made manifest (Gal. 3:19); and that happens when it is
confronted by the law. Then sin is revived (7:9). The law
gives sin "opportunity" and thus helps to set it free (7:8).
In what follows Paul has occasion to deal with that point at
length. For the present he contents himself with the concise

affirmation that the law came in to increase sin. That apparent paradox is explained in the next statement, "but where sin increased, grace abounded all the more."

Thereby the situation is entirely changed. If it had looked as if the law worked hand in hand with sin, it is now made clear that it works hand in hand with grace. Belonging to the old aeon, the law itself is indeed unable to overcome sin. Sin can be overcome only by Him who is stronger, by Christ. This much the law could do: it called sin into the arena of choice and enabled it to develop all its powers. But with that the mission of the law is fulfilled. From that point the battle must be taken over by grace. But through the very fact that the law enabled sin to mobilize all its powers, it did in that way contribute to its total overthrow and gave grace the greater possibility to triumph.

In the view that Paul thus gives as to the role of the law, there is entire harmony between the law and the gospel. If the law itself could overcome sin, and if righteousness and life could thus come through the law, the law would be against the promise of God. Then the law would be a way of salvation, competing with the gospel's way of salvation. But when thus misunderstood, the Law becomes a power of destruction, along with Wrath, Sin and Death. It becomes a tyrant which drives man to the fruitless attempt, with his own resources, to break the bondage of the old aeon. But thereby it only binds him more securely to the nature of the old aeon, and hinders him from accepting "the righteousness from God" which Christ brings. It keeps man from entering into the new age, the age of righteousness and life. It is this view of the law that Paul particularly opposes. Here he speaks of the law as belonging to the old aeon and apparently in the service of sin; but in actual fact the law is in concord with the gospel and contributes to its overwhelming victory by the very fact that it led sin to abound. The law as a way of salvation is nothing but an instrument of divine wrath, delivering man over to wrath. But in the true meaning, the law is a means of God's grace, for it does not keep man in its bondage, but gives him over to Christ that grace may abound all the more.

This is the way in which God brought mankind on towards the new aeon. At the beginning of that way stood the fall, which placed the whole race, as sinners, under the dominion of death. Into this situation the law entered. One might have expected that it would vanquish sin. But it rather drove sin to its supreme height. But at the same time it led on to the point where God, in Christ, revealed His overwhelming power and gave to our race a new beginning under a new head. Therein the goal is reached and God's intention is realized. That purpose of God, Paul explains in these words: "So that, as sin reigned in death, grace also might reign through righteousness to eternal life through Jesus Christ our Lord."

That is an extraordinarily expressive summary of the whole. Just as sin reigned in death, that is, in death's aeon, so now, through the new righteousness ($\delta\iota\kappa\alpha\iota\sigma\sigma\acute{\upsilon}\nu\eta$= $\delta\iota\kappa\alpha\iota\sigma\sigma\acute{\upsilon}\nu\eta$ $\theta\epsilon\sigma\hat{\upsilon}$) which God gives us in Christ, grace reigns "to eternal life," $\epsilon\iota\varsigma$ $\zeta\omega\grave{\eta}\nu$ $\alpha\iota\acute{\omega}\nu\iota\sigma\nu$. It is the life of the new aeon which has already begun here, and which shall be brought to fulfillment when Christ shall appear in glory (cf. the end of the Nicene Creed: "And I look for the resurrection of the dead and the life of the world [aeon] to come" $\zeta\omega\grave{\eta}\nu$ $\tau\sigma\hat{\upsilon}$ $\mu\acute{\epsilon}\lambda\lambda\sigma\nu\tau\sigma\varsigma$ $\alpha\iota\hat{\omega}\nu\sigma\varsigma$).

This chapter, like the next three, Paul closes with the words "through Jesus Christ our Lord." But it is for him not a merely formal ending. It is an expression of utmost importance. Paul cannot conclude any of these chapters in which he says how we are freed from the powers of destruction, without affirming that this liberation is given to us through Jesus Christ alone. Only through the fact that God sent Him as our Lord, our Kyrios, have all other lordships been overthrown. In the last verse of this chapter Paul twice uses the verb "reigned." This is the idea which has stood at the center of the whole discussion about Adam and Christ. The Greek word which is here used, βασιλεύειν, directs our thought immediately to the kingdom of God of which Jesus spoke, βασιλεία θεοῦ. It is this "kingdom of God" or "dominion of God" of which Paul speaks, when he sets the reign of life over against the reign of death. And in this kingdom of God, the reign of life, Jesus is *"Lord."*

VII

Free from Sin

6:1-23

The part of Romans with which we are now dealing discusses how he who through faith is righteous *shall live*. He who believes in Christ has, through Him, entered into the new age and now lives his life "in Christ." But what, exactly, does that mean?

In chapter 5 Paul gave his first answer to that question: He who through faith is righteous has, in Christ, been "freed from wrath." In the latter part of the chapter Paul let his view take in the two ages, the aeon of death under Adam and the aeon of life under Christ. Now in chapter 6 he returns to his central problem, and adds another answer: He who through faith is righteous shall live *"free from sin."*

The discussion in this chapter falls into two parts. The division between them is clear at first glance, from the fact that Paul lets each part begin with almost the same question. In verse 1 we read, "What shall we say then? Are we to continue in sin that grace may abound?" And in verse 15 we read, "What then? Are we to sin?" In the first part Paul shows that through baptism we have been incorporated into Christ and are thereby set free from the dominion of sin (1-14). In the second part he shows how this freedom from sin has been given to us, that we may thereafter serve righteousness (15-23).

1. FREE FROM SIN THROUGH BAPTISM
6:1-14

In the latter part of the preceding chapter Paul said, "Law came in, to increase the trespass; but where sin increased, grace abounded all the more." There Paul said that the role of the law was to increase sin. But at the same time the law is set into relationship with grace, for where sin is increased by the law, there grace has the opportunity to abound the more. Paul's thought here is quite different from that which is customary when the attempt is made to show a positive relation between the law and grace. It is usually said that the law prepares for grace and leads on to it, because only he who tries to fulfill the demands of the law can count on receiving God's grace and favor. In this sense one hears about "morality as the way to religion." Or a more psychological explanation is given, which says that the law empties man of all that is his own and thereby makes room for grace; it makes man humble, and therefore receptive to grace. But, as we have said, the view of the law which Paul gave in the foregoing is quite different: the law increases sin and misery, but thereby the mercy of God is appealed to the more. The grace of God is mighty not only in man's weakness, but also in man's sin. And the greater sin is, the more grace can triumph.

"Where sin increased, grace abounded all the more." That is a true and inescapable word; but it is also a perilous word. We are moving close to an abyss—one step to the side, and all that Paul has won, by what has preceded, can be lost. For it would be easy to conclude that, if what Paul

says is true, then for us to sin is a very simple way to grace.
So it would look as if the whole matter rests in our own
hands, though in a way contrary to what we used to think.
Sin seems to be the cause of the action of grace. So the
question arises, "Are we to continue in sin that grace may
abound?"

Already in 3:8 Paul had met a similar question, "Why
not do evil that good may come?" Then it was the truthfulness of God which was under consideration; it appeared
the more clearly through our falseness. Now the question
has to do with God's grace, which abounds the more through
our sin. Again Paul rejects the suggestion, as he did on the
former occasion. "By no means!" But what reason does he
give? Strikingly enough, he points to the new aeon and
what has taken place in it. Through Christ we have been
freed from sin once for all. With Him we have passed out
of the relationship in which sin reigns; so Paul can say,
"How can we who died to sin still live in it?" (vs. 2). Thus
Paul's chief argument against the suggestion is this: *through
Christ we have been set free from sin.*

In fuller exposition of this, Paul refers first to *baptism.*
He who has been baptized into Christ has thereby been received into a real fellowship of death and life with Him.
Here we again have use for what Paul said at the close of
the fifth chapter, when he set Adam and Christ in juxtaposition; for only against that background can we understand
what he says here about baptism.

"In Adam" we all belonged to the same organism. As
human beings we are members of *one* body, which, through
its head, Adam, stands under the reign of sin and death.
That which is true of the head is also true of each member

of the body. All participate in Adam's sin and in Adam's death

But now, through baptism, we have been incorporated into Christ. That means that we are henceforth not merely members in the great organism of humanity; we are members in "the body of Christ" (σῶμα Χριστοῦ). "By *one* Spirit we were all baptized into *one* body" (I Cor. 12:13). Then that which is true of Him who is the head and the chief is true of us, when we have become part of that body. Christ's death is our death, and Christ's resurrection is our resurrection. It is of this fellowship of death and life with Christ, established through baptism, that Paul speaks when he says, "Do you not know that all of us who have been baptized into Christ Jesus were baptized into his death? We were buried therefore with him by baptism into death, so that as Christ was raised from the dead by the glory of the Father, we too might walk in newness of life" (vss. 3-4).

It is immediately evident that in these words Paul makes reference to the external form of the rite of baptism. When he who is baptized is immersed in the water, the act signifies burial "with Christ"; and when he again comes up out of the water, that signifies resurrection "with Christ." But it would be an utter misinterpretation if, for that reason, one were to characterize Paul's view of baptism as "symbolical," in the sense in which that word is generally used. For, according to Paul, in baptism we have to do with realities, not merely with symbolical representations. That which baptism symbolizes also actually *happens*, and precisely through baptism. For the very purpose of pointing out this real fact in baptism, Paul uses the forceful words "we have been united" with Christ, "in a death like his and . . . a resurrection like his" (vs. 5). The verb is chosen with the thought that we were not formerly members in Christ's body; but we became such through baptism and henceforth belong inseparably with the Head. Or, to use another, kindred way of saying it, the verb is chosen with the thought that we are branches which did not formerly belong to Christ, the vine; but we were ingrafted into the vine and have been united with it in growth, so that we are henceforth a part of the vine and derive our nourishment and strength from it.

"We died to sin," says Paul (vs. 2). When and how did that take place? It happened in and through baptism, according to the apostle. Therein the Christian died with Christ, and was buried with Him; and furthermore, he therein also arose with Him. To understand what that signifies as to the status of the Christian, we must remember what it was that took place through the death and resurrection of Christ. In the death of Christ the regnant power of sin was broken; all the dominions and powers of the old aeon were cast down. And in the resurrection of Christ the new aeon began. Since the Christian shares in the death and resurrection of Christ, all of this is also true of him: he has been delivered from the dominion of darkness and transferred to the kingdom of Christ (Col. 1:13).

But now that he lives "in Christ" and belongs to "the body of Christ," there is another body that must die. Paul speaks of it expressively as the "body of sin" (τὸ σῶμα τῆς ἁμαρτίας); it is this body to which man formerly belonged, when he was under the dominion of sin and death. Beside this, Paul introduces another closely related concept, when he speaks of "the old man," ὁ παλαιὸς ἄνθρωπος. This fits definitely into his view of the two aeons. "The old man" is the man who belongs to "the old aeon" and is characterized by its nature. As to this "old man" it is said that he has been

crucified with Christ (συνεσταυρώθη). For "we know that
our old self was crucified with him so that the sinful body
might be destroyed, and we might no longer be enslaved to
sin" (vs. 6).

This crucifying of the old man, this destroying of the
sinful body, is, however, only the negative side of baptism.
It is that of which Paul says, "We have been united with
him in a *death* like his." But baptism also has its positive
side; we are also "united with him in a *resurrection* like his."
Through baptism the place of "the old man" has been taken
by "the new man," by the man who belongs to "the new
aeon" and is characterized by its nature. To be sure, Paul
does not here use the precise expression "the new man," ὁ
καινὸς ἄνθρωπος; but he speaks with full clarity about the
fact. There is even a glint of the term itself when he says,
"So that as Christ was raised from the dead by the glory of
the Father, we too might walk *in newness of life,*" ἐν καινότητι
ζωῆς. Those last words have seemed difficult to many, leaving them uncertain as to the correct meaning. But if we look
at them in their context, these words reveal an exceptionally
simple and clear intention, just as they stand. The matter
of which they speak is *the nature and manner of the life
which belongs to the new aeon.* Through baptism we have
been received into the new age, which began in the resurrection of Christ. He who has been baptized into Christ has
been incorporated into Him; he is "in Christ." II Corinthians 5:17 is the best conceivable commentary on the point
under discussion. "If any one is in Christ, he is a new creation; the old has passed away, behold, the new has come."
He who, through baptism, is in Christ is a new creation, a
new man, formed according to the nature of the new aeon.
All the old, which belonged to the dominion of death, has

passed away. Now he lives and acts ἐν καινότητι ζωῆς, "in newness of life," in the nature which corresponds to the resurrection aeon, the aeon of life.

The central thought for Paul, when he speaks of baptism, is thus *the participation of the baptized in the death and resurrection of Christ.* But by that we are confronted with a significant problem.

From the study of comparative religions, we know the role played, in the Greek mystery religions, by the concept of deity that dies and returns again to life. Those religions said that man's salvation consisted in the fact that, by an act of mystic union with the god, man became a sharer in the god's death and resurrection. That was the end sought through the initiations and cultic rites of the mystery religions. From this fact some scholars—particularly a couple of decades ago—arrived at the theory that Paul took over this whole idea from the Hellenistic world, and passed it on in what he said about the Christian's participation in the death and resurrection of Christ. It was thought that we could, in large measure, identify Paul's view with the other, and use this other as a means of understanding the apostle.

It is not to be denied that that study did make real contribution to the understanding of Paul's thought, particularly his manner of expression and his thought-forms. There is no doubt that he made use of words and idioms which were current in the surrounding Hellenism. But it would nevertheless be a most serious mistake to conclude therefore that the content of his thought was of the same type as that which characterized these mystery religions. The truth is quite the opposite. We meet the contrast at almost every point. It is enough to give a single illustration. The mystery religions thought of a mystic union with the god. But in

what Paul says about participation in the death and resurrection of Christ, there is not even a trace of mysticism.
We really obscure Paul's thought if we speak of his "Christ-
mysticism." Here we get great help from the parallel
between Adam and Christ. Paul says that humanity participates in Adam's sin and death; but in Paul's thought there
is certainly no "Adam-mysticism." That participation is not
mediated by any mystical experience of oneness. It rests
on the fact that our race stands in organic unity with Adam,
the head of the race. In like manner, we participate in
Christ. There is no idea at all of a mystical experience of
unity. Such a concept belongs to a thought-world quite different from Paul's. Nor is the meaning that the Christian
immerses himself in contemplation of the death and resurrection of Christ, until he is so at one with them that he
knows Christ's death as his own death and Christ's resurrection as his also. So to understand Paul is to misunderstand him. The truth is not that, through some endeavor on
our part, Christ and that which happened in Him are to be
introduced into our lives. The truth is rather that, by God's
action, we are included in and made sharers of that which
befell Christ. That of which Paul speaks is a simple and un-
mystical reality. God has made Christ the head of a new
humanity; and into that new organic relationship he has
brought us through baptism.

But just what does Paul understand by this participation
in Christ's death and resurrection? The problems raised by
that question are not insignificant.

Some have suggested that Paul here affirms a "contemporaneousness," a "paradoxical contemporaneousness" between Christ and one who believes in Him. Indeed, it has
been suggested that the category of time, belonging only

to the old aeon, plays no role in the new aeon. But such an interpretation is not true to Paul. Paul has not ceased to take time into account. He knows very well that Christ died at a precise point in human history, and that a certain period of time had elapsed between that event and the date when Paul writes this epistle to the Romans. It is no challenging problem for him that believing Christians were not contemporaneous with Christ. The death and resurrection of Christ do not need to be "contemporary" with a Christian to be able to bring their blessing to him. Here too the parallel between Adam and Christ can show us the way. I am not, according to Paul, "contemporary" with Adam; and yet I stand in relation with him and bear the condemnation which comes from him. And we can add that already through him, through his action, it was determined that I even now, should stand under the dominion of sin and death. We are indeed remote from each other in time. That fact is not abolished; but neither are the results of his actions on me abolished. The same is true as to life "in Christ." The separation in time does not prevent me from being, even now, a real member in "the body of Christ," in σῶμα Χριστοῦ; and as such I share in His death and resurrection.

Another explanation suggests that this sharing or fellowship must be understood exclusively as a fellowship with the exalted, spiritual Christ. Behind such a suggestion there generally lies a spiritualizing tendency. Particularly if one understands this fellowship as a relationship "with the Lord exalted above space and time" does he clash with Paul's meaning. Paul thinks definitely of a relationship with a specific man, Jesus Christ, who lived on earth, suffered under Pontius Pilate, was crucified, dead, and buried; and on the third day rose again from the dead. It is with Him that we, through baptism, have been incorporated; and what we share with Him is just that which befell Him during His life on earth, in time and space. Our "old man" has been crucified with Him; we have been baptized into His death; and thereby we have been buried with Him. But in baptism we have also been "united with him in a resurrection like his" to "walk in newness of life."

Paul has here spoken fully about baptism and its meaning. But we should not forget that that is not the main theme of this chapter. When he entered upon this point it was not primarily to give an explanation of baptism. The reason for the discussion was the question, "Are we to continue in sin that grace may abound?" The strongest answer with which he could meet that question was precisely by referring to baptism and what happens through it. There we died, with Christ, from the old aeon and all that belongs to it. But sin belongs with just that from which we have died. So he says, "How can we who died to sin still live in it?" Furthermore, Christ did not suffer and remain in its power; He has arisen to a new life. And that too is included in our fellowship with Him. We died to sin, that we might live His life, the life of the new age, "that we might walk in newness of life."

That thought has been present with Paul all the time he has been speaking of baptism. Now he goes back to the point with which he started. If our "old man" has been crucified and our "sinful body" destroyed, the inevitable result is that we shall "no longer be enslaved to sin" (vs. 6). The basis on which all rests is this: through Christ we have been made *free from sin.*

In what sense can Paul say of the Christian that he is free from sin? During the last half-century, theology has made that question the object of much study; and theologians have come to widely diverse answers. One notable interpretation has energetically asserted that Paul makes himself the champion for a forthright doctrine of *sinlessness*. In support of this view, its advocates have referred particularly to this chapter, with its clear and pointed declaration that the Christian is totally "free from sin." This declaration has been understood in this way. Paul is persuaded that the life of the Christian is so transformed that there can no longer be any place for sin. At Damascus he himself had experienced a total break with his earlier life. From that moment the old life had been for him a thing of the past, and something absolutely new had taken its place. Under the impression that Christ would soon come again, Paul, in "splendid optimism" and "mighty doctrinairism," had generalized his own personal experience and supposed that, for all Christians, sin belonged to the irrevocable past. According to him, the nature of the Christian is so completely changed that he cannot sin any more. This interpretation, then, says that according to Paul, the Christian, from the time of his conversion, is able to live his life without sin or fault, and that in normal circumstances he is a sinless man.

Of course it has been impossible for men not to see that Paul utters many warnings to Christians and admonishes them to battle against sin. So he clearly recognizes that sin is a possibility in the life of the Christian, indeed, is a reality as to which the Christian must ever be active. How is that to be reconciled with the averred sinlessness? Men have attempted to meet the issue by distinguishing between theory and practice, between the ideal and the real. It is said that, in theory, Paul defends the idea of the Christian's sinlessness; but in practice it cannot be maintained. The ideal is that for the Christian there can be no sin; but when Paul looks at the actual situation within the churches, he cannot fail to see that the fact is quite different, for there is much sin. It is then that he changes from idealizing indicatives to commands and admonitions.

We are here confronted with a problem of utmost importance for the understanding of Paul's view: *Does Paul anywhere assert that the Christian is sinless? Does he ever affirm a doctrine of sinlessness?*

To begin with, it must be stressed with all earnestness that Paul actually means that the Christian is *"free from sin."* That is a declaration which permits no limitation at all. To believe in Christ is to pass out of the reign of sin and enter into the reign of righteousness. It is not true to Paul's thought when it is said, as it often is, that he who through faith is righteous is actually free from sin's guilt, but not from its power. These two cannot thus be separated, according to Paul's view; and when he says "free from sin," he means especially that the Christian is free from sin's power.

But it is equally clear that the view stated above, which sees in this chapter a doctrine of sinlessness, is totally wrong. That that interpretation cannot be sustained can at once be seen from the fact that his indicative declarations and his imperative admonitions stand side by side. Paul has no sense of tension between them. On the contrary, the one rests on the other. The indicative and the imperative do not clash. It is not the case that Paul turns to exhortations when he cannot sustain his declarations. Quite the reverse, the imperative is spoken because the indicative is true. Just because Paul can say to the Christians, "You are dead to sin" (vs. 11), and only because he can say that, he can also say, "Let not sin therefore reign in your mortal bodies, to make you obey their passions" (vs. 12). He does not say that we ought properly to be "free from sin," but since, alas, it is evident that such is not the case, I must admonish you to fight against sin. He rather says: you actually are "free from sin"; *therefore* fight against sin, stand against it!

The fact of the matter is that "free from sin" and "sinless" are two very different things. If one were to ask Paul whether the Christian is "free from sin," he would answer with an unconditional affirmative. Were one further to ask him whether the Christian is "sinless," he would answer with an unconditional negative. Wherein lies the difference? Clearly in the fact that two different concepts of sin underlie these two expressions. The idea of sinlessness springs from a moralistic view of sin. It regards sin as a moral misstep which, it thinks, the Christian has been enabled to avoid by his new spiritual state, by the new "habitus" of the soul, given to him through his conversion. By means of this new possession man can become a pattern of virtue, in whom moral lapses are no longer found. But when Paul says that the Christian is "free from sin," he is speaking about something entirely different. To him sin is not basically separate moral missteps; but *sin is a power under whose bondage man lives.* It is to set forth this character of Sin as a hostile *power* that we capitalize the word. In this way we may be helped to escape a moralistic view of sin which seems to be hard to root out. That the Christian is "free from sin" means to Paul that by Christ sin is cast down from its throne. His thought is not at all that we in ourselves come to mastery over sin, so that it is less and less evident in us as we gradually grow toward sinlessness. Freedom from sin is rather a fruit of the work of Christ; it is by Him that sin is cast down and vanquished. He who believes in Christ no longer lives under the dominion of sin. He has found another Lord, to whom he stands in obedience.

Herein lies the reason why Paul can speak so unreservedly about the Christian's freedom from sin. If he had his mind fixed on the individual and his moral achievements, no "grand optimism of faith" and no "mighty doctrinairism" could have so beclouded his judgment that he would have proclaimed the Christian's sinlessness. But since his mind is fixed on what has happened through Christ, he can say with full confidence that he who is justified through Christ is "free from sin." There are no limitations in the victory which Christ has won. In the death of Christ sin suffered the definitive loss of its right to rule. "The death he died he died to sin, once for all, but the life he lives he lives to God" (vs. 10).

This also sheds light on the immediately preceding verses, "For he who has died is freed from sin. But if we have died with Christ, we believe that we shall also live with him. For we know that Christ being raised from the dead will never die again; death no longer has dominion over him" (vss. 7-9).

Men have found particular difficulty with the statement that "he who has died is freed from sin." It has seemed foreign to Paul's context; so it has been looked upon as a current saying that he took up and used here. It has even been called "a foreign element." But certainly the difficulty has been greatly exaggerated. For the truth is that this statement fits well into the context, if only it is rightly understood. Whenever Paul speaks of sin in this chapter, he thinks of sin as a *power*, as a *ruler*. He is far from the view that sees in sin an incidental expression of man's free will. Sin is not a matter which is at the disposal of man's freedom, so that he can assent to it one time and withhold assent another. When sin is viewed as a *power*, that means that it is not man who rules over sin, but sin who rules over him. "Every one who commits sin is a slave to sin," he is δοῦλος τῆς ἁμαρτίας. These words in John 8:34 express exactly Paul's view of the relation between sinful man and sin. Man is the slave, and sin is lord. And when it is asked how Paul thinks man can be freed from this bondage, we can quote further from the passage in John, "If the Son makes you free, you will be free indeed" (ἐλεύθεροι ἔσεσθε). Christ, who is the stronger, has conquered the strong, and taken his prey from him. Sin no longer has any authority or rule over those who through faith belong to Christ. It has lost its right to those who have died with Christ and risen again with Him. They have thereby been "freed from sin" (ἐλεύθεροι ἀπὸ τῆς ἁμαρτίας, ἐλευθερωθέντες ἀπὸ τῆς ἁμαρτίας, vss. 18, 22). Through God's judgment of justification, which is at the same time an act of justification, they have been freed from their position of subordination to sin. They are rightly released from service to sin, no longer standing under the tyrant's dominion.

Here is the meaning of the expression that at first glance seems peculiar, δεδικαίωται ἀπὸ τῆς ἁμαρτίας. It is not a "foreign element" which happened to be used here, though alien to the setting. It says just what Paul intended to say here. It says that he who has died with Christ is thereby set free from his obligation to serve the ruler, sin. We meet quite a parallel expression in the beginning of chapter 7, where Paul says that through Christ we die unto the law. When one, by attention to the context, in which an alleged "foreign element" is found, can show that the statement in question is an integral part of Paul's course of thought, that fact is in a certain measure an evidence that our interpretation is correct.

The expression we are considering is also of special interest because it shows how close justification and deliverance are, in Paul's thought. The entire line of thought in the first eight chapters of Romans could be summed up in this way: Since we are thus justified through faith, we are free from Wrath, Sin, the Law, and Death. "Since we are justified by faith" summarizes the first four chapters (cf. how Paul uses them in that way, in 5:1); and "free from Wrath, Sin, the Law, and Death," summarizes the next four. But this does not mean that justification is one thing and deliverance from these hostile powers another. Justification *is* at the same time liberation from these tyrants. They who believe in Christ are "justified by faith" and "justified from sin." They are δικαιωθέντες ἐκ πίστεως and δικαιωθέντες ἀπὸ τῆς ἁμαρτίας, that is, ἐλευθερωθέντες ἀπὸ τῆς ἁμαρτίας (vss. 18, 22).

Paul's starting point is a *fact*. The Christian has been baptized. Through baptism he is made a member of Christ. But that fact is not something which belongs only to the past; its results reach on throughout life. If Christ died to sin once for all and now lives His life for God, and if through baptism the Christian has been incorporated into Christ, he must have regard to that fact through the rest of his life. He may not live as if it never happened. Paul commands him to remember this fact and to draw the proper consequences therefrom. "So you also must consider yourselves dead to sin and alive to God in Christ Jesus" (vs. 11).

Here the realistic character of Paul's thinking is evident. When it is said of the Christian that he is "free from sin," it might easily be thought to mean that henceforth he lives his life in a sphere exalted above the circumstances of ordinary life; that sin and temptations no longer give him any trouble. But Paul has not fallen into any such starry-eyed idealism:

that becomes entirely clear in the verses that follow. Paul
knows that the battle continues. The Christian ever finds
himself on the front line, between the forces that fight
against each other. The outpost which he occupies is always
exposed to sin's attack. In measured terms Paul describes
the Christian's position between the contending parties: "Let
not sin therefore reign in your mortal bodies, to make you
obey their passions. Do not yield your members to sin as
instruments of wickedness, but yield yourselves to God as
men who have been brought from death to life, and your
members to God as instruments of righteousness" (vss. 12,
13).

The Christian has been "brought from death to life."
Formerly his outpost was situated in enemy territory where
death was in power. But now it has been captured and included in life's domain. Formerly he was the slave of sin,
but now through Christ he is "free from sin." And this newly
won freedom he is commanded to use to fight earnestly
against sin. Here it becomes very clear how fundamentally
they have misunderstood Paul, who think there is a tension
between his proclamation that the Christian is "free from
sin" and his admonitions to fight against sin. How could
man fight against sin, as long as he is the slave of sin and
bound in its service? Only after he is freed by Christ from
his captivity can he belong to the army whose mission it is
to fight sin.

A Christian lives "in Christ" (ἐν Χριστῷ Ἰησοῦ vs. 11).
Thereby he has come over on God's side in the battle. He is
"alive to God," as we read in verse 11. In his own person he
represents an actual factor which has been transferred from
the sphere of power of sin and death. Then it would seem
to be a self-evident consequence—so self-evident that it

should hardly be necessary to point it out—that we must "not let sin reign in our mortal bodies." Yet Paul considers it necessary to say it; and he has his reasons. If the Christian's life could be determined exclusively by the fact that he lives "in Christ," such an admonition would be superfluous. But the Christian's situation is more complicated than that. He really does live "in Christ," and so he is a member in "the body of Christ"; but at the same time he lives "in the flesh" (Gal. 2:20), and so is a member of Adam, of the body of the old fallen humanity. Here sin still has its hold on him; it seeks to regain control of that which it has lost, that it may have man in its power. It is definitely not superfluous to give the Christian the admonition, "Let not sin reign in your mortal bodies, to make you obey their passions."

In another way Paul shows how realistically he views the present status of the Christian. He speaks of how the Christian's life is "hid with Christ in God" (Col. 3:3). But that is not a reason for him to turn away from mundane reality, as if that has nothing to do with our life with God. On the contrary, the arena of our battle is in the world, in our mortal bodies. It is these "members" of ours, which were formerly enlisted in the service of sin and used by it as weapons of unrighteousness (ὅπλα ἀδικίας) which are now to be enlisted in God's service as weapons of righteousness (ὅπλα δικαιοσύνης). There is in Paul none of that familiar spiritualizing and superspirituality. He contends earnestly that our mundane life is the place where we must serve God. It is here that sin makes its attack, and it is here that it must be resisted. "Let not sin therefore reign in your mortal bodies, to make you obey their passions." If sin gets a foothold here, there is soon an end to the Christian's "freedom from sin."

Paul closes this section with a word of encouragement,

"Sin will have no dominion over you, since you are not under law but under grace" (vs. 14). These words contain, at the same time, both an explanation and an assurance. This is the explanation: Since Christ is our Lord, our κύριος, sin is no longer to have lordship over us (οὐ κυριεύσει). But there is also an assurance: Sin will not regain its dominion over you. Why not? Paul replies, "Since you are not under law." As long as we live under the law, there can be no talk of freedom from sin. Paul has expressed himself as to the function of the law in 5:20. The law came in "to increase the trespass." To live under the law is to be bound to sin, in the highest degree, and to stand under its dominion. In I Corinthians 15:56 Paul can say explicitly that it is the law which gives sin its strength (ὁ δύναμις τῆς ἁμαρτίας ὁ νόμος). Like sin, the law belongs to the old aeon. Through Christ we have departed therefrom, and been freed from all the destructive powers that rule there. After Christ has become our Lord, we are no longer under the law, but under grace. And to live under grace is to be "free from sin."

At the same time that this is a word of encouragement to the Christian, who is ever in the fight against sin, this is also the final answer to the question with which the chapter began: "Are we to continue in sin that grace may abound?" That question was legalism's criticism of Paul. When it heard what he said about grace, it could understand it only as indulgence of sin. But Paul has now come to his reply: The law binds man, but grace makes him "free from sin."

2. FREE FROM SIN TO SERVE RIGHTEOUSNESS
6:15-23

In the earlier half of this chapter Paul has given final rejection to the idea raised in its opening question, "Are we to continue in sin that grace may abound?" He has shown the absurdity of such an idea. That which is characteristic of the Christian is rather the very fact that he is free from sin. He has died to sin. How can he then live in it? It does not seem necessary to add anything else. The matter is left in no uncertainty.

But now Paul surprises us by again taking up the same issue almost from the beginning. He asks, "What then? Are we to sin because we are not under law but under grace?" (vs. 15). At first glance the question seems superfluous to us. But Paul knows how difficult it is to bring men to understand a consistent preaching of grace; and especially to keep them from drawing false conclusions from it. Especially perilous seems the statement that we are not under the law, with which he concluded the preceding discussion. The law is surely the force that opposes sin, forbidding it and attempting to keep it within bounds. If we now say that the Christian is "free from sin," and is to fight against it, but at the same time add that he is also "free from the law" and no longer under its dominion, is not the actual result only this, that we break down the condemnations which keep sin within bounds, and give sin free rein? Whatever one may say about the law, that sin can find occasion in it, it is after all primarily the law which God has set up against sin. If the law is then voided, what is there left that can effectively stand up against sin? Paul himself has said that there was sin in the world before there was any law, but sin is not counted where there is no law (5:13). Even if the law is not able to prevent sin, it has at least the result that man must take sin seriously. Where there is no law, sin can be considered a relatively guiltless trifle; but when man is set under God's holy law, such a possibility vanishes. He cannot

but see that sin is something frightfully serious, for which
he must give account. The law has the effect that, when
man sins, he does so with bad conscience. But when he is
no longer under the law, it would seem that the result could
easily be that he continues in sin, but now he does so with
good conscience, so to say. There is no longer any to accuse
or condemn him. Even if he sins, he stands under grace
anyway, and he always has access to God's forgiveness.

But is that really what comes of Paul's preaching? If so,
the condemnation of it would be inescapable. So it is not
surprising that Paul is not ready to turn away from the
question, after a single discussion of it. He is clearly right.
If this matter is to be made clear, one must not hesitate to
take it up again and again for discussion, that light may
continually be shed on it from new approaches.

And Paul has still another reason for discussing this question further. For if the above inferences were correct, exactly
the same condemnation would rest on his position as he
directed against the Jews for their trust in the fact that they
were God's people. When the Jew says, "Even if we sin, we
are still Thine," and when he expects God to judge his sin
differently from that of the Gentiles, Paul rejects that belief
by saying, "God shows no partiality" (2:11). But now it
can be asked whether the Christian—who is not under the
law, but under grace, and who therefore does not have to
take sin so seriously—does not come disturbingly close to
the position of the Jew. Does he not, like the Jew, expect
God to show him partiality? The Jew puts his confidence in
the law; and the Christian puts his in grace. But, despite
the differences, is not the case fundamentally the same with
both? Both expect God to show partiality to them because
they are His.

So it is not a fictitious problem that Paul here discusses. It is a problem which inevitably arises out of his insistence that the Christian is not under the law. Indeed we can go one step further and say that that issue is already implicit in the statement that, through Christ, sin has been cast down from its position of power. The very fact that the Christian considers himself "free from sin" may lead him to take sin less seriously. Sin no longer has power and the right of command over him. If he does happen to yield, that need not have tragic consequences for him, as long as he is under the dominion of grace. That that is not merely a concocted thought can be seen from many a case in church history. We could think particularly of the position of Gnosticism on this matter. A Gnostic, as a "spiritual" man, is "free from sin" permanently. Sin no longer has any part in him; in the inner man he is clean and undefiled. So sin has ceased to be a danger for him. He no longer has to take it seriously. Henceforth it can do no more than put its spots on the outward man; but it is not the outward that is of ultimate importance. "For as gold which is cast into the dirt does not lose its beauty, but maintains its own nature, because the dirt cannot injure it, so they suffer no harm and do not lose their spiritual nature, by any acts at all which they do. Therefore even the most perfect among them do, without fear, everything that is forbidden" (Irenaeus, *Contra haeres* I, chap. 2). In that way the Gnostics can draw libertinism out of their sinlessness.

It is against such distortions and false conclusions from his proclamation that the Christian is "free from sin," that Paul here protects himself. And he must do so for two different reasons. Here too, as often, he has to fight on two fronts. On the one hand, he has to stand against those who seriously think that they can draw such conclusions from his proclamation of the gospel, and use their freedom for their own ends. He must repulse such pretended disciples, who actually seize his proclamation of grace, but only to make laxity out of grace. But on the other hand, he must also withstand those who take a diametrically opposite position, who so misconstrue his position, because they can thereby the better maintain their legalism. Here they who hold to the law (οἱ ἐκ νόμου) play their biggest trump. They can point to Paul's statement that the Christian is free from the law, and say that, according to Paul, it makes no difference how people live, since it is only the law that is concerned about that; but he has done away with the law, so that the only thing that matters is that one stands under grace, for it gives him assurance that his sins will no longer be considered sins, but are forgiven by God.

What does Paul have to say against that? Here, as in the beginning of the chapter, he rejects the position with "By no means!" (μὴ γένοιτο). But he must here do more than point out that the Christian is "free from sin"; for the idea "free from" is too negative for the present purpose. The positive complement must be advanced, if he is to avoid just such misinterpretation as he is right now in the process of rejecting. That is what he now gives, as he says that the Christian is *free from sin to serve righteousness.*

Only when this positive complement has been added does the expression "free from sin" have unequivocal significance; it is thereby differentiated from a "freedom" which would leave scope for sin. Paul knows well that man can never be free in an absolute sense. He knows that even when man considers himself free and his own master, he is actually a servant; and the power which he serves is undoubtedly sin. It is quite characteristic of bondage to sin, that he who lives in it thinks himself free and his own master. If freedom from sin means nothing more than just freedom, the result really is that man is still under the dominion ot sin and more securely bound in its thralldom. One may remember the words of Jesus, "When the unclean spirit has gone out of a man, he passes through waterless places seeking rest, but he finds none. Then he says, 'I will return to my house from which I came.' And when he comes he finds it empty, swept, and put in order. Then he goes and brings with him seven other spirits more evil than himself, and they enter and dwell there; and the last state of that man becomes worse than the first" (Matt. 12:43-45). An empty, unqualified freedom gives sin its best chance to get man under its dominion. For the Christian the throne from which sin has been removed is never left unoccupied. That place has been taken by righteousness.

When Paul speaks ot the Christian's freedom—freedom from sin and freedom from law—one must note how constantly he fights on both of the fronts recently mentioned: against legalism and against libertinism, that is, against legalistic bondage and against false freedom to do anything at all. An outstanding example of this double battle is found in the fifth chapter of Galatians. Its first verse says, "For freedom Christ has set us free; stand fast therefore, and do not submit again to a yoke of slavery." That is said *against legalism.* It is seriously meant that the Christian is *free.* That is the gift which Christ has won for him. Under no circumstances must the Christian let himself be robbed of that. But later in the chapter we read, "You were called to freedom, brethren; only do not use your freedom as an opportunity for the flesh." That is said *against libertinism,* against the false freedom to do anything at all.

Paul takes position on the same fronts here. The Christian is "free from sin," and he is so just because he is not under the law, but under grace. On that Paul insists, with utmost emphasis, against every sort of legalism. But he is not championing an unqualified freedom; so he adds that this freedom is given to the Christian that he may serve righteousness. Thus he closes the door against all false conclusions of a libertinist tendency.

The idea that man could be free, in the sense that he can be lord of his own life, is nothing but a chimera. To live in service to one power or another is a position from which man can never escape. The only question is *which* power he serves, the power of sin or the power of righteousness. Freedom from the one means service of the other, and service of the one precludes service of the other. When it is said about the Christian that, through Christ, he is "free from sin," that does not mean that he is free, in an absolute sense; it means rather that he is committed to the service of righteousness. And therein we have the definitive answer to the question of the Christian's status as to sin: He is in the service of righteousness; how could he at the same time be in the service of sin, which is the opposite of righteousness? "Do you not know that if you yield yourselves to any one as obedient slaves, you are slaves of the one whom you obey, either of sin, which leads to death, or of obedience, which leads to righteousness?" (vs. 16). There is no middle ground; if one lives in service to righteousness, he is by that very fact *not* in the service of sin. One could express Paul's thought by the words of Jesus, "No one can serve two masters; for either he will hate the one and love the other, or he will be devoted to the one and despise the other" (Matt.

6:24). None can serve both righteousness and sin.

When Paul, speaking of the two powers, in the service of one of which each of us is, says that the service of the one excludes service to the other, he uses the word "obedience" to designate that power which stands over against sin. We should probably have expected him to speak of the opposition between sin and God, of service to sin or service to God. That was the contrast with which he was dealing in the first half of this chapter: Christ died to sin, but lives to God (vs. 10); so we also must consider ourselves dead to sin and alive to God (vs. 11); so we must not yield our members to serve sin, but we and our members must serve God (vs. 13). The fact of course is that it is of this same contrast that Paul is still speaking. But it is to point out the more sharply the impossibility of serving both that he now uses "obedience" to express the opposition to sin. Sin is by nature disobedience to God. How then could one possibly serve God and sin at the same time? One cannot simultaneously obey God and disobey Him. The only drawback to using "obey" for this purpose is the fact that, immediately preceding this, he has used the same word to express man's dependency to the power under whose sway he lives, whether that be God or sin. Indeed, after he now uses "obedience" for the present purpose, he goes back to "instruments of righteousness" to designate service to God.

It is customary to understand Paul to be referring here to a choice that man has. He does not have any absolute freedom, of course. It is not within his choice whether he will be his own master, or serve one or another of the powers mentioned. He is not asked whether he will be master or servant. As to that, his sole possibility is to obey another. But, it is said, it is for him to choose *whom* he will obey, sin

or righteousness, sin or God. At this point, it is held, the
decision lies in man's own hands. But when he has made
his choice, inescapable consequences follow therefrom. If
he chooses sin, he becomes the slave of sin; if he chooses
righteousness, he must accept the consequences of that
choice and live a righteous and holy life. This is supposed
to be what Paul means to say to Christians: You have made
your choice to serve God and righteousness; now let your
manner of life show that you are in earnest.

But such an interpretation is by no means true to Paul's
meaning. He is not talking at all about such a choice. There
was a time when his readers were the servants of sin, and
traveling the way that leads to death. But now they live
under another master, righteousness. But Paul does not
praise *them* for having made a better and happier choice;
he thanks *God* for taking them out of the old bondage.
"Thanks be to God, that you who were once slaves of sin
have become obedient from the heart to the standard of
teaching to which you were committed." That the time of
bondage is past is not due to *their* action or choice, but to
the action which God effected through Christ, and to the
election of grace whereby God has incorporated them into
Christ, through baptism, making them participants in Christ's
death and resurrection.

But the Christian teaching ($\delta\iota\delta\alpha\chi\acute{\eta}$) is not only the proclamation about God's action in Christ; it is *also the pattern
or type* ($\tau\acute{\upsilon}\pi\sigma\varsigma$) *in keeping with which the whole life of the
Christian is to be shaped*. That is a thought which is singu-
larly characteristic of Paul. In chapter 12, where he turns
to admonitions, we see how he carries that idea out in more
detail. In all the foregoing exposition, he has shown what
it means that God has, through Christ, overcome the bond-

age of the old aeon and brought in the new aeon, with justification and life. It is to this that he ties up his exhortations,
all of which he sums up in the sentence, "Do not be conformed to this world but be transformed by the renewal of
your mind" (12:2). To the new aeon the new man is to
conform, with new mind and manner of life. The life of
the Christian is not something independent in relation to
the work which God has effected in him through Christ.
This is rather the pattern which must set its stamp on the
life of the Christian. He lives under "the righteousness of
God"; therefore his entire life must bear the mark of righteousness. God has taken the Christian out of servitude to
sin, and brought him under the molding influence of "the
righteousness of God"; and for this the apostle expresses his
gratitude to God. This is the "obedience to the faith" about
which Paul spoke earlier (1:5).

The situation of the Christian is described very simply
by Paul: *He is a slave who has changed masters.* Formerly
he stood under the dominion of sin; now he is set free from
sin, but bound in the service of righteousness. What Paul
wishes to stress is that the Christian in his entirety is a bond-
slave to righteousness. This absolute subjection he illustrates
by reference to the prior status under sin; for that, too, was
a total bondage. To be sure, Paul is aware that this parallel
has only a severely limited validity and that the comparison
is actually defective in some respects. To begin with, there
is a difference as wide as the heavens between the two forms
of bond service spoken of. The service of sin is *an actual
bondage,* and the service of righteousness and of God is *an
actual freedom.* Properly it ought to be unnecessary to offer
still further proof to Christians that their status as servants
of righteousness automatically excludes service to sin. That

ought to be self-evident. But in reality the situation is more complicated than that. The Christians live their life on the border between the two aeons. They live "in Christ"; but have not thereby ceased to share the fate of the children of Adam. They live "in the spirit"; but they still experience the drag of the flesh. Because of the weakness of the flesh, there is need for such admonitions as Paul gives them. Half apologetically, Paul declares that he speaks in human terms (ἀνθρώπινον λέγω), and that his manner of e₊ression is due more to their limitations than to the nature of that of which he speaks. He reminds them of the condition of their old life, and calls upon them to learn how matters stand in their new life. He speaks to them as if they were more at home in the world of sin than in the world of grace and righteousness. "For just as you once yielded your members to impurity and to greater and greater iniquity, so now yield your members to righteousness for sanctification."

"No one can serve two masters," least of all if they are in conflict with each other. He who is in the pay of one commander must fight against the other. Paul applies that to the Christian, set in his outpost to battle against the enemy. As long as he was under the dominion of sin, it was sin that he served. While that was true he did not labor for righteousness; he was "free in regard to righteousness." Should there not now be a corresponding truth, since he has come into the dominion of righteousness? He is now a servant of righteousness, and that means that he is free from sin.

Paul is of course speaking in definitely human terms when, beside the expression "free from sin," he sets up the other, "free from righteousness"; as if he were discussing two evenly matched realities, and as if freedom meant the same kind of thing in both cases. And yet the parallel between

the old life and the new, between service to sin and to righteousness, is singularly instructive. It is actually true that
one sees better what service to righteousness means to the
Christian, when it is compared with what the service of sin
means to the natural man. With what inner urge and spon-
taneity, with what eagerness and joy, the natural man gives
himself to the service of sin, even though it means to him
genuine bondage. Is there any good reason why the Christian should be more slothful and indifferent, less willing and
joyous, in the service of God, which means genuine freedom
to him? And yet the words of Jesus in Luke 16:8 are relevant
here, "The sons of this world (οἱ υἱοὶ τοῦ αἰῶνος τούτου) are
wiser in their own generation than the sons of light." The
children of the new aeon have much to learn from the children of this age, both in wisdom and in foresight, in energy
and willingness of service.

That which is true of the old life is true of the new,
mutatis mutandis. But to guard against any misunderstanding of this parallel, Paul reminds his readers of the diametrically opposite goals to which the two kinds of service lead:
the service of sin leads to death, but the service of righteousness leads to eternal life. Both the parallel and the limits of
its applicability come to light clearly when Paul says, "When
you were slaves of sin, you were free in regard to righteousness. But then what return did you get from the things of
which you are now ashamed? The end of those things is
death. But now that you have been set free from sin and
have become slaves of God, the return you get is sanctification and its end, eternal life."

Finally, a word as to the unity of this chapter. Many
have made the complaint that there is no unitary course of
thought here. H. Lietzmann says, "From verses 6 to 23 one

finds no ongoing unity of thought." Still more emphatically
A. Jülicher expresses his dissatisfaction: "Nowhere else in
Romans do we find so many words about a single matter,
and so unclear an advance of thought as in chapter 6. It is
simply the sign of a certain confusion. At the high point
which he reached in 5:12-21 which knows no transitions or
connecting links between before and now, Paul was not
able to find the resolving word, that for his moral renewal
man has been awarded his time on earth; and that the difference between before and now is not simply sin or simply
righteousness, but that the old is 'ever deeper into sin,' and
the new is 'ever freer from sin and more fully into complete
righteousness.' In the effort to hold to the unconditional
opposition Paul uses two concepts which, with less consistency than truth, he so twists that they, instead of constituting
a proof of the actual presence of the new righteousness in
the Christian, only appeal to the Christian's pride, to his
sense of honor in his experience of his moral energy. . . . As
for the weakness of the proof offered in chapter 6, we do
not need to take that up at all. Though we should have
expected it, from 5:12-21, Paul does not show that sin has
ceased in the new man. He does not show that the justified
are sinless. He has only presented an argument for an 'ought'
of a new sort. The questions expressed in verses 1 and 15
are so helpful to this that the failure in logic is easily
concealed."

To such a conclusion one inevitably comes, if he begins
with the assumption that Paul's task here is to affirm the
Christian's sinlessness, in a moralistic sense. Then what he
says about freedom from sin seems to be an enthusiastic
overstatement; and his imperatives appear not as a logical
consequence, but, in relation to the truth of the situation, a

real twisting of the original line of thought which he found himself unable to carry through. To such a view Paul's thought in the whole of this chapter seems to be a planless wandering, hither and yon, without logic or goal. The only surprising thing is that Paul is not himself able to hit upon the simple little idea with which Jülicher thinks he can correct and improve on the apostle's thought, the "resolving word," as Jülicher says. When any interpretation results in such difficulties, we have every reason to raise question as to its correctness.

The exposition which we have presented has shown that the assumption on which Jülicher's construction rests is false. When Paul says that he who is in Christ is "free from sin," he does not, on the one hand, assert the Christian's sinlessness, in the usual sense of the word; nor, on the other hand, does he mean that the Christian is only relatively righteous, as he was formerly only relatively in bondage to sin, and that his task is to approach closer and closer to sinlessness by the exercise of his moral energy. No, Paul actually means just what he says, that, through the fact that the Christian belongs to Christ, he has been made "free from sin." According to the apostle, there is here an absolute boundary which must not, under any circumstances, be blurred or relativized. Man formerly stood under the dominion of sin; now, since "the righteousness of God" has been revealed through Christ, man has, through faith in Him, been received into the kingdom of righteousness. And since Christ is his Lord ($\kappa\acute{\upsilon}\rho\iota\sigma$), the Christian no longer stands under the dominion ($\kappa\upsilon\rho\iota\acute{\sigma}\tau\eta\varsigma$) of sin. He is "free from sin," justly absolved from servitude to sin. From his new Lord, Christ, he has received authority to fight against his former ruler and tyrant, sin, which continues to do all in its power to get man back again into its dominion.

When one is aware of these basic ideas, which mutually condition each other, the sixth chapter no longer presents any peculiar difficulties. Throughout the whole chapter there runs, like a red cord, the thought that the Christian is "free from sin." Through baptism he has *"died to sin"* (vs. 2). He who has died is *"freed from sin"* (vs. 7). Just as Christ died to sin once for all, so we must consider ourselves *"dead to sin"* (vs. 11). And finally Paul twice describes the Christian by using the expression "freed from sin" (ἐλευθερω- θέντες ἀπὸ τῆς ἁμαρτίας, vss. 18, 22). That is the basic thought of the chapter. By the constant repetition of the statements that the Christian is "free from sin" and "dead to sin," a great cohesiveness is given to this chapter. It affirms that, through faith in Christ, the Christian is free from all the powers of destruction that rule in the old aeon— Wrath, Sin, the Law, and Death.

Side by side with this there runs another thought, throughout the chapter: the Christian's life is *a constant battle with sin*. That this thought is brought forth here is due to the fact that both of the major divisions of this chapter begin with the question whether the Christian shall sin. Shall he continue in sin? At the same time that Paul declares that the Christian is free from sin, he stresses the necessity for him to cease from sin and to battle against it. "How can we who died to sin still live in it?" (vs. 2). We have died with Christ so that we might no longer be enslaved to sin (vs. 6). Since we now live for God in Christ, sin no longer has power over us. Our sinful bodies must not reign; they must be withstood and subdued (vs. 12). As long as sin was our master, we had to heed it and do its bidding (vs. 16).

But now that we have another Lord, who has brought "the righteousness of God" to us, we, as the bond servants of righteousness, must battle against sin, which is both His foe and ours.

It is not only true that these two lines of thought run parallel here; they belong together inseparably. Only when both are in mind do we have a correct picture of the status of the Christian with reference to sin. This unity of the two ideas is expressed when Paul says that the Christian's freedom from sin is the reason why he must fight against sin. Precisely because we are "free from sin," we have to fight against it. Many have argued that if we are free from sin, we no longer need to fight against it. Paul's idea is the direct opposite to this. He who is not free from sin cannot fight against it, for he is the slave of sin. That which he does serves sin. Only he who, through Christ, has been freed from sin *can* enter the battle against it; and he, because of his status as a slave of righteousness, is obligated to join in that battle. Seen in this light, this chapter is marked by a manifest unity; it shows an entirely consistent development. The reason why interpretations have so often gone astray here is probably due to the fact that sin has not been understood as Paul saw it, a power of destruction which holds man in bondage, until Christ comes and sets him free. Many have viewed sin in a moralistic way. Let us point out here too—as we have done already, and shall do again—that we capitalize such words as Wrath, Sin, Law, Righteousness, etc., for the purpose of keeping us constantly aware that these are powers to which man stands in the relation of obedience. The fact that, in the interpretation here presented, there is a clear unity and an organic progress of thought is strong evidence for the correctness of the view.

In the last verse of the sixth chapter, Paul takes us back to the basic idea of the second division of the epistle: He who through faith is righteous *shall live*. He who believes in Christ has thereby escaped from death, which rules in the old age; he has become a *sharer in the life of the new aeon, eternal life*. The great contrast, there as in 5:12-21, is between death and life; between death, which through sin gained its lordship over all things human, and life, which is God's gift, in which we are made sharers through Christ. That great contrast is perennially true. Here it is simply being viewed in the light of the role of sin. So Paul says, "The wages of sin is death, but the free gift of God is eternal life" (ζωὴ αἰώνιος, the life of the new aeon, which begins here, but comes to full consummation in glory). When he refers to sin, Paul speaks of a wage. The wage which sin pays its slaves is that it delivers them over to death; and thereby they receive what they have deserved. But Paul does not use the same word as to God; for God does not merely pay wages or a deserved recompense to His bond servants. He bestows on them a free gift, which excludes any thought of merit and reward. Not because of our merit or because of our labors, but through Christ are we "free from sin" and sharers in eternal life. That is ours only "in Christ" and because He is our Lord. For that reason Paul concludes this chapter, like the others in the second division of the epistle, with the words in Christ Jesus our Lord."

VIII

Free from the Law

"For freedom Christ has set us free." These words of Galatians 5:1 might be used as a caption for the second division of Romans, chapters 5-8. Before Christ came the whole of mankind was sunk in bondage to the powers of destruction. Because of his sin and alienation from God man had fallen under the *wrath of God. Sin* ruled over him, and the law only contributed to the increase of sin, heightening it to the degree of actual transgression. So the *law* also became a destructive power that surrenders man to the power of *death*. According to Paul there is an intimate relation between these powers of destruction. This relation is expressed concisely and significantly in I Corinthians 15:56: "The sting of death is sin, and the power of sin is the law" (τὸ δὲ κέντρον τοῦ θανάτου ἡ ἁμαρτία, ἡ δὲ δύναμις τῆς ἁμαρτίας ὁ νόμος). To Paul death is "the last enemy" (I Cor. 15:26), the terrifying ruler who gathers in his hands all threads of the old aeon; it bears the scepter in absolute sovereignty. But death has that power only with the help of sin. Sin is the weapon, the "sting," which death uses to bring humanity under its dominion. But sin, in turn, would not have such power, were it not for the law. Only after the law had come could sin abound as actual sin; so Paul can call the law simply "the power of sin." When these powers hold together, man is lost beyond redemption.

But to that hopeless situation God made an end when He gave Christ as Saviour. In chapters 5-8, Paul takes up the discussion of these powers, one by one. In chapter 5 he shows how the Christian is "free from wrath." In the sixth chapter he shows how the Christian is "free from sin." It is now time to speak of the law. In the seventh chapter Paul will show that the Christian is also *"free from the law."* This is, in a way, the most important and the hardest point in the discussion. It is relatively easy to understand that, through the salvation effected by Christ, the Christian is free from the other powers, Wrath, Sin, and Death. Where any of these still rule, salvation is not complete. But we may be somewhat surprised to find the law listed among these powers of destruction. A Christian is God's servant, for whom the will of God is something high and holy, which he wants to heed in all things. But since the law is the document that expresses God's will, under which the Christian would and must live, the question arises, Does that not mean that the life of the Christian is and must be "under the law"? Even though, for the natural man who sets himself against God's will, the law can be destructive and have the character of a power of destruction, still it would seem that for the Christian, who has a spirit of willingness, the law is a helping and saving power, under which it is an advantage and blessing to live.

But with this inquiry in mind, we should note that the passage referred to in Galatians 5:1—"For freedom Christ has set us free; stand fast therefore, and do not submit again to a yoke of slavery"—speaks specifically of the Christian's

freedom from the law, and affirms the peril of placing the
Christian life "under the law." In Galatians 4:3-4, Paul
speaks of how we were formerly under bondage to the
powers of this world, and how, in the fullness of time, God
brought this bondage to an end by sending His Son and
placing Him under the law. The purpose God had in mind
is stated thus: *"to redeem those who were under the law."*
It is a central thought with Paul that the Christian no longer
stands under the law, that he is "free from the law" through
Christ. One cannot continue under the law without con-
tinuing under the old bondage. He who stands under the
law also stands under sin. Therefore we could never be
justified by way of the law. If justification is to mean anything, we must accept in all seriousness the statement that
the Christian is "free from the law." If we continue in
bondage to the law, we are still under the wrath of God
and belong to the old aeon, which falls short of the righteousness of God. As justified, we are free from the law. We
are not under the law, but under grace. Paul has certified
that again and again, in what has gone before (especially
in 6:14); and now he turns to make that clearer, and to reinforce it.

The word about the Christian's freedom from the law is
an imperative word, which must under no conditions be
weakened. But it is also a perilous word; for it might be
understood to say that the Christian may remain in sin, or
at least that he need not be much concerned about it. But
that danger is reduced by what Paul has said in chapter 6.
Hence, without fear of being misunderstood, he can now
take up the great theme of the Christian's freedom from
the law.

1. "Dead to the Law" through Christ
7:1-6

Just as in 6:1, Paul at once made mention of ἁμαρτία (sin), the word which supplied the dominating concept of the whole chapter, so he here, in 7:1, sets the word νόμος (the law) almost at the very beginning, thereby indicating what is to be discussed in this chapter.

To understand aright the meaning of the seventh chapter, one needs to note the thoroughgoing parallelism in the exposition of these two chapters. We here set some of the most striking parallels side by side.

Chapter 6	Chapter 7
vs. 1, ἡ ἁμαρτία (sin)	vs. 1, ὁ νόμος (the law)
vs. 2, ἀπεθάνομεν τῇ ἁμαρτίᾳ ("We died to sin")	vs. 4, ἐθανατώθητε τῷ νόμῳ ("You have died to the law")
vs. 4, ἐν καινότητι ζωῆς περιπατήσωμεν ("that we might walk in newness of life")	vs. 6, ἐν καινότητι πνεύματος δουλεύειν ("that we serve in the new life of the Spirit")
vs. 7, ὁ ἀποθανὼν δεδικαίωται ἀπὸ τῆς ἁμαρτίας ("He who has died is free from sin")	vs. 6, κατηργήθημεν ἀπὸ τοῦ νόμου, ἀποθανόντες ἐν ᾧ κατειχόμεθα ("We are discharged from the law, dead to that which held us captive")
vs. 18, ἐλευθερωθέντες ἀπὸ τῆς ἁμαρτίας ("having been set free from sin")	vs. 3, ἐλευθέρα ἀπὸ τοῦ νόμου ("free from the law")

It is at least clear from this comparison that Paul's thought in chapter 7 follows a course similar to that in chapter 6. The same categories are used, being simply applied to different matter.

When, in chapter 6, Paul speaks of the Christian's liberation from bondage under sin, he could say interchangeably, "We are free from sin" or "We have died to sin." This liberation has come through the death of Christ, and through the fact that by baptism we have become sharers in His death. In verse 7 this is all summed up in the sentence, "He who has died is free from sin." Now, in chapter 7, Paul takes up the question of the Christian's relation to the law; and his thesis is that, through Christ, we are also "free from the law." But can one actually be freed from the law in the same sense and in the same manner as he is freed from wrath and sin? First of all, *can one die to the law?* It is this which Paul affirms with utmost emphasis. He who knows the law—and it is to such that Paul speaks—knows that the law rules (κυριεύει) over man as long as he lives; but death sets a limit to the relevance of the law. Only through death can one be freed from the law. In verses 2 and 3 an example is given to show how the dominion of the law, its ability to rule as man's lord, is terminated by death: "Thus a married woman is bound by law to her husband as long as he lives; but if her husband dies she is discharged from the law concerning the husband. Accordingly, she will be called an adulteress if she lives with another man while her husband is alive. But if her husband dies, she is free from that law, and if she marries another man she is not an adulteress." The interpretation of these verses has presented great difficulties, particularly when they are viewed in connection with those that follow, where one looks for light as to their meaning. In whatever sense they have been understood, it seemed that all could not be brought into harmony. So some have asked what Paul can be aiming at with so peculiar and apparently stumbling a comparison. He speaks first about a married woman, and her husband who dies; and that she is thereby free to give herself to another man. But then, in the second member of the comparison, he speaks about us, about Christ who dies, and about Another to whom we are now to belong, the risen Christ. That which some have found perplexing is especially the following: what Paul is saying is not that we are free from Him who died, but that we are free from the law. But if that be it, the comparison seems quite misleading. So some have suggested another interpretation—that the law is compared with the first husband, and Christ to the second. The law was our first lord; but Christ is the Lord to whom we now belong, since we have been set free from our former allegiance. Thereupon all sorts of ideas have advanced about "spiritual marriage with Christ."

But here, as in other places, many have conjured up quite unnecessary problems. The situation is really very simple. Paul is affirming *only one thing*, just what verse 1 says—*that death ends the sway of the law*. That is all that Paul intends to say here. He did not choose marriage as an example because it is a particularly good illustration of our relation to Christ, but only because it illustrates so definitely that *death puts an end to the force of the law*. How else could that be illustrated? About the law's relationship to one who is dead we can hardly speak, for we know nothing about that. He is no longer among us on earth so that we might decide whether death has changed his relation to the law. So, to show that death releases from the law, Paul chooses as an illustration a case in which a person was bound by a law, but through the intervention of death, was set free therefrom while still on earth. It is a situation in which the living can be said to be 'freed from the law. The illustration concerns a wife who was bound by the law (who by the law was bound to her husband); so that if she evades the law, she is called an adulteress. But then, by the intervention of death, she was "freed from the law." There is no other way to escape from the sway of the law; but death has this effect, that it removes man from the pale of the law. Every one who knows the law can see, by this example, how death really sets a limit to the relevance of the law. It has been affirmed that Paul here happens to make use of a misleading example, having chanced on a poor comparison or allegory. But we must rather insist that it is an exceptionally good illustration, if only we understand it as Paul plainly requires, throughout this line of thought, that it be understood.

It is, then, indubitable that one can die to the law. Paul has shown that clearly in this illustration. And that is exactly what has happened to Christians, according to Paul. They were formerly under the law. The law was the power which had complete command of them and placed them under condemnation. But now *a death had intervened.* Christ has died, and they have died with Him; and the result is that they are henceforth free from the law. Hence Paul continues, "Likewise, my brethren, you have died to the law through the body of Christ, so that you may belong to another, to him who has been raised from the dead in order that we may bear fruit for God."

When men interpret this as an allegory, they do have difficulty with what the apostle says here. "Application to the Christian does not fit with the illustration. If it were really to apply, it would be the law that dies. But, in the illustration, man dies to the law, and yet is free to enter a new relationship" (Althaus). They who think like that feel that, if the illustration were consistent, it would run about as follows: The law corresponds to the first husband, in the example; so it is the law that dies. The Christian corresponds to the surviving wife. Through the death of the law the Christian is free from his first allegiance, "marriage" with the law, and free to enter a new marriage with the risen Christ, who corresponds to the second husband. But Paul does not say anything of the kind. According to him, it is not the law that dies, but Christ, and the Christian with Him. Nor does Paul speak of any "marriage" with the law. It is clear that we have here no allegory.

To Paul there can be no thought of the law dying. It is not a case of the Christian's decision to regard the law as repealed and nonexistent. No one is really "freed from the law" in any such way; the claim of the law would continue undiminished. Nor can it be said that, with the coming of Christ, the law was outdated and abolished. The law continues, and it constantly lays its claim on man, regardless of whether he acknowledges it or not. One does not escape the sway of the law by neglecting its mandate. The law does not die. There is only one way to liberation. Only in the fact that the Christian has died with Christ is he really and truly set beyond the realm of the law. Paul's emphasis lies on this genuine liberation. The parallel with chapter 6 is here especially enlightening. When he was there discussing the liberation of the Christian from sin, Paul raised an analogous question. The conclusion to which he came was as follows: "He who has died is freed—really freed—from sin" (6:7). Now, in chapter 7, he comes to an entirely similar result with reference to the law. The law no longer rules over him, for he belongs to Another, he has another Lord, the Lord Jesus Christ who arose from the dead.

But it is this very expression, "You have died to the law
. . . . *so that you may belong to another,*" which has given
men occasion to think that this passage must be interpreted
as an allegory. In the illustration one reads about the married woman who, when her husband died, was free to give
herself to another. Does not Paul here indicate that Christ
is the "other" to whom the Christian henceforth belongs?
And does he not thereby show that he is presenting an allegory? In answer it must be said that the verbiage, "that
you may belong to another," is clearly influenced by what
was said about the woman who is free to give herself to
another. But the idea that we belong either under the law
or under Christ, Paul has already advanced, apart from the
illustration here taken from the area of marital law. When
one is dead to sin, he lives for God in Christ Jesus. Paul has
said that in 6:11 (cf. 6:22). Now he says the same as to
the law. When one has died to the law, he lives for Christ
and belongs to Him. This is the same idea as that which
we meet in Galatians 2:19-20: "For I through the law died
to the law, that I might live to God. I have been crucified
with Christ; it is no longer I who live, but Christ who lives
in me." That Paul, when he wants to set forth this idea
which is so familiar for him—and that he should set it forth
right here is clear from the above-mentioned parallel with
chapter 6—allows it to take on a certain coloring from the
illustration which he now uses, is not in any way surprising.
It is most natural to see here an incidental play on words,
such as we often find in him. But it must certainly be called
unjustified for us, on that account, to call all this an allegory,
and thereby rob the line of thought of its clear and simple
meaning.

There is still another word which deserves special notice

in this context. When Paul wants to state how it happened that the Christian died to the law, he says that it came about "through the body of Christ," διὰ τοῦ σώματος τοῦ Χριστοῦ. Paul is manifestly thinking of Christ's death. But what is the reason for this peculiar and special emphasis on the body of Christ, that *it* was through it that we died to the law? Many are the suggestions, more or less artificial, which have been advanced to answer that question. But the correct explanation is easy to find, if we only remember what σῶμα Χριστοῦ, what "the body of Christ" means to Paul. Then it becomes clear that here too his thought runs parallel with that in chapter 6. There, too, he spoke of the Christian's participation in the death of Christ, saying that that is effected through baptism. In baptism we are incorporated into Christ, made members of "the body of Christ." "By one Spirit we were all baptized into one body" (I Cor. 12:23). When Christ died, when His body was given for us in death, then we "through his body" died to sin (chap. 6) and died to the law (chap. 7). In 6:11 Paul stated the result of Christ's death with reference to the Christian's relation to sin: "So you also must consider yourselves dead to sin and alive to God in Christ Jesus." Now he draws a like conclusion as to the Christian's relation to the law: "Likewise, my brethren, you have died to the law through the body of Christ, so that you may belong to another, to him who has been raised from the dead in order that we may bear fruit for God."

The law demands that man be the servant of God and obey His will. But as long as man stands under the law, there is no "fruit for God." That there can be only when man, with Christ, dies to the law. Here we may find one of the reasons why Paul insists so earnestly on freedom from the law. He does not do so because a lawless life appeals to him, but because it is only when man is free from the law that he can really bear fruit for God; and that is the goal of the work of Christ and of the Christian life, the life "in Christ."

That idea is further developed in the two verses that follow, where Paul says, "While we were living in the flesh, our sinful passions, aroused by the law, were at work in our members to bear fruit for death. But now we are discharged from the law, dead to that which held us captive, so that we serve not under the old written code but in the new life of the Spirit" (vss. 5-6).

Paul is speaking about *what we formerly were* and *what we now are;* but all the time the issue is the role which the law plays here. In describing our *former state*, he uses an expression with double meaning, "while we were living in the flesh," ὅτε ἦμεν ἐν τῇ σάρκι. By itself that expression could simply mean our life in time. But Paul here clearly uses it in contrast with the Christian life. Some translations are quite right in reading "while we were still in a carnal way of life." What role did the law play then? It aroused our sinful passions, with the result that we bore fruit for death.

That far everything is clear and simple. But when Paul now goes further and describes the *present status* of the Christian, and the role of the law in the Christian life, he does it in a way that has often disturbed his theological interpreters. When it is said about our former status that "we were living in the flesh," we might expect that it would be said, as to our present status, that we henceforth "live in the Spirit." Indeed, verse 6 rightly says that "we now serve in the new life of the Spirit." But beyond that we might expect that the role of the law would be the opposite of its

place in the old life. Now that we live in the Spirit, we might
think, the law is no longer a power of destruction, but a
helper by our side; through the Spirit we have received the
ability to fulfill the law in a new way, and the law gives us
indications how the Christian life ought to be "the third use
of the law." If we start with a current theological tradition,
it would be natural for us to explain Paul's view in such
terms. But that is not what Paul says; he rather says the
opposite. Not even in the Christian life is the law able to
bring forth fruit for God. If the law, "while we were living
in the flesh," was a great power which provoked and increased sin, but was not able to bring forth anything good,
so now, in the new life, it suffers from the same impotence.
There is no law that can give life. The law belongs to what
Paul calls "the old written code." The law belongs to the
old aeon. It is one of the powers of destruction to which
man stands in bondage; and therefore it is a foremost mark
of the Christian life that we are now "discharged from the
law." Through Christ we have died to all the old hostile
powers, from "that which held us captive." Only after this
negative thing has been said about the law does Paul continue, "We serve not under the old written code but in the
new life of the Spirit."

Paul has spoken about the Christian's "before and now,"
about *what we were in the past* and *what we are now.* In
so doing he has indicated his outline for what he wishes to
develop. As he proceeds we find the same temporal contrast.
First, in verses 7-13, he discusses *what the Christian was
before.* This is naturally enough expressed in the past tense.
Then, in verses 14-25, he sets forth *what the Christian is now;*
and beginning with verse 14, Paul quite rightly writes in the
present tense.

In these two situations the law has an essentially different meaning and status. The Christian's past, on which he can look back, signifies his bondage in the old aeon. Then the law had a mighty power, but it was a power to destroy. It is of this that Paul speaks in the first part of this section. We might say that verses 7-13 discuss *the law in the circumstances of the old aeon,* or *the power of the law to provoke and increase sin.* But now, in the new aeon, the law has lost its power, and that in all respects. To begin with, and above all, the law is no longer a power of destruction to the Christian; he has died to the law. Of that Paul has spoken sufficiently in the foregoing. But the law is not a saving power for the Christian either; it is no δύναμις εἰς σωτηρίαν. In the final section of the chapter, verses 14-25, Paul discusses *the law in the situation of the new aeon,* that is, *the impotence of the law to bring forth that which is good.*

2. THE POWER OF THE LAW TO PROVOKE AND INCREASE SIN
7:7-13

Paul begins his exposition with the question, "What then shall we say? That the law is sin?" That question may seem to us to be strange and superfluous. But for Paul it is not superfluous. To see how natural that question is for him, and how necessary it is for him to raise it, we need only to note how, in what has gone before, he has set sin and the law immediately beside each other, as closely related powers of destruction. Again and again the law and sin have appeared in close bond, working together to a common end. When the law comes in, the result is that the power of sin is increased (5:20). Beside the statement that the Christian is "free from sin" Paul has placed the other, that he is also "free from the law." In one connection he has declared that freedom from the law also means freedom from sin; for in 6:14 he says, "Sin will have no dominion over you, since you are not under law." Does not that imply that he who lives under the law is at the same time surrendered to sin? And as, in 6:11, Paul says that only he who is "dead to sin" can live for God, so he can say, in 7:4, that only he who has "died to the law" can bear fruit for God.

What is the meaning of all this? Does it not seem as if Paul is speaking of one and the same thing? Is there not at least such an infiltration between the law and sin, that we may practically say that the two are one? It is not necessary forcibly to introduce the idea that sinister misinterpreters of his thought compel him to confront this question. The presence of this issue is clearly enough at hand in what has gone before. That Paul states the question so forthrightly, and discusses it in thoroughgoing manner, shows how eager he is to leave the matter in no uncertainty at all.

So then, "Is the law sin?" His answer is, "By no means!" Quite the contrary, the law is that power which would oppose sin. And yet there is an intimate relation between the law and sin. Sin would not be what it is, if the law did not exist. Paul begins with the statement of this relationship, saying, "Yet, if it had not been for the law, I should not have known sin. I should not have known what it is to covet if the law had not said, 'You shall not covet.'"

Here we immediately take notice of a peculiarity in this statement. Except for the personal note in the introduction, this is the first time in the epistle where Paul speaks in the first person singular; and he continues to do so throughout chapter 7. What can be the reason for that? It is clearly not Paul's intention to present the following explanation as a subjective confession, true only for him and without valid-

ity as to others in general. On the contrary, the singular
form and the general compass are immediately included in
each other. But we shall not be in error if we assume that
the use of the personal form is due to the fact that Paul here
comes to an issue which, in the most proper sense, is the
problem of his own life. It is the question of the Christian's
relation to the law, the question as to the law in the contexts
of the old and new aeons.

When Paul says that he would not have known sin, if it
had not been for the law, that does not mean only that it is
the law which teaches us the difference between right and
wrong, and that without the criterion of the law we should
not know rightly what is sin. He means that sin would not
have been the power that it actually is in the life of man, if
the law had not helped to that end. There is indeed sin,
without the law, but it slumbers. It is present as an evil
covetousness; but it has not had opportunity to reveal itself.
Man does not realize what a frightful power has him under
its might and rules him. But then the law comes and exposes
sin that was heretofore hidden. The commandment confronts man with its "You shall not covet." But what is the
result? Not that covetousness vanishes, but on the contrary,
it is brought out of seclusion. Just as the sun's rays call forth
the possibilities that are in the seed and bring them to full
growth, so the law calls forth the sin that slumbers. Now it
has opportunity to develop its inherent possibilities; and the
result is conscious opposition to God. *It is in relation to the
law, that sin grows powerful in man.*

Paul expresses this by saying that the law gives sin its
"opportunity," ἀφορμή. "But sin, finding opportunity in the
commandment, wrought in me all kinds of covetousness."
Sin takes the law into its service, so to say. The very com-

mandment becomes a means which sin uses to its own purpose. If sin was formerly relatively weak and powerless, it
can now exercise its control over man, with the help of the
law. We could here apply literally the statement that "the
power of sin is the law" (I Cor. 15:56); for without the law,
sin would not have had such power. Paul even goes so far
as to say, "Apart from the law, sin lies dead," χωρὶς νόμου
ἁμαρτία νεκρά. He describes dramatically the difference
which the entry of the law makes in the life of man. "I was
once alive apart from the law, but when the commandment
came, sin revived and I died." Man's condition without the
law can be characterized as a life, at least as a relative life:
"I was alive," but sin lay dead, it slumbered. But then the
law comes in; the commandment comes with its requirements, and especially with its prohibitions—and *then sin
revives.*

All of this is said from the viewpoint of the old aeon.
That is the result the law effects, when it comes in, whether
it be in the life of the individual or in the race. For what
Paul here says about himself is equally true of every man
and of mankind as a whole (cf. 5:13, 20). The effect of the
law is that is *arouses sin to activity,* and in a sense *provokes*
it. For man being what he is, his encounter with the law
always has the effect of giving sin "opportunity." Only when
he is faced with the law does man become a sinner in earnest, and the result of the entry of the law into his life is
unfailing; he is given over to death. Sin is revived, but man
dies.

So the law or the commandment is the occasion of death
to man. *The law takes its place among the powers that destroy.* But it takes a particular place among these. Sin and
death are by nature simply powers of destruction. As to

FREE FROM THE LAW 7:7-13

them all is simple. Without any qualifications, they are powers of evil, which have the destruction of man as their original purpose. But Paul does not say that about the law. It is not, by nature and original purpose, a power of destruction. Its primary aim is to make man responsive to the will of God. But in actual fact it *becomes* a power that destroys, because sin finds "opportunity" through it. This double character, this discrepancy between the law's original purpose and its real effect, Paul expresses clearly when he says, "The very commandment which promised life proved to be death to me. For sin, finding opportunity in the commandment, deceived me and by it killed me." That is the peculiar thing about the position of the law, that it is the opponent of sin, yet at the same time it can be used as a means to deliver man up to sin and death. The law would keep man from sin; yet it is precisely through the law that sin is able to deceive him and get him into its power.

But Paul does not mean to say that God intended one thing through the law, but its effect actually turned out to be different and contrary. What he says here about the law also fits organically into his central idea that the law was given "so that the whole world may be held accountable to God" (3:19). When the law, which was given for life, leads to death and becomes a power of destruction which increases sin to transgression, it effects in that way that which God wants done against sin and the sinner. Like the wrath of God, the law also represents God's "strange work," which He must carry out, that He may later effect His "proper work," the work of which the gospel is the message. The law is the means by which sin brings man to death. God can permit sin to use the law in this way, He can permit it to kill man, because in His "proper work," in justification, He gives life to the dead.

Paul had lived "under the law"; but contrary to familiar presentations, that had not been a heavy and uncomfortable burden. On the contrary, he was one of the righteous of whom the first Psalm says, "His delight is in the law of the Lord, and in his law doth he meditate day and night." In his pre-Christian period, the law wore a wonderful aura for Paul. He looked up to it just as the idealist looks up to his ideal. When, on the Damascus road, he came to see that the law was a false way of salvation, and that it was not a saving power but a power of destruction, it might have been expected that his love for the law would be changed into enmity, and that he would thereafter speak of it in derogatory terms. But that was not the case at all. Even for Paul, the Christian, there is a peculiar glory about the law. It continues to be an expression of God's holy will: "So the law is holy, and the commandment is holy and just and good."

But is it not contradictory that God's holy and good will brings death and ruin? If that be the case, can it any longer be called good? Therefore, to what he has said, Paul adds, "Did that which is good, then, bring death to me?" He immediately answers, "By no means!" It is not properly the law that kills; for if there were no sin, the law would not be a power of destruction to me. It is rather sin that proved to be death to me. To be sure, sin alone could not have brought about so absolute a destruction as is now man's fate. That is the result of the joint effect of sin and the law. It is, as Paul has just said (vs. 11), sin killed me through the commandment, that is, through the law. It was through the law that sin got such power, for "the power of sin is the law." But it is also true that it was in this way that it was first made manifest what a frightful power sin is, when it worked death in me "through what is good." The law has by no means failed in its mission. For God's very purpose for the law was that, through it, sin "might become sinful beyond measure."

Paul has spoken of the law's ability to bring forth sin and give it power, so that it becomes "sinful beyond measure." By reason of its relation to sin, the law becomes a destroying power—something which, in its own nature, it is not. From that destroying power Christ has saved us. He who is in Christ is "free from the law," just as he is "free from sin." These two powers belong together, and co-operate in man's destruction. Only liberation from both means real salvation. Because of this it is easy to understand Paul's insistence upon the Christian's freedom from the law.

But as yet only one side of the matter has been presented. It might be said that Paul is certainly right in saying that the law evokes and gives power to sin; and also in saying that the law brings man to death, when it confronts him. But, as Paul says, God gives life to the dead; He makes the sinner righteous. Does not that give the law a wholly different position and meaning to the Christian? Does one really need to speak about the Christian's freedom from the law? Is it not enough that he is free from sin? When the law comes to him who has escaped the bondage of sin, there is no longer the fatal co-operation between the law and sin. If, in the hand of sin, the law becomes an instrument of death, it ought to be a means of life when it is in God's hand. If, in the unconverted man under the bondage of sin, the law has the power to call forth the evil, then, in the believer who is thereby free from sin, it ought to have the power to call forth the good. Is it then necessary that the Christian be free from the law? Is not the law rather his faithful companion and counselor on the way to life? It is to that question that Paul addresses himself in the latter part of chapter 7. He speaks there of the impotence of the law to call forth the good.

3. THE IMPOTENCE OF THE LAW TO CALL FORTH THE GOOD
7:14-25

The section of the epistle which we now take up is perhaps the most discussed and fought over part of Romans. It presents us with one of the greatest problems in the New Testament. It was already recognized in the first Christian century; and since that time it has never come to rest. Through the centuries the battle has been waged as to what this peculiar passage means. The issue may be stated as follows: Who is the "I" to whom Paul here refers when he says, "I am carnal, sold under sin" (vs. 14); or "I know that nothing good dwells within me, that is, in my flesh. I can will what is right, but I cannot do it" (vs. 18)? Confronted with such a statement, interpreters ask whether the reference is to a converted person, or to the unconverted. Or, since Paul says "I," and speaks more or less in his own name, is he speaking of his pre-Christian experience or of his experience as a Christian? The Greek church fathers generally understood Paul here to refer to those not yet Christian, to those still under the law. But Augustine, partly due to his struggle against Pelagius, was convinced that these statements are made about the Christian. This view was accepted by the church of the Middle Ages; and—though understood differently—by Luther and the other Reformers. It was Pietism that first rejected this interpretation, declaring that Paul's statement can only refer to the unconverted, to the unregenerate man. For Pietism, with its view of the meaning of the Christian life and of sanctification, it was utterly inconceivable that Paul might speak in this way about his new life as a Christian; he is rather talking here of the discord which ruled his life while he was under the law.

It looks as if one faces insuperable difficulties, no matter which of these interpretations he accepts. In favor of the view of the Reformers is the fact that, if one comes to the passage without prior assumptions, it would seem from the text that Paul has hitherto been speaking of something which is past, but now speaks of the present. As he has, up to this point, written in the past tense, he here uses the present. But we are immediately troubled by the question whether Paul can really be talking so depreciatingly about his life as a Christian. Can he really have so low a judgment as to Christ's ability to overcome sin in his life? And how can the picture here presented be reconciled with what Paul usually says about the Christian life? In this connection chapter 7 has often been contrasted with chapter 8. In the latter Paul is manifestly speaking about the Christian; but, it has been said, here the outlook is entirely different from that of chapter 7. It is not of the weakness of the flesh, but of the power of the Spirit, that chapter 8 speaks. In general, chapter 7 is not speaking of the Spirit, *pneuma*. But the distinctive thing about the Christian is that he has received the Spirit, and of that chapter 8 has much to say. Is it then conceivable that these two chapters refer to the same person or to the same stage of experience? Are we not compelled to divide them and say that chapter 7 characterizes man's pre-Christian stage, while chapter 8 describes the experience of the Christian?

But no less difficulty faces us if we, by such considerations, are led to conclude that the view stated is correct; that the passage under consideration applies to Paul's pre-Christian experience, to his life as a Pharisee under the law. For then we must ask how the picture here given can be reconciled with that which Paul elsewhere gives of the man who is without Christ. It is only necessary to compare this passage with Romans 1:18—3:20. Nor does that which Paul is saying in 7:14-25 agree with what he says elsewhere about his life as a Pharisee. It is enough to call to mind what he says in Philippians 3:6 as to righteousness under the law: he had been "blameless." Which ever way one turns, then, the result seems to be that this passage is incompatible with views expressed elsewhere.

In the effort at reconciliation, many in recent times have suggested the following solution. Paul, it is said, is certainly speaking about man under the law, that is, of man before and without Christ; but it is of man under the law, not as he sees himself, but as faith sees him. So Paul now looks with Christian eyes on his former state. He discerns the discord which was actually present, but which he did not then see. But there is not much help in such a view either. Does Paul really so think of life apart from Christ that he can say of it what we read in verse 20, "It is no longer I that do it, but sin which dwells within me"; or, as in verse 25, "So then, I of myself serve the law of God with my mind, but with my flesh I serve the law of sin"? And there is still another question which the suggested solution cannot answer. Can anyone really think Paul capable of such a theatrical outcry—as it would have to be characterized, if Paul is here speaking of something which lies definitely in the past—as we find in 7:24, "Wretched man that I am! Who will deliver me from this body of death?"

Nevertheless, despite such difficulties, today's exegesis generally takes this position, which can be said to be a modification of the pietistic interpretation mentioned above. It is held that Paul is here discussing "the unregenerate man," man under the law as faith sees him. As to this interpretation there is agreement in recent monographs on this chapter (cf. W. Kümmel, *Römer 7 und die Bekehrung des Paulus*, 1929; R. Bultmann, *Römer 7 und die Anthropologie des Paulus*, 1932; P. Althaus, *Paulus und Luther über den Menschen*, 1938). To what degree this kind of interpretation has been accepted can be seen from the fact that an exegete like R. Bultmann, who is no defender of pietism in general, can say as to the meaning of this seventh chapter of Romans, "It seems to me that sufficient discussion has been given to this problem. There can no longer be any doubt as to the answer. It is fundamentally the status of man under the law which is characterized here, and that as it is seen through the eyes of one whom Christ has freed from the law." That affirmation is so categorical that it might seem as if the matter is now entirely clear and settled. But that is far from the case. The above-mentioned difficulties remain. Closer examination shows that the view which Bultmann calls the only one possible is burdened with so many and great difficulties that it cannot be sustained. Inasmuch as it has been so widely accepted, it may not be out of place here to present certain arguments which show that it is untenable.

First of all, against the proposed interpretation we must mention the context in which Paul makes the statements which are under discussion. Throughout chapters 5-8 the subject is the meaning of *the Christian life*. The question to which Paul is here giving answer is what it means to "live in Christ." That answer is fourfold: it means to be free from

Wrath, Sin, the Law, and Death. The passage now undei discussion is the concluding part of the third affirmation, which speaks of *the Christian's freedom from the law.* We cannot help asking how Paul could suddenly turn, in that context, to a description of the anguished and discordant status of the soul of the man who is under the law. It is indeed very significant that the suggested interpretation has to regard chapter 7 as a great parenthesis. It falls entirely outside of the frame of the subject which Paul is discussing. It is said that after his digression, Paul "returns," in chapter 8, to his real theme. Brunner's formulation is very enlightening, when he takes up the discussion of chapter 8. He says, "The theme is indeed the same which has been under development ever since chapter 5, *except of course for the great interruption in the seventh chapter:* it is the new life, the life of and in the righteousness of God, by faith in the reconciliation through Christ. In a sudden turn, Paul breaks away from his consideration of man under the law. Again we find a 'now' as a signal for the new line of thought, or better, for the line of thought that is again taken up." Brunner has stated the message of chapters 5-8 entirely correctly. That he cannot fit chapter 7 into this context, but must speak of "the great interruption of chapter 7," is due to the fact that he finds in it only a description of man's pre-Christian life under the law. With such a view it is quite impossible to see a single line of thought. Chapter 7 inevitably becomes a "foreign element." This must be judged a very weighty objection to such an interpretation.

Also against this interpretation we must point out the fact mentioned above, that Paul, after consistently writing in the past tense in verses 7-13, goes over to the present tense, beginning with verse 14, and continues to use it con-

sistently to the end of the chapter. Just before entering upon
the section under consideration, Paul spoke of *what we once
were* (vs. 5) and of *what we henceforth are, as Christians*
(vs. 6). By so doing, it would seem, he supplied his outline
for that which was to follow. Therefore if the reader, without preconceived view, had let the text speak as it actually
is, he would not have construed verses 14-25 as anything
else but a characterization of the present life of the Christian.
He would not have been confronted by the difficulty of
reconciling what the apostle says here with assumptions as
to the Christian life, to which the reader had come for other
reasons. P. Althaus says, "Although expressed in the present
tense, what is here presented is clearly something past."
Whence that clearness comes he does not show. The only
explanation he gives is to add, "for it discusses man under
the law." But that is just the point which was to be determined, for it was doubtful. To ignore so easily what the
words actually say is hardly justified.

Against this interpretation it must also be said that it
flagrantly violates Paul's own thought, as we know it from
what he says elsewhere. That is so evident that it is admitted
even by representatives of this interpretation. Let a pair of
examples suffice. W. Kümmel, one of the advocates for this
view, says, "There can be no doubt that, in Romans 7:14ff.,
there is ascribed to man a natural harmony with the spiritual
law, *which Paul does not recognize elsewhere*." P. Althaus
concedes, "It is true that *Paul has not elsewhere in his epistles spoken in this way* about νοῦς, reason. It is rather true
that a whole series of passages shows that νοῦς, or 'the heart,'
is included in man's ruin." Althaus' interpretation of Romans
7 makes it necessary for him to make a difference between
the Spirit by which God activates every man, through His

law, on the one hand, and the Holy Spirit which only Christ gives, on the other. But at the same time he has to admit that Paul "nowhere speaks expressly of God's action by the Spirit, without which man would not be man." To set forth such a concept of the general activity of the Spirit is, according to Althaus, one of the most urgent tasks confronting theology today.

Finally, against this interpretation it must be said that it has recourse to explanations which manifestly clash with what the text says clearly. Here too we can find illustrations in Althaus. He says, "Is it not true that, in the same heart, desire for the good and desire for the evil live, mysteriously and painfully, side by side?" "Paul has dared to see and characterize man in his contradiction. The picture seems intolerably contradictory: man hears the law with desire, and does the evil with desire." "Man's lack is *not* that he would not find joy in the good, that he would not desire and will it, but *that* he assents to it, desires and wills it—and yet, as man, does *not* will it, and therefore does *not* do it; that he rejoices in the commandment—and avoids it and wishes it did not exist, because he desires the evil."

This is what we meet, when a contemporary expositor undertakes to explain the discord and anguish which characterize man under the law. Here everything fits into the scheme, for man under the law is declared to be "Man in Revolt." It is held that his whole spiritual existence is split; two clashing souls dwell in his breast. He both will and will not do the good. He has a desire for the good, but also a desire for the evil. But where does *Paul* say anything like that? Where has he said that the man of whom he here speaks has a desire for the evil? It is here declared that he hates it. Where has Paul said that the man here characterized both wills to do and not to do the good? He says the very opposite, and that with all emphasis. Throughout this passage it is affirmed that the will is directed only to the good. What Paul laments is not that the will simultaneously desires something else, but that the will is not effected in corresponding action. It is only on the basis of the fact that the will is singly directed to the good that he can say that he "delights in the law of God." Only because he would not do evil, but hates it, can Paul say, "It is no longer I that do it." If there were such a schism in the will as Althaus says, so that at one and the same time it does not will evil and yet wills it, Paul could not thus absolve his "I" from the action. Against the statement of Althaus, that man affirms, desires, and wills the good, and yet, as the same man, does not will the good, and therefore does not do it, stands Paul's statement, "I do not the good that I want, but the evil that I do no want is what I do" (vs. 19). Althaus stands on the assumption that if I do not the good, it is because I do not want to do it. But Paul laments that, although I want to do the good, it is not done. According to Althaus, the man here characterized delights in the law, and yet wishes that there were no law, because he desires the evil. But Paul does not speak of a man like that. He speaks of a man who truly and simply desires the good and has his mind set to serve the law of God (vs. 25).

What has been said is enough to show the impossibility of construing 7:14-25 as a description of the divided state of soul of man under the law. Since, as we have seen, we encounter so much difficulty and so many exceptions in almost every verse, and since, to make the interpretation fit, it is necessary to take such liberties with what the text says, we have inescapable evidence that the interpretation is *false*.

For it is surely true that no one can hold that the text, if it be not forced, agrees with the suggested interpretation.

The result, then, is that *chapter 7:14-25 does not refer to the pre-Christian life.* That means that we must, with all seriousness, seek for the proper role of this passage in the inclusive context which Paul is developing through chapters 5-8. Like the rest of these chapters, chapter 7 treats of *the Christian life.*

At once the question arises whether Paul is here describing a divided and discordant state of the soul which characterizes the Christian life. The answer to that question must be negative, and that because it confronts us with a false alternative. It is not the case that Paul, in anthropological or psychological interest, has given a description of a certain state of soul, and that our task is simply to determine whether it is the spiritual experience of the unconverted or of the converted that he has pictured. It is because it has become habitual to construe the issue in this way, that an essential fact has tended to slip from view, namely, that Paul addresses himself completely to the question of the position and meaning of *the law.* But it has been customary to assume that Paul is here presenting a general picture of the average Christian and pre-Christian experience, respectively. But if we are right in holding that he is here speaking of the Christian life, it must be affirmed with utmost emphasis that, according to Paul, the soul of the Christian is not characterized by division and discord. As we saw above, the idea of the divided will—that man both wills and does not will the good, that he desires both the good and the evil— is not at home in the mind of Paul. It is falsely read into his words.

But when we have rejected this false view about division

and disharmony in the Christian life, we must at once add that that view has glimpsed a certain truth, even though it did not rightly grasp it. For Paul does undeniably have in mind a certain duality in the Christian life. But he does not think of a divided will or a discord in the soul. He has in mind the tension which exists, in the Christian life, between will and action, between intention and performance. With *that* dualism in the Christian life Paul is well acquainted. It is an expression of the Christian's status as participant in the new aeon even while, at the same time, he is also in the old. Earlier, in the sixth chapter, we saw the effect of this double status on the Christian's relation to sin. "In Christ" he is "free from sin"; and yet sin has not vanished from his life. He still lives "in the flesh," and there sin finds its point of contact. The Christian is not only a member "in Christ," but he continues to be also a member "in Adam." Therefore his life is a constant battle against sin. The situation is the same here, when Paul speaks of the Christian's relation to the law. The same dualism obtains here. When finally the new aeon has come to consummation, there will be no tension between will and performance. But as long as the Christian is not only "in Christ," but also "in the flesh," that tension remains. The will to do the right is always present in him; but he steadily falls short in performance. The Christian's yearning and prayer are that the will of God may "be done on earth as it is in heaven." But in all that he does, experience shows it does not happen that way on earth. "In the Spirit," he delights in God's will; but still he knows by experience what it is to continue to live "in the flesh." "The flesh" exercises its effect, with the result that the will is not carried through to corresponding performance. "I do not do the good I want, but the evil I do not want is what I do" (vs. 19).

Some have reacted against the thought that "the flesh" continues to have such power in the Christian life that it can hinder the will from being translated into corresponding action. That is one of the reasons why many have preferred to interpret Paul's words as applying, not to the Christian, but to life before one is a Christian. It is held that the unbeliever is indeed not able to do the good that he would; but Paul can hardly have meant that the will of the Christian, who has received "the Spirit," can be hindered by "the flesh" from doing the good. Such a line of reasoning only shows how far such a view is from Paul's thought. For he is speaking just of the Christian; nor is this the only place where he says the same. See, for instance, Galatians 5:17, where there is no doubt that he refers to the Christian: "The desires of the flesh are against the Spirit, and the desires of the Spirit are against the flesh; for *these are opposed to each other, to prevent you from doing what you would.*" Since Paul, in Galatians, can say that about the Christian, why should it be impossible for him to say it in Romans 7:14-25?

But even some, who have understood that Paul here speaks of the Christian, have felt that he is painting in dark colors. So they have thought that what Paul says here cannot be true of actual Christian life; that the power of the Spirit is actually more effective than that. Even though Paul does here speak of the Christian life, says this view, he does so because "he does not now take into account the supernatural power of liberation which the regenerate man has available through his fellowship with Christ, namely, the Spirit of God. In other words, as he now describes the regenerate, he does so only in terms of the purely subjective side of such a man's situation; that is, he takes cognizance of the fact that the regenerate man has received a new direction of

will so that it is in harmony with the requirement of the law.
. . . The apostle here does not go beyond what the Christian
is and is capable of when standing, as it were, on his own
legs, with his new will, but isolated from the influence of
the Spirit and confronted with the demand of the law" (S.
Odland). That view says that Paul attempts an abstraction;
he does not describe the Christian's actual situation, but
speaks of him apart from the very thing which is characteristic of the Christian, namely, that he has received the Spirit.
He is held to be speaking of the Christian "standing, as it
were, on his own legs"; but the very thing that is characteristic of the Christian is that he does *not* "stand on his own
legs," and that he is *not* "isolated from the influence of the
Spirit."

No, it is not Paul, but his interpreters, who have attempted an abstraction. They start with an assumption as
to the meaning of the Christian life. Beginning with the fact
that the Christian has received the Spirit, they draw the in-
ference that "the flesh" no longer plays any role; so they
describe the Christian life in terms that are not true to the
actual situation. Paul does speak here of the Christian, but
not in an abstract way. He describes the actual situation of
the Christian as it is in the midst of the present aeon. The
Christian—in this present world: there we face the dualism
and the tension in the Christian's status. As a Christian he
belongs to Christ and lives his life "in Christ"; but as one
who belongs to the old aeon, he still lives "in the flesh." That
dualism is not found in chapter 7 alone, although many see
it here particularly, and what is said here has received particular opposition. The very same dualism faces us in both
chapter 6 and chapter 8. The parallelism in these three
chapters can be outlined thus:

Chapter 6: We are *free from sin*—yet we must battle against it.

Chapter 7: We are *free from the law*—yet we are not righteous according to its criterion.

Chapter 8: We are *free from death*—yet we long for the redemption of our bodies.

Only if we heed both sides of such facts can we give a true picture of the Christian life; for it is conditioned by the fact that the Christian belongs at the same time to both the new and the old aeons. Again the fruitfulness of the aeon-concept is seen in that it changes the "foreign element" which other interpretations find in chapter 7—for if that chapter does apply to the *non-Christian*, it is out of harmony with a context which speaks throughout of the *Christian* life—into an organic link in a logically progressive line of thought. And it also removes the difficulty which especially confronted every interpretation which regarded 7:14-25 as descriptive of the Christian life; for the dualism encountered here is no longer a problem, as soon as it is seen that it is not the expression of a divided and discordant soul—anything like that is clearly not true of the Christian life—but of the Christian's double situation due to his position in the two aeons.

The result of the foregoing exposition can be summed up in the following points:

1) 7:14-25 applies to *the Christian life*. It is thus an organic part of the inclusive view which speaks in chapters 5-8, discussing consistently the meaning of the Christian life ($\zeta\acute{\eta}\sigma\epsilon\tau\alpha\iota$—$\acute{\epsilon}\nu$ $X\rho\iota\sigma\tau\tilde{\wp}$).

2) It speaks of the position of *the law* in the Christian life. It is seen to be essentially negative, since even the Christian cannot attain to righteousness by way of the law.

It is in a wholly different way that he receives the righteousness of God. He is *free from the law*. Thus this passage
belongs to the context of chapter 7, whose theme and caption are just these words, "free from the law" (ἐλεύθερος ἀπὸ
τοῦ νόμου).

3) The reason for the impotence of the law is the fact
that the Christian, even though through Christ he belongs
to the new aeon, still lives *in the old aeon, "in the flesh."* The
impotence of the law goes back to the conflict between
πνεῦμα and σάρξ.

Here we have the key to chapter 7:14-25. If we start
here, this passage no longer presents any problem. We have
already indicated, in one context or another, what it means.
Beyond this we need only a brief discussion.

What is the reason why the law is impotent to call forth
the good? Paul answers that it is because humanity, to
which the law speaks, is *carnal*. "We know that the law is
spiritual; but I am carnal, sold under sin" (vs. 14). Here we
are confronted directly by the contrast between "spirit" and
"flesh," between πνεῦμα and σάρξ. At first glance it may
seem surprising that Paul divides their respective roles as
he does. The law is called "spiritual," πνευματικός; man, the
Christian man, is called "carnal," σάρκινος. Would we not
naturally have expected the direct opposite? The law, with
all its works, belongs to the old aeon (5:20) which is not
spiritual but carnal. But, according to Paul, the Christian
is spiritual (8:9; cf. Gal. 6:1). Would it not have been more
natural, therefore, to base the Christian's freedom from the
law on the fact that, as a spiritual man, he is lifted above the
law, which belongs only to the old aeon? It is a fact that
Gnostics and "fanatics" in all ages have argued in just this
way, to show that the law has no relevance to the Christian.

So it is of special interest to note that Paul here says just the opposite.

The Christian has no right to set himself above the law. It is not in that sense that he is *"free from the law."* It is true that the law belongs to the old aeon, and must serve its purpose therein; but it does not follow that the law itself is carnal. It must not be forgotten that the law is *God's.* The law is given by God, and is an expression of His holy will. It is actually *spiritual.* As God's own word, it is living and powerful, and should by its spiritual nature be effective unto life. Paul has just said about the commandment that it "promised life" (vs. 10). But the law confronts a humanity that is "carnal, sold under sin." That fact robs the law of its power, so that it cannot bring forth the good. We saw, above, that the law actually is a power, a δύναμις; but when it meets sin, it becomes a destroying power. That is the only power which the law now has; for it has lost the ability to evoke the good and effect righteousness, by reason of the carnal which it meets in man. Paul is insistent to point out that the fault is not in the law. "The law is holy, and the commandment is holy and just and good," he says in verse 12. And now he adds that "the law is spiritual." Precisely when he affirms the law's power to provoke and increase sin, and its impotence to effect righteousness and life, and just when he proclaims that the Christian is utterly "free from the law," he will not permit any shadow to rest on the law. It is because of man's sin and his "carnal" state that the law is a destroying power and a shadow that can make nothing perfect (cf. Heb. 7:18-19; 10:1). And here the Christian is not an exception. He is indeed "in Christ," and therefore a new man, a spiritual man; but he has not thereby ceased to be a child of Adam, a being of flesh and blood, a man of carnal nature. It is that which deprives the law of its δύναμις to effect the good. In 8:3 Paul returns to this thought; there he says that the impotence of the law (τὸ ἀδύνατον τοῦ νόμου) is due to the fact that it was "weakened by the flesh."

It ought to be noted that when Paul speaks of the Christian's carnal state he uses the word σάρκινος, and not σαρκικός. The Christian is no longer "carnal" in the sense of "carnal minded." Rather is he "carnal" in the sense that he still lives in the flesh (ἐν σαρκί) and participates in its condition. It is the latter sense which is expressed by the word σάρκινος. Sin is always most definitely a reality in his life. Together with the whole race, he is "sold under sin." Even though through Christ he has been made "free from sin," so that it is no longer his lord, nevertheless, as long as this life lasts, he still lives under the condition of sin. He belongs to a human society which is marked by sin. He lives as a sinner among sinners, not as a sinless saint among sinners.

That is the enigmatical in the Christian life. The Christian is at the same time "free from sin," and yet subject to the condition of sin. He is not "carnally minded," and yet the flesh sets its mark on all that he does. No corresponding enigma rests on the natural man. There is a natural concurrence between will and action. The natural man is "carnally minded"; and, in agreement therewith, his conduct is also "carnal." For that reason one is apt to go forthwith from the will to the deed, to conclude that, if one actually will, he can also carry that will into action. But, as to the Christian, Paul says, "I do not understand my own actions. For I do not do what I want, but I do the very thing I hate" (vs. 15). A Christian constantly experiences that the will of God, which he inwardly wishes to be done, is nevertheless not done on earth as it should be; that even in the Christian's own conduct it is not effected. When the Christian sees his own behavior and what it results in in this world, he has to say that this is not what he wanted to do. He would that God's will "be done on earth, as in heaven"; but the old way persists here on earth, and his own behavior is only a link in a life that is all too human; it is carnal and sinful. The reason for this Paul expresses in this way. "For I know that nothing good dwells within me, that is, in my flesh" (vs. 18). Action here never comes to correspond with that will, because of the inescapably carnal character of all human conduct, even of the Christian's conduct. "I can will what is right, but I cannot do it. For I do not do the good I want, but the evil I do not want is what I do" (vss. 18-19).

What does this mean as to the Christian's relation to the law? It implies a recognition that the law is right. "Now if I do what I do not want, I agree that the law is good" (vs. 16). Inwardly, in my will I am at one with the law. But, one may ask, what does that mean as to my ego? Paul answers, "So then it is no longer I that do it, but sin which dwells within me" (vs. 17). And in verse 20 that idea is repeated in virtually the same words. Here is one of those places which show with special clarity that Paul is speaking of the Christian. As to the non-Christian he recognizes no such difference between the self and the indwelling sin. Significantly enough, he uses the word οὐκέτι, "no longer": "It is no longer I that do it, but sin which dwells within me." In the struggle between God's will, expressed in the law, and sin, the self stands on God's side. And yet the Christian cannot declare himself free from participation in sin, for it does not come to him simply as an external force; rather must he confess that sin dwells in him, present in his carnal nature.

Such is the Christian's relation to this aeon. He has the will to do the good, but sin is present with him. In the inward man he desires God's law; but in the realistic situation in which he lives, sin occurs (vss. 21-23). With his heart he serves the law of God; but since he constantly shares in the old aeon, he continues in an inclusive context in which with his flesh he serves the law (vs. 25). He is a member in σῶμα Χριστοῦ, in "the body of Christ"; but since he still lives in the flesh, he is at the same time a member in the body of the natural humanity, which is subject to sin and death. It is this dualism which forces from Paul the much discussed—and often misunderstood—cry, ταλαίπωρος ἐγὼ ἄνθρωπος. τίς με ῥύσεται ἐκ τοῦ σώματος τοῦ θανάτου τούτου; "Wretched man that I am! Who will deliver me from this body of death?" (vs. 24). The meaning of that cry is immediately clear. As long as this life lasts, there continues the tension between the old aeon and the new, between the heart and the members, in the life of the Christian. As long as he still lives "in the flesh," and is thus a member in the body of death, which mankind under Adam, its head, is, there remains the tension between being "in Christ" and being "in the flesh." When we thus understand the real meaning of this cry, we see that there is not a bit of theatrical declamation in it. It expresses what every Christian must know in this tension between the two aeons. Though his inner desire and prayer are that God's will "be done on earth, as it is in heaven," he sees that evil has its abode here on earth. Is it not natural that he yearns to be freed from this body of death? Must he not reach forward in hope toward the time "when the perishable puts on the imperishable, and the mortal puts on immortality" (I Cor. 15:54)?

But in that cry there is nothing of doubt or despair.

Therefore Paul goes on immediately to thanksgiving, "Thanks be to God through Jesus Christ our Lord!" (vs. 25). Paul has reached the conclusion of his discussion of the Christian's freedom from the law. Of this, as of all else, he affirms that we have it "through Jesus Christ our Lord." Through Him the victory is already won. Through Him we may look forward with full confidence to the day of final redemption.

Finally, a word as to the role which 7:14-25 has to fill in the context.

In the foregoing, Paul has shown that the Christian is "free from the law." That is quite in line with the central thought of the epistle. It is of course not through the law that man becomes righteous before God. The mission of the law is something other than to justify and give life. It convinces man of sin, and it drives sin to its height; it stops every mouth, and makes the whole world stand in guilt before God. When God justifies man and gives him life, it is something wholly other than the law which is operative. In that it is exclusively a matter of what God does in Christ. A Christian is free from the law principally in the sense that he has been justified entirely without the co-operation of the law.

Thus it is that the Christian life comes about. But when once that life is present, the situation appears changed. Everyone who has followed Paul's foregoing presentation sees at once that man, left to himself, cannot fulfill the requirement of the law; so he cannot in that way become righteous. But when one has become righteous through Christ, have not new possibilities opened for him? The characteristic fact for the Christian is just this, that he is never left to himself. He lives his life "in Christ," and new powers come to him through that relationship. Can one not say that the ability, which man lacks by nature, is given to him through faith? Can one not say that Christ gives him the power to keep the law, so that he can really stand before God as righteous in this way?

To speak in such a way about the Christians' ability to fulfill the law, and thus to stand as righteous before God is nothing less than again to bring in the law, by a back door, as a way of salvation. Here the passage, 7:14-25, fills the important function of showing that the law can never, under any circumstances, be a way of salvation, *not even for the Christian.* If he were to be judged according to the law, he would be lost, for "by the works of the law shall no flesh be justified." Through the law no man, not even the Christian, becomes righteous. *The righteousness which the Christian has in his new life is not "the righteousness of the law."* Only when we realize this do we see in what basic sense the Christian is free from the law. It is not in this sense that Christ is our righteousness, namely, that He gives us power to keep the law, and we then become righteous by keeping it. Were that the case, there would be no fundamental difference between righteousness by the law and righteousness by faith, between δικαιοσύνη ἐκ νόμου and δικαιοσύνη ἐκ πίστεως. Every thought of that kind Paul excludes by this passage, 7:14-25. The works of the Christian in this aeon are no basis for his righteousness. But that only makes the gospel stand out the more in its overwhelming greatness. The gospel is not just a means for the establishment of the righteousness of the law; but the gospel of Christ is *the very righteousness of God.* To be "in Christ" is full and complete righteousness; that is to be justified apart from the law. That is to be "free from the law," without reservation.

IX

Free from Death

The dark shadow of death hangs over the old aeon. The idea of death has also rested on all that Paul has said in chapters 5-7, as he showed how the Christian is free from the destroying powers that rule in the old aeon. Even though, in those chapters, he was speaking primarily of Wrath, Sin, and the Law, the thought about Death has always lain in the background. In general one cannot draw a sharp line of demarcation between the different powers of destruction. They belong together; where one of them is, the others are also at hand. But this is especially true of death, which is always present among the destroying powers. It is "the last enemy," which includes all the others. So we saw, in chapter 5, how Paul let the discussion of the Christian's freedom from wrath broaden out into a consideration of the contrast between the dominion of death and of life. And in chapter 6, where the central issue is the Christian's freedom from sin, Paul shows that bondage to sin ends finally in death (δοῦλοι ἁμαρτίας εἰς θάνατον, vs. 16; τὸ τέλος ἐκείνων θάνατος, vs. 21; τὰ ὀψώνια τῆς ἁμαρτίας θάνατος vs. 23). And as to chapter 7, which speaks primarily of the Christian's freedom from the law, there too the discussion culminates in a word about death, about "this body of death" (7:24). To this thought which was always present, but in the background, chapter 8 now gives separate discussion. Paul here turns back to his starting point in 5:12-21. Only when he reaches chapter 8 does he carry to its conclusion the comparison of Adam and Christ, of which he spoke in the earlier passage.

We have said more than once (25ff.; 213f.) that difficulty in understanding Paul is due, in large part, to the fact that we come to him with a wholly different mode of thought from that which he uses. We are in the habit of thinking in individualistic and atomistic categories. We begin with the idea that we are individuals, distinct persons who live in proximity to others. When Paul speaks of Adam and Christ as present realities, with real significance for us, the question arises how Adam, an individual who, according to Paul, lived at the beginning of the human race, and how Christ, an individual who lived over 1900 years ago, can have actual significance for us. We perhaps look for a psychological explanation and say that by his sin Adam became a bad example for those who came after him; and that Christ, by His holiness, became a suggestive example for those who believe in Him. But Paul thinks in a wholly different way. To him Adam stands at the beginning of human history, not merely as a separate individual, but as the head of his race, as the head of the entire old humanity. And as "in Adam" we were all subjected to *death*, so we are now to *live* "in Christ," for He is the head of the new humanity.

In the attempt to avoid an individualism which clearly makes impossible a right understanding of Paul, some have laid hold on the idea of a "collectivity." It is held that Paul thinks not of individuals, but of collectivity. But the gain in this way is slight, because even the collectivity is usually conceived in the light of an individualistic starting point. To a line of thought orientated in this way, the collectivity is looked upon as a sum of individuals. If we begin with such sociological alternatives as "individual or collectivity," we shall not arrive at what Paul has in mind. The only way to understand him is to take seriously, on the one hand, the idea of *the body of sin and death* of which we are by nature ("in Adam") members; and on the other hand, *the body of Christ*, into which we are incorporated by faith and baptism. Only thus can we discern what Paul has in mind when, in chapter 8, he speaks of *death;* for his thought here too has been greatly obscured by the individualistic point of view. To Paul death is not merely an occurrence which cuts off the life of the individual; but death is a universal power which rules over the life of mankind, an all-powerful ruler who has mastered all that belongs to man.

In Genesis Paul read that transgression would lead to death: "In the day that thou eatest thereof *thou shalt surely die*" (Gen. 2:17). That is the lot of the whole human race "in Adam." But now death has met its master in Christ. In Him is found the antithesis to the transgression, namely "the righteousness of God"; and it bears its fruit unto life. Therefore it is said of him who is "in Christ," of him who through faith is righteous, that he *"shall live."* Here *life* is, in deepest sense, against *death*. They who hitherto, throughout the whole of life, have been slaves to death, have been freed by Christ from this frightful ruler, and have been received into life (cf. Heb. 2:15). Here we see how, in chapter 8, Paul draws the ultimate conclusion of his theme, that the Christian, he who through faith is righteous, shall live: he describes the Christian life not only as free from wrath, sin, and the law, but also as *"free from death."*

It is important to notice the parallel between Paul's thought in chapter 8 and his discussion in the three preceding chapters. That parallel might seem to be relatively external; but it deserves notice as an indication of the closely knit thought of the second part of the epistle.

The parallel presents itself definitely at the very beginning. In each of these four chapters the subject is the freedom of the Christian, treated in each in a special way with reference to a particular power of destruction. In each case Paul points out something special through which the freedom is effected: (1) The Christian is free from *wrath*. That fact Paul bases on *God's love* in Christ (chap. 5). (2) The Christian is free from *sin*. Here Paul refers to *baptism*; by it we have been incorporated into "the body of Christ," that the "body of sin" may be destroyed (chap. 6). (3) The Christian is free from *the law*. Here Paul refers to the death of Christ; in the "body of Christ" we have died unto the law (chap. 7). (4) The Christian is free from *death*. Here Paul refers to the *Spirit*, πνεῦμα; the Spirit of Christ is the power which makes alive (chap. 8). That parallelism is not merely coincidental or external. It is evidence for the fact that in these four chapters it is one and the same subject which is under discussion. Just as the powers of destruction are inseparably bound together, being really expressions of one and the same reality which wastes man's life, so also are those things in which Paul trusts for victory over the destroying forces, only different expressions for one and the same redeeming reality. That God's love was manifested to us through the death of Christ, that in baptism we were received into the "body of Christ," sharing with Him in death and life, and that the Spirit of Christ was given to us as the power which gives life to the dead—all these are basically one and the same fact. These are only different expressions for that which God did when He gave us Christ as "righteousness from God." The simplest way to set forth this parallelism is by setting down, side by side, the captions under which we have summed up the introductions to the several chapters:

> "Saved from the wrath of God by God's love" (5:1-11)
> "Free from sin, through baptism" (6:1-14)
> "Free from the law, through the death of Christ" (7:1-6)

Now to these, we must add:

> "Free from death, through the Spirit" (8:1-11)

But this parallelism found in the introductions also prevails throughout the discussions that follow them. Even though the wording "free from" may appear negative, the freedom of the Christian means something wholly positive to Paul. As in chapter 6 he says, "Free from sin to become slaves of righteousness," so he now says, "Free from death that you may have life" (8:12-17).

And furthermore, we see here again the oft-mentioned dualism in the Christian life, which rises out of the Christian's relation to the two aeons. When chapter 6 says that the Christian is "free from sin," it does not follow that he no longer has anything to do with sin, and no longer has to battle against it; on the contrary, just because the Christian has been delivered from the tyrant Sin, he must no longer stand in bondage to it. For the very reason that he belongs to the new aeon, his new life, as long as he still lives in the flesh, in the old aeon, must mean a constant battle against sin. And when chapter 7 says that he who is "in Christ" is "free from the law," it does not mean that he is, so to say, "through" with the law, so that he no longer has to give it any thought, or that he now keeps it in such a way that he can be righteous by means of it. From the point of view of the law, the Christian continues to be a sinner, as long as the old aeon lasts. At the same time as he has, through Christ, become participant in "righteousness from God," and has thereby been received into the new aeon, he still lives in the old. This dualism which Paul sees in the Christian life has been expressed in this striking way: the Christian is *simul justus et peccator*, he is righteous and a sinner at the same time. And now comes chapter 8 to underscore this dualism in the area which it discusses. The Christian is "free from death." The Spirit has been given to him, and the Spirit gives life. But as long as the Christian lives in the old aeon, he still lives under the condition of death, though with the prospect of eternal life before him. Therefore, just because Paul is talking of the Christian's freedom from death, he speaks of the sufferings of this present time and the glory of the aeon that is to come (8:18-30). And in conclusion he lets this chapter, and with it the second part of the letter, sound forth a song of praise to God for His love manifested in Christ, from which no power shall be able to separate us (8:31-39). God's love in Christ, with which chapter 5 began, thus also becomes Paul's final word in this connection.

The line of thought in chapter 8 falls into four divisions: (1) Free from death, through the Spirit (1-11). (2) Free from death, that we may have life (12-17). (2) The sufferings of this present aeon and the glory of the aeon that is to come (18-30). (4) Conclusion: God's love in Christ (31-39).

1. Free from Death through the Spirit
8:1-11

In direct connection with what was said in chapter 7 about the Christian's relation to the law, Paul now proceeds, "There is therefore now no condemnation for those who are in Christ Jesus" (vs. 1). That which would have been able to condemn them was the law. "By the works of the law shall no flesh be justified." That declaration, in 3:20, has been supported in many ways by what chapter 7 has said. Especially has it there been made clear that even the Christian cannot become righteous through the law. Before the law all men come only to stand as sinners. From its point of view there is no distinction, whether it be the natural man who stands there as a manifest sinner, or a Christian who stands there as *simul justus et peccator*, as one who is righteous but a sinner at the same time; for the Christian too is a sinner, and the righteousness he has is not "righteousness by the law," but "the righteousness of faith," not δικαιοσύνη ἐκ νόμου, but δικαιοσύνη ἐκ πίστεως. Before the law the Christian has no righteousness to which he could appeal. Were he to be judged, either according to what he naturally was, or according to what he was able to do with the help of faith, he would in either case be condemned, not justified. He would be judged by the law. But now Paul can nevertheless say that there is no condemnation for the Christian. Why not? The reason has been given in the preceding chapter: the Christian is "free from the law." It is not from the law that he hopes for justification; so he does not have to fear that the law will condemn him. He is "in Christ," and that means that he is beyond the pale of the law's power, being neither condemned nor justified by it. He hopes for nothing from the law, and fears nothing. For him the law is completely eliminated, as far as righteousness and freedom, condemnation and the wrath of God are concerned. Through the death of Christ, or through "the body of Christ," as it is expressed in 7:4, he has died unto the law; and he no longer lives for himself. Christ lives in him (8:10; cf. Gal. 2:19-20), and he is "in Christ." Thereby the situation is totally changed. There is no longer any condemnation, for to be "in Christ" is full and complete righteousness.

Once before, in this letter, Paul spoke about condemnation, κατάκριμα. That was in 5:16, 18. There were contrasted the "condemnation" which came through Adam, and the "justification" which came through Christ; and the latter was called "justification to life," δικαίωσις ζωῆς. It is that idea which Paul takes up again here. "Justification to life," which we have "in Christ," excludes at the same time all condemnation and all death. For the Christian these are powers that have been deposed.

What does it mean to be "in Christ"? The answer has been given in the three preceding chapters; and he goes on with it here. To be "in Christ" means to be free from Wrath, Sin, the Law, and Death. All that is now gathered up by Paul in the first two verses of this chapter. In verse 1 he says that there is no condemnation for those who are in Christ Jesus. The "condemnation" here mentioned is only another name for the wrath of God. In verse 2 he mentions sin, the law and death as that from which I have been freed by life in Christ. Here Paul contrasts two different laws or orders. To live "in Christ" is to come in under "the law of the Spirit," and that involves freedom from "the law of sin and death." Here law confronts law. But "law" is here given a meaning which is out of the ordinary. The thought is not about a law of the same sort as that from which we are set

311

free, but of a law in the general sense of a new order.

This new law or order, under which we are placed through Christ, is now defined more closely in three ways: (1) It is "the law of the *Spirit*." He who believes in Christ has received the Spirit of God and of Christ. The Spirit dwells in him (5:5; 8:9, 11; I Cor. 3:16; Gal. 4:6) and is now the driving power in his life (8:14; Gal. 5:18). The Spirit is the sphere of his whole new life "in Christ." The Christian "lives in the Spirit, and walks in the Spirit" (Gal. 5:25). Just as his ordinary human life is a life ἐν σαρκί, "in the flesh," so his life in the inner man lives ἐν πνεύματι, "in the Spirit." It is the Spirit which marks his life and is his pledge of the glory that is to come (II Cor. 1:22). (2) It is the law of life. As death holds sway in the old aeon, so life rules in the new, over those who are "in Christ." The Spirit and life belong immediately together, for "it is the Spirit that gives life" (John 6:63; II Cor. 3:6). (3) It is the law, or order, which is given "*in Christ Jesus*." For the same reason that Paul ends each of these chapters, 5-8, with practically these same words, he introduces them here, when he wants to state concisely the new situation. In a characterization of this situation there must be no failure to make clear that this is not something that comes to us automatically; that it is given to us only "in Christ," and is a reality in us only in the degree that we are "in Him."

All these ideas Paul now gathers up in a single statement, by adding genitive to genitive, and then finally adding "in Christ Jesus." He thus builds up a formulation which is hard to translate directly; but in Greek the very piling up of affirmations is peculiarly effective, ὁ νόμος τοῦ πνεύματος τῆς ζωῆς ἐν Χριστῷ Ἰησοῦ.

The new order has vanquished the old and thus "set me

free from the law of sin and death" (vs. 2). As to freedom from sin and the law, Paul has said enough in what has gone before. The new thought here is "freedom from death," ἐλεύθερος ἀπὸ τοῦ θανάτου. That is the theme of chapter 8.

In chapter 7 we heard both about the law's power and its impotence. It has the power to kill, but not to give life. Its power is the power to destroy, consisting in the fact that it can call forth sin, increase its intensity and make sin exceedingly sinful. In contrast with this, we see its impotence, as soon as the issue is victory over sin and the evoking of the good. When Paul now refers again to the law, he is thinking of its impotence, not of its power. He speaks of τὸ ἀδύνατον τοῦ νόμου. From what has gone before we know the reason for the law's impotence and inadequacy. The law is indeed spiritual; but man, to whom it speaks, is carnal by nature. That is true of all that is human. There is indeed a distinction between the natural man, who is carnally minded (σαρκικός), and the Christian, who is spiritually minded. But that distinction is of no consequence in this connection, since even the Christian is a child of Adam, of carnal nature, even though not carnally minded—σάρκινος, even though not σαρκικός.

Thus the law is entirely excluded in the matter of the victory over sin. That takes place χωρὶς νόμου, "apart from law" (3:21), by God's own intervention. "For God has done what the law, weakened by the flesh, could not do: sending his own Son in the likeness of sinful flesh and for sin, he condemned sin in the flesh" (vs. 3). So God here deals with mankind, no longer through the law, but through His own Son. As to the sending of the Son into the world, Paul uses a very peculiar expression. He says that God sent Him "in the form of sinful flesh" or, as another translation reads, "in the likeness of sinful flesh." That is a peculiar expression; but we shall see at once that it has good reason. Paul could simply have written ἐν σαρκί, "in the flesh," for it is just that which is the issue. It is true of God's own intervention by which God's own Son came "in the flesh." It is true of the incarnation of the Son—that and nothing else. But Paul does not stop with a general reference to "the flesh"; he speaks of it as "sinful flesh." For it was to be right *in sin's own realm* that the Son was to bring sin to judgment, overcome it and take away its power. It is therefore important that with Christ it is actually a matter of "sinful flesh," of σὰρξ ἁμαρτίας.

Paul is concerned to affirm that when Christ came into the world, He actually stood under the same conditions as we, and under the same destroying powers as had man in bondage. Wrath, Sin, the Law, and Death were not unknown to Him. He stood under wrath when He to redeem us from the curse *Himself became a curse* (Gal. 3:13). He stood under sin, for *"he made him to be sin who knew no sin*, so that in him we might become the righteousness of God" (II Cor. 5:21). He has stood under the law, for "when the time had fully come, God sent forth his Son, born of a woman, *born under the law*, to redeem those who were under the law" (Gal. 4:4). And in Hebrews 2:14 it is said that God made Him subject to death, "that through death he might destroy him who has the power of death." Paul could have said the same. If in any respect Christ had not been made subject to any one of these destroying powers, it would not have been completely deprived of its power or rightly brought to judgment. It is for that reason that Paul chooses to go as far as possible in affirming that Christ also actual'y was subject to the power of sin. Otherwise there would be a measure of unreality about it all. If Christ had been subject to the power of wrath, the law, and death, but had not had the whole weight of sin resting on Him, He would have been free from that which gives death its sting and makes it the absolute ruler that it is.

Paul is firmly convinced that, in some way, Christ stood under the power of sin. But here a special difficulty arises. For it is just as clear to Paul that sin had no place in Christ. He says of Him that He "knew no sin" (II Cor. 5:21). Paul can therefore not use the absolute expression σὰρξ ἁμαρτίας, "sinful flesh"; for that would mean that Christ was subject to the power of sin in the same way as we who are sinners. Paul wants to come as close to that as possible without falling into conflict with the sinlessness of Christ, of which he is utterly certain. He comes close to the dividing line; but he does not step over it. He says ἐν ὁμοιώματι σαρκὸς ἁμαρτίας, "in the form of sinful flesh," or "in the likeness of sinful flesh." In that expression there is no trace of docetism. Christ's carnal nature was no unreality, but simple, tangible fact. He shared all our conditions. He was under the same powers of destruction. Out of "the flesh" arose for Him the same temptations as for us. But in all this He was master of sin. It is not without right that it has been said that Paul here uses a definite choice of expression; but he had reason to choose his words with care. For he here deals with two relationships which seem to be in conflict, but as to neither of which he must go too far: on the one hand, the sinlessness of Christ, and on the other hand, that Christ was placed under the same conditions and under the same powers as we.

Christ overcame sin in its own realm, in the flesh, when He himself came in the form of sinful flesh. Through His death, God condemned sin and took away its power; but He thereby also deposed that power which, by the strength of sin, had ascended the throne in the old aeon and, with un-limited sway, ruled over mankind in the weakness of the flesh—namely, death. For these two, *sin* and death, belong together inseparably; they stand and fall together.

That is the way it went, when God put an end to the old order, to "the law of sin and death." For those who are in Christ, all the old is done away: no condemnation (wrath), no sin, no law, and no death has now power over them. They have been received into a wholly new order. The life of the old aeon, characterized by the fact that it is a life in the flesh and "according to the flesh," is, for them, something left behind. Through Christ they are now placed under the new order of the Spirit. They "walk not according to the flesh but according to the Spirit."

The purpose for which God through Christ deposed the old powers and brought in the new order is stated by Paul in this way: "In order that the just requirement of the law might be fulfilled in us, who walk not according to the flesh but according to the Spirit" (vs. 4). These words have often occasioned misunderstanding. It has been held that Paul here says expressly that the believer has been so changed that he can, by his works, fulfill all the requirements of the law. And is not that furthermore stated as the goal of the work of Christ? Paul says *ἵνα*, "*in order that* the just require-ment of the law might be fulfilled in us." According to that interpretation, this would be Paul's meaning: the law sets forth God's demands of us, and only if they are met in every point can we stand as righteous before God. But no one *can* by nature fulfill the requirements of the law in that way; the weakness of the flesh makes that impossible for him. But in this situation God comes to him with help. He gives him Christ, and He gives him the Spirit. Thereby he receives

the ability which he formerly lacked. Now, by the strength
that God has given him, he can fulfill the requirements of
the law. Thus righteousness is finally attained. The relation
between the law and the gospel is accordingly understood
in this way, that the law is the goal and the gospel is the
means to that goal.

But such an interpretation flies directly in the face of
Paul's whole view. On the contrary, it is just such a view
that he opposes. He has never considered it the mission of
the gospel to make possible "righteousness by the law."
"Righteousness by the law" never ceases to be, for Paul, an
expression of the false way of salvation. But it must further
be pointed out that this interpretation is also directly opposed
to what Paul says in the passage under discussion. That this is
true is obscured in some measure by the expression "the just
requirement of the law," as our translation renders δικαίωμα
τοῦ νόμου.

But what is the meaning of the law's δικαίωμα? To be
able to answer that question correctly, it ought to be observed
that this word stands in contrast with the law's κατάκριμα,
the "condemnation" of which verse 1 speaks. Paul has, in
an earlier passage, set these two in juxtaposition (5:16, 18).
There he spoke of the condemnation, the κατάκριμα, which
came through Adam, and of the status of righteousness, the
δικαίωμα, which came through Christ.

What is the end and purpose of the law? It can be said
to be twofold, in this way. (1) The law is the expression
of God's holy will. The end for which it works is that "the
righteousness of God" shall prevail. We should note that
this is something quite different from "righteousness by the
law," δικαιοσύνη ἐκ νόμου. The law is not working for *that*
end. On the contrary, Paul has stressed most emphatically

that the law itself testifies *against* righteousness by the law
and for the righteousness of faith (cf. 149, 173). If one asks
about the ultimate purpose of the law, he should not forget
this positive mission to bear witness to "the righteousness
of God." It is with this in mind that Paul says that "the
law is holy, and the commandment is holy and just and
good" (7:12); and in 7:10 he makes the simple declaration
that the commandment was given unto life, ἡ ἐντολὴ ἡ εἰς
ζωήν. Primarily, then, the law is in the service of life. It
bears witness to "the righteousness of God" which includes
life. *That is the δικαίωμα of the law.*

(2) But when the law confronts man's sin, it becomes
a condemning law. In the old aeon this becomes the law's
sole function. "The very commandment which promised life
proved to be death to me." God's holy law becomes a destroying power. It evokes and increases sin, and sets all
things human under the wrath and condemnation of God.
It fulfills its office to the condemnation of all unrighteousness
of man, and equally of all legalistic righteousness, for that
is not the righteousness God would have established among
us. Paul stresses the fact that this is exactly God's *purpose*
for the law. It was given *in order that* sin might become
sinful beyond measure (7:13), *in order that* every mouth
may be stopped, and the whole world may be held accountable to God (3:19). Thus the law became "the dispensation
of condemnation" (II Cor. 3:9). *That is the κατάκριμα of
the law.*

The law can condemn; but it does not have the power
to effect righteousness. Thus there is something which the
law would bring about, but cannot. It aims at righteousness
and its whole tendency is toward that end; but it is unable
to realize it. It is given for the sake of life, but it brings

about death. Its ultimate meaning and purpose are not to require that which is evil; and yet its effect is that that which is evil is increased. So the law does not reach its goal, but rather leads to the opposite. But "God has done what the law, weakened by the flesh, could not do," when He gave us Christ. What the law intended, but could not effect, is now brought about; but—note well—without the co-operation of the law. From the κατάκριμα of the law, from condemnation by the law, we Christians are free. Now the δικαίωμα of the law is in effect, but not any longer through the law itself, but through Christ. It is precisely when the law leaves the stage that righteousness is fulfilled; but it is not righteousness by the law, but true righteousness, "the righteousness of God," δικαιοσύνη θεοῦ. The law always expresses God's will; and where the δικαιοσύνη θεοῦ is, there the will of God is realized, *there the law's δικαίωμα is fulfilled.* It is fulfilled "in us who walk not according to the flesh, but according to the Spirit." It is fulfilled in us for the very reason that we are no longer under the law, but under grace. The righteousness of God has been manifested among us through Christ, and life has been given to us. Therein the goal of the law is realized, that which the law intended, but could not effect. The status of righteousness which the law sought to bring about, but could not, is now realized among us since "righteousness from God" has come to us.

Thus the deepest purpose of the law has been fulfilled. Against sin the law rises up in condemnation. But as to the life which is lived under "the righteousness of God," Paul says, "Against such there is no law" (Gal. 5:23). When we are "in Christ," the law's positive purpose, its δικαίωμα, is fulfilled in us, not by our keeping of the law, but through Christ, and by the fact that we "are in Him." Here we see the consequences of what Paul said in chapter 7, that Christ does not merely give us power to fulfill the demands of righteousness, but that He is Himself our righteousness. He is "the righteousness from God" which, by faith, becomes our righteousness. They who are "in Christ" are by that very fact righteous, and not by a keeping of the law made possible by that fact. Their righteousness consists in the fact, pure and simple, that they no longer live of themselves but "are in Christ." *Therein, and not through any keeping of the law is the δικαίωμα of the law fulfilled.*

That is the most positive thing that Paul says about the law. The δικαίωμα of the law has been fulfilled in us through Christ. The law and faith do not stand over against each other as enemies. Just as the law testifies to the righteousness of faith, so faith is the fulfillment of the law's δικαίωμα. Here we see the ultimate reason why Paul could answer the question, "Do we then overthrow the law by this faith?" (3:31) with his exclamation, "On the contrary, we uphold the law!"

Before we knew Christ we walked according to the flesh. Such is the ordinary, natural life of man. All that pertains to man is "flesh," for all that is human is in itself impotence and nothingness. In the concept "flesh" is included all that belongs by nature to man's life, from the lowest to the highest. "The flesh" is therefore not—as men have thought under the influence of ancient ways of thinking—a lower part of man against which man could place the spiritual side of his nature. The spirit of man also is comprehended in the carnal. It is precisely in his spiritual striving and condition that it is manifest that man is "flesh." But to us who are by nature "flesh," Christ has come and made us partakers in the divine life; that is "Spirit."

Here Paul sets up a great either—or: either we are carnal

and walk according to the flesh—and that is *death;* or we are "in Christ," we are spiritual and walk according to the Spirit—and that is *life.* He who is carnal has his mind (φρόνημα), his thoughts, his desire and constant yearning directed to that which belongs to "the flesh." His every thought is conditioned by his own carnal self. In everything he seeks only his own. He has thought and interest for nothing but the selfish, carnal life. He strives only for that which can please himself. He does not concern himself about God and His will. Therefore Paul adds, "For the mind that is set on the flesh is hostile to God; it does not submit to God's law, indeed it cannot; and those who are in the flesh cannot please God" (vss. 7-8). But, on the contrary, the Christian's mind and heart are directed to the things of the Spirit. He no longer lives for himself, but Christ lives in him; and though he still lives in the flesh, he nevertheless lives "by faith in the Son of God" (Gal. 2:20). And that means that he has the mind of Christ (I Cor. 2:16) or the Spirit of Christ, the νοῦς or πνεῦμα of Christ. Thus a thoroughgoing change has taken place in his whole existence: he is no longer carnally minded, but spiritually minded. To the very roots of his being he is another person. To be sure, sin still dwells in his flesh (ἡ οἰκοῦσα ἐν ἐμοὶ ἁμαρτία, 7:20; cf. 7:17f.); but that is not the deepest force in his life. The Spirit of God and of Christ has found abode in him, Paul says, and it is that which has made the Christian a *spiritual* man. So Paul can say to the Christians, "You are not in the flesh, you are in the Spirit, if the Spirit of God really dwells in you" (πνεῦμα θεοῦ οἰκεῖ ἐν ὑμῖν, vs. 9). And that is so genuinely true that he can add, "Any one who does not have the Spirit of Christ does not belong to him." One cannot belong to Christ without sharing in His death and resurrection and having His Spirit resident in him.

The contrast between flesh and spirit is at the same time the contrast between death and life. "To set the mind on the flesh is death, but to set the mind on the Spirit is life and peace" (vs. 6). This great contrast concerns the Christian, and it might seem that he must be wholly within the realm of the Spirit. As we have just noted, Paul can say to the Christians, "You are not in the flesh, you are in the Spirit." But the fact is not so simple as that. The Christian stands *between the two aeons*. He still lives "in the flesh," with all the sin and weakness that that involves; but at the same time he lives "in the Spirit," with all that involves of righteousness and life. The Christian is *simul justus et peccator*, both righteous and sinner at the same time. Therefore he stands, at the same time, under death and under life. The outer man, the body, Paul says, is dead *because of sin;* but the spirit is alive *because of righteousness* (vs. 10). That is the status of the Christian as long as he lives "in the flesh," that is, in this earthly existence. Here is the same dualism we observed in chapter 7.

At one time Christ lived here "in the flesh" and was subject to death; but "according to the Spirit of holiness" (κατά πνεῦμα ἁγιωσύνης) He was raised for our justification (1:4; 4:25). In this present life, the Christians are subject to death, as He was; but that which happened to Him, who is the head and the beginning of a new humanity, shall also some day happen to those who are His members. Therefore Paul says to the Christians, "If the Spirit of him who raised Jesus from the dead dwells in you, he who raised Christ Jesus from the dead will give life to your mortal bodies also through his Spirit which dwells in you" (vs. 11).

Here Paul looks forward to the world of the consumma-

tion. *Through the Spirit the Christian is free from death.*
But as yet that freedom is his only as something assured for
him in the future. He has the beginning of it in the resurrection of Christ, for therein the resurrection aeon has already
begun; and it is that beginning which God will carry forward to consummation in glory. Then there will no longer
be any tension between the "mortal body" and the spirit
which is life. And the reason why that tension will cease is
not that the spirit is to be freed from the body—as many,
under the influence of the Greek way of thinking, have held
—but rather that the Spirit will give life to the body. The
natural man, who belongs only to the old aeon, is "carnal"
in his total existence. Both his body, and also what we
usually speak of as his "spirit" are nothing but "flesh," according to Paul. For σάρξ, "the flesh," sets its mark on everything in the old aeon. But when one, through faith in Christ,
is received into the new aeon which gets its character from
the Spirit, πνεῦμα, that means first of all that the Spirit is
given to him. As a human being he is still "flesh"; but he is
no longer only flesh, but also spirit, because *the Spirit of
God dwells in him.* The Christian is thus a spiritual man.
And yet he cannot be called "spiritual" in the same degree
as the natural man is "carnal." With the latter *everything*
is "carnal." With the Christian the Spirit has come to dwell;
and in view of that the Christian can be called "spiritual."
But in his "flesh" and members sin is still present all the
time. So the result of the indwelling of the Spirit is a tension
which was not found in man as long as he was only carnal;
there is now the struggle between flesh and spirit. That
tension we saw in the discussion in 7:14-25; and we shall
encounter it throughout the entire eighth chapter. It was
that tension which evoked from Paul the dry, "Wretched

man that I am! Who will deliver me from this body of
death?" (7:24). The Christian has received the Spirit, and
He is a reality in his life; but he lives on in the body of sin
and death, which keeps the Spirit from ruling completely.
"The Spirit is willing, but the flesh is weak." Therefore the
Christian life is never more than partial in this life; but for
that reason the yearning of the Christian reaches forward
toward the eternal consummation.

Far from thinking that man's status in the consummation
is a "pure spirituality," Paul rather thinks of the body as
belonging to the full life of the spirit. He is of course sure
that "flesh and bood cannot inherit the kingdom of God"
(I Cor. 15:50), for that which belongs to the present aeon
has nothing to do with the new aeon. In the new aeon the
Spirit is to rule without limitation; but that does not mean
that the bodily is to pass away. It is to be transformed into
keeping with the spiritual character of the new aeon. For
that reason Paul speaks of a spiritual body (I Cor. 15:44).
With the natural man in this world, both his body and spirit
are "carnal" in character. Even so, for the Christian, both
body and spirit will bear the character of "the Spirit" in the
new life. Even his mortal body shall be made alive. That
is the result of his membership in Christ, the risen One. It
is the result of the indwelling of the Spirit of Him who
raised Christ from the dead.

As long as earthly life lasts, the Christian stands between
the dominions of death and of life. Both aeons meet in his
life and impress the characters of both on it. The Christian
lives "in the flesh," but not "according to the flesh" (II Cor.
10:2-3); he lives "according to the Spirit." The outward
man bears evidence that he lives in the old aeon. Therefore
the body is subject to death, because of sin (τὸ σῶμα νεκρὸν

διὰ ἁμαρτίαν); but in spirit, the Christian even now belongs to the new aeon, so it can be said of him that "the spirit is alive because of righteousness (τὸ πνεῦμα ζωὴ διὰ δικαιοσύνην.) "In Adam," and by reason of participation in his sin, the Christian stands under the dominion of death; but "in Christ," and by reason of participation in His righteousness, life has been given to him.

2. FREE FROM DEATH, THAT WE MAY HAVE LIFE
8:12-17

The Christian has escaped from that ruler, death. But the intention is that he is actually to *live*. If death has been deposed, we are to let it be deposed in our lives, and no longer shape our lives according to its demand.

We here call to mind again the dualism in the Christian life, to which Paul has referred again and again in the foregoing. In the sixth chapter, for example, he declared that the Christian is "free from sin"; and from that he immediately drew the conclusion that the Christian must battle against sin and all that would bind us to it. Out of the indicative, Paul educes an imperative. Through Christ we *are* free from sin; and *for that very reason* we are to fight against it. By Christ we have been snatched out of our bondage to sin; and *for that very reason* we must always fight against sin when it attempts to reconquer what it has lost. The same dualism emerges here, where Paul speaks of the Christian's freedom from death. Through Christ the Christian has actually been freed from death; but that does not mean that there is no longer any possibility for death to threaten him. He has not yet reached the condition where "death shall be no more . . . for the former things have passed away" (Rev. 21:4). The life of the Christian is still lived all the time in the scope of the first creation. He still lives "in the flesh," and there death has its chance to lay hold, when it strives to regain its power over him. Out of the flesh come all sorts of claims on him; and if he were to follow these, the result would be that he would be carried straight back along the way to bondage under death. It is therefore imperative to resist these claims and reject them as unjustified. Just as, in chapter 6, Paul was concerned to show that the Christian is truly free from sin, so that it can no longer come with any warranted claim on him (cf. pp. 243f.), so he is now concerned to show that, in like manner, the Christian's freedom from death means that the flesh can no longer come with any justifiable claim. "So then, brethren, we are debtors, not to the flesh, to live according to the flesh—for if you live according to the flesh you will die, but if by the Spirit you put to death the deeds of the body you will live" (vss. 12-13).

So there are two different ways to live. Man can "live according to the flesh" or "live according to the Spirit." As to the former manner of life, it must be said that it is not really life. On the contrary, in its basic nature it is quite the opposite. Therefore Paul says, "If you live according to the flesh you will *die*." In that case one does not speak of what is properly life. When we hear Paul speaking here about a life which is really death, our thoughts turn automatically to the famous words of Augustine: "Such was my life—was that life?"

Man can really live only by living "according to the Spirit"; but that means to "put to death the deeds of the body." Here Paul speaks of *"the body,"* where we should have expected him to speak of *"the flesh"* and of putting it to death; for "the flesh" is the antithesis of "the Spirit." In fact it is that antithesis which Paul has in mind. But it is not difficult to see the reasons why he here uses the word "body" and refers to "the deeds of the body." He has just said that the Christian's outward man belongs to the old aeon. The body is subject to death because of sin, even though the spirit is alive because of righteousness. With his "mortal body" the Christian lives in an order where death reigns. It is here—in his mortal body—that the Christian must carry on his battle against the flesh and death. Here we find additional light on 7:23 where Paul speaks of a "law in his members" which is at war with the law in the Christian's mind. Perhaps we can now see better why Paul longs for deliverance from "this body of death" (7:24).

Since the Christian has received the Spirit, Paul calls on him to "walk in the Spirit" and let the Spirit permeate all of his life. To be sure, it is true that in the Christian life the Spirit and the flesh are at war with each other; but the intention certainly is not that the flesh is still to have any right to direct the Christian. He has entered into the reign of the Spirit and is putting to death "the deeds of the body." Paul's idea here is the same as that which, in Galatians, 5:16, he expresses in this way: "Walk by the Spirit, and do not gratify the desires of the flesh."

That the Christian is able to carry on that battle against the flesh and death is due to the fact that he does not wage it alone and in his own strength. When the tyrant death is cast down from his throne, the place is not left vacant in the Christian's life. The place has been taken by the Spirit of God which is "the Lord and Giver of life," for "it is the Spirit that gives life" (John 6:63). Thereby the Christian has come to a life that is *life* indeed. The meaning is made clear in the theme of this epistle: "He who through faith is righteous *shall live*." He who believes in Christ has thereby been taken out of the old aeon, the aeon of the flesh. So he no longer stands under the dominion of *death*. He has now been received into the new aeon, the aeon of the Spirit, where *life* reigns. And though he still lives "in the flesh" and therefore finds himself in the old aeon, he there carries on the battle of the new aeon; he battles for the Spirit, against the flesh. He "lives in the Spirit," "walks in the Spirit," and "puts to death the deeds of the body"; and in all this he has the promise of eternal life, the life of the aeon to come.

Here the declaration applies that "that which is born of the flesh is flesh, and that which is born of the Spirit is Spirit" (John 3:6). According to the flesh we are *the children of Adam*, but as they who have been born of the Spirit, we are *the children of God*. In the prologue of the Gospel according to John it is said "to all who received him, who believed in his name, he gave power to become children of God; who were born, not of blood nor of the will of the flesh nor of the will of man, but of God" (John 1:12-13). In like manner Paul here couples the reception of the Spirit with sonship, "For all who are led by the Spirit of God are sons of God." In the spirit of sonship we can, without fear and in full confidence, draw near to God as our Father, for "the Spirit himself bears witness with our spirit that we are children of God."

Herewith really everything is bestowed, for as the children of God we are also heirs. With the words "children—heirs" Paul has, in an extraordinary way, described the Christian life in its two aspects, its *present* and its *future*. "Now *are* we the children of God"; we *are* heirs; the inheritance is already ours. But at the same time he looks toward the future. "It does not yet appear what we shall be" (I John 3:2). We have not yet received the inheritance. As the first fruit Christ has already received it and has entered into the new aeon of the resurrection. But thereby something real has been attained for us also, for everything that concerns Christ also concerns us who belong to Him through faith. We are "heirs of God and fellow heirs with Christ." Notice ought to be taken of the particle, σνν, repeated three times in verse 17. First the apostle declares that we are *fellow* heirs with Christ (σνγκληρονόμοι). And then he goes on to two other compounds with σνν, "we suffer with him" (σνμπάσχομεν), and "we may also be glorified with him" (σννδοξασθῶμεν). In these Paul's emphasis on both present and future in relation to Christ comes to expression. In this life it is of primary importance that we are participants with Him in His suffering. But in the life that is to come we are made participants in His glory; only then shall we enter into the inheritance which has already been assured for us.

It is not the suffering but the glory that is the goal. But for the Christian, as for Christ himself, the way to glorification, to participation in God's δόξα, is through suffering. In the fact that the suffering is a suffering *with* Christ it has received its inescapable place in the Christian life. As long as this aeon lasts, the suffering also lasts; the glory waits in the aeon that is to come. Of that the next section speaks.

3. THE SUFFERING OF THE PRESENT AEON AND THE GLORY OF THE COMING AEON
8:18-30

In the foregoing, Paul has shown how, through Christ, we have been removed from the power of death and received into the new life. But can he actually sustain that view of the Christian life? Death has clearly not yet lost its grip on the Christian. As long as he lives on this earth, he has definite experience that he is still in death's country. To

that fact the sufferings which come to him bear their unequivocal witness. To such objections Paul can answer simply
by pointing to the coming glory. It is so great, beyond measure, that it sheds its clarifying light over the present life with
its suffering. "I consider that the sufferings of this present
time are not worth comparing with the glory that is to be
revealed to us" (vs. 18). The seed of the glory that is to
be lies in the suffering that is here. It is the same idea which
Paul expresses in this way, in II Corinthians 4:17, "This
slight momentary affliction is preparing for us an eternal
weight of glory beyond all comparison." The suffering itself
assures no glory. Paul is quite free of any such thought of
compensation. That which makes the Christian's suffering
a preparation for glory is the fact that it is a suffering *with
Christ*. The fellowship of suffering with Christ here in time
prepares the way for the fellowship of glory with Him in
eternity.

It is clear from the way he expresses himself that Paul is
speaking of the two aeons. "The sufferings of the present
time" means simply the suffering of this aeon. ὁ νῦν χαιρός is
a familiar parallel expression for ὁ αἰὼν οὗτος. And "the glory
that is to be" bears a glimpse of "the aeon that is to come."
In ἡ μέλλουσα δόξα we can see ὁ αἰὼν ὁ μέλλων. In the coming aeon the tension, which has marked the Christian life
in this world, will be resolved. But for that reason the present suffering is not work compared with the glory which will
then be revealed to us. The victory of life over death has
already been won. Therefore this present life with all its
infirmity reaches ahead, with sighs and yearning, towards
the final manifestation of the glory.

Paul speaks in this section about a threefold groaning:
(1) the whole creation groans (vss. 19-22); (2) the Christian

groans (vss. 23-25); and (3) the Spirit himself groans (vss. 26-27). To these Paul adds (4) a word about the fulfillment of God's eternal purpose (vss. 28-30).

(1) The groaning of creation

Through man's sin death has come into the world and won its dominion here. That has its primary relevance to mankind. But it was not man alone, but the world in which he lives, that was subjected to death. The ground is cursed because of him (Gen. 3:17). The whole existence in which we are involved stands in bondage to corruption. But there is hope for it too. Just because it was made subject to corruption *because of man,* there is hope that it may some time, together with man, be saved from corruption. The old world was cursed on account of man's *unrighteousness.* But since *"the righteousness of God"* has been revealed through Christ, it brings with it a promise of a new world. II Peter 3:13 says "According to his promise we wait for new heavens and a new earth in which righteousness dwells" (cf. Isa. 65:17; Rev. 21:1). Paul views the matter in exactly the same way. There is a bond between man and creation, as we know it by our usual experience in the old aeon; and the new humanity has its counterpart in the new creation as it will be revealed when the new aeon comes in glory and fulfillment.

That is what Paul has in mind when he says, "The creation waits with eager longing for the revealing of the sons of God; for the creation was subjected to futility, not of its own will but by the will of him who subjected it in hope; because the creation itself will be set free from its bondage to decay and obtain the glorious liberty of the children of God. We know that the whole creation has been groaning in travail together until now" (vss. 19-22).

According to Paul, the whole course of the world moves toward a very definite goal, that is, the freedom which belongs to the glory of the children of God (ἡ ἐλευθερία τῆς δόξης τῶν τέκνων τοῦ θεοῦ). As yet that glory and that freedom have not been revealed. Christ has indeed already entered into His glory, and it is true of those who believe in Christ that they live in Christ and are, through Him, free from all destroying powers; but as yet their "life is hid with Christ in God" (Col. 3:3).

The redemption of mankind is also to be the redemption of creation. For Paul the two go hand in hand and are inseparably united. Just as God, on the day of resurrection, will give man a body which corresponds to the new aeon of glory, a "spiritual body," so He will create a corresponding new cosmos, "new heavens and a new earth." So the consummation will not come by any automatic process of development. God does indeed lead the whole creation on toward a goal which He has fixed definitely; but the consummation will come through His own mighty action; and it will concern not only individuals, but it will have cosmic meaning and cosmic dimensions. Only then, in union with this total fulfillment, will "the revealing of the sons of God" take place.

(2) The Christian's groaning

The whole creation groans in travail. "And not only the creation," Paul adds. The Christian also groans and waits for sonship. We might ask why he has to groan and yearn for adoption. It is already his, is it not? Verse 14 says, "All who are led by the Spirit of God are sons of God." And in verse 16 we read, "It is the Spirit himself that bears witness with our spirit that we are children of God." Is it necessary, then, for the Christian to groan and wait for sonship?

The answer to that question has really been given in what has gone before, when, for instance, Paul spoke in verse 17 about the dualism and tension that mark the Christian life. That idea is now taken up for further development. The Christian has been made an heir of God and a fellow heir with Christ; but he has not yet received the inheritance. He has received the Spirit, but as yet only as a first fruit and guarantee of the glory that is to be. Only the earnest-money, a first payment, so to say, has been given him. The matter is indeed thereby assured, but the full possession is not yet his. Though the Christian has received the Spirit and already lives in the security of sonship, he still has to wait, as long as he lives "in the flesh," stretching forward to the fulfillment, to that which Paul calls "the revealing of the sons of God."

What is it that is still lacking in this sonship? Paul says it is "the redemption of our bodies." That statement has often been thought to mean that Paul was expressing a longing for entire liberation from his body, from corporeality in general. That is a misinterpretation. Paul does not yearn for liberation from the body as such, but for redemption from this body of *death* in which we live here. That is what he says expressly in 7:24, "Who shall deliver me from this body of death?" He yearns for deliverance from the bondage to corruption, in which the outward man is placed as long as the old aeon lasts. Only when "this body of death" has given place to the new spiritual body of the resurrection, only "when the perishable puts on the imperishable, and the mortal puts on immortality" (I Cor. 15:54), can we properly speak of "the revealing of the sons of God."

This shows how realistically Paul views the Christian life. Chapters 7 and 8 have sometimes been contrasted to

each other, with the idea that the former is concerned exclusively with the weakness of the flesh, and the latter with
the power of the Spirit. What Paul says about the groaning
of the Christian contradicts such a view. Paul has painted
for us no enthusiast's overdrawn picture of the present power
of the Christian life. He knows very well to what limits that
is bound in this world. He knows how to differentiate between that which has already been given and that which
must wait for fulfillment. To say it concisely, he is able to
distinguish between the *present* and the *future* in the Christian life. The Christian *is* already saved. It would be false
to speak of salvation as something that is yet to come. But
it would be equally false to say that it has already come fully.
Paul combines these two aspects when he says "in this hope
are we saved." "We are saved"—that is the *present* of the
Christian life; he who is "in Christ" has already received the
gift of salvation. But, on the other hand, we have that gift
only "in this hope"—that is the *future* of the Christian life.
It is of the nature of hope that its object lies in the future.
"Hope that is seen is not hope."

The Christian hope sees its realization in the future, not
in so far as that has already begun here, but in so far as the
full manifestation is still to come. There is an incomplete-
ness in the Christian life on earth. In II Corinthians 5:7
Paul refers to that when he says, "We walk by faith, not by
sight." It is the same contrast that meets us in the passage
under discussion, though Paul here uses "hope" in place of
"faith." But the truth is the same, in both ways of saying it.
Faith is directed to that which is not seen (Heb. 11:1), and
the same is true of hope. "Who hopes for what he sees?"
The faith and hope of the Christian reach forward toward
that which lies beyond the veil, toward that which does not

yet appear. The Christian's true home is in the life that is
to come, which is not yet revealed. To that his yearning and
hope reach out. So Paul concludes, "If we hope for what
we do not see, we wait for it with patience." The Christian
knows that he is away from the Lord as long as he is at home
in the body (II Cor. 5:6); therefore he groans and waits for
the redemption of the body, therefore he waits for the life
of the coming aeon. That is what the Christian's groaning
means to Paul.

(3) The groaning of the Spirit

It is the tension between the old aeon and the new, between the suffering of this present time and the glory that
is to be, that marks the Christian life on this earth and calls
forth its groaning and its longing. The Christian still lives
in this aeon with all that presses upon him and causes suffering and need; but before him opens the prospect of eternal
glory. Can he help recognizing the limitations of the present
or longing for the consummation? Here we see how erroneous are views which have understood Paul's view of the
Christian life to mean that it has already attained to fulfillment. On the contrary, Paul is clearly aware that, in this
aeon, the Christian life is weighted down with great weak-
nesses and infirmities. And that is made even clearer by
what he now says about the groaning of the Spirit.

Paul has again and again pointed out that, in this aeon,
the Christian is bound to "this body of death," and that his
outward man is conditioned by the circumstances of this
life. In this relationship to the old aeon lay the explanation,
in chapter 7, of the tension between will and action in the
Christian, between the law of his mind and the law that
rules in his members. It might seem natural to think that

the life of the Christian could be divided into inner and outer spheres; that the weakness due to "the flesh" concerns only the latter, the Christian's external relationship with the world; and that the inner man, in its relationship with God, is so transformed that weakness gives way before the power of the Spirit. But in Paul we find quite another view of the inner life of the Christian. For right here Paul speaks of "our weakness." It is not only in the outer life of the Christian that weakness grips him. It is a tragic reality even in his inner life, in his life with God, in his very prayer life. "We do not know how to pray as we ought." But here the Spirit enters to help us in our weakness. Even as creation groans, as the Christian groans, so *the Spirit himself groans* (ὡσαύτως καὶ τὸ πνεῦμα), for "the Spirit himself intercedes for us with sighs too deep for words." The Spirit himself makes intercession for us with groans without words. And even though no Christian can understand the groaning of the Spirit, the Spirit's wordless language, God, who searches the heart, understands. "He who searches the hearts of men knows what is the mind of the Spirit, because the Spirit intercedes for the saints according to the will of God."

This, then, is what "the saints" are like. Even in their inner life there is much of weakness; but the Spirit comes to help them in their weakness, even though they cannot understand how. But that is far from the time of consummation. Even as they themselves must groan and wait for "the redemption of the body," so the Spirit cf God also groans in like manner, when it has found abode in them. The Spirit also groans and intercedes for the day of fulfillment, when the sons of God shall be revealed in glory, and God's eternal purpose shall come to consummation.

(4) The consummation of God's eternal purpose

Ever since verse 18 Paul has been speaking about the suffering of this present time and the glory that is to be revealed. He has a final word to add here. As long as one looks at the two aeons simply as two realities which can be set side by side and compared, that which happens to the Christian, while he still lives in the old aeon, always takes on a negative aspect. It is something that he must endure while he waits for the glory that is to be. But why should he have to wait anyway? The powers of destruction have been brought to judgment and deposed, have they not? Why does the Christian have to have so much to do with them in this life? Does it not really look as if, even though they have in principle been overcome, the destroying powers still have the advantage in the struggle? Even though the Christian is not confined to this aeon, but has the vision of that which is to come, he is easily tempted to view the present and its suffering with worldly eyes.

In an earlier connection (pp. 24f.) we saw how the thought of the two aeons involves an enormous widening of perspective, in comparison with the mundane view which is customary among us. While a secularized outlook regards *this* world as all there is, and operates with the short perspective that follows therefrom, faith in the age that is to come opens a view, unending perspective. Now, in the passage under consideration, we see Paul *widening the perspective still further*. The present age is not the first, as its comparison with that which is to come might suggest. Just as the present aeon is to be followed by an eternity, it has already been preceded by an eternity. Only when we see our present existence set in God's activity, which goes from eternity to eternity, do we get it in right perspective. Then

man comes to see that *everything* that comes to the Christian
in this life—and consequently the sufferings of the present
too—must work together for good to him.

Thus all that is negative in this life is seen to have a positive purpose in the execution of God's eternal plan. Super-
ficially the sufferings inseparable from the present age and
the inescapable struggle against the powers of destruction,
in which the Christian is here involved, seem to hinder and
oppose God's purpose for the Christian. These are the fac-
tors that keep God's will from ever being "done on earth, as
it is in heaven"—even in the Christian. But in actual fact
these things too, that seem to frustrate God's purpose, come
to serve its accomplishments. The result is that nothing in
this life can harm the Christian. Even the onslaught of the
powers of destruction belongs to that which must work together for good.

When Paul here speaks of the Christian, he uses a characterization which deserves notice for two reasons. He says,
"To those who love God, (τοῖς ἀγαπῶσιν τὸν θεόν), all things
work together for good."

What primarily makes the expression noteworthy is the
fact that Paul usually seems to avoid talking of man's love
to God. For instance, one cannot point out a single place in
his writings where the noun "love," ἀγάπη, clearly means
love to God. The explanation is not hard to find. "Love,"
ἀγάπη, is for Paul primarily the love which God showed to
us in giving His Son for us (5:5-8). This "love of God in
Christ Jesus" (8:39) is, as we earlier pointed out (p. 199),
so overwhelming a reality to Paul that he generally refrains
from using the same high word to express our love to God.
A few times he does use the verbal expression "to love God"
(ἀγαπᾶν τὸν θεόν). Except here, it is found only twice in his

writings (I Cor. 2:9; 8:3; cf. τῶν ἀγαπώντων τὸν κύριον, Eph.
6:24). Here, then, is one of the very few places where Paul
speaks of the Christian's love to God. Of course it would
be a misunderstanding to think that Paul in any way wants
to thrust aside the reality spoken of in the expression "love
to God." Schlatter is right in saying, "Even if Paul does not
speak about the Christian's love, he always speaks in love."
And as for the Christian, he does love God and "loves our
Lord Jesus Christ"; and to Paul that is something which is
so characteristic that the expression "those who love God"
is sufficient as a name for Christians.

The sentence, "Everything works together for good to
those who love God," presents still another problem. On
what does the Christian rest his certainty that all that comes
to him must work together for good? Does Paul mean that
the Christian is to let his confidence rest in himself, in his
love to God? That would be to come into conflict with all
that he has always affirmed. It is as if Paul realizes that
there is possibility of misunderstanding here. So he adds
another expression which definitely excludes any such interpretation. Beside the words "to those who love God" and
in explanation of them, he adds "who are called according
to his purpose." The situation is as follows. The Christians
love God; that expression can be used as a name for them
and to characterize their inner status; but it says nothing as
to why all things must work together for their good. The
reason for that is not found in them, but in God; not in their
subjective state, but in God's objective, eternal purpose.
They who love God have not brought that about themselves;
it has been given to them through the calling that has come
to them from God, which has its basis in His eternal purpose.

After Paul has thus raised the question from the level of

the subjective in man to the objective plan in the divine purpose, he goes on with a series of sentences which might be characterized as *the most objective* to be found in the New Testament: "For those whom he foreknew he also predestined to be conformed to the image of his Son, in order that he might be the first-born among many brethren. And those whom he predestined he also called; and those whom he called he also justified; and those whom he justified he also glorified."

These are mighty affirmations which are closely knit together and stretch *from eternity—through time—to eternity*. The concept of the two aeons is here transcended. *Before* the old aeon stands God's eternal purpose. "Before the foundation of the world" God fixed his purpose of election. It is that which now moves on toward realization in the world, when God calls and justifies men. And it is that which He will bring to consummation in eternity, when He glorifies them. Paul would thus show how everything—from the eternal election to the final glory—is utterly in God's hand. There is place for neither chance nor arbitrariness.

Of those who are "in Christ" it is true that, from eternity, God knew them as His own. "He chose us in him before the foundation of the world" (Eph. 1:4). And as to those whom He thus knew and chose, it is further said, them "he also predestined to be conformed to the image of his Son." When the sufferings of this present time come to the Christian, it is not only because alien powers of destruction attack him. He is not given up to the play of hostile powers, but what happens to him is only what God foreordained for him. Christ was also at one time placed under these powers of destruction; but now, ever since the time of His resurrection, He has entered into glory. In both of these respects we are predestined to be conformed to His likeness, united with Him in the same death and in the same resurrection (6:5). We are so apt to see in the sufferings of the present only an obstacle to God's will and purpose, thinking that God's purpose can apply only to the glory. But Christ's path went through suffering to glory. Therefore God has also predestined those who are "in Christ" to go the same way. God has predestined them to "suffer with him in order that they may be glorified with him" (8:17).

The first two links in this chain of thought belong to eternity. They are concerned with God's eternal purpose "before the foundation of the world." But that which God purposed in eternity He carries out here in time. "Those whom he predestined he also called." When man is reached by God's call through the gospel, that is not by chance. It means rather that God's eternal purpose for him begins to take concrete form. He is brought into relation with Christ, is incorporated into Him, becomes a member of "the body of Christ"; and thereby the "righteousness of God," which was revealed through Christ, becomes a reality in his life. Therefore Paul goes on, "and those whom he called he also justified."

Here the chain of God's actions culminates for the time being. Paul has carried the line of thought forward to the point where the Christian now finds himself. The Christian is justified. Henceforth he stands as one who is righteous through Christ. And now there appears to him one stage more, which crowns all those that have gone before, the final consummation. We remember that it is said of him who through faith is righteous that he *"shall live."* He is to share in the life of the new aeon; glory awaits him. And therewith one takes the step from time to eternity. This last

step Paul makes, and that in a way that must arouse notice
and surprise. All the other steps have dealt with the past and
the present. Paul can therefore say that God has effected
all these. From eternity God *has* foreknown and chosen
those who now believe in Christ. He *has* foreordained them
to be conformed to the likeness of His Son; He *has* called
them and justified them. But when Paul now turns to speak
of their *glorification,* he treats of something which, unlike
all the foregoing, has not yet taken place, but is still to be.
We might therefore expect that Paul would now change
from the past tense to the future, and say "those whom he
justified he *will* also glorify in eternity." But that is not
what Paul says. Even of this last step he speaks as of something that has already happened, and ends the series in this
way, "and those whom he justified *he also glorified.*" Instead
of the future we were expecting he uses an aorist, ἐδόξασεν.

For this reason some interpreters have come to the conclusion that Paul does not refer here to the "glorifying" or
the "glory" (δόξα) which comes at the end of the Christian
life and is not revealed in its fullness until eternity. They
hold that Paul rather means here an inner process of transformation that goes on in the Christian, which he may himself sense. It comes as a result of the indwelling of the Spirit
and can, in a sense, be spoken of as a "glorifying." (Thus
Zahn spoke of "a renewing of life effected by the reception
of the Spirit"; and Jülicher said that "the process of glorification within us has already begun.") But it is abundantly
clear that this is a misinterpretation. Ever since verse 18
Paul has set over against each other "the suffering of this
present time" and "the glory that is to be revealed." The
line of thought that started there is now brought to its culmination with the explanation "those whom he justified he

also glorified." There is no room to doubt that with these words Paul actually refers to "the glory that is to be revealed," ἡ μέλλουσα δόξα.

Likewise, on the other side, it can be said to be a misinterpretation when others have held that Paul here makes a "triumphant anticipation" and speaks of that which is still to come as if it had already arrived. Every such fictional "as if" is totally alien to Paul. He speaks of a reality which both *has* come and *is to* come. But how shall this strange doubleness of meaning be understood. The explanation lies in the relation between the two aeons and the peculiar way in which they reach into each other. Again and again (cf. p. 328) we have had occasion to speak of the present and the future in the Christian life, and how these two constitute an indissoluble unity. So, for example, Paul includes both in a single expression when he says (8:24), "In this hope were we saved." Salvation is already here as an indubitable, present reality; it *has* been given to us through Christ. And yet hope stretches forward to it as to something which *is to be* fulfilled only in eternity. There is another parallel, even closer to the double sense in the passage now under discussion, when Paul says (5:2) that we rejoice in God's glory (δόξα θεοῦ), but as yet only in hope (cf. p. 334). We have the more reason to call that passage to mind because Paul not only speaks there of the "glory," but also of "the sufferings of this present time." He says, "More than that, we rejoice in our sufferings," (5:3). Thus in chapter 5 he already touches on the problem to whose fuller discussion he comes back in 8:18-30. With Christ the new aeon has entered into the world as a reality, that is, as something that is actually present in it. Therefore when it is said of the Christian that he lives in both aeons, we must be on guard against understanding this to mean that in the present he lives *only* in the old aeon, and that the new aeon is *only* something that is still in the future.

Again and again, in the foregoing, we have seen how the two aeons reach into each other. Though the new aeon has come through Christ, the old aeon remains. Generally the stress has been laid on the fact that the Christian still lives in the old aeon, even though he belongs to the new. But it is now necessary to stress the other side too. Even though the Christian still lives in the old aeon, nevertheless the new aeon is present in his life as a mighty reality. The Christian does not live in the present aeon "as if nothing had happened." On the contrary, something utterly overwhelming has happened through Christ, whereby the old existence has been utterly transformed. This manifests itself most clearly in this, that even "the sufferings of this present time" have been comprehended in that which works for the Christian's good, so that he can actually rejoice in them. "The sufferings of this present time" are a part of the Christian's being conformed to the likeness of Christ; for that likeness includes both suffering with Him and being glorified with Him.

From verse 18 and on, the thought of "the sufferings of this present time" has governed Paul's discussion. That idea is, to be sure, not the subject of *direct* consideration in verses 28-30. In these verses it is set aside so definitely that it is not mentioned at all, as Paul talks of God's dealing with the Christian here on earth. The only glimpse of it is seen in the statement that the Christian is conformed to the likeness of His Son. Yet it continues to be present as a point of orientation in the mind of the apostle; it makes its contribution to the way in which he formulates even this passage. That such is the case is likewise clear from the fact that it again

344

comes to expression in the passage that follows next. It has not been forgotten, but is present in latent form all the time. In verse 18 Paul says that the sufferings of this present time are not worth comparing with the glory that is to be. Now that he comes to the end of his discussion of that point, concluding with his statement about the coming glory, he says nothing further about the sufferings. They have lost their negative aspect. But in that very fact it is manifest that the new aeon is a mighty reality in the life of the Christian on this earth, and that the "glorifying" has already begun. Paul therefore has all reason to say, "Those whom he justified *he also glorified*." But that which has been begun here is to be brought to consummation in eternity. Only then will they share fully in the glory of God, in δόξα θεοῦ. Especially as regards the "glorifying" do the present and the future reach into each other—for the Christian as for Christ himself, of whom it is said, "*Now* is the Son of man glorified, and in him God is glorified; if God is glorified in him, God *will* also glorify him" (John 13:31-32); and again, "I *have* glorified it, and I *will* glorify it again" (John 12:28).

In 7:24 Paul says, "Wretched man that I am! Who will deliver me from this body of death?" The answer to that question follows immediately in the thanksgiving, "Thanks be to God through Jesus Christ our Lord!" Only if the question and the answer are taken together do we have a striking expression of the Christian's status in this world. That has received further light in chapter 8. This has shown us how the Christian continues to live in "this body of death," subject to "the sufferings of this present time"; he must still groan and wait for sonship, the redemption of his body. But in all this he is, through Christ, "free from death" and is already participant in the glory that shall be brought to

consummation in eternity. Therefore in the midst of the
sufferings of this present time he can thank and praise God
for the victory that has already been given. Though he is
still in this body of death Paul can say, as he does in I Corinthians 15:57, "Thanks be to God who gives us the victory
through our Lord Jesus Christ!" Even so he also concludes
the eighth chapter with a jubilant thanksgiving to God for
the victory over all the powers of destruction, that has been
bestowed on us through the love of God in Christ Jesus our
Lord.

4. CONCLUSION: VICTORY THROUGH THE LOVE OF GOD IN CHRIST
8:31-39

In part two of his letter to the Romans, Paul set himself
the task to show what it means that he who believes in
Christ *"shall live."* He has shown that, through Christ, we
are free from the destroying powers which held the old
humanity in bondage. He has shown how these powers, one
after another, lost their dominion, including "the last enemy,"
death, which he discussed in chapter 8. In their overthrow
life has now been revealed in all its power. ὁ δίκαιος ἐκ
πίστεως ζήσεται, "he who through faith is righteous *shall live.*"
Life has been given to him through Jesus Christ our Lord.

Paul has come to the end of that presentation and can
now sum up the result. Whereas he has hitherto discussed
each question separately and at length, he can now gather
all up in one inclusive view of the great gift that has been
given to us through Christ. So Paul lets it all sound forth in
a jubilant song of praise to the love of God in Christ, who
gained for us a victory great beyond all measure.

"What shall we then say to this? If God is for us, who
is against us?" That there are plenty of powers ready to

stand against the Christian, Paul has shown fully in what
has gone before; but he has also shown that they cannot prevail. Like everything else they must work together for the
Christian's good. The reason for this is that *God is for us.*
And that God is for us does not merely mean that He is
graciously disposed toward us. Above all it means that He
is for us in what He *does.* God has acted for our benefit in
giving His Son for us. That is love in deed and in truth.
And now Paul can add, "He who did not spare his own Son
but gave him up for us all, will he not also give us all things
with him?" With Christ *all* has been given to us. We should
note how Paul here speaks in universals, in words that exclude any limitation. There is *no* condemnation for those
who are in Christ Jesus; *no* power can stand against us; *none*
can bring any charge against us; *nothing* can separate us
from the love of Christ. *All* is given to us through Christ: *all
things* must work together for good to those who love God;
in *all* things we are more than conquerors through Him who
loved us.

Paul further asks, "Who shall bring any charge against
God's elect?" To bring charge against God's elect is an act
without basis. He who does so fights against God himself.
It is not against us, but against God's eternal purpose, that
he rises up. θεὸς ὁ δικαιῶν, "It is God who justifies." When
God moves to effect His eternal purpose, who can hinder
Him? There is a limitless security in the fact that all that
happens to the Christian in this world has its basis in God's
eternal act of election.

And another question: "Who is to condemn?" There *is*
no condemnation to those that are in Christ Jesus. All that
Christ has done had the purpose of freeing us from condemnation. His death had that purpose, and even more His

resurrection (cf. 5:10). The same Christ who came into the world for us and offered himself in our place, the same Christ who bore our sin and took our condemnation upon himself, now enters in before God for our sake; He is at the right hand of God and intercedes for us.

And finally, a fourth question: "Who shall separate us from the love of Christ? Shall tribulation, or distress, or persecution, or famine, or nakedness, or peril, or sword?" Once again Paul comes back to the thought of "the sufferings of this present time." So far are these from being able to separate us from the fellowship of Christ that, on the contrary, this fellowship comes to expression in these very sufferings. The Christian is incorporated with Christ in the sharing of suffering and death. For that reason Paul can apply to the Christian the words of the psalm, "For thy sake we are being killed all the day long; we are regarded as sheep to be slaughtered" (Ps. 44:22). If our suffering is "for the sake of Christ" and "with Christ," it can only increase our oneness with Him.

In all the uncertainty that marks this earthly life there is still something which is absolutely fixed and certain, namely, God's election and Christ's love. Both of these are equally eternal and immovable. In this second part of the epistle Paul has said much about the powers, the δυνάμεις, which rule in this world, and about the Christian's freedom from them. When he now, finally, looks back at them, he does so only to point out what an *overwhelming victory over* these powers God has given us through Christ. When death, "the last enemy," has been conquered, there is definitely an end to the dominion of these destroying powers. Now no powers or dominions (δυνάμεις, ἀρχαί) can prevail in this world or in the world to come, and no creature whatever

348

can separate us from the love of God in Christ Jesus our Lord.

"In Christ Jesus our Lord"—with these words Paul ends the eighth chapter, as he ended the three that preceded. By the fact that He has become our Lord, all other dominions have lost their power. "In Him" life, the life of the new aeon, eternal life, has been given to us.

PART THREE

The Righteousness of Faith Is Not against
the Promise of God
9:1–11:36

It might seem that in the first two parts of the epistle Paul has entirely exhausted the theme with which he began in 1:17, "He who through faith is righteous shall live." In the first four chapters he gives the picture of him who through faith is righteous; and in the next four he shows what it means to say that he "shall live." The line of thought is carried through rigorously, and it might seem that there is in this context no place for further issues. We might therefore expect Paul to bring the letter to a close now in the usual manner, with certain exhortations. But he does not do so. Instead of that, he enters upon another main part consisting of three weighty chapters, 9-11, about the rejection of Israel.

What place does this fill in the unity of the whole epistle? Is it only a digression or an appendix which was added even though it has nothing to do with the main theme of the letter? Or does it have a definite role to fill in the unity of Romans?

There has been great lack of clarity on this point. It has generally been held that personal reasons, rather than content, lead Paul here to take up the problem of the rejection of Israel. It is thought that, beside the theme which he has now concluded, he turns to another matter which has been very close to his heart; he can no longer hold himself back from it. The idea of his own people's rejection must have been an unendurable thought to Paul, the Jewish Christian; and now that his main theme has been discussed, he cannot avoid turning to this new theme. This theme must have been inescapable to him personally; but with the main theme of the epistle it has nothing to do, strictly speaking. As support for this view, attention is called to the deeply personal tone of the words with which these chapters are introduced (9:1-3). Here Paul himself explains that this question has caused him "great sorrow and unceasing anguish"; that he could actually wish himself accursed and cut off from Christ if that could help his kinsmen by race.

Beside the difficulty of seeing the place of this part in the total message of the letter has been the difficulty in deciding what these chapters are. What does Paul intend to do in them? Let it suffice to recall here three familiar answers to this question. (1) It is said that Paul sets forth his doctrine of predestination in these chapters. Some have simply called this part of the epistle the *locus classicus de praedestinatione*. (2) These chapters have been said to present Paul's theodicy. (3) And they have been said to contain his philosophy of history.

These answers are all alike mistaken. (1) The *locus classicus de praedestinatione* is in 8:28-30. There we learn what was Paul's view of God's eternal election, of its accomplishment in time, and of its consummation in glory. If one uses chapters 9-11 as his point of departure in studying Paul's view of predestination, he ends with a false picture of it. (2) Paul knows nothing of a theodicy. To defend the action of God before the bar of human reason is utterly alien to him. That would be little better than to dispute with God. The

idea of a theodicy belongs in a world of thought wholly different from Paul's. It can never occur to him to call God
to account; no more would he seek to defend God's actions,
as if they needed to be defended before men. Against all
who would call God to account, it is enough for him to recall
that God is God and they are men. Every theodicy is a
blasphemy. To attempt to defend God's action is to attack
Him in His deity. To look upon this part of the epistle as
attempting to give a theodicy, a justification of God's way
of dealing, is to close the door to an understanding of it. (3)
But it is just as erroneous to say that Paul here sets forth his
philosophy of history. For Paul never gives himself to anything of that kind, in the accepted sense of the term. When
he introduces this part of the letter he is not attempting an
inclusive historical view of how God controls the direction
of the world and leads that which happens on toward its
goal. His reasons are quite different. The question as to the
rejection of Israel is of much more vital significance than
the chance to use it as a point of departure for a speculation
about the philosophy of history.

Under such circumstances it must be our first task to
inquire whether this third main part of the epistle does not,
despite all said to the contrary, constitute an organic part
in the total message of the letter, and whether it does not
have a very definite function to fill in the unity of the epistle.
Careful examination shows that that is indubitably the case.

In what has preceded Paul has spoken of how God has
given Christ to us, and how through Him the new aeon has
come. The new aeon is the time of *fulfillment*, for *all God's
promises are fulfilled in Christ.* "For all the promises of God
find their Yes in him. That is why we utter the Amen through
him" (II Cor. 1:20). But now a vital point arises: the prom-

ises were given *to Israel*. What extraordinary advantage had God not given to this people? He had elected this people before all others and said, "Israel is my son, my first-born" (Exod. 4:22). From the mercy seat, the place of God's gracious presence among His people, He had revealed His glory, His δόξα (cf. p. 157). With Israel He had established and renewed His covenant. The law and the temple worship were further evidence of Israel's special election. And to these were added all the promises that pointed forward to Him who was to come. And finally, as the greatest advantage of all, out of Israel should come Christ, the Saviour of the world. All these Paul gathers up in these words, "They are Israelites, and to them belong the sonship, the glory, the covenants, the giving of the law, the worship, and the promises; to them belong the patriarchs, and of their race, according to the flesh, is the Christ. God who is over all be blessed forever. Amen" (vss. 4-5).

Why does Paul set forth all these advantages of Israel? To make the mystery of the rejection of Israel truly great and inconceivable. How was it possible that this Israel, to which God had given such advantages, could now be rejected? And even harder is it to comprehend that this rejection should fall upon Israel in the very moment when God acts to fulfill His promises in Christ. Paul here faces the same fact as that which the Gospel of John expresses in this way, "He came unto his own, and they that were his own received him not" (John 1:11). But the problem is even more pointed than that for Paul. Not only does Israel reject her own Messiah, but thereby Israel seems to suffer the loss of that which God had promised. It is more than a matter of human unfaithfulness. The greater problem is that *God's word of promise seems to have lost its validity*. Once before, in this letter, Paul touched upon the same question, when, in 3:3-4, he asked "Does their faithlessness nullify the faithfulness of God?" and answered, "By no means! Let God be true though every man be false." In the very faithlessness of man God glorifies His faithfulness. But is not that idea now refuted by the facts? For the facts speak of Israel's rejection because of her faithlessness. Does not that mean that God has revoked the promises He made to the fathers? Paul seems to have fallen into an inescapable dilemma in which he will have to choose between these alternatives: *either* the gospel which he has proclaimed, that is, the gospel of the righteousness of faith revealed through Christ, *or* God's truthfulness and faithfulness. Is the righteousness of faith then actually contrary to God's promises, so that God thereby takes back the promises that He had formerly given? If that were the case, it would mean a catastrophe for all of Paul's preaching. Would it not be the most striking refutation of Paul's preaching, if its content were that, in the very moment that He is ready to fulfill His promises, God breaks them? As long as that issue remains unanswered, all that has preceded hangs in the air.

Because of what has been said we can affirm that chapters 9-11 are by no means to be regarded as a digression or a chance appendix which lacks organic connection with the main message of the letter. On the contrary, they are an essential part of the letter, and fulfill a very definite and necessary function in its total context. Our task is to show that there is no contradiction between the righteousness of faith and the promises of God. As long as there is any appearance of such a contradiction, Paul's gospel must appear doubtful.

Being thus able to confirm the fact that it is a very substantial necessity which impels Paul to take up this subject, we should also say that he is indeed concerned with this problem in a very personal way. Paul knows himself deeply at one with his people, and he is at pains to affirm that fact in this connection. Otherwise some might think that he, who has been prepared to be the apostle to the Gentiles, is no longer moved by a deep solidarity with Israel, but can look calmly on her rejection. Such an idea Paul will not permit. Therefore he avows that the fate of his people causes him great sorrow and unceasing anguish; and he emphasizes that declaration by calling the Holy Spirit to witness. Indeed, he makes the direct declaration that he would be willing to be accursed and cut off from Christ, if that could help his kinsmen after the flesh. That is no mere boast; it is a true statement of his sense of solidarity with his people. It is a word dictated by love's will to fullest self-sacrifice, if that can minister to the redemption of his brethren. In Exodus 32:32 Paul has read how Moses prayed for his people, who were threatened with rejection by the Lord, "Forgive their sin; and if not, blot me, I pray thee, out of thy book." Paul knows just such a solidarity with his kinsmen. He calls them his "brethren." That word is usually employed to indicate the unity of Christians. When Paul uses it here of his fellow members in Israel, it is very expressive of his bond with them. But he adds at once that it is a kinship κατὰ σάρκα, "according to the flesh." That is true too of Christ's relation to Israel. "According to the flesh," κατὰ σάρκα, He belongs to Israel; but "according to the Spirit," κατὰ πνεῦμα, He is "God who is over all, blessed forever."

As to this sentence—ὁ ὢν ἐπὶ πάντων θεὸς εὐλογητὸς εἰς τοὺς αἰῶνας, ἀμήν, (vs. 5)—interpretations have varied. Grammatically it is simplest to construe these words as in apposition to Christ, of whom Paul has just been speaking. But against this the point is made that this would then be the only place where Paul uses the name of God directly for Christ. To avoid this, it has been proposed to put a period after the statement about Christ as of the race of Israel according to the flesh, and to understand that which follows as an independent doxology, directed to God. The meaning would then be, "From them came Christ, according to the flesh.—God who is over all be blessed forever. Amen." But even if we overlook the manifest straining in that attempted interpretation, it must be pointed out that the assumption on which it rests is shaky, that is, the statement that this would be the only place where Paul speaks directly of Christ as God. That cannot be maintained. Paul is aware that God has exalted Christ "and bestowed on him the name which is above every name"; God has given Him the name which belongs only to God—the name LORD, *Kyrios* (Phil. 2:9-11; cf. p. 54). Thus is removed every reason for the grammatically most natural interpretation of verse 5.

Thus in this third part of the epistle Paul intends to show that the righteousness of faith is not contrary to God's prom‑ ises. To that end he presents three main arguments. (1) He who gave the promises is God himself, who is sovereign. Thus all depends on whom God has chosen to be "the children of promise." When God gave the promises He determined that they should belong to those who believe in Christ. (2) When Israel, directly contrary to God, seeks for righteous‑ ness by the way of works, she makes herself responsible for her rejection. (3) And yet that rejection is not final and decisive. By this very rejection God brings about the situa‑ tion necessary for Israel's final salvation.

In keeping with this line of thought, Paul's exposition

falls into three parts. (1) The promises belong only to those who believe (9:6-29). (2) Israel's rejection is due to herself (9:30—10:21). (3) The rejection is the way to Israel's final salvation (11:1-36.)

X

The Promise Only to Believers

9:6-29

1. IN THE VERY PROMISE GOD SHOWS HIS SOVEREIGNTY
9:6-13

Two things are unshakably fixed for Paul: (1) that God
gave His promises to Israel, and He never breaks them; and
(2) that these promises of God have now been fulfilled in
Christ.

But how are these two points to be reconciled with the
evident fact that Israel has in large measure rejected Christ
and has for that reason been rejected by God? Does not
that mean pretty nearly the same as if God has taken back
His promises, at least as far as Israel is concerned? And
while Paul speaks of the great advantages which God gave
Israel, he has to confess that the rejection of Israel causes
him "great sorrow and unceasing anguish." What is that
but an acknowledgment that God has broken His promise to
Israel? But Paul rejects any such ideas energetically, "It is
not as though the word of God had failed." He will not have
what he has said misunderstood in that manner. Of course
the promises to Israel remain secure. But, Paul holds, "Not
all who descended from Israel belong to Israel." We must
distinguish "Israel according to the flesh" from "Israel ac-

cording to the spirit." Only to the latter, only to the spiritual
Israel were the promises given. But now Israel according
to the flesh seeks to appropriate the promises and use them
as the basis of claims on God. They hold defiantly that they
belong to the peculiar people, because they are children of
Abraham. But Paul does not admit that. *Against men's
claims he sets God's sovereignty.* Men think that they can
use God's promises as basis for claims on God; they think
they can thus obligate God. But instead, God's sovereignty
is manifest in the very promises; they show that He is above
all human claims.

But what does it really mean that God is sovereign in
His promises? It does not mean that He gives them a general validity, that He fulfills or does not fulfill them as events
in general determine. It means that, when He gives His
promises, He determines in His own freedom to whom the
promises are given. Paul illustrates that by recalling what
God did when He gave His promises to Abraham and the
patriarchs. When the promise was given to Abraham and to
his children, it would have been easy to conclude that it
applied to all his progeny. That is what the Jews thought.
Since they were children of Abraham, they held that the
promises were theirs as a matter of course. But it is not so.
"Not all are children of Abraham because they are his descendants," Paul says. From the viewpoint of nature, one
might think that the promise was as valid for Ishmael as for
Isaac, for both were Abraham's sons. But God gave the promise to Isaac, "Your descendants will be reckoned through
Isaac" (cf. Gen. 21:12). Even when He gave the promise,
God showed that there is a distinction between those who
are born according to the flesh and those who are born in
the strength of the promise (Gal. 4:23). So it was not by

virtue of natural descent that Isaac became the heir of Abraham's blessing, but through special divine promise; only in that way was he a "child of promise." He became that, not by virtue of what he himself was, but by what God would make him. From this concrete example Paul now draws the general statement, "It is not the children of the flesh who are the children of God, but the children of promise are reckoned as descendants."

Now it would be easy to conclude that the promise belonged to Isaac and his posterity. But in the very next generation it is shown that an act of election on God's part is involved; and here it is impossible to point to a human quality as the reason for the choice. It might be thought, in the case of Isaac, that the basis of his election was the advantage he had in being the son of the free woman, whereas Ishmael was the son of the bondwoman. But when Paul now turns to the choice of Jacob above Esau, there can be no such idea. We see how insistent Paul is to remove any factor which might be considered a basis for the choice. Both sons had the same father and the same mother; they were twins; and they were alike in all aspects of their status. There is nothing to advance as the basis of a distinction between them. And furthermore, the word of God which shaped their fate was spoken before they were born, "though they were not yet born and had done nothing ·either good or bad." But though they were so alike, the outcome fo₊ each was so different that Scripture says "Jacob I loved, but Esau I hated" (cf. Mal. 1:2f.). Why was there this difference? Paul answers, "In order that God's purpose of election might continue, not because of works but because of his call" (vs. 11).

Summing up, we may say that God is sovereign in His

promise. He gives it to whom He will, allowing no one to prescribe rules for it. And so, in this sovereignty, even before He gave the promise, He reserved it for the spiritual Israel, for Israel κατὰ πνεῦμα. That, in other words, is to say that He meant the promise for those who believe. The promise and faith belong inseparably together; that Paul has already pointed out. In 4:16 it is said, "That is why it depends on faith, in order that the promise may rest on grace and be guaranteed to all his descendants" (cf. p. 177f.). So, far from any contradiction between the righteousness of faith and God's promise, faith is the necessary presupposition on which the promise stands. For it is only the righteousness of faith that lets all rest on the free mercy of God. Faith is to hold fast to God's promise; therefore only he who believes is a "child of promise," τέκνον τῆς ἐπαγγελίας.

2. GOD'S SOVEREIGNTY IN MERCY AND IN WRATH
9:14-29

In the preceding examples Paul has shown that everything depends on God's will and election, and nothing on our works. "Not because of works but because of his call," Paul sums up the result of his discussion (vs. 11). That God chose Abraham, Isaac, and Jacob, and gave them His promise, did not depend on anything in them; Jacob was not even born when God chose Him and established His promise for him. That choice depended solely on God's gracious will. That is of the nature of grace and promise. If it depended on anything else than God and His will's free choice, grace would not be grace and the promise would not be promise.

But when everything is thus placed in God's hand, human reason rises up to say that that is not just. Can it be right not to take cognizance of human character and works? In a just world order, must it not be precisely such things, and not some arbitrary volition of God, that decides the fate of man? Paul is aware that these questions, and others like them, can be raised against him, and he meets them with the following word, "Is there injustice on God's part?" Here, as in 3:5, the apostle speaks "in a human way." And here, as there, he replies, "By no means!" In his reply two things are implied. In the first place, he rejects any idea of unrighteousness in connection with God. In God's action there is no place for arbitrariness that knows no rule. The whole matter under discussion is how the righteousness of God, the δικαιοσύνη θεοῦ, is manifested; and in such there is no place for ἀδικία, for unrighteousness. But in Paul's "By no means!" there is a more fundamental fact. Paul does not merely answer the question with a negative. He denies the propriety of the framing of the question.

The question asked comes quite close to the traditional issue in theodicy. It is of particular interest to see how Paul, by his answer, completely rejects the issue. Otherwise we should have expected that, when the question was raised, he would have presented an array of arguments to defend the righteousness of God. But there is not a trace of that in Paul. We get the impression that the problem of theodicy does not even exist for him—and that for good reasons. For there is a basic fault in all that concerns theodicy: it measures God by human standards. But when man sets out to judge God's dealings by man's own standards, the results cannot be other than the conclusion that God's goodness is faulty.

Paul proceeds in a wholly different manner. When he is faced with the question of the justice or injustice of God's dealings, he does not enter at all on any argument on the level of that issue. He simply disallows the question. But he points out that that at which man now takes offense is in entire harmony with the way God has always acted. Of that the Scriptures bear witness; for God says to Moses, "I will have mercy on whom I have mercy, and I will have compassion on whom I have compassion" (cf. Exod. 33:19). God is absolutely free and sovereign in his mercy. No one can claim it, and no one can earn it by works. It can only be received as a freely proffered gift. If God's mercy had had its cause in man's character, it would really not be mercy. "So it depends not upon man's will or exertion, but upon God's mercy." God's mercy depends on God's mercy; that is to say that no reason can ever be given for it than that God will have mercy. For the love of God there is no explanation except that He loves and He "is love."

But if God is sovereign in His mercy, so that He gives it to whom He will, that also implies, on the other hand, that He can withhold it. Otherwise God's love and mercy would not be free. It would be something which would be extended to man because of a natural necessity, so to say, so that God could not do otherwise. That God "has mercy upon whomever he wills" is only one side of the matter. We cannot separate that from the other side, "He hardens the heart of whomever he wills" (vs. 18). Scripture also gives example of this. "For the scripture says to Pharaoh, 'I have raised you up for the very purpose of showing my power in you, so that my name may be proclaimed in all the earth'" (cf. Exod. 9:16). When men in enmity rise up against God, they think they are acting in their own autonomy and thus limit God's power and thwart His plans. He is making them obdurate and hard, as He did with Pharaoh. For even in that situation can they avoid filling the place which God has assigned to them in His world plan. For there is place not only for the "vessels of mercy," whom God by His eternal election has destined for glory, but also for the "vessels of wrath" who are prepared for destruction. All must serve His purpose, in one way or another. For God has servants of different sorts; some serve Him from the heart, but others must be compelled against their will to serve Him. One can see that in the case of Pharaoh. He meant to frustrate the will of God when he hardened himself against it; but God had raised him up for the very purpose of showing His power in him. Paul is utterly in earnest in saying that it is God who hardens. We have already met a kindred thought in 1:24, 26, 28, where we read that God gives men up to sin. When man turns to sin, he does so of his own volition; but at the same time the wrath of God commits him to it (cf. pp. 109ff.). When a man hardens his heart against God, it is God who hardens him "to show his wrath and to make known his power" on the vessels of wrath. So there are no limits to God's sovereignty; it is revealed both in His mercy and in His wrath. In both cases His will moves forward victoriously. "So then he has mercy upon whomever he wills, and he hardens the heart of whomever he wills."

But if this is the situation, if everything depends on God's will and purpose, another question arises, What happens then to man's responsibility? Is it possible to say that he is to blame for anything? It is God's will which stands concealed behind everything. "Why does he still find fault? For who can resist his will?" Here we see again how Paul sets forth a question, not to answer it, but to dissolve it. We should perhaps have been glad to have from Paul an explanation on the time-honored questions how God's omni-

potence and sovereignty are related to man's "free will," or
how God's eternal plan can be harmonized with responsibility and guilt in man. But we look to Paul in vain for
answers to these questions. That is not because he has not
yet clearly enough thought his way through these issues; it
is rather because he rejects the questions as improper. Behind them lies a dialectic which Paul rejects. Men think
that if everything rests in God's hand and depends on His
will, there is then nothing that rests with man; so there can
no longer be talk of his responsibility and guilt. Paul does
not admit that alternative. He can affirm both points at the
same time: the basis of Israel's rejection lies in God's purpose; but, in the next passage, he says Israel is herself responsible for her rejection. Where is the mistake, when men try
to answer questions like those raised above? It lies in the
attempt to draw the line between the roles of God and man.
But that means that man puts God on the same plane with
man. Every attempt of this kind to give a theoretical answer to such questions therefore comes to involve an attack
on God's deity. There is consequently no wonder that Paul
refrains from answering these questions. The only answer
he gives is to recognize that God is on God's plane and man
is on man's. "Who are you, a man, to answer back to God?
Will what is molded say to its molder, 'Why have you made
me thus?' Has the potter no right over the clay, to make of
the same lump one vessel for beauty and another for menial
use?"

In the nature of the case there is something incongruous
in man's attempt to confront God and call Him to judgment.
Man against his Creator! Man, who is in God's hand as clay
is in the potter's! By reminding man who he is, and who
God is, Paul shows him the incongruity of answering back

to God—and of attempting to defend Him. Here there is room for no thought of a theodicy. It is disallowed by a reference to God's unsearchable election. A theodicy assumes that *man* is central. Predestination shows that that is false. The chief significance of the concept of predestination is that it makes *God* central, as it should.

The concept of predestination is the most theocentric idea there is. When it becomes clear that man's salvation does not rest on his own works or exertions, but alone on the fact that it has pleased God, in His divine purpose, to take man out of this age of death and place him with Christ in the new age of the resurrection life, then it becomes genuinely clear that all really depends on *God's free grace*. All human claims are thereby dismissed. The issue is not what man is or does, but what God does with him.

But even this concept, which expresses God's sovereignty better than any other, can also be distorted in an egocentric way. That happens when, instead of directing our attention on God's action, we direct it on man and his fate; when we interpret predestination, as it were, from below. That is to give it a meaning quite alien to Paul's. It becomes a speculative theory about how one group is saved and another rejected. That is to change it into its diametrical opposite. Instead of allowing it to dismiss all such speculations, because the matter lies entirely in God's hand, it becomes an attempt on man's part to intrude into the secrets of the divine majesty. If the idea of a theodicy means that God is pulled down to man's level and has to be defended before the bar of human reason, such a changed and distorted concept of predestination means that man thinks himself able to ascend to God's own level and examine His thoughts and purposes. To use Luther's fitting expression, that is "to climb up to the divine majesty"; that is speculation of the kind that is denied to man. Such an idea of predestination is nothing less than an attack on God. When predestination is so conceived as to limit the inclusiveness of grace, it is a falsification. The great and legitimate service of the concept of predestination is to affirm, against all human pretensions, that God's grace is really free grace on the part of God. Beyond that Paul does not go, and beyond that we ought not to go. Paul's idea of predestination is not a theory that solves the riddles of this life; it is an expression of the faith that puts life and its insoluble mysteries into the hand of God.

To put it concisely, Paul does not at all attempt a rational answer to the problem of theodicy; he attempts rather to dissolve and repulse questions of that kind. The clay does not dispute with the potter. Man has no authority to call God to account. He can neither earn God's mercy by well-doing, nor frustrate His will by opposition. The error of both theodicy and a rational doctrine of predestination consists in this, that it sets up the very questions which Paul deems improper and to be rejected. That is exactly what a true theocentric concept of predestination rejects, as it puts all things without exception into God's hand.

In the foregoing Paul has drawn examples from Israel's history to show how God acted, both in election and the giving of His promises, and in rejecting and hardening men's hearts. As to the former, Paul drew his illustrations from the history of the patriarchs; the classic example of hardening and rejection is Pharaoh.

Now the application must be made to Paul's own day. Indeed it was a problem of his day, the rejection of Israel, which caused him to look back to God's history with Israel. Now he returns to the original problem, after he has drawn from the past the right categories for dealing with it. And since it is the rejection of Israel that presents the problem, there naturally comes into the foreground that which has been said about Pharaoh, about the hardening of his heart and his rejection. Very properly Paul makes verses 22-23 to parallel verse 17. According to the latter, God had a double purpose and a double result, when He hardened Pharaoh's heart: (1) It gave God opportunity to show His power, and (2) God's name was thereby proclaimed in all the earth. That is the thought which now marks Paul's discussion of this problem.

As long as this age lasts "vessels of wrath" will always be found side by side with "vessels of mercy." Why does God permit that? Why does He not shatter the useless vessels? He has His purpose when He spares them and still has patience with them, in His longsuffering. Like Pharaoh in his day, Israel is now a "vessel of wrath." And God still has the same double purpose in rejecting: (1) Thereby He intends to show His wrath and make known His power. Israel has refused to believe that God could reject His people. The Israelite considers himself safe in his natural relationship to this peculiar people. But now he is to experience the manifestation of God's wrath and power upon himself and his people. (2) But God also has another purpose; and for Paul that is the chief matter in this connection: He will make known the riches of His glory for the "vessels of mercy." Precisely through Israel's hardening, through the fact that Israel rejected her Messiah and was herself rejected, the gospel has gone forth into all the world, and there it has made "vessels of mercy" both of Jews and, even more, of Gentiles.

We should note this coupling, so characteristic for Paul,

between Israel's rejection and the salvation of the world—
a thought to which he comes back particularly in chapter
11, "Their transgression means riches for the world" (vs. 12).
"Their rejection means the reconciliation of the world" (vs.
15). The natural branches were broken off the tree of Israel
to make room for the Gentiles (vs. 19). The Gentiles received mercy because of Israel's disobedience (vs. 30).

In 9:22-23 there is a difficulty of language which we
ought to note. At first glance it looks as if these verses contain only detached subordinate clauses that qualify no main
clause. Origen had already faced this difficulty, and he tried
to solve it by textual changes. It has been common to resolve the difficulty by freely supplying a concluding inter-
rogatory clause. But there is a much simpler possibility,
namely, that verse 23 contains the main clause in question.
It begins with a strongly accented καί "*and.*" The problem
is then reduced to the fact that, because it already appears
in the relative clause, Paul does not repeat in the main clause
the verb which it has in common with the relative clause.
Such abbreviations are not rare with Paul, and some of them
are more labored in nature than the one we now deal with;
for example, 4:16, literally translated, reads "therefore of
faith, in order that by grace, that the promise may be stead-
fast" (cf. p. 178). As in that case one need not be uncertain of the meaning, because the verb is missing, so too in
the case now before us. Perhaps verses 22-23 could be ren-
dered most correctly as follows, "If God, to show his wrath
and make known his power, in his longsuffering, had patience with the vessels of wrath which were ready for destruction, so [he also had it] in order to make known the
riches of his glory for the vessels of mercy, which he has
prepared beforehand for glory."

When Paul looks at the situation as it confronts him in his own day, he sees two things: (1) He sees an Israel which, at least for the present, is rejected by God and must be described as a "vessel of wrath." (2) But beyond that he sees that, instead, God has made himself new "vessels of mercy" of those Jews who have come to faith, and of the great numbers of Gentiles who have been won through Paul's preaching. Therefore he immediately adds the relative clause in verse 24, "to be such vessels of mercy he has also called us, not from the Jews only, but also from the Gentiles." The greater part of Israel has thus become a "vessel of wrath." But they who believe on Christ, be they Jews or Gentiles, are "vessels of mercy." That God has determined in His sovereign will and election. Since He determined this beforehand as to us Christians, He has also called us to faith.

Thus Paul has come forward with the first answer to the question appearing in verse 6, whether the righteousness of faith is contrary to God's word of promise. Would it be contrary to God's promise, if the greater part of Israel should be rejected, and only a remnant of Israel, together with Gentiles, be accepted as the people of God? On the contrary, is it not *just that* which the promise portended? The Jew is agitated because the Gentiles are called. He insists that Israel, and Israel alone, is God's people. But what does Scripture say? "Those who were not my people I will call 'my people,' and her who was not beloved I will call 'my beloved.' And in every place where it was said to them, 'You are not my people,' they will be called 'sons of the living God'" (cf. Hos. 2:23; 1:10). To the prophet these words meant the Jews; but through their insistence that they belonged to God's peculiar people they had lost the right to appeal to this promise, which belonged now to the Gentiles

instead. The Jews come with their claim that Israel in its
entirety be saved. But what does Scripture say? "Isaiah
cries out concerning Israel: 'Though the number of the sons
of Israel be as the sand of the sea, only a remnant of them
shall be saved.'" Is it not just that which is now fulfilled?
The remnant, τὸ ὑπόλειμμα—that means Paul and his kinsmen
who with him have come to believe in Christ. And even
this, that a remnant be saved, is not something that Israel
can claim because of itself. All human claims are definitely
excluded. God has so ordered it that it does not depend on
anyone's works, but only on Him who calls (9:12). And for
God's call there is no other reason than God's free mercy.
That there is any "remnant" at all depends exclusively on
God's mercy, for "if the Lord of hosts had not left us children, we would have fared like Sodom and been made like
Gomorrah."

How could God more completely fulfill His promise, to
the very point, than in what He has done through Christ
and the people of God gathered around Him, consisting of
a remnant of Israel side by side with Gentiles, who have
come to faith in Him?

XI

Israel's Rejection Her Own Fault

9:30–10:21

Paul distinguishes between two groups of men, "vessels of wrath" and "vessels of mercy." And now he asks, "What shall we say, then?" That is, in other words, "What is the result of this as it concerns the Jews and the Gentiles?" Formerly they were all without exception, "vessels of wrath." In the first three chapters of the epistle Paul has shown that all, both Gentiles and Jews, stood under the wrath of God. The result of that introductory analysis Paul could sum up, in 3:23. "All have sinned and fall short of the glory of God" (δόξα θεοῦ). But in the same chapter it is said that "the righteousness of God" is offered to *all* without distinction. What is the result of that offer? That Israel is rejected and the Gentiles are accepted. Israel is a "vessel of wrath," the Gentiles become "vessels of mercy." Even after "the righteousness of God" is revealed through Christ, Israel still stands under the wrath of God: but the Gentiles receive the mercy of God. What makes that so amazing is not only that God once chose Israel to be His people, but above all the fact that the Jews sought after righteousness with all their might, while the Gentiles did not seek it.

When, in chapter 1, Paul had to characterize the condi-

tion of the *Gentiles*, he could do so with one word, "unrighteousness," ἀδικία. Their life was marked by indifference to
unrighteousness. They did not seek the will of God, but
suppressed the truth in unrighteousness (1:18). Paul did not
lighten the picture of the life of the heathen; he painted it
as it was. Truth compelled him to say that they did not seek
after righteousness. And yet God gave them to share in the
righteousness now revealed, "the righteousness of faith," ἡ
δικαιοσύνη ἡ ἐκ πίστεως.

But the *Jews* were characterized by a manifest *zeal* for
righteousness. That was the great pathos of their life. They
actually pursued after righteousness. And yet they must now
stand without, when God reveals His righteousness. They
stand there without any righteousness. Why? Because the
only real righteousness is the righteousness of faith, δικαιοσύνη
ἐκ πίστεως. However much Israel strives after righteousness,
she *cannot* attain to it, because she seeks it by way of the
law. In 9:16 Paul has said that "it depends not upon man's
will or exertion, but upon God's mercy." That is confirmed
here. Had it depended on the will or the exertion of man,
the result would have been the opposite. Then the Jews,
who sought after righteousness, would have found it; and
the Gentiles, who did not seek it, would have been rejected.
But God has proceeded in quite the opposite way.

Here we may see how closely these two passages, 9:6-29
and 9:30—10:21, belong to each other.

The great question to which Paul addresses himself in
chapters 9-11 is whether the righteousness of God is contrary to God's promise. Does not the rejection of Israel show
that God has taken back His promise? Paul's first answer,
contained in 9:6-29, is this: It is precisely in His promise
that God shows His sovereignty. And in His sovereignty

God has determined that the promise is to those who believe. Only they are the "children of promise"; only οἱ ἐκ πίστεως are τέκνα τῆς ἐπαγγελίας. Be it noted that God's sovereignty shows itself above all in the fact that He will *give*. But therefore that which He gives has to be accepted as a gift of His mercy. He never permits man to come presenting claims; that conflicts with His divine majesty. Only in faith can His gift be received.

To this is immediately added the second answer, in 9:30 —10:21. If God has determined that righteousness shall belong to those who believe, and only to them, then in the nature of the case Israel cannot be participant in that righteousness, since she seeks to win it by way of the law. If God has promised to give His gift in the east, and they push westward with might and main, all their striving only carries further and further away from righteousness. So Israel's rejection is her own fault.

What thus happens to Israel and to the Gentiles in the present moment gives Paul occasion, with Isaiah, to speak of the cornerstone that became a stumbling stone, about the stumbling stone that became the cornerstone. Paul here puts together two different sayings, namely, Isaiah 8:14 which speaks of the stone that should cause Israel to fall, and Isaiah 28:16 which tells how the Lord placed in Zion a precious cornerstone on which His congregation should build in faith. From of old men had understood this word about the cornerstone as referring to the Messiah. These two sayings together now become for Paul—and not for him alone, it was a familiar early Christian idea, cf. I Peter 2:6-8—a testimony as to the double result of Christ's coming into the world, the fall of some and the rising of others (cf. Luke 2:34). They are at the same time a testimony *against* righteousness by the law

and *for* the righteousness of faith. For those who push
ahead in their own strength and with trust in their own
works, for οἱ ἐκ νόμου, Christ becomes a stone on which they
stumble and fall; but for those who believe, for οἱ ἐκ πίστεως,
He becomes the cornerstone which God has set, upon which
they can build without fear of being put to shame. Thus it
has happened that the Gentiles who had no righteousness to
which to appeal, have become "vessels of mercy," σκεύη
ἐλέους, while the Jews, who sought after righteousness, stumbled over Christ and became "vessels of wrath," σκεύη ὀργῆς

Just as Paul did not at all seek to brighten the picture of
the condition of the Gentiles, when he discusses their acceptance, so he does not speak depreciatingly of the Jews, when
he deals with their rejection. On the contrary, he begins
the tenth chapter with some warm, personal words, which
show his inner fellow feeling with them, "Brethren, my
heart's desire and prayer to God for them is that they may
be saved." And beside that, he bears a very favorable testimony to them, from the human point of view. "I bear them
witness that they have a zeal for God." Paul would not deny
that the Jews were very earnest about their religion. He
would not at all label it simply as hypocrisy. He sees "a zeal
for God" (ζῆλος θεοῦ). But that does not help them, for
Paul must add, "but it is not enlightened." Zeal for God
that is not enlightened can carry man very far from God.
And that is just what happened to the Jews. When God
revealed His righteousness, through Christ, they could not
accept it just because they had such a zeal for righteousness,
the righteousness of the law, δικαιοσύνη ἐκ νόμου. That which
was their advantage became their downfall. In their zeal
they were so preoccupied with thoughts of all the works of
righteousness which they themselves would offer that they

could not see that God now offered them a wholly new righteousness. δικαιοσύνη θεοῦ is so strange to them that they cannot understand, says Paul. "Being ignorant of the right-eousness that comes from God, and seeking to establish their own, they did not submit to God's righteousness." The Jews pile up their own righteousness, τὴν ἰδίαν δικαιοσύνην, and therefore will not submit to the righteousness of God, which comes from above and is given as a free gift of God's mercy.

With this, Paul is again back with his old theme, the contrast between righteousness by law and righteousness through faith, between δικαιοσύνη ἐκ νόμου and δικαιοσύνη ἐκ πίστεως. When God revealed His righteousness in Christ, He put a definite end to the law as a way of salvation. "Christ is the end of the law, that every one who has faith may be justified." There is no longer any righteousness built from below, with its point of origin in man, in his works or in his character. Man has no righteousness of his own. *Without* the law and *without* man's co-operation, God's new right-eousness has been revealed, and it belongs to each and every one who believes. This is exactly the same thought which Paul set forth in 3:21. That passage and the one we now examine are at one in emphasizing two things: (1) that this righteousness is revealed *"apart from law"* (χωρὶς νόμου in 3:21 equals τέλος νόμου Χριστός in 10:4); and (2) that it is given to each and every one who believes (εἰς πάντας τοὺς πιστεύοντας in 3:22 equals παντὶ τῷ πιστεύοντι in 10:4).

Thus in Christ the dominion of the law is brought to an end. Yet that does not mean that the way is thereby opened for lawlessness and unrighteousness; it means that he who believes in Christ has passed from one kind of righteousness to another, from a worthless righteousness to one that is true, from righteousness by law to the righteousness of God,

which is the same as righteousness through faith. With full
confidence Paul can tell how through Christ there is really
an end to the law, because the inner intention of the law—
which it is not able to effect—is realized through faith. In
3:31 Paul asks, "Do we then overthrow the law by this faith?"
And his answer says, "By no means! On the contrary, we
uphold the law" (cf. p. 166). Nor is the law overthrown
here. The law has a double function: (1) It is to stop every
mouth and overthrow all boasting; and faith does that, because faith excludes all human claims; and (2) the law
demands righteousness; and in faith man has the true righteousness, "righteousness from God." At a certain point in
history God sent Christ. That was the beginning of something new. But it also marked the end of the old; the day of
the law is past. Christ is the end of the law, the terminus of
the law, the law's τέλος. And yet this must not be construed
as an ordinary historical judgment, to the effect that the law
ceased to function at a given point in time. The statement
about the τέλος of the law applies only to those who have
through Christ been made sharers in the righteousness of
the law. Otherwise, outside of the realm of faith, the law
still rules.

That there is an absolute contrast between righteousness
by law and righteousness through faith Paul finds certified
in Scripture. As to *righteousness by law*, δικαιοσύνη ἐκ νόμου
we read, in Leviticus 18:5, that the man who practices that
righteousness shall live by it. In righteousness by law all
depends on man's works. But *righteousness by faith*, ἡ ἐκ
πίστεως δικαιοσύνη, speaks in entirely different manner. For
this too Paul can find support in Scripture, for instance, in
Deuteronomy 30:11-14 (and Ps. 107:26). In Deuteronomy
we read, "For this commandment which I command thee

this day, it is not too hard for thee, neither is it far off. It is not in heaven, that thou shouldest say, 'Who shall go up for us to heaven, and bring it unto us, and make us to hear it, that we may do it?' Neither is it beyond the sea, that thou shouldest say, 'Who shall go over the sea for us, and bring it unto us, and make us to hear it, that we may do it?' But the word is very nigh unto thee, in thy mouth, and in thy heart, that thou mayest do it." If we ask as to the *literal* meaning of that passage, there can be no doubt that it refers to the *commandment*. That is entirely clear, both from the opening sentence, and from the thrice repeated "that thou mayest do it." This literal meaning Paul knows very well indeed. Without doubt this was a cardinal passage for him during his time as a Pharisee. But after he came to know Christ, after the veil was removed, it dawned upon him that there is here another and deeper meaning too. *God's* meaning is not exhausted in the purely literal significance. He wished here to speak to us beforehand about Christ and the righteousness that comes through faith in Him. It is thus of the righteousness of faith that He speaks, "Do not say in your heart, 'Who will ascend into heaven?'" that is, it is not necessary to bring Christ down from heaven. He has come down to us himself, and by the incarnation He has taken up His abode among us. Nor does one need to ask, "Who will descend into the abyss?" that is, to bring Christ up from the dead. He is no longer in the kingdom of death. He is risen, and as such He is with us.

Through the *incarnation* and the *resurrection* Christ is near us; He is immediately with us. If, according to Paul, Deuteronomy 30:12-13, in its deeper meaning, refers to Christ, he understands verse 14 in the same manner, "the word is very nigh unto thee, in thy mouth, and in thy heart."

"That is, the word of faith which we preach," says Paul. In
its literal meaning this passage refers to the law, but in the
deeper sense, intended by God beforehand, it refers to "the
word of faith." Christ has come from heaven, He has arisen
from the dead, salvation is at hand, and the word about this
salvation is immediately near us. To set forth *how* near this
word is to us, the Old Testament passage quoted uses two
different expressions: (1) the word is in thy mouth—ἐν τῷ
στόματί σου, and (2) the word is in thy heart—ἐν τῇ καρδίᾳ
σου. Paul lays hold of both expressions and bases on them
a statement about the significance which the mouth's confession and the heart's faith have for salvation: "If you confess
with your lips (ἐν τῷ στόματί σου) that Jesus is Lord and
believe in your heart (ἐν τῇ καρδίᾳ σου) that God raised him
from the dead, you will be saved. For man believes with his
heart and so is justified, and he confesses with his lips and
so is saved" (vss. 9-10). This statement has special interest
because it shows us on what Paul thinks the matter really
rests in Christianity.

Surprise has sometimes been expressed that Paul here
stops with such outward things as confession with the mouth
and belief in the resurrection of Christ. Is Christianity actually only a matter of agreement with a statement of a doctrinal confession? The meaning of faith has been explained
as trust, *fiducia*. Even though Paul here speaks of the belief
of the heart, is not belief that Christ arose from the dead,
belief in the *fact* of the resurrection, after all the acceptance
of an external event in history? But to hold that a proclaimed
fact is true is not the same as trust in the heart.

Against this it must said that for Paul the confession of
the mouth and the faith of the heart are by no means external;
on the contrary, they express what is inmost and deepest in

Christianity. (1) *A Christian is one who confesses that Jesus is Lord.* God has exalted Jesus and given Him a name that is above every name, that all may "confess that Jesus Christ is Lord" (Phil. 2:9-11). That is the central confession of Christianity. God has given Christ divine honor and power and made Him *Lord* over all. "He disarmed the principalities and powers (τὰς ἀρχὰς καὶ τὰς ἐξουσίας) and made a public example of them, triumphing over them" (Col. 2:15). To be a Christian is to have Christ as one's Lord, and thereby be freed from all other lords and powers. That is certainly nothing external. (2) *A Christian is one who believes that God raised Christ from the dead.* To Paul the resurrection is the center of Christianity. In 1:4 Paul has said that Christ, who was the seed of David according to the flesh, was designated "Son of God with power" according to the Spirit; and, Paul adds, that happened by His resurrection from the dead. Thereby He became the first fruit; and belonging to Him through faith we too have become participants in the new age of the resurrection. And this is not something merely outward, either. It means a transformation of our whole existence. If Christ had not risen from the dead, we should still be in death's realm. To be a Christian is to have a risen Lord, and through Him to share in the resurrection life.

To confess Christ as Lord and to believe in His resurrection are not two different things; they are basically one and the same. It is the same word of faith which is near us, in our mouth and in our heart. The reason Paul here uses both expressions is that he is referring to the Old Testament quotation in which both are found. Nor should verse 10 be interpreted as if it speaks of two different things, as if Paul makes righteousness depend on the faith of the heart and salvation on the confession of the mouth. When he says here, "Man believes with his heart and so is justified, and he confesses with his lips and so is saved," he is using a rhythmic parallelism of the sort very common in the Old Testament. In the development of thought he is presenting it is natural for Paul to couple righteousness and faith—all the time, in what goes before, he has been operating with both terms side by side as he spoke of "the righteousness of faith," δικαιοσύνη ἐκ πίστεως—and similarly to couple salvation and confession of Christ as Lord, our Kyrios. To see how easy it is for Paul to couple the last two terms, we need only recall that each of the chapters 5-8, which say that the Christian *shall live or be saved* (ζωή=σωτηρία), he closes with a reference to "Jesus Christ, our Lord." It is a formal coupling which ought not to be used as reason for positive conclusions. The purpose of what has just been said is to guard against using this rhythmic parallelism as the basis for dogmatic distinctions in a way that does violence to its true significance.

Paul has set the two ways of salvation in sharp antithesis with each other—the way of law and the way of faith. Both could not be valid at the same time. With the coming of Christ, judgment is pronounced against righteousness by the law. "For Christ is the end of the law, that every one who has faith may be justified" (vs. 4). And now Paul can turn back to his quotation from Isaiah 28:16 (in 9:33), "He who believes in him will not be put to shame." Faith in Christ is henceforth the only way of salvation. It is not the case that the Jews can be saved through the law and the Gentiles through faith. No, "there is no distinction between Jew and Greek; the same Lord is Lord of all and bestows his riches upon all who call upon him." This, then, is the way of salvation for whomsoever: to believe in Christ, to call upon His

name, and to confess Him as Lord. Once again Paul turns
to Scripture for support, "Every one who calls upon the
name of the Lord will be saved" (Joel 2:32). That prophetic
word, which refers to God himself, Paul applies to Christ.
He can do so because he knows that God has exalted Christ
and given Him the name which is above every name. God's
own name, the LORD, belongs also to Christ; and the prayers
and invocation of the church are addressed to Him in the
same way as to God. Luther has given striking expression
to the same view, in these words:

> Ask ye, Who is this?
> Jesus Christ it is,
> Of Sabaoth Lord,
> And there's none other God.

Ever since Christ came salvation is dependent on faith
in Him and the confession of Him as Lord. But Israel does
not confess Christ as her Lord. Israel does not believe in
Him. What is the reason that Israel takes this position? Paul
wants to show the exact point where the difficulty lies.
Therefore his mind runs back through the steps that lead
one to faith and confession: (1) One cannot confess him in
whom one does not believe; (2) one cannot believe in him
of whom one has not heard; (3) one cannot hear without a
preacher; (4) no preachers come unless God sends them.
What, then, is the reason why Israel does not confess Christ
as her Lord? Paul examines the different possibilities, and
from Scripture he brings forth his answer on each point. Is
the reason for Israel's turning aside perhaps that God sent
her no messengers? No, God has certainly taken care that
the gospel should come to Israel. It is written, "How beauti-
ful are the feet of those who preach good news!" (Isa. 52:7).
The reason for Israel's alienation lies in herself. The message

which is preached demands faith; the gospel demands that one submit himself to it in "the obedience of faith" (cf. 1:5, ὑπακοὴ πίστεως). But Israel has refused to go along in that, "They have not all heeded the gospel," οὐ πάντες ὑπήκουσαν τῷ εὐαγγελίῳ; or, as Paul expresses it in 10:3, "They did not submit to God's righteousness." Paul finds that confirmed in Isaiah 53:1, where we read, "Who has believed what he has heard from us." Once more Paul looks back at the steps that prepare the way for faith, and says, "So faith comes from what is heard (ἐξ ἀκοῆς), and what is heard comes by the preaching of Christ" (vs. 17).

On His part, God has done everything that man might come to faith. In Christ He has laid the basis for His message; and He has sent forth His heralds to proclaim the message, that Israel might hear it. But now it depends whether Israel believes the message she has heard. Or could it be that Israel has not heard the message? That is the only point to which Paul has not yet given answer. The second of the steps mentioned says that one cannot believe in him of whom he has not heard. Recognizing this, Paul says, "I ask, have they not heard?" Indeed they have. The heralds of Christ have gone forth with His gospel into all the earth. So widely has the word been proclaimed that, when Paul wants to state the fact, he can do so in the words of Psalm 19. As the witness of the heavens that declare His glory is not a voice or a language that is not heard, so the messengers of the gospel have not come with a word which is not heard. "Their voice is gone out to all the earth, and their words to the end of the world" (vs. 18; cf. Ps. 19:4).

So it is quite beyond doubt that Israel has *heard* the message. But why has she not believed? Faith comes by hearing (ἐξ ἀκοῆς). To bring the matter still closer, Paul adds another question which does not arise directly from the preceding outline. He has already run through the various possibilities, and, in so doing, gone back to the second step mentioned: one cannot believe in him of whom he has not heard. But Israel *has heard,* and yet does not believe. "Again I ask, did Israel not *understand?*" The answer to that Paul finds in Israel's own Scriptures, in "the law and the prophets." In "the law"—in the Song of Moses, Deuteronomy 32:21—Paul had read how, by her apostasy, Israel had aroused God to jealousy and anger, and how God would therefore move Israel to jealousy and anger "with those who are not a people, with a foolish nation." That word has now been fulfilled. The Gentiles, who were not God's people, have now been accepted as God's people (cf. 9:25-26). The "foolish" Gentiles had both heard and *understood* the gospel, and thereby had come to faith. Under such circumstances it cannot be said that Israel could not have understood the message she heard. God has spoken so plainly that even the Gentiles understand. Paul has dealt at such length with this point, to show that Israel did understand, and the reason for her disbelief must lie elsewhere. Later, in 11:11, 14, Paul returns to the thought that, by His grace to the Gentiles, God will move Israel to jealousy and envy—a very important thought for Paul's answer to the question of the rejection of Israel.

Now Paul adds an expression from "the prophets." In Isaiah 65:1 it is written, "I have let myself be manifest to those who did not ask for me; I have let myself be found by those who did not seek me." There may be doubt whether this statement referred to the Gentiles in its original use by the prophet. But Paul at any rate so interprets it, and he finds support in the prophet's following word about "a nation that was not called by my name." But even though the opposite be correct, the vital thing for Paul is not the "historic" meaning of the passage, but what *God* meant thereby, what He wants to say to us through this word (cf. p. 83). As to this it is entirely clear to Paul that these words must apply to the Gentiles. God has here declared beforehand how it was to be in the day that has now come. God has let himself be found by those who did not seek Him and been revealed to those who did not ask for Him. Is not that precisely what has now happened to the Gentiles? Already in 9:30, Paul has said exactly the same thing, "that Gentiles who did not pursue righteousness have attained it, that is, righteousness through faith."

So it stands with the Gentiles. "But of Israel he says, 'All day long I have held out my hands to a disobedient and contrary people.'" One can hear and yet not heed. That is just the case with Israel. She has heard the gospel of the righteousness of God, but has refused to submit to it, rather holding fast to her own righteousness, righteousness by the law. God has made righteousness and salvation depend on faith. Only they who believe are the "children of promise," only οἱ ἐκ πίστεως are τέκνα τῆς ἐπαγγελίας. Therefore he who does not believe must be rejected. Israel does not believe, therefore rejection is inescapable. Israel has both heard and understood the message—but rejected it in disobedience and unbelief. Therefore she has now been rejected herself. That has taken place in entire harmony with Scripture and prophecy. So the rejection of the Jews is not a point against Paul's gospel; it rather bears witness for it.

XII

Israel's Rejection Not Final

Is the righteousness of faith contrary to God's promise?
That is the question which Paul is discussing in chapters
9-11. It might appear that such is really the case. For the
result of the revelation of the righteousness of God in Christ
was the rejection of Israel, the Israel to which all God's
promises had been given. Against this, however, Paul aims
to show that the righteousness of faith is not at all in conflict
with God's promise. In the preceding chapters he has discussed the issue from two points of view. Now, in chapter
11, he adds a third. It is easy to see that this is also a necessary point. If Paul had omitted it, he would not have
given adequate consideration to his problem. A look back
over what he has presented shows that this is the case. How
far has Paul gotten with his answer?

In his first answer (9:6-29) he has spoken of God's sovereignty: God chooses whom He will, and whom He will He
rejects, and man can present himself with no claims on God.

In his second answer (9:30—10:21) he has shown that
the rejection of Israel is her own fault. When God makes
His promises depend on faith, but Israel seeks her righteous-

ness by the law, the only possible result is the rejection of Israel.

What would the situation be if Paul added nothing more? It would mean that Israel's rejection is final; that God intended it that way, and Israel deserved it. But that is not what Paul means to say. Israel's present rejection is of course an incontrovertible fact, the inescapable consequence of Israel's rejection of the Messiah. Paul starts from that fact as one which must be seen aright; but his interest in it is more than theoretical. He does not merely accept it as an irrevocable fact, about which nothing can be done, which one simply has to include in a total theological view. On the contrary, as we saw earlier, this is a matter which, under certain conditions, could shake his theological view to its base, or even demolish it—that is, if the conclusion were that God breaks His promises. Against such a conclusion, Paul has thus far said two things: (1) that God did not give His promises to Israel according to the flesh, but to those who believe (οἱ ἐκ πίστεως); and (2) that Israel broke with the order which God established. So it cannot be said that God breaks His promises, when He rejects Israel according to the flesh. Yet a peculiar obscurity still confronts us: of what use was all God's procedure with His peculiar people, if, when the fullness of times has come, they are simply to be rejected? That is a question which absolutely demands an answer. And it is that problem which Paul now discusses in chapter 11: "I ask, then, *has God rejected his people?*" The answer is an absolute no. The rejection of Israel is not final, for (1) *there is even now a remnant of Israel* which is not rejected (vss. 1-10); (2) *the fall of Israel became the salvation of the Gentiles,* and therein there is already an intimation of her final acceptance (vss. 11-24); and (3) it will, in the last place, be shown that *the rejection is the way to Israel's salvation;* it is the means which God in His unfathomable wisdom lays hold of to bring Israel back to the right (vss. 25-26).

1. Even Now There Is a Remnant
11:1-10

Paul immediately comes to the crux of the matter by opening the eleventh chapter with the question, "Has God rejected his people?" There he gives concisely what is the core of the issue which has been under discussion from the beginning of the ninth chapter. God once chose Israel and made her His peculiar people. Has He now given up that choice and rejected His people finally? In the most decisive manner Paul rejects that thought. As his first argument against it he points out that there is even now a remnant to which God's promise is already fulfilled.

To understand Paul's use of the concept λεῖμμα, "remnant" or "remainder," it is important to keep two things in mind, namely, that, in the first place, Paul takes that idea from the Old Testament where it already plays a singularly important role (cf., for example, Isa. 6:13; 10:20-22); and, in the second place, here as elsewhere, he is not thinking in modern, individualistic categories. If we were to approach what he says, with our current presuppositions we should be apt to understand him in some such way as the following. *Viewed as a people,* God has of course rejected Israel. But that does not mean that all individuals in Israel are rejected. The best illustration to the contrary is Paul himself. He was of course an Israelite, of the seed of Abraham and the tribe of Benjamin. But he is not the only one in Israel who came to believe. Though the number of believers in Israel seems small in comparison with the total of Gentiles who accepted the gospel in faith, yet it is by no means insignificant. It is as in the time of Elijah. He thought that all the nation had fallen away and only he remained true. But God gives him his answer, "I have kept for myself seven thousand men who have not bowed to Baal." Even though God has rejected Israel as a people, there are yet many individuals who believe, and to these He now shows His faithfulness, which He could not show to Israel as a people.

But such an interpretation is in direct conflict with Paul's clearly expressed meaning. The question is not the attitude of God to certain individual members of Israel, but His attitude to *His people:* "Has God rejected his people?" Paul answers, "By no means!" He expressed his certainty with a reference to Psalm 94:14, *"God has not rejected his people whom he foreknew."* Even if the great majority in Israel has fallen under God's judgment of rejection, Israel still exists as the people of God; it continues in the "remnant." Ever since God chose Israel and made her His people, there has always been a spiritual Israel. It is this Israel, this people of God, which continued through the ages, as a watercourse which is sometimes broad and sometimes narrow. In the day of Elijah there was a remnant of only seven thousand, but that remnant at that time consituted the spiritual Israel, and was as such the bearer of God's promises to Israel. And the same is true of Paul's day, "So too at the present time there is a remnant" (vs. 5). In the fact that in every age God takes care that there shall be such a remnant, He shows that He has not rejected His people.

But that does not depend on the character of the people or on the qualifications of the individual. It depends wholly and alone on God's purpose and election. It is God who makes the "remnant" by His choice. "If the Lord of hosts had not left us children, we would have fared like Sodom and Gomorrah," says Paul (9:29), in agreement with Isaiah 1:9. The very existence of the "remnant" is a witness to God's election and His faithfulness to His covenant. That people whom He foresaw He cannot reject; and when He cannot give the whole people His blessing, He takes care that there is always a "remnant" to receive it. In the same manner God had said to Elijah, "I have kept for myself seven thousand men." It is God who sees to it that there is a "remnant."

"Remnant" and "election," λεῖμμα and ἐκλογή are thus interchangeable concepts. A "remnant" is not just a group of separate individuals, taken out of a people doomed to overthrow; it is itself the chosen people, it is Israel *in nuce*. It is the seed which, after the winter, will bear the harvest. In the "remnant" Israel lives on as the people of God, but in such a way that all human pretensions are excluded, and all is left absolutely in God's hand. God's free and sovereign grace decides who shall belong to the "remnant"; for it is implicit in this concept that not all of Israel, but only that part thereof, which God in His grace has determined, shall be bearer of the promise to Israel. Therefore Paul says that the remnant which now is, is "chosen by grace" (κατ' ἐκλογὴν χάριτος); and he adds, "But if it is by grace, it is no longer on the basis of works; otherwise grace would no longer be grace." Israel thought that, as God's chosen people, they could come with claims on God and need not depend wholly on grace. That was the very reason why "Israel according to the flesh" had to be rejected. But according to God's election, the "remnant" had been brought to faith in Christ. It comes before God with no claims; it knows it is wholly de-

pendent on God's grace. Therefore, as the spiritual Israel,
it now receives the fulfillment of the promise.

Paul can sum up the result in the following words, "What
Israel sought it failed to obtain. The elect obtained it, but
the rest were hardened." "The elect" here means the same
as "the remnant"; ἡ ἐκλογή=τὸ λεῖμμα. The smaller part of
Israel, the "remnant" entered into the inheritance from the
fathers. The larger part of Israel holds fast to its righteousness by the law, and therefore it is hardened. To them Paul
can apply the word of Scripture, "God gave them a spirit
of stupor, eyes that should not see and ears that should not
hear" (cf. Isa. 29-10, and Deut. 29:4). God lets His promises come to fulfillment in Christ, but Israel lies deep in
sleep, so that they do not see it. The Messiah is at hand,
but Israel's eyes are darkened, so that they cannot see Him
and recognize Him as their Messiah. The gospel is preached
over all the earth; Israel hears it (10:18), and yet does not
hear it, for hearing has not brought obedience; from ἀκοή no
ὑπακοή has come. The very thing that was Israel's strength
and boast, her zeal for God and for righteousness, leads to
her fall. It is with them as the psalm says, "Their table before them becomes a snare" (69:22).

2. ISRAEL'S FALL BECAME THE GENTILES' SALVATION
11:11-24

Paul can say, at the same time, that God has rejected
Israel and that He has not rejected her. That depends on
which Israel he is speaking of. The Israel of promise has not
been rejected; it is ever the people of God, "the remnant."
But "Israel according to the flesh" has been rejected. In
what has just preceded, Paul has thought mainly of "the
remnant" which, by its very existence, testifies that God has

not rejected His people. Now he turns his attention to
"Israel according to the flesh," which has been rejected; he
asks, "Have they stumbled so as to fall?" Are the fall and
the rejection God's ultimate purpose for the people of Israel?
Paul answers, "By no means! But through their transgression
salvation has come to the Gentiles, so as to make Israel
jealous" (vs. 11).

The first result of the fall of the Jews was that salvation
came to the Gentiles. When the Jews rejected Paul's preaching, when he testified to them that Jesus was the Christ, he
could say to them, "From now on I will go to the Gentiles"
(Acts 18:6). That was the actual result of Israel's fall. But
just now Paul is not so much concerned with the gain which
came to the Gentiles through Israel's fall, as with what the
conversion of the Gentiles would mean to Israel. And as to
this it is Paul's conviction that it will urge Israel on to envy.
When the Jews come to see that their own Messiah is recognized by the Gentiles, that cannot help but arrest their
thought. If the only possibility were that the Jews would
not recognize the Messiah, the whole matter could soon
have been forgotten. But now there stands a constant reminder before them, when the Gentiles show that the Messiah for whom Israel had waited had now come, and the
Gentiles recognize themselves as His people. When the
Gentiles converted to Christ call themselves "Christians"
($X\rho\iota\sigma\tau\iota\alpha\nu o\iota$, Acts 11:26), the name they use rests on the Old
Testament name, Messiah. The name "the Christians" simply
means "the messianic congregation," "the messianic people."
But it was precisely for the age of the Messiah that the Jews
waited. It is the hope of *Israel* which has come to fulfillment
for the Christians. It is the God of *Israel* on whom the Gentiles have come to believe. It is the promises originally

given to *Israel* which the Gentiles now inherit. How could they who belonged to Israel see all this without a pang in the heart? It is to these and similar thoughts that Paul gives expression when he says that the Jews will be aroused to envy by the fact that salvation has come to the Gentiles.

At the present moment Israel, as the people of God, is represented by τὸ λεῖμμα, by a small remnant. But to Paul that is not the normal condition. He looks forward to the time when Israel, numbering a great multitude, will come to believe in Christ; and he contemplates with great joy the blessing which will follow as a result. "Now if their transgression means riches for the world, and if their failure (ἥττημα) means riches for the Gentiles, how much more will their full inclusion (πλήρωμα) mean!" (vs. 12). The consummation can come only when *all* of Israel is saved.

Before taking up this matter for final discussion Paul turns to the Gentiles to speak to them about the Jews and about the relations of his apostleship to them. It is precisely with the Jews in mind that he regards his apostleship to the Gentiles so highly. He knows that the best service that he can just now render to the Jews is to preach the gospel to the Gentiles; for he thereby awakens the Jews to envy. The office to which he is called is not for the good of the Gentiles. alone, but of the Jews as well, for those who are "his own flesh and blood." Paul here considers Israel "according to the flesh," Israel κατὰ σάρκα, and expects that good will come to them through his work among the Gentiles. He is himself a fellow worker for the conversion of Israel, even though his be the indirect way, through his work with the Gentiles. He looks forward to the time when not only a remnant but the whole of Israel as a people, when not only a λεῖμμα but the πλήρωμα, will accept Christ in faith; and he considers his own work a preparation for that end. For by His act of election God has once for all coupled His relation to the world with Israel. Israel has been involved in the great turning points of God's history with mankind; and Israel will be included in the consummation. Her rejection is coupled with the reconciliation of the world, and her acceptance will be the harbinger of the final consummation (vs. 15).

Paul here lets us see what election by God means in its total outreach. It is no longer necessary to ask what good was served by the fact that God chose Israel as His peculiar people, since He later rejected her. No, even with reference to Israel as a people it is true that God has not "rejected his people." When God chose Abraham and the patriarchs, He put an ineffaceable mark on Israel; He gave her, so to say, a "character indelebilis." Thereafter Israel can never be other than a "peculiar people," "the people of God." Not even her present alienation can change that, for God has faithfully bound himself to Israel, and her faithlessness cannot nullify God's faithfulness (3:3). The Gentile Christians should remember that; otherwise they might easily look down on Israel as forsaken by God, because she happens now to be rejected. But her rejection is not final; in its time it will be transcended in her ultimate acceptance.

God's choice has once for all made Israel a "holy" people. Not holy, to be sure, in the sense that all her members are righteous and holy in manner of life; but holy in the sense that this people has, in a special way, been sanctified and separated unto God. Paul expresses this with two different figures: (1) "If the dough offered as first fruits is holy, so is the whole lump." The dough that is the first fruits signifies Abraham and the fathers. (2) To this Paul adds the other figure. It says the same thing, but it lends itself better to what Paul is about to say, "If the root is holy, so are the branches." God sanctified the root by His choice. From that holy root Israel has grown. This tree is holy in its entirety; but this does not mean that the fact of belonging to Israel is itself enough to shield anyone from God's wrath. In 2:25—3:8 Paul has specifically said the opposite. Branches of the holy tree may become useless and be cut off; and that is what has now happened to a large part of the people of Israel.

But even in the face of what has been said, we seem to confront a difficulty. Has Paul not here contradicted what he said earlier on the same matter? When the Jew trusts in circumcision and his belonging to this holy people, Paul dissents with utmost vigor. But is he not now taking practically the same position which he earlier criticized?

But this contradiction is only apparent. The Jew comes to God with his *claims*. It is that which Paul censures. The grace and election of God can never serve as the basis for human pretensions. But on the other hand, man's faithlessness can never nullify God's faithfulness. Paul also pointed out that side of the matter in the earlier context (3:3; cf. pp. 136f.), thereby pointing ahead to what he is now saying. But here, in chapter 11, he is not discussing a proud Israel that trusts in its advantage; to a rejected Israel he is affirming God's faithfulness, despite everything. Here there is no thought of human pretensions, but of God's free grace based on the choice of His sovereign will.

The illustration of the tree and the branches Paul now applies to the relation between a rejected Israel and the Gentiles who have come to faith. The branches that are pruned away illustrate the rejection of Israel. Not all branches have been cut off, but a great part of them. In their place other branches, brought from a wild olive tree, have been grafted; and they illustrate the acceptance of believing Gentiles into the people of God.

This illustration has special interest because it makes clear Paul's view of the relation between Israel and the Christian church. We might have expected a different illustration, that God had the unfruitful tree cut down, and in its place planted a new one by the hand of Christ. But that is not what Paul means. The tree remains; it is. a holy and noble tree. What has happened is only that some useless branches have been removed and other branches have been put in their place. It has rightly been pointed out that what Paul says is not characteristic of the usual grafting technique. But that does not trouble Paul. It is not by observing what happens in nature that Paul has come to his conception of the point he is presenting. And he is not using the illustration to prove that God's way of acting is justified. The *matter* which he is presenting quite rises above the illustration he uses. Israel is the tree; Israel is God's people. Into this people are introduced and ingrafted the Gentiles who come to faith in Christ and are saved. Salvation consists in the very fact that they are thus ingrafted. It is not their faith that sustains the people of God, but the people of God that sustains them. According to Paul, the Christian church has its roots in the Old Testament, in God's choice of the fathers. Through that choice the root was sanctified. Thus the people of God came into being; and they will continue through all time. Despite the alienation of Israel, God has not pulled up the root, for it is a holy root. In the fullness of times God let a Branch come up out of this noble root (Isa. 11). When through baptism the Gentiles are incorporated into Christ, that means at the same time that they are grafted into the spiritual Israel. So, from that point of view, Christians are not a new race; they are rather the continuation, the legitimate continuation, of God's Old Testament people.

The Christian church is the true Israel. It has grown up out of Israel's holy root, and it includes, in part, "the remnant" of Israel (the natural branches which were not broken off), and, in part, those Gentiles who come to believe in Christ (the ingrafted branches). For the Gentiles who were not God's people (9:25), but have now been accepted as members thereof, of the spiritual Israel, through the grace of God, this should be the occasion of humble gratitude. They had no advantage which they could claim; they came from a wild olive tree and were ingrafted among the natural branches. All that they are they have received through that new fellowship; that is, to use Paul's figure, "they have come to share with the natural branches in the vital root of the cultivated olive tree.' Ought not that to be enough to exclude all self-exaltation above the natural branches? "If you do boast, remember it is not you that support the root, but the root that supports you" (vs. 18). And yet the temptation to self-exaltation is very near. Paul continues his discussion with the Gentile Christians. "You will say, 'Branches were broken off, so that I might be grafted in'" (vs. 19). In a way, that is true. Paul has himself asserted that it was through Israel's fall that salvation came to the Gentiles (vs. 11). But what was it that caused Israel's fall? It was their unbelief; or, in other words, Israel fell because they trusted in their advantage, and were not disposed to accept all by the free grace of God. "They were broken off because of their unbelief, but you stand fast only through faith. So do not become proud, but stand in awe." Paul knows that the same temptation that caused Israel's fall also confronts the Christian and constitutes a grave peril for him. The Jew says, "I belong to God's own people." He puts his confidence in circumcision and the promises to the fathers. In his complacency he refuses faith. But in exactly similar manner, the Christian is tempted to say, "I belong to the spiritual Israel." He is tempted to put his confidence in his own faith, his Christianity.

It is as if Paul had sensed how much disturbance would come about among Christians through the very subject of faith. It is as if he knew the extent to which faith itself, the very opposite of self-reliance and pride, would be made to serve human complacency. There is really no great difference, in principle, whether one reposes his confidence in his belonging to the Israel chosen by God, or in his belonging to Christianity, whether one puts his trust in his works or in his faith. In either case a man is resting on himself and the superiority of his position. But the only thing on which the Christian can build is *the goodness of God*, God's free grace, the sovereign will of His love, His unmerited mercy. But everything is lost if the Christian thinks he can build on his faith as if it were the basis of a superiority in him. It is notable that in this connection Paul specifically refrains from using the word faith. In verse 23, in reference to the Jews, he speaks of "persisting in unbelief." It would have seemed most natural, in contrast with that, to speak of how a Christian "persists in faith." But Paul refrains from using the expression, though it suggests itself. He says, rather, that the Christian continues in God's kindness. To the Gentiles he says, "Note then the kindness and the severity of God: severity toward those who have fallen, but kindness to you, *provided you continue in his kindness;* otherwise you too will be cut off. And even the others, if they do not persist

in their unbelief, will be grafted in" (vss. 22-23). Pride and
self-exaltation are unbelief; that is to put one's confidence
in oneself, as if one's own superiority were the reason for
acceptance by God. That is to reverse the relation between
the tree and the branches, between the root and the
branches, as if the branches bore the root, rather than the
opposite. In that way one does not build on the cornerstone,
Christ, but on himself; and then Christ becomes the stone
that makes men stumble.

To "continue in the goodness of God" is possible only by
living in awe (vs. 20). There is a relation between faith and
fear. There is in some a certainty of salvation which rests
only on one's certainty as to oneself; one is sure of oneself.
But to build on oneself in that way is to stumble on Christ
and to fall. That is what had happened with the Jews. But
the very same thing can happen to the Christian; and it must
happen to him if he exalts himself. If he puts his confidence
in his own excellence as a Christian, he will be cut off. "For
if God did not spare the natural branches, neither will he
spare you," Paul says (vs. 21). Just as the Jews, persisting
in unbelief, made way for the Gentiles, so the situation
could again be reversed, if the Christian, in a feeling of self-
importance, puts his trust in anything else than the unmerited grace of God.

Paul has set forth the fall of Israel as a warning example
to the Christians. But his final word in this connection is a
word of hope as to Israel. "God has the power to graft them
in again. For if you have been cut off from what is by nature a wild olive tree, and grafted, contrary to nature, into
a cultivated olive tree, how much more will these natural
branches be grafted back into their own olive tree." There-

with Paul prepares for his ultimate answer to the question of Israel's rejection, to which he now turns.

3. REJECTION IS GOD'S WAY TO ISRAEL'S SALVATION
11:25-36

The problem of Israel's rejection emerges directly from what Paul has been saying. He had to ask himself how the fact of Israel's rejection can be reconciled with God's promises. If these cannot be reconciled, Paul's whole message collapses. He cannot hold that, in the moment of fulfillment, God simply *breaks* His promise. To be able to maintain his message he must show how, in spite of everything, the rejection of Israel can be harmonized with God's promises and is part of God's plan of salvation.

How far has Paul gotten with his answer to this problem?

In chapters 9-10, he has shown how God in His sovereignty determined that the promise should belong only to those who believe. When Israel refused to believe, and held fast to righteousness by the law, she herself is to blame for losing the promises. To this, chapter 11 adds an important consideration. It is not the case that God has simply rejected His people. Only in a limited sense can one speak of the rejection of Israel. That God did not absolutely reject His people is evident from the fact that even at this time there is a "remnant" of Israel, to which God has fulfilled His promises. God has laid a cornerstone, Christ, in Zion. The intention was that man should build thereon in faith. The "remnant" did so, and thus was saved. But in the large, except for the "remnant," Israel found the cornerstone a stone of offense. Israel has stumbled over it and fallen. She has rejected the Messiah, and therefore she has herself been rejected. So the question arises whether her fall is perma-

nent. Is the rejection final? No, says Paul. God has used
the fall as a means to His purposes, and these do not aim at
destruction but at salvation. In the first place, Israel's fall
has worked out to the gain of the Gentiles. When Israel
rejected the gospel, it passed over to the Gentiles; when
Israel rejected the Messiah, He became the Christ of the
Gentiles. Thus the promise was fulfilled, "The root of Jesse
shall come, he who rises to rule the Gentiles: in him shall
the Gentiles hope" (cf. 15:12). But beyond that, the fall of
Israel will work out to blessing for Israel too. This will
naturally not come immediately, but in an indirect way,
through that which has happend to the Gentiles: for thereby, Paul hopes, Israel will be awakened to envy.

Now only one step remains for Paul before he reaches
his goal. There is one answer more which he must present,
and that is *the principal answer*, for which all that has preceded is only preparatory. The importance of this answer
Paul himself suggests by the way he introduces it. Earnestly
and solemnly he explains that he must now proclaim a divine
secret, a "mystery." By a special revelation from God it has
been made known to him; and he will now disclose it to his
readers, that, in these vital questions, they may not have to
rely only on their own speculations and human wisdom. The
content of the secret is that hardening has come upon part
of Israel (ἀπὸ μέρους) for the present, and it will continue
till the full number (πλήρωμα) of the Gentiles come in. But
when that has taken place, the turn will come to Israel as a
people. Then it will no longer be a "remnant" but Israel's
πλήρωμα, "all Israel," will enter into the kingdom of God.
All Israel, πᾶς Ἰσραήλ will be saved.

About the unfaithful Jews it can at one time be said that
they are "enemies" of God and "beloved" of God. "As re-

gards the gospel they are enemies of God," for they reject the gospel and do not want to know about it. But the peculiar thing in this connection is that God himself has put the stone of offense in their way, on which they must stumble and fall, as long as they seek a righteousness of themselves. "But as regards his election they are beloved." The hostility that obtains between them and God cannot destroy God's love. "For the gifts and the call of God are irrevocable." God's promises to the fathers always stand fast. They will have a glorious fulfillment, when *all* Israel is again accepted.

God's way of salvation for Israel goes through unbelief to faith, through fall to restoration, through contingent rejection to final acceptance. But why this indirect way? Was it necessary? Could God not have brought Israel to salvation without it? First it must be said that that kind of reasoning about possibilities and necessity are wholly alien to Paul's line of thought. Nothing is further from Paul's mind than to try to show the necessity of God's ways. He would not speak of how God should or must act. He notes how God has in fact acted, and that is what he tries to present. The starting point for him is a *fact:* Israel *is* at present rejected. But in the present situation Paul sees a divine purpose, a mystery, which God has disclosed to him; and in that, man could say in another sense, there is a *divine necessity*, for God never acts arbitrarily. It is not in arbitrariness that God has rejected Israel. *Israel must be rejected that she may be accepted;* that is the content of the mystery of which he has just spoken. The hardening and rejection of Israel are a preparatory step to her acceptance. Rejection is the way in which God carries Israel on toward salvation. It is to a certain extent the consequence of His election of the fathers. God leads each one on the way that is necessary for him.

For Israel the way goes through rejection to salvation.

But wherein lies the difference between Israel and the Gentiles, since they are taken by God on different ways to the same goal? *The Gentiles* stood simply and exclusively under *the wrath of God,* but have now become the object of *His mercy;* through the gospel they share in the righteousness of God revealed in Christ. This a clear example of the justification of sinners. They had nothing in themselves on which they could build, nothing of which they were capable to which they could appeal; they simply had to accept what was given to them for nothing, in grace—and that is what faith means. But with *the Jews* the situation is not so clear and simple. They had much to which to appeal. They had the law and a relative righteousness; they had the fathers, circumcision, the promises, etc. Under such circumstances, how can the new righteousness come to them?

Before God there are two kinds of men, and only two kinds: "vessels of wrath" and "vessels of mercy." We read of them in 9:22-23: σκεύη ὀργῆς and σκεύη ἐλέους. In that alternative the Gentiles fit entirely; they were "vessels of wrath," but by the grace of God they had become "vessels of mercy." But the Jews? They did not apply the alternative to themselves. Of course they were not "vessels of wrath"; they were God's own people! Yet, on the other hand, they were not willing to be simply "vessels of mercy." That could be all right for Gentiles who had nothing to appeal to. Mercy and wrath are the two ways in which God meets men. He who will not accept God's mercy stands under God's wrath. There are these two possibilities, but no third. But Israel wanted a third, different from the other two. If Israel had been willing simply to accept God's mercy, without pretensions or thought of merit, they too would *immediately* have become "vessels of mercy," as well as the Gentiles. No indirect way is necessary on God's side. But Israel has so much in which she trusted: "They are Israelites, and to them belong the sonship, the glory, the covenants, the giving of the law, the worship and the promises; to them belong the patriarchs" (9:4f.). That which was Israel's advantage, and surely an advantage not to be scorned, became her destruction. For she put her hope on these and thought it unnecessary to descend to the place of the Gentiles, just as if she had no real advantage to appeal to. So she refused to become a "vessel of mercy," which owes everything to the mercy of God alone. But she did not escape the consequences; she became a "vessel of wrath," and was rejected.

But that which, in human judgment, is both Israel's responsibility and her tragedy, is, with God, *the way to Israel's salvation.* There is no other way. Israel must first be cast down from her self-confidence. She must come to see how multitudes of Gentiles enter into God's kingdom, while Israel, who thought herself better than the Gentiles, has no part in it. She has to experience something of that which Jesus expressed in the words, "Many will come from east and west and sit at table with Abraham, Isaac, and Jacob, in the kingdom of heaven, while the sons of the kingdom will be thrown into the outer darkness" (Matt. 8:11f.). But when Israel has been cast down from her pedestal and lies there rejected, when she is only a "vessel of wrath" before God, then she will finally be ready for the action of God by which He will make her a "vessel of mercy." Israel in her pride will not accept mercy, at any rate not the same mercy as the Gentiles receive. So God has now given Israel up to disobedience, and allowed rejection to fall on the Jews, "that by the mercy shown [to the Gentiles] they also may receive mercy" (vs. 31).

Thus every difference between Jew and Gentile has been removed. That for which Paul has contended throughout the epistle receives its crowning and seal in his final word about Israel's rejection and her salvation. "There is no distinction; since all have sinned and fall short of the glory of God, they are justified by his grace as a gift, through the redemption which is in Christ Jesus," Paul has said in 3:22-24, at the high point of his transition from the old aeon to the new. He says exactly the same thing here, and emphasizes it by what has happened to the Gentiles and the Jews. On the part of man, of Jews and Gentiles alike, there is only disobedience. On the part of God, to Jews and Gentiles alike, there is mercy. "For God has consigned all men to disobedience, that he may have mercy upon all" (vs. 32).

God has granted Paul a glimpse into His plan, and Paul stands filled with wonder, "O the depth of the riches and wisdom and knowledge of God! How unsearchable are his judgments and how inscrutable his ways!" God's thoughts and ways are entirely different from man's. He takes counsel of no man, and without His revelation and guidance no one can know why He acts as He does. Who could have fathomed this, that God would use even man's disobedience as a means for effecting His saving will. And in it all God's mercy triumphs. He does not suffer anyone to appear before Him with pretensions. "Who has given a gift to him that he might be repaid?" All depends on His sovereign will. It is at once the source and the goal of all, "For from him and through him and to him are all things. To him be glory forever. Amen."

PART FOUR

The Life of Him Who through Faith Is Righteous
12:1–15:13

Beginning with chapter 12 Paul turns to *exhortations*
The first word here, παρακαλῶ, "I appeal to you," stands as
a rubric and superscription for all of the part that follows,
indicating that we now come to a new section of the letter.
That does not mean that Paul now takes up something wholly
new which has no relation to what has already been said.
On the contrary, he continues in the same sphere as before.
That which was the theme of what preceded—"he who
through faith is righteous shall live"—is also the theme of
these exhortations. We here have an illustration of the
matchless logic which controls Paul's thought.

This fact needs to be emphasized the more because it
has often been said that the matters to which Paul now turns
stand in a very loose and external relation with what he has
presented up to this point. And furthermore, it has also been
asserted that only a loose connection binds together the
contents of this part, one exhortation following another in
a motley series, just as they happen to come to Paul's mind.
So both the external relation of this part to the rest and the
internal connections within it are said to be weak. But as
to both of these affirmations it must be said that they are
manifestly contrary to fact. In that which is to follow it will
become clear that this concluding section of the epistle only
draws the conclusions as to the manner of life of the Chris-

tian from that which Paul has already presented. And it will also be manifest that the relation of the constituent parts of this section of the letter is built up in keeping with definite structural plan.

That there has been such difficulty in discovering the consistency that obtains here may be due, at least in part, to the fact that in recent centuries it has been customary to draw a sharp line between "doctrine" and "life." But such a differentiation is alien to Paul. A doctrine, a gospel, which has no significance for man's life and conduct is not a real gospel; and life and conduct which are not based on that which comes to us in the gospel are not Christian life and Christian conduct.

In the consideration of the first two verses of chapter 12 we shall find occasion to point out more fully the intimate relation between the hortatory part of this epistle and the rest. We therefore limit ourselves now to a brief sketch of the relationships within the section to which we now turn.

The issue concerns the Christian's *conduct.* How is that to be shaped? Paul's answer says that it must be molded and shaped in harmony with the new aeon. That may be called the basic rule of Pauline ethics. That basic rule emerges in concise and concentrated form in the first two verses of chapter 12. But just what does it mean? Paul sets forth two characteristic marks of the new life: it is a life "in Christ," and it is a life "in love." We should note Paul's art in presenting them. In discussing them anew he reverses the order. First he speaks about life in love, and how love is the fulfilling of the law: and only then comes the concluding exhortation, "Put on the Lord Jesus Christ." By this chiasmus the statement about living and acting "in Christ" comes to be both the first and last in this section.

When Paul has thus, by his exhortations, presented the characteristic quality of the life of one who through faith is righteous, he turns to a special problem which has clearly been particularly real in the church at Rome, namely, the relation between the weak and the strong. But even what he says as to that is not unrelated to his central theme; it rather illustrates by one special problem what it means to "walk in love" (κατὰ ἀγάπην περιπατεῖν, 14:15).

What has been said shows that Paul's exhortations too are controlled by a rigorous consistency. His line of thought here falls into two main divisions: (1) conduct in harmony with the new aeon (12:1–13:14); (2) the weak and the strong (14:1–15:13).

XIII

Conduct in the New Aeon

12:1–13:14

Chapters 12-13 contain the fullest exposition that we have of Paul's central view of the ethical life of the Christian, of the conduct of one who through faith is righteous. We may say that these chapters give a brief summary of Paul's ethics. What we see first is how immediately the ethical requirements are bound to the new situation which Christ brought; they grow directly out of it. It has been possible to note the same again and again in the earlier parts of the letter. It will suffice to recall a single illustration, in 6:4. Paul there spoke of how, through baptism, we are incorporated into Christ and united with Him in participation in His death and resurrection. From that he immediately drew the conclusion that we should "walk in newness of life," ἐν καινότητι ζωῆς περιπατήσωμεν. In that statement in chapter 6 Paul has, so to say, given the formula for that which is now to be discussed. Since we have been justified, i.e., been taken out of the dominion of death in the old aeon, and been received with Christ into the new aeon of life, we should now "walk in newness of life," to quote Paul verbatim. We should put our conduct into harmony with the new aeon. That is the basic rule in Paul's ethics; and it is that which is unfolded further in the first two verses of chapter 12.

415

1. The Basic Rule of Paul's Ethics
12:1-2

The reason why we put this caption over these two verses is that they contain an idea which steadily and always emerges in Paul's thought in different contexts. It is clearly of central significance for him, because it concerns the shaping of the Christian life. In Galatians 5:25 he says, "If we live by the Spirit, let us also walk by the Spirit." That statement is entirely in line with the thought of the letter to the Romans with its emphasis that "he who through faith is righteous *shall live*." Life is given to him by the Spirit, the Spirit of God and of Christ, as we heard in chapter 8. But where the Spirit of Christ lives and works, a new mode of life results. Even that is implicit in what Paul says in 1:16, that the gospel is the power of God; this power also manifests itself in that it transforms man's ways and conduct. But we should observe carefully that it is not we who help the gospel to have this transforming power in our life; it is the power of the gospel which renews and transforms us. What God has done through Christ is primary. Because this has happened the Christian's conduct is to be different from what it was formerly. In this sense the gospel, the "doctrine" (διδαχή), is both the pattern according to which the life of the Christian is to be shaped (cf. p. 256), and the power that transforms. We find the same idea in I Thessalonians 2:12, where Paul writes, "God calls you into his own kingdom and glory"; and there Paul exhorts Christians to "lead a life worthy of God" (ἀξίως τοῦ θεοῦ περιπατεῖν). And when Paul turns to exhortation, in Ephesians 4:1, his first admonition is "lead a life worthy of the calling to which you have been called," ἀξίως περιπατῆσαι τῆς κλήσεως. Or, to give one more example, in Colossians 2:6, we read, "As therefore you received Christ Jesus the Lord, so live in him"; ἐν αὐτῷ περιπατεῖτε. Everywhere it is the same: God has done something for us, we have received something from Him, we have received His call, we have received Christ or the Spirit; so we are to live a life that is in harmony with what we have thus received.

Now, after this survey, we turn to the first two verses of chapter 12, to see how they give expression to Paul's basic rule of ethics. First of all the apostle refers to God's mercy which the church has experienced. All that he has thus far said about the new aeon and its blessings has its basis in God's mercy. "It depends not upon man's will or exertion, but upon God's mercy" (9:16). It was because of His mercy that God did not spare His own Son, but gave Him for all of us; and it is because of the same that He would now give us all things with Him (8:32).

It is to those who have experienced the mercy of God that Paul speaks here. Out of this comes his exhortation that in life and conduct they show the fruits of what has been given to them by this divine mercy; that they therefore present their bodies as a living sacrifice, holy and acceptable to God. That he speaks especially of presenting our "bodies" to God will awaken no surprise if we remember how he has spoken of the body of sin and death, and that in the sixth chapter he said that that body and those members, which formerly served as instruments of unrighteousness, should henceforth be devoted to God's service as instruments of righteousness (6:13, 19). It is God who has placed us in this temporal existence. Hence it is here amidst present reality, in this life conditioned by corporeality, that we are to serve God, and not in an incorporeal existence conceived in dreams or painted in fancies. God has given us definite tasks, in which body and members are to serve Him. Nor is it surprising that Paul calls this a "living" sacrifice. The thought of "life" runs through the whole epistle. "He who through faith is righteous shall *live*"; and his sacrifice is therefore living, holy, acceptable to God, a real and true service to God, ἡ λογικὴ λατρεία. Any spiritualizing of the meaning of Christian service is contrary to Paul's intentions; he speaks specifically of our bodies and members as given to the service of God.

With this, Paul has come to the point where he can give exact formulation to his basic rule of ethics. We find it in the second verse, "Do not be conformed to this world, but be transformed by the renewal of your mind, that you may prove what is the will of God, what is good and acceptable and perfect." Christians should remember that they already belong to the new aeon, and that that fact has definite consequences for their manner of life. By the mercy of God, through Christ, they have been saved from the present evil aeon (cf. Gal. 1:4), in which Wrath, Sin, the Law, and Death carry on their harsh rule. It will therefore not do for them to live on in the old nature, just as if nothing had happened through Christ. Paul has touched on this thought before. In 6:2 he said, "How can we who died to sin still live in it?" The same applies to the Christian's relation to the other destroying powers too, and indeed to his relation to the old aeon as a whole. He has died to it; through Christ he has left it. But if he has left the old aeon and entered into the new, his mind must not remain with the old and be conformed to it. His mind and conduct must not bear the mark of this age; a genuine *metamorphosis of mind and conduct* must take place. Paul expresses it in that very way. He says μεταμορφοῦσθε, "be transformed by the renewal of

418

your mind." The mind and memory, reason and emotion, indeed, everything in the Christian's life, the inmost and the more outward, from the highest to the lowest, all must be included in this metamorphosis into harmony with the new aeon.

The old aeon, ὁ αἰὼν οὗτος, Paul here calls by name, but not the new, ὁ καινὸς αἰών. But the latter is glimpsed in the expression ἡ ἀνακαίνωσις τοῦ νοός, "the renewal of your mind"; for the new man with the new mind, the mind of Christ, corresponds to the new aeon (6:4; cf. p. 235; I Cor. 2:16).

Through baptism the Christian has been incorporated into Christ. Thereby the basis has been laid for the transformation of which Paul speaks (cf. 6:4). But since the Christian must live his life in this world and serve God in its relationships, the temptation always arises to be conformed to the nature of this world and to copy its fashion (σχῆμα). But that must not be allowed to happen. Here Paul's words in I Corinthians 5:7 are applicable, "Cleanse out the old leaven." And in Ephesians 5:7f. we read, "Therefore do not associate with them, for once you were darkness, but now you are light in the Lord; walk as children of light." It is indeed in this world that the Christian must serve God, but not with a mind that belongs to this world and is conformed to its nature. He must serve God with a mind that bears the mark of the new aeon, of membership in Christ. In the midst of this aeon he must live the life of the new aeon as God's child, "without blemish in the midst of a crooked and perverse generation" (Phil. 2:15).

According to Paul, "the renewing of the mind" also includes a new ethical judgment. The Christian has received the ability to prove what God's will is in the concrete situation. He has received a new mind for God's will, for that which is good and acceptable and perfect. He no longer judges according to the manner and standard of this world. His aim is that God's will be done.

But just what does it mean to walk in harmony with the new aeon? Paul answers that it means to *walk in Christ* (vss. 3-8), or, what really means the same, to *walk in love* (vss. 9-21).

2. TO WALK IN CHRIST
12:3-8

The conduct of the Christian is to be determined by the fact that he *is in Christ*. "If any one is in Christ, he is a new creation" (II Cor. 5:17). That must set its mark on all of his life, on all that he does or allows. But to be in Christ is to be a *member of the body of Christ*. A member without connection with the body would be nothing. It is a member only in relation to the body and its other members. It has its existence only by the fact that it is incorporated in the body and has its special function therein. So it is with the Christian. By himself he is nothing. What he is, he is through belonging to Christ. In that relation his place is assigned to him, and he must respect its limits as determined by God. As to this, Paul says, "By the grace given unto me I bid every one among you not to think of himself more highly than he ought to think, but to think with sober judgment, each according to the measure of faith which God has assigned him. For as in one body we have many members, and all the members do not have the same function, so we, though many, are one body in Christ, and individually members one of another. [We have] gifts that differ according to the grace given to us" (vss. 3-6).

Here we have an illustration of the fact that the conduct of one who through faith is righteous is, and must be, different from that of one who belongs to the old aeon. In the latter it is the rule that each is to seek his own, his own power, promotion, and honor. While the Christian lives in this world it is easy for him to be conformed to its character, so that he uses for his own advancement the gifts and functions that were given to him. Even spiritual gifts, gifts of grace, can be misused in that way. It is against that that Paul warns when he admonishes the members of the church not to think more highly of themselves than they ought to think, but to think with sober judgment. Paul here uses a play on words which is not easy to render in translation: μὴ ὑπερφρονεῖν . . . ἀλλὰ φρονεῖν εἰς τὸ σωφρονεῖν. The final word, σωφρονεῖν, reminds us of one of the four cardinal virtues of ancient times, σωφροσύνη, moderation. But it is only the word that is common to both. All in all, Paul knows no "virtues"—despite Philippians 4:8. What he has in mind is something quite different in meaning. We shall speak of that later (p. 438).

The Christian must not strive to be everything. There is only one who comprises everything, Christ. God has determined "to unite all things in him, things in heaven and things on earth," as Ephesians 1:10 says; and in verses 22f. in the same chapter, we read, God "has made him the head over all things for the church which is his body, the fullness of him who fills all in all." So it is true of the Christian that he is only a member of that body. However richly equipped he may be, and however great the commission entrusted to him, he still is, and ever remains, only a member. In one respect there is utter similarity among the members, namely, in the fact that they are all members in one and the same body, none being either greater or less than the rest. But that does not mean that, in another sense, there is great difference among them. One member has one function, another has another; it is not the intention that all should be alike in this, or serve the same function. On the contrary, their manifoldness and differences are prerequisite for the meeting of all the different needs of the body.

When Paul here speaks of the body and the members, it is not merely a figure of speech; it is a *spiritual reality* to him. He means more than that, just as members of a body work together, so Christians should work together, with their diverse gifts and equipment. He means that we *are* one body in Christ, that we *are* members in our mutual relations. To Paul the σῶμα Χριστοῦ, "the body of Christ," is not a figure or a comparison, but an indisputable reality; and into that body we Christians have been placed as members. Through faith we belong to Christ; in baptism we have been fitted in with Christ and joined to Him (6:5), and are thereby actual members of His body. We "are *one* body in Christ," ἐν σῶμά ἐσμεν ἐν Χριστῷ. In Christ there is *oneness;* but that does not abolish *manifoldness* and *difference*. When we were joined to the body of Christ, we were given a special function to fulfill in its organism, the function of each being distinct from that given to other members; and we were given special gifts needed for our special function. We have "gifts that differ according to the grace given to us." God dispenses many different gifts, to each He gives something different. Any attempt to disregard these differences conflicts with God's will.

It is not the intention that the Christian is to use these gifts for his own enjoyment and advancement. Just as he must not lay his hand to that for which God has not equipped him, even though it might appeal to him and be more highly regarded by others, so too the gifts entrusted to him he must not use to gain luster and fame. The gifts are given to him that he may *serve* with them. Both a carnal pride, which thinks more highly of itself than is proper, and a false humility, which hides its talent, are equally reprehensible. When God bestows a gift, even though it be small, it is His will that it be used in His service and for building up the body of Christ (Eph. 4:12).

No one is superfluous. God has so arranged that the different members are each to serve the other with the gifts given to each; and thus they contribute to the growth of all. No member may exalt itself above the others, for all are indispensable. The church, which is the body of Christ, cannot exist and grow without prophecy, those who serve the congregation, ministry, those who rule, etc. (cf. the parallel and more detailed presentation of this in I Cor. 12). Each one ought to serve by means of his gift and in the special way indicated by it; but he must not forget that his gift is only one beside others which are just as necessary; he must use the gift in harmony with the measure which faith sets for it. In faith oneness in Christ is given; into that unity each gift and service is integrated and is thereby authenticated. In this way every member, every joint, has its contribution to make to the inclusive purpose— the upbuilding of the body of Christ. Thus the result is that "the whole body, joined and knit together by every joint with which it is supplied, when each part is working properly," "grows up into him who is the head, into Christ" (Eph. 4:15-16).

3. To Walk in Love
12:9-21

To walk "in Christ" is also to walk "in love." In Christ God has revealed His love to us (5:8). Therein lies the

basis of the new life, into which they who believe in Christ
are brought; and that life is characterized by the fact that
it is a life "in love." The Christian's conduct in love is only
a reflex of the love which Christ has shown to him. This
connection between Christ's love and the Christian's life in
love comes to particularly clear expression in Ephesians 5:2,
"Walk in love (περιπατεῖτε ἐν ἀγάπῃ), as Christ loved us and
gave himself for us." For Paul, then, the two expressions "in
Christ" and "in love" (ἐν Χριστῷ—ἐν ἀγάπῃ) coincide with
each other. Some examples will illustrate this. Paul, who
holds that all things must be done *in Christ,* can say, in
I Corinthians 16:14, "Let all that you do be done *in love.*"
And as Paul, in Romans 13:14, (cf. also Gal. 3:27) addresses
to the congregation the exhortation, "Put on the Lord Jesus
Christ," so, parallel with that, he says in Colossians 3:12, 14,
"Put on love." In Colossians 2:6 he says, "live in him"
(Christ); and in Ephesians 5:2 (cf. Rom. 14:15) the other
expression is used, "walk in love." About those who have
received Christ, Colossians 2:7 says, "rooted and built up
in him" (Christ); in Ephesians 3:17 we find "rooted and
grounded in love." As Christ is the *unity* in which the many
are built into *one* body, so it is love "which binds everything
together" (Col. 3:14). We may also call to mind the fifteenth
chapter of the Gospel according to John, the chapter about
the vine and the branches. There Jesus says interchangeably, "Abide in me" (vss. 4, 5, 6, 7) and "Abide in my love"
(vss. 9, 10). Love is, so to say, the circulation of the blood
in the body of Christ, through which all its parts and members are immediately related to each other and bound together in a oneness. It is love that makes the members share
each other's lot, bear each other's burdens, and share each

other's joy. Love flows from one to another; but ultimately it comes from Christ himself.

Under these conditions it is entirely natural for Paul to let his statement that he who through faith is righteous lives "in Christ" glide over into the statement that he lives "in love." So he starts the new section with the word "love," ἀγάπη. Since conduct in love is the outer expression for the hidden life "in Christ," there is always the danger that men clothe themselves in the outer garment of love, without really having love in their hearts. Therefore Paul's first admonition says, "Let love be genuine."

It is not by chance that Paul mentions love first. He does so elsewhere. When, for instance, in Galatians 5:22, he speaks of "the fruit of the Spirit," it is love which is named first. That love has that place does not mean that is only first in a series of comparable qualities, but that it includes the rest in itself. If love be unfeigned, all that to which Paul exhorts the church will follow.

As the section that immediately preceded had its counterpart in I Corinthians 12, so this one has its counterpart in I Corinthians 13. One needs only to make "love" the subject throughout 12:9-21, to see how close the contents of this section are to I Corinthians 13. It could then be paraphrased about as follows: "Love hates what is evil, but holds fast to what is good. It loves the brethren, and seeks to outdo them in showing honor. Love never flags in zeal; it is aglow in the Spirit; it serves the Lord. It rejoices in hope, is patient in tribulation, is constant in prayer. It contributes to the needs of the saints, and practices hospitality. Love blesses those who persecute it; it blesses and does not curse. Love rejoices with those who rejoice, and weeps with those who weep. Love lives in harmony with the brethren. It is not haughty, but associates with the lowly. It is never conceited. Love does not repay evil for evil. It takes thought for what is noble in the sight of all. If possible, so far as it depends on it, love lives peaceably with all. Love never avenges itself, but loves even an enemy, according to the Scriptures which say 'If your enemy is hungry, feed him; if he is thirsty, give him drink.' Love is not overcome by evil, but overcomes evil with good."

That which gives us a certain right to make such a paraphrase is the fact that, by these exhortations, Paul means to show what it means *to walk in love.* This is what love is like. That is the way it acts in life's varied situations. To these exhortations Paul adds a personal appeal: you have been *justified through faith;* therefore live a life suitable to that fact; walk in love!

4. THE CONDUCT OF THE CHRISTIAN IN THE ORDERS OF THIS WORLD
13:1-7

Again and again, in the preceding parts of the letter, we have been reminded of the tension in the life of the Christian due to the fact that it must be lived *in this aeon.* This aeon has its orders, quite apart from those that obtain in the new aeon. We remember, in his connection, what Jesus said to the disciples, "You know that the rulers of the Gentiles lord it over them, and their great men exercise authority over them. Not so shall it be among you" (Matt. 20:25f). In these orders which have their cause and existence in the present aeon, the Christian is a participant. It is in this world that he has to live as a Christian. How should he shape his life in relation to the orders of this world? That is the issue on which Paul expresses himself in the beginning of the thirteenth chapter. The answer that might readily suggest itself might be as follows: The Christian has been freed from all the powers that reign in the old aeon. Its "princes," "authorities," and "powers"—its ἀρχαί, ἐξουσίαι, δυνάμεις—have been overthrown and destroyed. Where Christ is Lord, there is no place for any other dominion. So the Christian should, as far as possible, separate himself from the orders of this world. His commonwealth is in heaven (Phil. 3:20); so he is free and without obligation as to all earthly citizenships. He no longer has to obey worldly powers. "Then the sons are free," we read in Matthew 17:26.

The first to find it hard to differentiate between the freedom of the Christian and earthly freedom are not people of today, or even the "fanatics" of Reformation days. That difficulty has presented itself throughout Christian history. But Paul has done what he can to keep such anarchistic conclusions from being drawn from what he has said about freedom. It is indeed true that the destroying powers of the old aeon have been deposed. The Christian is actually free from these ἐξουσίαι. Paul does not retract a word of what he has said about that. But it is no less true that God has placed the Christian in this world and subjected him to the ruling powers. Paul uses the same term, ἐξουσίαι, for the powers that rule here. Here Paul takes a most emphatic position against the fanatical view which makes the gospel into a law for society. That form of legalism too is to be rejected. The two aeons do interpenetrate, but that does not mean that they may arbitrarily be confused. One must not take that which belongs to the new aeon and apply it simply as a law for the old. "Let every person be subject to the governing authorities," Paul begins; and the reason he states

is that *they have been instituted by God.* "For there is no
authority except from God, and those that exist have been
instituted by God." That does not say that all the authorities
do will agree with God's will. There are good and bad authorities, God-fearing and godless governments. There are
some authorities that use their powers in harmony with God's
will, and others that misuse their powers and tramp the will
of God under their feet. But Paul is not now talking about
such distinctions. He is speaking of that which all authorities have in common, namely, that they are instituted by
God. That there are governments in the world is not an arbitrary invention of man's; it is a fact ordained by God. Thus
it is God who grants power to the governments. It does not
at all follow that actions of the governments are ethically
approved. God uses even unworthy and culpable men as
means to the accomplishment of His purposes (cf. Acts 4:24-
28). But on the other hand the offenses of governments do
not undo the fact that it is God who has given the power—
even the power which they now misuse—and that He can
use even unrighteousness for the accomplishment of His
purpose. "Therefore he who resists the authorities resists
what God has appointed, and those who resist will incur
judgment." If a Christian, trusting in his freedom from the
powers of this world, thinks that he is absolved from obedience to the authorities that govern, he resists not only the
authorities, but that which God has ordained. He thereby
calls down upon himself, not only punishment by the authorities, but also the judgment of God. If God has ordained
that the Christian is to live his life in *this* world, in *this* aeon,
the Christian must not pretend that he already lives in the
glorified state of the new aeon. If God has placed him in
this existence with its orders, it is not the intention that he

shall set himself above them and arbitrarily claim a state of glory in advance. When at last the new aeon comes into its glory, the power of earthly authorities will be past, for it belongs to those things of the old world which will cease to be. But as long as the present aeon endures, the power and authority of government will last, for God has ordained them for this aeon.

There has been surprise that Paul is able to speak with such positive appreciation of the state and its functions, especially since the state in which he lived was a heathen state. Some have sought to explain his appraisal by referring to favorable experiences he personally had with Roman authorities. The great persecution of Christians had not yet begun. Some have questioned whether he would have been able to stand by his positive judgment after the persecutions came. As to such it must be said that his judgment did not rest on accidental experiences and impressions; it is part of his total theological outlook. He is not here giving casuistic counsels how his readers should act towards the authorities in different situations; he is setting forth the basic Christian view about worldly government. In so doing he is aware both of its positive powers and of its limits.

Paul recognizes the problematical in worldly orders; they belong to a world which is judged and to pass away. But it is in this world that the Christian has to live his life. The positive significance of the ruler is that he is a *servant* of God (διάκονος θεοῦ, vs. 4; λειτουργὸς θεοῦ, vs. 6). The limitation lies in the fact that such authority belongs to the old aeon and has relevance only to it. The earthly ruler is *the servant of God in the aeon of wrath*. It is the instrument of God's wrath, and as such it bears the sword which, by the will of God, is to be used to combat evil. For the ruler "does not bear the sword in vain; he is the servant of God to execute his wrath ($ἔκδικος εἰς ὀργήν$ vs. 4) on the wrong-doer." He who does what is good does not bring the sword down on himself. For him the ruler "is God's servant for your good." What would the result be if the Christian set himself up against the ruler? It would mean that he set himself up against the power which God uses to execute His wrath in this world.

In this view of earthly government and its function there is nothing that needs to be modified, depending on whether he who holds the authority uses it well or badly. The Christians did not have to wait for the coming of persecutions to know that the heathen state could use its power against them. Paul, like all other Christians, knew that it was an officer of the Roman government, Pontius Pilate, who handed Christ over to be crucified. But that did not change his view of the ruler, that God has entrusted a special function to him. That only shows that Jesus also had to suffer wrath in the present aeon. It adds nothing new to what has been set forth, when a ruler uses his power to persecute Christians. It only shows that the Christian can no more avoid suffering wrath here than could Christ.

Persecution at the hands of rulers is but a special form of "the sufferings of this present time" which the Christian is called upon to undergo in fellowship with Christ. He who believes in Christ has, through Him been "freed from wrath" (chapter 5), but that does not mean that he does not have to suffer the wrath which is still at work in the present aeon. Here, with reference to Wrath, tension and dualism in the Christian life arises, like that which we earlier noted with reference to Sin, the Law, and Death (cf. p. 296).

The Christian, far from standing in hostility to earthly

authorities, is the only one who is able to give them the esteem and honor due them. Others must regard them as a necessary and useful arrangement for the advantage of human society; the Christian knows that "there is no authority except from God." In the earthly ruler he sees a servant of God, with only a limited function within the aeon of wrath, but withal a servant of God. He sees him as one who carries out the work of God in this world. It is indeed God's "alien" work, His wrath; but it is still God's work. For that reason it does not satisfy Paul if the Christian merely bows outwardly to the ruler. Paul calls for an inner subjection. "Therefore one must be subject, not only to avoid God's wrath but also for the sake of conscience," that is, for the sake of God. In both the outward and the inward, the Christian is called to live in this aeon as the child of the coming aeon, and therefore to give to each and every one what is his due. "Pay all of them their dues, taxes to whom taxes are due, revenue to whom revenue is due, respect to whom respect is due, honor to whom honor is due."

5. LOVE, THE FULFILLMENT OF THE LAW
13:8-10

The task which Paul has set himself in the fourth part of the epistle is to show the character of the conduct of him who through faith is righteous. It is a life in harmony with the new aeon. He who through faith is righteous walks "in Christ" and "in love." Such a life he has to carry on in the midst of the old aeon and its orders. It is impossible for the Christian to be indifferent to these orders. To be sure, the earthly and civil righteousness must not be confused with the righteousness of the new aeon, the righteousness of God. But it would be bad if the Christian, who shares in the righteousness of God, were not even to measure up to the demand which human righteousness lays upon him. In the passage we have just considered, Paul has been at pains to present the Christian view of government and the attitude of the Christian to it.

Before he returns to what is for him the chief matter in this connection, namely, that the life of the Christian is determined by the fact that he walks "in Christ" and "in love," he sums up, in a concise expression, the position of the Christian as to civil righteousness: "Owe no one anything." The Christian must not, on the ground of any superior spirituality, excuse himself from any justified human demand; that is Paul's basic rule as to the Christian's civic relationships.

From this he goes back to the subject of love, with the unique formulation, "Owe no one anything—except to love one another." One can satisfy earthly, civil claims; but love's claims are never fulfilled. Taxes and revenues can be paid, so that they are no longer owed. One can show respect and honor to those to whom they are due, so that one no longer owes anything further in these matters. But as to love to his neighbor the Christian is always under obligation, however far he may have gone. Love can never be "fulfilled," but it is itself "the fulfillment of the law." Paul says, "He who loves his neighbor has fulfilled the law. The commandments, 'You shall not commit adultery, You shall not kill, You shall not steal, You shall not covet,' and any other commandment, are summed up in this sentence, 'You shall love your neighbor as yourself.' Love does no wrong to a neighbor; therefore love is the fulfilling of the law."

The statement that love is the fulfillment of the law confronts us with two problems. In the first place, does not the law, then, in spite of all that Paul has said against righteousness by the law, have the last word? And, furthermore, if love is the fulfilling of the law, how does it happen that Paul does not go beyond such manifestly negative statements?

Is it really to say enough about love if we say that it does no wrong to a neighbor? Should it not rather have been affirmed that love does everything that is good? Is it not by the positive that love is the fulfillment of the law? These questions are very closely related, and they all arise from the same misunderstanding of Paul's view.

As to the first question it has been said, "That Paul here, as in 8:4, speaks quite naturally of 'the fulfillment of the law' as something worthy of man's striving, and seems to have forgotten chapter 7 and 10:4, is characteristic of his unschematic way of expressing himself. He means that the Jews' ideal as to the fulfillment of the law, which the Jews can never attain to, is achieved by the Christian through works of love. But it is only in name, not in fact that the ideal is the same in both cases: in one case it is a faithfulness to the law that works casuistically; in the other, it is the work of the Spirit of God without reference to the law which is 'dead'" (Lietzmann). Is that really a correct interpretation of Paul's view? Does he mean that when he speaks of "the fulfillment of the law"? The answer must be in the negative When Paul speaks of the law and its fulfillment, his starting point is not the Jewish ideal of the fulfillment of the law. Here, as in 8:4, he thinks of God's holy will; that that is to be fulfilled is not merely a Jewish demand.

But furthermore—and here we come to the second issue— it ought to be noted that for Paul the law does not at all play the role of a positive ideal which is to be realized by man. The idea that the natural man lacks the capacity to fulfill

the law, but that by the aid of the Spirit the Christian receives the ability to achieve it, is completely foreign to Paul's
thought. It is not in that way that he speaks of the fulfillment of the law. For Paul the law is essentially God's restraint on sin. From that fact comes the negative quality
which always characterizes the law. It forbids sin and aims
to limit it. "You shall not" is the basic form of the law; it
expresses the limits which the law raises against sin. Even
when Paul speaks of that which is most positive in the law,
for instance, when in 8:4 he speaks of the law's δικαίωμα, the
negative quality is present; for the demand of the law is that
there be no unrighteousness. The law does not set up any
positive ideal of its own, and this is essential if there is to
be a harmonious relation between the law and the gospel.
Earlier Paul has shown that the law forbids sin, but is not
able to prevent it. On the contrary, when the law confronts
the carnal man, sin comes to life. When the law says, "You
shall not covet," the result is that covetousness is aroused
and grows strong (cf. p. 277). But what the law aimed
at, but could not effect, that "God has done"; that God
achieved among us through Christ (cf. p. 316). It is
not because we received new powers and can now, by their
help, fulfill all the different precepts of the law, that the
law's δικαίωμα has been fulfilled; it is because God's righteousness has been revealed. To believe in Christ is full and
complete righteousness. Therefore Christ is the end (τέλος)
of the law unto righteousness for every one who believes
(10:4). In exactly the same sense it can here be said that
love is the fulfillment of the law. There is no tension at all
between these two affirmations; on the contrary they are
both expressions of the same truth. Where Christ is, there
is righteousness; there is no room for the unrighteousness

against which the law is directed. And so it is with love. The law speaks against the different manifestations of sin and says, "You shall not commit adultery, You shall not kill, You shall not steal," etc. But *where love is, the things which the law forbids do not occur.* There is no longer anything for the law to condemn. There are indeed not "the works of the law," there is no righteousness by the law; but there is the fruit of the Spirit. "The fruit of the Spirit is love, joy, peace, patience, kindness, goodness, faithfulness, gentleness, self-control," it is said in Galatians 5:22f. And the apostle adds, "against such there is no law." We should notice the negative formulation. The law is *against* sin, but *not against* life "in Christ" and "in love." To live "in Christ," to walk "in love," is something entirely different from living under the law and striving to fulfill all its requirements; and yet the law is fulfilled in it. Therefore it can be said at the same time that the Christian is *"free from the law"* and that in him *the law is fulfilled.* Not by fulfillment of law is the law fulfilled, but by life "in Christ" and "in love." It is in this sense, and only in this sense, that "love is the fulfilling of the law."

6. Put on the Lord Jesus Christ
13:11-14

He who through faith is righteous is to live a life in keeping with the new aeon—that was the starting point for Paul's admonitions. The Christian must not conform himself to the character of the old aeon; his mind must be transformed into harmony with the new (12:2). Now Paul comes to the end of all his exhortations, and his thought returns to the starting point.

The Christian lives on the frontier between the two

aeons, and his entire existence is marked by that fact. He is
still in the old aeon, but the new sheds its light on his life,
and that life is a moving forward toward the new day. The
life of the Christian in this world looks forward to the day
of salvation as something that is to come. In one sense we
may indeed speak of salvation as already present, but it will
not be complete before the eschatological consummation. It
is of this eschatological salvation that Paul speaks when he
says, "Salvation is nearer to us now than when we first believed." Every step which the Christian takes carries him
closer to "the day of the Lord," closer to the day of the revelation of the glory of the Lord, which also will include the
manifestation of the glory of the children of God. When the
Christian sees how time runs on, he ought thereby to be made
mindful that "it is full time . . . to awake from sleep. . . . The
night is far gone, the day is at hand."

When, earlier in his letter, Paul spoke of the old aeon,
he characterized it as the aeon of sin and death, as the age
that stands under the wrath of God. Now he compares it
with night. As long as the old aeon lasts, the night continues.
But a turning point has come, through Christ. He has come
to us as the dawn of day from on high (Luke 1:78). The
old aeon is of course not yet past; the night continues, but it
moves on swiftly toward daybreak. They who believe in
Christ no longer belong to the night; they live in the early
rays of morning, having seen the first light of sunrise. "The
night is far gone, the day is at hand." That fact has impli-
cations as to the manner of their life and conduct. Having
seen the dawn of the new, they may no longer remain in the
darkness of night. Paul says, "Let us then cast off the works
of darkness and put on the armor of light." The works of
darkness are to be cast off. That is the same as what Paul

calls "the works of the flesh," in Galatians 5:19. In that place Paul illustrates with mention of such things as carousing, drunkenness, unchastity, licentiousness, dissention, envy, all of which belong to the aeon of sin and death and stand under the wrath of God. In place of such things the Christian is to put on the armor of light, or, as Paul says in verse 14, "put on the Lord Jesus Christ."

According to Paul, the entire Christian life can be described as a constant putting off and putting on. That begins with baptism. "As many of you as were baptized into Christ have put on Christ" (Gal. 3:27). But that which happened in baptism must ever take place anew. All that belongs to the old aeon must be cast off; all that belongs to the new aeon must be put on. The Christian must put off the old man and put on the new. He must put off "the works of the flesh": "Make no provision for the flesh, to gratify its desires" (vs. 14), or for anything connected with the old "body of death" (6:6). He must rather put on the Lord Jesus Christ. The Christian, who once lived "in the flesh" ($\dot{\epsilon}\nu$ $\tau\hat{\eta}$ $\sigma\alpha\rho\kappa\acute{\iota}$, 7:5), now lives "in Christ."

Thus Paul sums up all his exhortations as to the Christian life in a single one: "Put on the Lord Jesus Christ." That includes all the others: the Christian lives "in Christ" and walks "in Christ." To walk thus in Christ is what it means to "conduct ourselves becomingly as in the day" ($\dot{\omega}\varsigma$ $\dot{\epsilon}\nu$ $\dot{\eta}\mu\dot{\epsilon}\rho\alpha$ $\pi\epsilon\rho\iota\pi\alpha\tau\epsilon\hat{\iota}\nu$); to walk in keeping with the new aeon.

7. CHARACTERISTICS OF PAUL'S ETHICS

There is a possibility of a misunderstanding in our earlier statement that chapters 12-13 contain Paul's ethics in brief summary. It might be thought to mean that we here have in Paul's writing his counterpart of that which usually goes under the title of "ethics," and that he accordingly gives his answer to the questions which Greek philosophy, for instance, raised. That would indubitably be a misinterpretation. One searches Paul's writings in vain for answers to these problems. What he presents in these chapters must not be regarded as ethics, like that found in the Greek philosophers. If that is what is meant by "ethics," we could say that Paul has no ethics. To make his view as clear as possible in this area, it may be helpful, by way of conclusion, to gather up in a number of points certain characteristics of Pauline ethics.

(1) Paul's ethics is an ethics of *the mind*. In the very beginning of chapter 12 we read that the issue is that the Christian's mind must be transformed in harmony with the new aeon. But if we use the word "mind," which is used in a variety of senses, we must guard against two likely misinterpretations. In the first place, for Paul there is no contrast or tension between mind and action. In Paul's ethics everything depends on the renewing of the mind; but it is just as true to say that everything depends on action in the actual world in which God has placed us. When Paul speaks of the renewal of the mind, in almost the same breath he also speaks of presenting the body as a sacrifice to God (12:1-2). It would not be possible to disavow more strongly a spiritualizing view of mind. And, in the second place, when Paul refers to the renewal of the mind, he means, as the above implies, something entirely different from Aristotle's ἕξις or the *habitus* of the Middle Ages.

(2) Paul's ethics cannot be expressed in any of the generally accepted ethical categories, such as *"virtue," "duty," "the greatest good."* The concept of "virtue" (ἀρετή), which is basic for Greek ethics, is completely foreign to Paul. Even

Philippians 4:8 does not justify a contrary view. That the concept has, by its very nature, no place in Paul's thought is easy to see. The starting point for his ethics, we remember, is not what man is able to offer God, but what God does for man. Paul does indeed speak of obligations (1:14; 13:7, 8; 15:1); but his attitude to the law makes it false to understand his ethics as an ethics of duty. And finally, he accepts no form of eudaemonistic ethics, even of a religiously colored eudaemonism. He does not look upon God as "the greatest good," or the total of all desired goods, but as Lord, absolute in what He requires and absolute in what He gives.

(3) Paul's ethics is *a social ethics*. It does not regard the Christian as an isolated individual, on whom certain ethical demands rest. It sees him as a member in a great, organic whole, the body of Christ. The individual member gets its task from its place in the body and from its relation to the other members.

(4) It follows that Paul's ethics is not an *equalitarian ethics*. It recognizes no uniformity or sameness. Any such idea is excluded by the fact that the Christian is a member in the body of Christ; and members do not all have the same function. It is precisely in the difference and manifoldness of endowment and function that the organic relationship finds expression. Because they are different, the members are dependent on each other and can mutually support and help each other.

(5) With the idea of the right ethical behavior there is usually associated the idea of something deserving (cf. that concept in Kant). With Paul every such thought is excluded. His is not an ethics of *deserving*, but of *serving*.

(6) This rests on the fact that his is an *ethic of justification*. It describes the conduct of those who through faith are

439

righteous. But justification bars any thought of merit. Man's justifiction rests exclusively on the action of God. It is in this that his ethical action has its basis. For that reason the imperative rests on the indicative.

(7) Paul's ethics is an *ethics of the new aeon.* The life of one who through faith is righteous gets its character from the fact that he belongs to the new aeon. The life of the Christian on earth is throughout conditioned by the contrast between the two aeons, their simultaneous existence, and their interpenetration of each other.

(8) Paul's ethics is *a Christ ethics.* Christ is central, not only for the gospel of what God has done for the salvation of man, but also for the ethical life. The Christian life is a life and conduct ἐν Χριστῷ.

(9) Paul's ethics is *an ethics of love.* When he speaks of "the fruit of the Spirit," he mentions love first, because that includes all the rest. Love, ἀγάπη, is the bond that holds together all members in the body of Christ and makes all serve each other.

XIV

The Weak and the Strong

14:1–15:13

Unlike Paul's other letters, this one gives but little attention to concrete problems in the life of the congregation. There is of course a natural explanation for that. His other letters were written to churches which he himself had established and which looked to him as a spiritual father. The occasion for those letters was, in many cases, some disturbances which had arisen, which Paul sought to correct with his counsel and instructions. But as to the church at Rome he is in a different situation. It was as yet largely strange to him, so it was natural that he should exercise great self-restraint as to the inner concerns of that congregation. So, up to the point now reached, the whole letter has maintained a definitely objective character (cf. p. 4).

Now, for the first time, we come to a section of the letter which is addressed directly to a special situation in the church at Rome. There was a group in the church which, because of conscience and religious convictions, wanted to refrain from the use of certain foods and esteemed "one day better than another" (14:2, 5, 21). This group was described as "the weak" by the majority of the congregation, which had no qualms about these matters. The issue was what attitude the church should take to "the weak."

What was the reason why this group refrained from these things? To that question we can give no absolutely certain answer. Paul does not say anything on that point. He clearly assumes that the issue was so well known to the congregation that he does not need to stop to describe it. This at least is clear, that it was not a group of Jewish Christians who wanted to force Jewish ways on the church. That is evident from the fact that in Judaism there was no commandment not to eat meat or drink wine. We know the position which Paul always takes against efforts to bind the Christian church with Jewish shackles. In Galatians 2:5 he says, "To them we did not yield submission even for a moment." When the issue was the Christian's freedom from the law, Paul was inflexible. Some have thought that the abstention of "the weak" was related to a widespread religious vegetarianism in antiquity, rooting in the dualism of the Hellenistic view of existence. But that interpretation is also doubtless wrong. With a view so basically at variance with the Christian view Paul certainly would not have exercised the patience that he now shows to "the weak." The truth probably is that the weak abstained from meat and wine that they might not be contaminated by things that were "unclean" because they had been offered to idols. If that be the case, we have here a parallel to the issue in I Corinthians 8.

To us it may seem a small matter about which there was so much ado in the congregation at Rome. Paul also thinks it a small matter. He agrees with the majority that the qualms of "the weak" are quite baseless: "I know and am persuaded in the Lord Jesus that nothing is unclean in itself" (14:14; cf. the parallel in I Cor. 8:4: "We know that 'an idol has no real existence.'"). And yet Paul gives the issue singularly earnest consideration. For it threatens to cause *a rift* in the church, and that is a most serious matter.

How then should the congregation act toward "the weak," whose anxious nature created a disturbance in the church? Paul answers, "As for the man who is weak in faith, welcome him." Do not despise him, but receive him as a brother, for he too is a genuine member of the church. "Welcome him," "but"—Paul adds—"not for disputes over opinions." It would be easy to think that the strong should welcome the weak, that they might persuade them of the inferiority of their view, and make them like "the strong." But Paul will not agree to that. Fellowship among Christians is not to be based on questioning and disputing, toward the result that the one adopts the other's view and accepts it as the norm of action. Such a sameness is not a Christian ideal. Acceptance ought not to rest on such secondary considerations. Christians are not all alike, nor should they be. Nietzsche was not the first to discover that difference is proper (cf. his statement, "Men are not alike, nor should they be so"). Paul, in a far deeper sense, defended the propriety of difference. God has given faith to one in larger measure than to another. The one is "strong in faith," the other "weak in faith." But "the weak" also has the place which God has assigned to him in the church, and it is not the intention that he is to copy "the strong."

Paul is clearly well informed as to the discussions afoot in the church at Rome; and it seems as if the congregation, to avoid a rift, had asked Paul for an authoritative statement as to what the Christian ought to do. They wanted to have a simple procedure, a clear answer to the question whether a Christian ought to abstain from meat and wine, or to eat and drink what is set before him, without asking questions. Paul himself agrees with the view of "the strong." He knows that nothing is unclean in itself, so a Christian may, without qualms, "eat anything." What we might have expected, from such a starting point, would be that Paul would seek to persuade "the weak" that their scruples were baseless, and so to avoid a schism. That is probably what was expected of him. But Paul proceeds in an entirely different manner. He says they should let each one be what he is and act as he does; there is place for both groups in the church, for "the weak" as well as for "the strong."

Paul here contends for Christian freedom, for the right of both weak and strong. "One believes he may eat anything, while the weak man eats only vegetables" (vs. 2). "One man esteems one day as better than another, while another man esteems all days alike." But the chief thing is that "every one be fully convinced in his own mind" (vs. 5). This is not just an arbitrary indulgence, by which Paul lets both groups continue side by side in the church. On the contrary, it is manifest that it is only in this way that he can be true to the gospel. But if he had prescribed a Christian course of action, as was desired of him, it would have involved a surrender of the evangelical position. That would have been the result, whichever side he had espoused. If he had declared that all Christians were to follow the example "of the weak" and abstain from eating meat and drinking wine, the legalistic character of such an enactment would be clear. Or, if he had chosen the other position and decreed that all Christians should, without misgivings, eat meat and drink wine, the result would likewise have been a victory for legalism. To be Christian would have meant to follow certain outward usages, to eat, or not to eat. Against this Paul says, "The kingdom of God does not mean food and drink, but righteousness and peace and joy in the Holy Spirit" (vs. 17).

Instead of taking one side against the other, he calls each to account for attack against the other. "The strong" has a certain natural tendency to look down on "the weak." The latter has a tendency to pass judgment on those who are not as solicitously careful as he himself. Therefore Paul admonishes both, "Let not him who eats despise him who abstains, and let not him who abstains pass judgment on him who eats" (vs. 3). The chief purpose of the passage 14:1–15:13 is to evoke in the congregation a considerate treatment of "the weak" in his solicitude, even though it is objectively seen to be uncalled for. It is interesting to note that it is particularly on "the strong," whose freer course is entirely justified, that Paul calls for protection of "the weak." He knows very well that, in issues between the strong and the weak, the latter is by no means always the wronged party. On the contrary it often happens that in his very weakness he has an effective weapon for making the circumstances comply with his view. Not infrequently it is the weak who is the real tyrant. In his judgment of others he finds a compensation for his weakness. Therefore Paul turns to "the weak" first and says, "Who are you to pass judgment on the servant of another? It is before his own master that he stands or falls. And he will be upheld, for the Master is able to make him stand." When people set themselves to judge others, they stretch forth their hand to something which God has reserved to himself and to Christ. Judgment is the Lord's, it belongs to God and to Christ. But to us the admonition applies, "Judge not" (Matt. 7:1).

In Christianity the vital thing is that one belongs to the

Lord through faith, not on the outer fact that one eats or abstains from eating. Faith is the thing that is true of all Christians, the fact that unites them all, be they weak or strong in that faith. "He who eats, eats in honor of the Lord, since he gives thanks to God." A Christian no longer lives to himself; he lives for his Lord, and Christ lives in him. In life and in death he belongs to his Lord. That was the purpose in Christ's death and resurrection, that we should become His and He become our Lord. But if He is our Lord, we are no longer to be judged by men. It is before the judgment seat of God that we must give account of our life, not before men. Thus Paul has come back to his starting point: "Why do you pass judgment on your brother? Or you, why do you despise your brother?" (vs. 10). To judge and despise, to despise and judge—that is the constant dialectic between "the weak" and "the strong." But before the judgment seat of God all such human pretensions must fall.

Thus Paul has repudiated all tendencies to sameness in the Christian life. Just as uniformity is impossible because Christians are members of the body of Christ and not all have the same functions, so it is also impossible because there is a difference between "the weak" and "the strong." Inwardly the weak is not the same as the strong. Therefore it is not intended that his action is to be the same as that of the latter. Each is to act according to the measure of faith given to him, and give account accordingly. The fundamental thing for the Christian, be he weak or strong, is always the same, namely, that what he does he does in the Lord, or, what is the same, he does in love.

In the foregoing we have seen what it means to "walk in Christ" and "walk in love." When Paul now (vss. 13-23) addresses himself to the strong, to teach them to be con-

siderate of the weak, he has occasion to give a concrete illustration of what it means to "*walk in love.*" The position
of the strong is itself right, when he uses his freedom. But
he is not alone in the world. Beside him stands the weak
brother. What effect does his action have on that brother?
When the latter observes his free action, he may be influenced in either of two directions. *Either* he is tempted to
judge; of that Paul has spoken in what precedes. *Or* he is
tempted to act in the same way; and that fact makes the
conduct of the strong questionable, even though it is right
in itself. For what is the result, if the weak thus imitates
him? The result is that he does so with bad conscience.
Thus one Christian can cause another to fall. It is true that
"nothing is unclean in itself; but it is unclean for any one
who thinks it unclean." When the strong, who knows this,
exercises his freedom, he does right; he acts in faith. But
his weak brother stands beside him; he looks on and is
tempted by the example to do something for which his faith
has not given him the inner stability. Each one is to act in
keeping with the measure of faith given to him. But what
he now does does not agree with his weak faith, so he is
guilty of sin, for "whatever does not proceed from faith is
sin" (vs. 23). But whose fault is it that he falls? The blame
rests on the strong, who acted without consideration for his
weak brother. By his conduct he caused the latter to stumble.
For "he who has doubts"—as the weak brother undeniably
has—"is condemned, if he eats, because he does not act from
faith."

When we now use the expression that one is an "offense"
to another, we usually mean that the latter disapproves of
what the former does, that he is aroused against him, and
pronounces judgment upon him. But it is not in that way

that Paul uses the word. He does not mean to say that the Christian is to be anxious what impression he is making, to ask whether he wins approval or not. In that sense it may rather be the Christian's responsibility to give offense to the world. When Paul here speaks of offense, he means something quite different, namely, that one can tempt another to go beyond what he is equal to, to go beyond what his faith approves, and thus to cause his brother to fall. In the life of Christians together, one can be the rock of offense on which another stumbles and falls. Therefore a Christian must always remember to consider his brethren. To a Christian who inconsiderately uses his freedom without inquiring whether it tempts others and causes them to fall, Paul says, "you are no longer walking in love," οὐκέτι κατὰ ἀγάπην περιπατεῖς (vs. 15). For it is the Christian's task to "pursue what makes for peace and for mutual upbuilding."

At the beginning of chapter 14 Paul gave his attention to the weak. He must desist from judging; he must learn that there are others who are not bound as he is, so that they can act as he cannot, without thereby giving him the right to deny their sincerity in the Christian life. It is not intended that the weak are to be lord over the faith and conduct of others, the less so since his own faith is weak. In the latest section, Paul has addressed himself to the strong. Of these he demands that they show regard for the weak and, for the sake of the latter, limit their own freedom rather than cause them to fall by a careless use of it. "It is right not to eat meat or drink wine or do anything that makes your brother stumble" (vs. 21). If in the beginning Paul laid down the rule that each is to be what he is, and to act as he does, that there is to be peace in the church for both the weak and the strong, he has now modified that rule somewhat. It is not so that the weak and the strong are merely to live side by side, each in his own way and without concern as to the other. On the contrary, he demands of the strong that he consider the weak and limit his own freedom for the sake of the weak.

Is it, then, the idea that when conduct must be accommodated to another, it is the strong who must do so? Yes, that is what Paul means. It is easier for the stronger to adjust his conduct to the weak, than the opposite, for he knows that "nothing is unclean in itself." So when he refrains from using his freedom, he knows that he does so, not because there is anything unclean in the exercise of his freedom, but he voluntarily assumes the self-restraint because of the brother's weakness. The weak, as long as he is weak, can only do one thing, namely, abstain. If he acts freely, without the inner certainty, he sins. But the strong can do two things: he can exercise his freedom or refrain from doing so. In either case he is free. It is for that reason that it is he who must make the accommodation of conduct to the other. The strong must be strong enough to bear the burden of the weak.

But is it really right to restrain the freedom which Christ gave us, and not exercise it? Is it not rather the very duty of the Christian to show his freedom before the world, and thereby show his faith? Paul answers, "The faith that you have, keep between yourself and God." There is no need to show one's faith, for faith is the relation between man and God, which belongs to one's hidden life. But when the matter at issue is one's relation with his fellow men, there is one inescapable necessity for the Christian, namely, to *walk in love.*

So there rests on the strong the duty to have regard for

the weak. "We who are strong ought to bear with the failings of the weak, and not to please ourselves; let each of us please his neighbor for his good, to edify him." That is exactly the same thought as that expressed in I Corinthians 10:23f., "'All things are lawful,' but not all things build up. Let no one seek his own good but the good of his neighbor." It is a basic characteristic of the Christian that he does not live to himself. In 14:7f. Paul said, "None of us lives to himself. . . . If we live, we live to the Lord." But to live for the Lord is also to live for one's neighbor, that he may be built up, built in as a stone in the temple. For the life of Christians together it is an inescapable rule that they "bear one another's burdens" (Gal. 6:2). But that rule applies particularly to those who are strong in faith. They have received greater strength just that they may bear the burdens of others.

The basis for this obligation Paul carries back, here just as in Philippians 2:4, to Christ himself. In Philippians we read, "Let each of you look not only to his own interests, but also to the interests of others. Have this mind among yourselves, which you have in Christ Jesus." And in Romans, "For Christ did not please himself; but, as it is written, 'The reproaches of those who reproached thee fell on me.'" He willingly accepted His sufferings, allowing the enemies of God to be His enemies, who heaped their reproaches on Him. But that which had been "written in former days," and which was fulfilled in Him, has a special message to us. It "was written for our instruction." For when Christians do not live only to themselves, but also for others, then every rift vanishes. They "live in such harmony with one another, in accord with Jesus Christ, that together with one voice [they] glorify the God and Father of our Lord Jesus Christ."

To build up a church which, without schism, but in one accord and with one voice glorifies God was the aim of Christ's work; and that is also to be the Christian's aim. With that in mind Paul adds, "Welcome one another, therefore, as Christ also welcomed you, for the glory of God."

With that Paul comes to the end of what he has to say about the weak and the strong. But now he broadens the perspective. All that he has said earlier about the gospel as "the power of God for salvation to every one who has faith, to the Jew first and also to the Greek," becomes an illustration of the fact that, from the ends of the earth, from Jews and Gentiles, Christ has gathered a united people which, in one accord and with one voice, praises God. "For I tell you that Christ became a servant to the circumcised to show God's truthfulness, in order to confirm the promises given to the patriarchs." In Christ all these promises have been fulfilled. In Him God has been true to His promises (ὁ θεὸς ἀληθής, 3:4). So the Jews may glorify God for his faithfulness, and the Gentiles may "glorify God for his mercy," because out of those who were "vessels of wrath" He has made "vessels of mercy," because He took those who were branches of the wild olive and grafted them into the cultivated tree (11:17, 24). Now the Gentiles can "rejoice with his people" Israel (vs. 10). From the root of Jesse, God has brought forth Christ. Thereby a new hope has been given, not only to Israel, but also to the Gentiles; "in him shall the Gentiles hope" (vs. 12).

XV

Conclusion

The theme of the epistle to the Romans—"He who through faith is righteous shall live"—has been treated from all sides. It culminated in the exposition of part four as to the conduct of the one "who through faith is righteous." Now that the matter which Paul set out to discuss has been made clear, it remains only for him to touch on certain personal urgencies on which the attitude of the congregation in Rome is important, and to express his greetings to the church in that city. Like the introduction to the epistle, this conclusion is also unusually rich in inclusiveness. It includes essentially two things: (1) Paul's travel plans; and (2) greetings and concluding words.

1. Paul's Travel Plans
15:14-33

Paul begins this section with a word which has a half-apologetic sound. He has ventured to write to this church, and above all, he has addressed incisive admonitions to it. But he has not done so because it was in special need of admonitions and correction at his hand. On his part he is persuaded that this church's members have such Christian insight that they are "able to instruct one another." It should be observed that when Paul says his admonitions may be superfluous, he does not imply that the situation is so good at Rome that exhortations are no longer necessary at all. As long as the church lives in this world it cannot dispense with mutual admonitions and reminders. If Paul has now written "very boldly" to the church in Rome, he has done so by virtue of the special commission which he received from God, his commission as apostle to the Gentiles (cf. 1:5f.). "In the priestly service of the gospel" he must "be a minister of Christ Jesus to the Gentiles . . . so that the offering of the Gentiles may be acceptable" to God. It was a task of overwhelming proportions which Paul had to render. He can speak of it without exalting himself, because it was all carried on "in Christ." For Paul is not talking about what he himself has achieved, but of what Christ has done through him.

In the apostleship committed to Paul lies both the *universality* of his work and that which sets its *limits*. His mission is "to win obedience from the Gentiles" (εἰς ὑπακοὴν ἐθνῶν, vs. 18; cf. how Paul, in 1:5, characterized his office: ἀποστολὴ εἰς ὑπακοὴν πίστεως ἐν πᾶσιν τοῖς ἔθνεσιν). His is a world-wide commission. Part of it he has already carried out: within an area which stretched from Jerusalem to Illyricum he had traveled from place to place, proclaiming the gospel and establishing Christian churches. Now that he has finished this first task, so that no part of it remains undone, he looks westward. In that direction an enormous field of labor awaits him. In Spain the name of Christ has not been preached. In that area Paul wishes to go on with his work; and on his way thither he intends to visit Rome.

But how can Paul think that he has finished his proclamation of the gospel in the East? What has been accomplished up to this time is that he has preached the Word in a series of cities and established churches. But these churches are still in the beginning stage and, furthermore, they are scattered around very sparsely. How can Paul then say that he has "fully preached the gospel" here? It would rather seem that there is room for much more work here, and that the care of these churches would give him more than enough to do, so that he would not need to look for a new field. The answer to this is also implicit in his apostolic office. His office was not the same as that of other preachers of the gospel. His task was to establish new congregations. As to that he says, he has made it his "ambition to preach the gospel, not where Christ has already been named, lest I build on another man's foundation." He has found the guiding star for his missionary work in Isaiah 52:15, which he repeats in the following form, "They shall see who have never been told of him, and they shall understand who have never heard of him."

When Paul explains that he does not wish to build on another man's foundation, that has been interpreted by many as an expression of his personal ambition. But the fact of the case is rather that his decision is in closest keeping with his special commission. The mission of the apostle to the Gentiles is to establish churches. Paul does not mean to set it up as a general rule that one should not build on a foundation laid by another. Here, as elsewhere, he upholds the idea that people's tasks are different. To one it is given to lay the foundation, to another to build on it; one has the commission to plant, another to water (I Cor. 3:6ff.). The mission committed to Paul is limited essentially to the laying of the foundation. In I Corinthians 3:10 Paul says as to this, "According to the commission of God given to me, like a skilled master-builder, I laid a foundation, and another man is building upon it." The apostle to the Gentiles must lay the foundation. When that has been done, when a Christian congregation is established in a city, when the Christian life flourishes and the light shines out over the surrounding area, then the apostle's work is, in a certain sense, finished. He has planted; now he must leave it to others to water. He has laid the foundation; he must leave it to others to raise the building thereon. He must hasten on and lay the foundation for new congregations. The world lies before him and new tasks always await him. It is this apostolic commission which now drives him on toward Spain. On the way he hopes to visit Rome, and there, with the help of the congregation, to be equipped for the journey that lies beyond (cf. p. 5).

But he must first go to Jerusalem. At the meeting of the apostles in Jerusalem, in A.D. 52, it had been agreed that the Gentile congregations would send help to the mother congregation in Jerusalem. "Which very thing I was eager to do," Paul writes in Galatians 2:10. How much care Paul had given to the organizing of that work of assistance we can see in I Corinthians 16:1-4 and in II Corinthians 8 and 9. But even though Paul had labored earnestly in that cause, the participation of the churches in Macedonia and Achaia had nevertheless been spontaneous. The support that had been contributed in this way—Paul calls it κοινωνία, "fellowship"—did not have the character of charity. The churches looked upon it rather as an obligation of gratitude, "for if the Gentiles have come to share in their spiritual blessings, they ought also to be of service to them in material blessings." Now the contribution has been gathered, and Paul is ready to go to Jerusalem to deliver it. He is aware of the dangers that threaten him on the journey. Therefore he appeals to the congregation in Rome for its prayers on his behalf.

2. GREETINGS AND CONCLUDING WORDS
16:1-27

In the opening verses of chapter 16 Paul commends to
them sister Phoebe, who is at the time on her way to Rome.
These verses are of interest in three ways: (1) they show us
how such a recommendation, usual in the early church, might
be expressed; (2) they give us the name of the person who,
from all appearances, had the task of taking Paul's letter to
the congregation in Rome; and (3) they complete the picture which we have of offices in the early church. Just as
there were the offices of bishop and deacons (Phil. 1:1), so
we learn here that there was also a feminine diaconate.
Phoebe was διάκονος in the church at Cenchreae, one of the
ports of Corinth.

When we now turn to his greetings (vss. 3-16), we are
at once surprised at the long list of names which we find.
Was Paul actually acquainted with so many of the members
of this church? It has been suggested, because of this question, that chapter 16 was originally a separate letter to one
of Paul's "own" congregations—perhaps most likely at Ephe-
sus. But the fact is, it seems, that, in letters to congregations
which he had established, Paul deliberately avoided sending
greetings to individuals. Where he knew practically all the
members of a church, to send greetings to some and not to
others would have caused discord. But there is no danger
of that in the church at Rome, because he knows only a few
of the members there and sends greetings specifically to
them.

After Paul has, in verses 17-20, given warning against
false teachers who might creep into the church and by fair
words turn it away from Christ, and after those who are with
Paul—we note in particular the name of Timothy who is

referred to in several of Paul's letters as sharing in them, and of Tertius who has served as Paul's secretary in the writing of this epistle—have added their greetings, the words of conclusion follow, in verses 25-27. They have the form of a doxology.

Views have differed as to the place of the doxology too, because of the varying testimony of the manuscripts. Some scholars have also, on linguistic grounds, doubted whether it belongs to Paul. But the arguments which have been advanced do not seem well founded, when examined closely. Parallels are to be found in Paul to practically everything on which discussion has dwelt.

In great sentences Paul here allows the total message of the Epistle to the Romans to pass before our eyes.

From eternity, before all aeons, God has, in His eternal purpose, bound salvation to Jesus Christ. This mystery, which was kept secret for long ages, has *now* been disclosed through Christ, testified to by the law and the prophets. God who reigns over all aeons (ὁ αἰώνιος θεός) has now caused this gospel to be proclaimed among all the Gentiles, to bring about obedience to the faith (cf. 1:5).

"To the only wise God (cf. 11:33) be glory for evermore through Jesus Christ! Amen."

ΩΙ Η ΔΟΞΑ ΕΙΣ ΤΟΤΣ ΑΙΩΝΑΣ ΤΩΝ ΑΙΩΝΩΝ

ΑΜΗΝ